Secrets of Economics Editors

Secrets of Economics Editors

edited by Michael Szenberg and Lall Ramrattan

foreword by Robert M. Solow

The MIT Press
Cambridge, MA
London, England

MIT Press books may be purchased at special quantity discounts for business or sales promotional use. For information, please email special_sales@mitpress.mit.edu or write to Special Sales Department, The MIT Press, 55 Hayward Street, Cambridge, MA 02142.

This book was set in Sabon by Toppan Best-set Premedia Limited. Printed and bound in the United States of America.

Library of Congress Cataloging-in-Publication Data

Secrets of economics editors / edited by Michael Szenberg and Lall Ramrattan ; foreword by Robert M. Solow.
    pages   cm
Includes bibliographical references and index.
ISBN 978-0-262-52546-6 (pbk. : alk. paper)
1. Economics—Periodicals. 2. Editing. 3. Editors. I. Szenberg, Michael. II. Ramrattan, Lall, 1951–
HB1.S43   2014
070.4′4933—dc23
2013020994

10 9 8 7 6 5 4 3 2 1

B'H

Dedicated to the memory of my sister, Esther, for bringing me to these shores;
to the memory of my father, Henoch, for his wisdom;
to my mother, Sara, for giving birth to me—twice;
to my children, Naomi and Avi, and
their spouses, Marc and Tova;
to my grandchildren,
Elki and Chaim, and Chanochi, Batya, Chanoch, Devorah, Ephraim, Ayala, and Jacob;
and to my wife, Miriam

And to the righteous, anonymous Austrian-German officer who took my immediate family to a hiding place just days before the last transport to Auschwitz, where most of my family perished

In Memoriam
To my late elder sister, Balwanty Deolall,
and my brother Deonarine Ramrattan,
who have always directed me on the traditional path

Contents

The Journal Editorial Cycle and Practices

Foreword

Robert M. Solow

I would have made a lousy journal editor. At the simplest level, these essays demonstrate convincingly that editing an economics journal is a formidable managerial project. Hundreds of submissions arrive each year. They have to be channeled to appropriate—knowledgeable but not too opinionated—associate editors and referees. In turn, the referees have to be nudged, cajoled, and flattered into producing fair and useful reviews, preferably in finite time. And records have to be kept every step of the way: where is each paper now, when did it get there, what has been received about it? The editor cannot afford to be caught in ignorance of the state of the system. To make it harder, some journals are owned by interfering publishers who know an inelastic demand when they see one. As for me, I could not manage my way out of a paper bag. Maybe that is why no one ever asked me to edit a journal.

All this is without mentioning the authors of those hundreds of papers. Their behavior was once summarized for me by a former editor of the *American Economic Review* (AER). He said that he could afford to accept about one in every ten papers submitted, and in so doing he created nine enemies and one ungrateful wretch.

Editors do much more than merely manage a flow of papers. Any reader of these essays will be struck by the seriousness with which these editors approach their task. They tend to know a lot about different area of economics and to care about the discipline and the profession. They think about the dual role of learned journals as records of ideas and research results and also as guarantors of intellectual quality, purveyors of a sort of Good Housekeeping Seal of Approval.

They also have to worry whether they are presiding over a dying industry that is on the verge of being rendered obsolete by online publishing and the ubiquity of the Web. Anyone attentive enough to have observed what has been happening over the years to the waistline of the

AER and the *Quarterly Journal of Economics* (*QJE*), for example, will wonder about that. Maybe it is just another aspect of general obesity, but maybe it is a sign of vitality. By contrast, I can remember how much I used to enjoy the old *Review of Economic Studies*, not only because it was alive and interesting but also because it came out only three times a year with just a handful of articles and a lot of white space on every page.

There is a subtler question that surfaces occasionally in the book and on which there are natural differences of opinion and practice. Editors, like other economists, may have strong views on methodological and substantive issues that are currently the source of controversy within the research community. Is it proper for an editor to favor papers that support his or her side of the dispute? Or the majority view? Or is it the editor's responsibility to see that the contents of the journal more or less reflect the distribution of opinion in the profession at large?

I can see valid arguments on both sides. One can maintain that editors are not chosen to be powerful protectors of whatever paradigm they happen to favor. They, or rather their journals, should be neutral, accepting or rejecting papers purely on the basis of merit. This is easier said than done: every partisan knows that giving the "correct" answer is a necessary if not sufficient sign of merit. An alternative view might say that no one wants monolithic journals, a little attitude makes for interesting reading, and since there is virtually free entry into the journal business, no serious work is likely to be excluded from publication. A thousand flowers can bloom without all blooming in the same journal. This is no trivial matter: promotion and tenure decisions often turn, for better or worse, on who published how many articles in which journals. (This saves senior members the trouble of actually reading the articles.) The current mainstream will naturally classify any dissenting journal as inferior, worth fewer tenure points (and sometimes the mainstream is right). Maybe it is a toss-up, but whichever way a journal goes, it should be up-front and explicit. Right now, I would say that the publication cards are stacked in favor of whatever the current fashion may be.

Maybe this book ought to be the first in a series. It could be an enlightening window into the sociology of knowledge to compare the practices and experiences of editors in economics with those in other fields—other social sciences, some natural sciences, history, philosophy. Here is one example. In the economics departments I knew well, the choice of a thesis topic was left to each student, almost as a rite of passage. In, say, chemistry departments, as I understand it, many or most doctoral students attach themselves to somebody's expensive laboratory, and they essentially carry out a piece of Professor X's project. Because many journal articles must arise from thesis research, this kind of institutional/cultural difference will affect what editors do and how they respond. There may be a reason for this difference in approach. It has sometimes seemed to me that in some sciences there is usually a well-defined set of unsolved problems waiting for a solution, not quite as well defined as a powerful mathematical conjecture looking for a proof but more in that direction than is usually the case in economics. If so, those sciences would function more like a group effort than economics does and perhaps be more cumulative, and the work of journal editors would somehow reflect this difference.

That is just one train of idle speculation set off by the chapters of this book. When I first saw the manuscript, I wondered who would want to read the reflections of a bunch of journal editors. Then I thought of the answer—anyone who ever edited a journal, served as an associate editor, refereed a paper, wrote and submitted a paper, or read an article and wondered why it was in the journal. That's just for starters.

Preface and Acknowledgments

Marcus Tullius Cicero wrote of Socrates that he called down philosophy from the skies and implanted it in the cities and homes of men. The purpose of this volume is to spread and extend the wisdom of the editors assembled here to all who are interested in the workings of scholarly journals. When the Danish architect Arne Jacobson designed St. Catherine's College in Oxford in the 1960s, he also designed the school's chairs, the dishes and cups used in its cafeterias, and even the gardens. When questioned about this, he responded: "God is in the details." The contributors to this volume provide a wide variety of details about navigating and jumping over the editorial hurdles of scholarly journals. Their insights allow knowledge to come to you.

We were prompted to focus on and explore the role of editors by an incident described in chapter 22, "An Instructive Case in Referencing, Priority Conflict, and Ethics: The Role of an Editor in a Scholarly Journal" (Michael Szenberg). When authors ask us how they should react if their papers are rejected, we advise them to adopt Szenberg life's motto: "Rejections energize me."[1] When faced with hardships and failures during World War II, Winston Churchill expressed a similar thought with his own mantra: "Keep buggering on."

At the MIT Press, we have been blessed to work with Jane A. Macdonald, an editor who has become a dear friend. Her suggestions were precise and unarguable, and they induced us to invest more time and expand the roster of editors, which strongly improved the final product. Thank you, Jane, and thanks also to assistant editor Emily Taber for giving the book a critical reading and for shepherding it through the four referees and the editorial board. Some of the chapters in this volume initially appeared in the *American Economist* when I was the editor; they are reprinted here with changes. We are grateful for permission to include them.

We are deeply indebted to Bob Solow, who again contributes a foreword, after he did the same for our *Franco Modigliani: A Mind That Never Rests,* which was translated into several languages.

I am profoundly grateful to Ben Friedman and Victor Fuchs for being my champions. I bow to you both.

My intellectual debt continues with the members of the executive board of Omicron Delta Epsilon, the honor society in economics, for being an important source of inspiration, encouragement, and support. Thanks to Professors Mary Ellen Benedict, Tina Das, Alan Grant, Paul W. Grimes, Stacey Jones, Katherine A. Nantz, Farhang Niroomand, Robert Rycroft, Joseph M. Santos, Ali Zadeh, and the coordinator of the ODE central office, Phyllis Carter. I am grateful for their collegiality and friendship. I am deeply indebted to Mary Ellen Benedict, department chair and distinguished teaching professor at Bowling Green State University, for her impeccable wisdom, big heart, and wit. I am particularly indebted to Farhang Niroomand, dean at the University of Houston-Victoria, for his wise advice on various matters over the years.

Pace University's library is a superbly run unit where efficiency and kindness dwell together. We are grateful to the Pace librarians—Adele Artola, Yakov Bibichkov, Steve Bobich, Wanda Castaner, Amernal Denton, Gladys Gonzalo, Alicia Joseph, Sanda Petre, Chloe Pinera, Rey Racelis, and Ann Wilberton—for being extraordinarily supportive.

Thanks are extended to my colleagues at Pace University—Lew Altfest, Burcin Col, Natalia Gershun, Elena Goldman, Aron Gottesman, Iuliana Ismailescu, Joe Salerno, and P. Viswanath. Most of all, I renew my indebtedness to Arthur Centonze, dean emeritus of Lubin School of Business, for his wise counsel and support. I owe an enormous debt of gratitude to two extraordinary individuals, Iuliana Ismailescu and Oscar Camargo, for their goodness of heart, enduring support, positive attitude, gracious good cheer, and friendship. They are a constant source of affection. I am deeply grateful to Tamara Kelly, associate director of communications and external relations at Pace, for being my linguistic anchor. I also want to recognize Elki and Chaim Herzog; Batya, Chanoch, and Ephraim Kunin; and Devora and Ayala Szenberg. They worked with diligence, character, good humor, exactitude, and patience. They all have lightened many a task. Their assistance was incalculable, and I am grateful to them.

My heart still warms with gratitude toward Sadia Afridi, Ester Robbins (Budek), Leo Faleev, Lisa Ferraro, Laura Garcia, Lisa Heffron Youel, Jennifer Loftus, Marina Slavina, Janet Ulman, and Aparna Vasudevan, my past talented and devoted graduate research assistants who have helped directly and indirectly in more ways that I can list to make this book the offspring of our partnership. Their input lives on in these pages.

We do not forget for a moment the arduous task of Julia Roca, who voluntarily undertook the preparation of this manuscript for publication; Iva Juric, who also prepared the index for *Franco Modigliani: A Mind That Never Rests*; and Aaron Ross, who continues to express his willingness to edit our writings. Julia, Iva, and Aaron are imbued with unremitting kindness and exactitude.

In addition, a number of former students deserve thanks for their invaluable inputs and assistance—Frank DiMeglio, Lorene Hiris, Richard Larocca, Tahany Naggar, Andrea Pascarelli, Cathyann Tully, and Alan Zimmerman. They have gone on to occupy educational and administrative positions at various universities.

And finally, to the many who have in their own special ways supported my efforts, I thank Michelle Cheung, Lloyd Duberry Jr., Hema Gajaraj, Anna Geller, Masha Gishin, Yelena Glants, Natalie Hedden, Aishwarya Kothapally, Olesya Kurilo, LiLi, Sandy Lundy-Resnick, Raizel Moskowitz, Larisa Parkhomovskaya, Umesh Patel, Joshua Pearl, Jigyasa Roy, Dhvani Shelat, and Justyna Tuniewicz.

Any institution, especially one of higher learning, is best led by individuals who combine toughness with humanity. Pace University is indeed fortunate to have at the present time leaders at its helm who embody these qualities—President Stephen J. Friedman and Provost Uday Sukhatme. My deep gratitude to Stephen for his rare combination of effective leadership, efficiency, humility, kindness, and cheerfulness.

I am blessed to have had everyone's help and support.

Michael Szenberg

Note

1. Some time ago, Melinda Beck, health columnist and editor at the *Wall Street Journal*, asked me how I arrived at this motto. My argument is that diligence and talent are important but that mental toughness, character, passion, and the desire to excel are more important. We need these qualities to cope with rejection. As a famous study once showed, successful people face more rejections than unsuccessful people. In fact, I welcome rejections because I believe that nature does not tolerate imbalances; therefore, acceptances must follow after rejections. Also, according to the first law of thermodynamics, energy can be neither created nor destroyed. It can only be transformed. So the negative energy of a rejection can be transformed into positive energy. Therefore, rejections energize me.

Introduction: What Editors Do and Want to Tell Us

Michael Watts

Being named the editor of a respected academic journal is a clear signal of ability and professional esteem on many dimensions, in almost all cases including a long and well-known record of scholarship in a field or sub-field. The past and present editors who have contributed chapters to this volume are a highly successful group of mostly senior economists, many of whom describe themselves as opinionated. Given that, the editors of the volume undoubtedly anticipated and faced a cat-herding problem. Judging by the range of topics represented in the chapters, including some issues and experiences discussed in only one or a few of the chapters, they quite sensibly appear to have offered contributors general suggestions on topics related to editing journals and allowed them more than usual latitude to write on special and even personal issues and concerns.

Some chapters are mostly sanguine reflections on what was accomplished by the writers or their journals, although they often include suggestions on how to deal with some of the persistent and well-known problems that face editors. Several contributors devote considerable space to the key role that was played by their predecessors and mentors in founding or strengthening the journals they later took over or for bringing them into roles that led them to become editors. Among others, such encomiums go out to Joseph Stiglitz, Karl Brunner, Gordon Tullock, René Stulz, and Ingrid Rima.

Other chapters feature complaints or explanations about special problems and sometimes personally painful experiences that can arise when economists serve as editors. Among the most serious issues in this category are accusations of various kinds of plagiarism, whether they are founded, unfounded, or uncertain. At a more routine and mundane level, editors also note frustrations with late or undelivered referee reports, slow resubmissions of revised manuscripts from authors, and in some cases limited resources.

Scattered across many of the chapters, although not featured as the major focus in any of them, are wide-ranging observations about the overall level of effectiveness of the system of academic journals in economics. These are offered from an insider's warts-and-all perspective. The consensus opinion on the general assessment is strongly positive—not surprisingly given the selection process for contributors to the volume. But at the same time, the writers are keenly aware of and concerned about the flaws and failings of the system and sometimes suggest at least partial remedies or policies for dealing with them. In several cases, the writers have already tried to address the problems with special initiatives or policies. A few notable successes are reported, but more often the initiatives lead to mixed or unsatisfactory results, due largely the persistent and deeply rooted nature of the problems.

Many common points are put forward on a wide range of topics across most of the chapters, including advice and pointed requests to authors who are submitting manuscripts, to referees, and to anyone who is thinking about serving as an editor or associate editor or perhaps even starting a new journal. On a few of these topics, there are notable differences of opinion—for example, in the discussion of the gate-keeping versus developmental and copyediting roles that editors and editorial staffs should play. Some of those disagreements reflect differences in the various journals' rankings, their intended audiences, and the personal beliefs of the different editors. For example, because the (usually invited) articles in the *Journal of Economic Perspectives* are intended to be accessible to economists who do not specialize in the subfields from which the articles are drawn, there is a greater emphasis on copyediting for those papers, which has led to a specialized editorial position and role at the journal. But even at other journals, editors note that they push authors to strengthen the writing in submitted papers (see especially Rubin and Dnes, chapter 12), with Campbell R. Harvey (chapter 4) putting special emphasis on abstracts and introductions, which he sees as keys to the "marketing" of papers.

Some of the chapters deal with the special history and challenges facing particular subfields and journals in those subfields. All of the editors of field journals are concerned about how their fields can become more accepted and influential in the discipline or at least maintain their current status.

Reading the chapters together, several overarching questions and at least partial answers to those questions emerge. In the final section of this introduction, I review and discuss what the editors say about three such questions:

1. Is the current system of journal publication and manuscript reviews working reasonably well, or is it underachieving, perhaps to the point of being biased or fundamentally flawed?

2. What can editors do, individually or perhaps with some degree of coordination, to make the journals work better?

3. What personal characteristics are most important for a good editor?

But first, I briefly discuss what the writers have to say about the ordinary and not-so-ordinary concerns that come with the job of editing an economics journal. The contributors use most of the pages of their chapters to address these points, and when they offer overall appraisals of the successes and failures of their journals, their own editorships, and the general process of publishing in economics journals, those appraisals are based on their knowledge of and experiences in dealing with the routine and nonroutine facets of serving as editor.

Issues from an Editor's Ordinary Business of Life

Authors

Journals and editors ultimately depend on the quantity and quality of manuscripts that are submitted for review, which presents a greater problem for lower-ranked journals than top-tier journals—most of which have been ranked in the top tier for decades. Despite that key difference in what editors of different journals have to work with, there is a strong consensus across these chapters—from editors of first-, second-, and even third-tier journals—on what authors can do (and should do more often) to submit work that has a higher chance of being published. The editors would like to see articles that are written more carefully and clearly. They would like authors to include key citations that show where the article fits into the existing literature, why it fits the journal to which it has been submitted, and who might be appropriate referees for the article (for example, see Rubin and Dnes, chapter 12). Several editors mention that they too often see papers—including many that have almost certainly been rejected earlier at other journals—that have not been updated to cite recent publications or key working papers.

A few editors warn authors not to oversell the contribution of their papers and not to be overly and unnecessarily critical of earlier works that reached different conclusions or used different analytical frameworks or different data. Describing how a paper advances or revises the current view of a topic does not require a condescending dismissal of earlier work on the subject. There are also several calls to stress content over technique. For example, Richard Friberg (chapter 2) suggests that, at least after tenure, authors should slow down in terms of the number of papers they try to publish so that they can do deeper and more innovative work.

After authors have received reviews and an editorial decision, they are encouraged to take referee comments seriously and respond to them clearly and directly, either in the revised paper or the cover letter for the resubmission. As noted earlier, revisions should be resubmitted on a timely basis.

When articles are rejected, as are most of papers submitted to all of the journals represented in this sample, authors are advised to allow time for the understandable disappointment and anger of the rejection to fade before considering an appeal or complaint to the editor. Authors are also asked to recognize some facts of life in the journal review process—including journals' space limitations, a "crap shoot" or "luck of the draw" element in referee assignments, and editorial "saturation points" in terms of the number of articles on a particular topic or technique that a journal is likely to accept.

Referees and the Review Process

Almost all of the editors report using desk rejections for papers that they view as being inappropriate for their journal or as falling too far below publication standards to justify using scarce staff and referee time. Some editors appear to use desk rejections far more than others, however. Most papers that make it through desk review are assigned to associate editors, who assign referees, but in some cases, associate editors add an additional level of desk review or suggest that the editor reconsider a desk rejection.

Good referees are a treasure to the discipline and particularly to editors and associate editors. But as noted earlier and again below in the discussion of structural problems and shortcomings with the journal process, some referees are problematic. The big issue is late reviews, including reviews that are promised but never delivered. Daniel Hamermesh (1994) reported that 5 percent of referee reports are never submitted and that another small percentage of reports are late, with referees often claiming the papers or reports were "lost" in various ways. Those rates would be higher if editors and associate editors did not spend such a large part of their time—as virtually all of the contributors to this volume discuss—in carefully choosing referees and reminding referees about overdue reports. Several writers also note that it is important to keep track of which referees are habitually prompt or slow and "easy or tough" in their recommendations to accept, reject, or revise.

Late and undelivered referee reports might be addressed by paying or paying more for referee reports. But even at journals that do pay, including the *American Economic Review*, the average hourly rate for a good referee report falls well below the minimum wage. This key role in the profession remains based on a service rationale and perhaps on recognition of that service at the referees' host institutions. Several of the editors, especially John Pencavel (chapter 5) and Daniel F. Spulber (chapter 8), thank most of the referees they have worked with for service above and beyond the call of the service role, not only in terms of making better decisions on which manuscripts to accept and reject but also in improving papers. Several editors note that they inform referees about the final decision on manuscripts they have reviewed, and a few send personal letters thanking referees for each report they submit, including reports on revised versions of papers.

There are notable differences in procedures for using referees to review revised manuscripts, however. Lawrence J. White (chapter 9), for example, says that he rarely asks referees to look at revisions. There is also variance in the number of referees that are typically assigned to review papers. Two is most common, but some journals use just one for many papers, and at least one journal typically uses three. Others use two referees with an associate editor or the editor acting as the third reader.

Some of the editors complain that referee reports too often address technical issues but not the overall significance of the paper. Fabrizio Zilibotti (chapter 6) writes that "In some fields, especially narrow ones, scratching each other's back is much too common" and recommends using at least one referee who is a generalist—someone "especially trustworthy because she or he is expected to give me the representative reaction of a mature general reader." Problems are also reported with referees who favor papers that use established procedures over innovative approaches and with others who suggest radical revisions that essentially direct authors to write different papers along lines the referees would have followed if they had written the papers themselves.

It is still common practice to keep the identities of referees unknown to authors, but many journals have abandoned the double-blind standard and do not try to keep referees from knowing the identity of manuscript authors, mainly because Internet searches of working papers usually make that impossible. A single-blind policy also saves considerable journal staff time (which in some cases means the editor's own time) by not requiring redaction of self-citations and other identifying passages.

In annual reports for their journals, editors usually report the average times from submission to first editorial response, from submission to acceptance, and from submission to final publication. Several editors argue that the time to first response is the best general measure of editorial efficiency in the review process because it is not affected by authors' lags in revising and resubmitting articles but still indicates how diligent the editorial staff is in completing desk reviews, assigning associate editors and referees, monitoring and prompting referees to complete reviews, and preparing reports to send to authors (see Ramarattan and Szenberg, chapter 24, for more details on this editorial cycle). Several editors also note that at least some offers to revise papers include an explicit warning that the revision may not be accepted, especially in cases where substantial revisions are suggested.

The Cash Nexus

There is relatively little discussion by the editors about specific financial policies at their journals, including journal subscription fees, article submission fees, or payments to referees, editors, and associate editors. Subscription fees are often set by publishers that own journals and may not be tied to revenue streams that the editors control. R. Preston McAfee (chapter 3) cites and sympathizes with Ted Bergstrom, who has complained about monopoly pricing for journals (and books) that are sold primarily to academic libraries. In some cases, subscription fees are tied to memberships and dues for professional associations, with association members receiving a discount on subscription rates or perhaps other benefits such as reduced or waived fees for submitting manuscripts. Zilibotti (chapter 6) reviews the decision to start the *Journal of the European Economic Association* when the European Economic Association "divorced" itself from Elsevier because it viewed Elsevier's pricing policies as "exploitative." Ties with professional associations can have important content implications, too. In some cases, the match between an association and a journal becomes incompatible over time, as Daniel W. Bromley (chapter 14) recounts for *Land Economics* and the real estate group Lambda Alpha International.

Some journals, including those published by the American Economic Association (AEA), pay editors and associate editors at levels that reflect estimates of salary-based opportunity costs. But most journals pay much less, and many pay nothing at all. As noted earlier, some journals pay modest amounts for referee reports, but most journals do not pay referees.

The transactions costs of journals' handling fees and payments are high, and authors are no doubt more willing to pay higher submission fees to higher-ranked journals. Smaller journals are therefore less likely to adopt fees and payments beyond a basic subscription fee for the journal.

Some journals were created as the publication outlet for a professional association, some were founded with financial sponsorship by a publisher, and others were sold to a publisher after operating independently for a time. In all of these cases, journals seek a higher or more stable resource base and often shift the transactions costs of handling financial payments and receipts to the sponsoring organization. Predictably, the general-interest journals sponsored by national associations of economics tend to be highly ranked journals in nations with large numbers of economists, compared to journals sponsored by regional (especially intranational) organizations or field journals.

One exceptional case in which a journal evolved into a major funding source for its host organization deserves note. At the *Journal of Economic Literature* (*JEL*), Pencavel (chapter 5) pushed for the AEA to keep ownership of *EconLit*—the bibliographic database developed largely by Mark Perlman that emerged from and eventually replaced part of the print version of *JEL* over time—rather than selling it to a commercial publisher. *EconLit* was initially licensed to libraries and other uses in a Silver Platter CD-ROM format and later in online formats provided by EBSCO and other companies. The AEA's financial success in doing this is sharply contrasted with the experiences of associations in other disciplines in a recent *Chronicle of Higher Education* article (Berrett 2012).

Out-of-the-Ordinary Editorial Issues and Problems

The chapters in this volume relate many cases in which editors or prospective editors faced a number of extraordinary situations, including starting a new journal or resurrecting an old one; responding to a new journal that was targeting the same readership and authors drawn from a particular subfield; dealing with disputes that arose with members of editorial boards, authors, referees, the journal's publisher, or other stakeholders; adapting to new technologies for handling manuscripts and referee reports or for publishing and distributing the journal; implementing or adapting to new pricing and marketing schemes, which often originate from the publisher; and at some journals facing occasional or more regular financial crises. For some of these events, there are relatively standard approaches that represent necessary if not sufficient responses. In launching a new journal, for example, the first issue and volume are crucial in attracting notice and readership, so prominent economists are usually invited to submit articles. A distinguished editorial board is named, and the editor—also someone well known in the field or subfield—often writes a short piece on the rationale and goals for the journal, noting its distinctive procedures and features. These approaches have been used at least since the 1960s, when there was a rapid increase in the number of economics journals being published.

Plagiarism

Based on an informal page count of content issues from chapters in this volume, the major issue facing editors that is not common enough to be considered part of the ordinary business of editing but also is not so rare that it can be ignored is plagiarism. A survey by Walter Enders and Gary A. Hoover (2004), cited by J. Barkley Rosser Jr. (chapter 21), looked at responses from 130 journal editors and reported that the average frequency of plagiarism at those journals was once every two years. All responsible journal editors have to look for and try to avoid these charges, and for the most part they succeed. But when charges arise, especially if they become public, they become a major drain on the resources of the journal and editor. And on a higher ground, Szenberg (chapter 22) argues that editors have an ethical responsibility to address these issues openly and fully, because of their impact on the professional reputations of authors, journals, and editors.

There are several kinds of plagiarism. Some cases are blatant and, once identified, undeniable. Examples include entire papers published by others, including those that are translated and taken entirely or almost entirely from journals printed in other languages. Sometimes long sections of work by others are taken from sources in the same language, with only the title and parts of the introduction and conclusion changed. Cases of self-plagiarism, in which all or major parts of an article are taken from an author's earlier and already published work—sometimes without citations—are often more difficult to establish. This is even harder to do when the other work has not yet appeared in print but has been simultaneously submitted to multiple journals in articles with different titles or when some part of the content is different at least in terms of wording if not substance. William E. Becker and Suzanne R. Becker (chapter 18) describe a different and unusual variant of self-citation that runs in the opposite direction. In this case, an author cites empirical results and data from his own earlier work, but the paper cited was never written and the data and programs that were reported with the self-citation were "not available."

Yet another form of plagiarism involves the deliberate failure to cite earlier work by other authors that features the writer's approaches and general results. The issue in these cases often is a matter of degree and judgment and centers on questions of how much a current article copies earlier work versus cases of truly independent discoveries such as the well-known examples of Isaac Newton and Gottfried Leibniz with the development of calculus, John R. Hicks and Eugen Slutsky with the separation of income and substitution effects, and the lawsuit brought by Fantasy, Inc. against the singer-songwriter John Fogerty, who was accused of self-plagiarism because one of his new songs (released by Warner Bros. Records) sounded too much like one of his older songs (released by Fantasy, Inc.).

Rosser says there is a general view that "editors are cowards or wimps for not more vigorously moving to punish plagiarists," but he points out "fear of litigation by one who is accused is complex. It is not always easy to prove plagiarism, and editors often disagree about what constitutes plagiarism." The survey of editors by Enders and Hoover (2004) reflects both facets of this problem. But several authors describe cases in which editors failed to deal with plagiarism effectively and directly. Zilibotti (chapter 6) discusses an editor who published a paper that was plagiarized from earlier work by others and, when the plagiarism was uncovered, only required the authors of the plagiarizing paper to publish a list of additional references that included the original work. Zilibotti writes that the editor's behavior in this case was similar to the episode of the capsized cruise ship *Costa Concordia*, in which the captain was "directly responsible for the disaster" but showed by his actions that "his sole concern was to leave the boat and swim ashore, abandoning many passengers trapped in the ship."

Special Initiatives

A much different kind of out-of-the-ordinary work done by editors—more positive and ultimately more important—reflects the entrepreneurial possibilities of the position. Editors often adopt and experiment with various kinds of special initiatives, and the contributors to this volume have done much of this kind of work. A selected set of those initiatives is listed and briefly described below. Many of these examples warrant notice on their own merits, but they also offer insights into the key roles that editors can play for a journal and for the profession as a whole.

During his tenure as editor at *Economic Inquiry*, McAfee (chapter 3) launched several experiments and reforms that he felt could more appropriately be tried at *Economic Inquiry* than at the very top journals, such as the *American Economic Review*, where he had previously served as a coeditor. The initiative that drew the most notice offered authors the choice to have articles either accepted or rejected, eliminating the required revise-and-resubmit option. Authors who choose this option still receive referee reports, and all of the authors of papers that were accepted under this option at the time McAfee wrote his chapter had made revisions before publication, even though they were not required to do so. The primary aim of the option is to cut down on the number of rounds of revisions and thereby speed up the review and acceptance process, but it also encourages authors to spend more time preparing a paper before submitting it. McAfee also instituted a much larger editorial board at *Economic Inquiry*, including numerous coeditors, specialized coeditors for particular fields, and associate editors. He also encouraged the submission of a few "humor and entertainment" articles, noting the precedent of Axel Leijonhufvud's 1973 *Western Economic Journal* article, "Life among the Econ," and several papers published at the *Journal of Political Economy* when George Stigler was the editor.

At the *Journal of Money, Credit, and Banking*, a replication project was conducted from 1982 to 1984 that required authors to submit their statistical programs and data along with each manuscript. The hope was that the requirement would significantly reduce the frequency and magnitude of errors, but attempts to replicate results using the data and programs provided by the authors found that "inadvertent errors in published empirical articles are a common-place rather than a rare occurrence. While correction of the errors did not affect the authors' conclusions in most studies, the errors make independent replication impossible unless the replicator errs in precisely the same way" (Dewald, Thursby, and Anderson 1986, 587–588). In their chapter here, William G. Dewald and Richard G. Anderson (chapter 13) conclude that

The situation is little better today. The economics profession seems trapped in a stable 'bad' equilibrium wherein replication is interpreted as an affront to the author and wherein no one questions the quality or accuracy of published results lest he or she also be questioned. Although some journals collect data, none requires its submission as a condition of publication, and few journals collect authors' programs.

Harvey (chapter 4) notes that at the same time that several top economics journals were implementing these policies related to replication and access to data sets and programs, the *Journal of Finance* held long discussions about doing something similar, but opposition to the policy was widespread, and it was not adopted. Harvey also notes that at least one top journal in economics, the *Quarterly Journal of Economics*, did not adopt a replication policy.

As mentioned earlier, at the *Journal of Economic Literature*, Pencavel (chapter 5) pushed for the AEA to keep ownership of *EconLit* rather than selling it to a publisher. He also modernized the classification system for article topics that is now used at *JEL* and at most economics journals and updated the review process for determining which journals would be listed by *JEL* and *EconLit* and which articles would be abstracted in *JEL*.

At the *Journal of the European Economic Association*, a *Papers and Proceedings* issue featuring short papers from invited sessions at the annual meetings of the association was "suppressed" because these papers had come to account for over half of the articles published in the journal each year and were viewed as "on average of lower quality and of less impact than regular submissions" (Zilibotti, chapter 6).

At *Macroeconomic Dynamics*, William A. Barnett (chapter 10) initiated the publication of interviews with leading economists and a Vintage Articles section that prints "old unpublished papers that have become citation classics" but that "often no longer can meet normal peer review in comparably high-quality journals" because they do not consider more recent research.

Spulber (chapter 8) at the *Journal of Economics and Management Strategy* writes survey articles to "prime the pump" for submissions on new topics and has published many special issues on such topics. Many of the other journals also feature special issues or symposiums with invited papers that sometimes are tied to conferences.

At *Land Economics*, Bromley (chapter 14) invited the submission of shorter (ten or fewer double-spaced pages) "speculations" papers but received only half a dozen such papers over a decade and a half.

At the *Journal of Finance* (*JF*), over a six-year term Harvey (chapter 4) handled 210 appeals, which he describes as "nightmares," from authors of rejected papers. Most of the appeals came during the first half of his tenure, but at that point he implemented the policy of allowing an author one appeal every three years. After finishing his term as the *JF* editor, Harvey accepted the position of editor for the American Finance Association's Digital Publishing Initiative. This involves posting electronic versions of articles published in *JF* in HTML versions that have the clean appearance of PDF copies and facilitating mobile delivery of the *JF* to smart phones and tablets in HTML5 and iOS (for Apple products) formats.

At the *Journal of Institutional Economics*, Geoffrey M. Hodgson (chapter 19) notes, editors are not allowed to submit "full-scale articles" for publication, and decisions to accept or reject papers are made by a vote of the five journal editors.

Issues Facing Journals in Subfields

Not all subfields are created equal. Some are much narrower than others. Some are firmly in the mainstream, and others are heterodox or tend to attract more heterodox economists. Some are cross-disciplinary, while others feature topics and methods that are regularly featured in the top-tier general-interest journals. These differences mean that editors of journals for different subfields face different challenges and opportunities.

The regional journals, particularly the international regional journals, warrant a further note, which is well stated by Zvi Eckstein, Esther Gal-Or, Thorvaldur Gylfason, Jürgen von Hagen, and Gerard Pfann (chapter 1): "European economics is not different from American economics," but at the same time "There are preferences, tendencies, and market phenomena that economists residing in different countries try to explain." Partly for that reason, some journals have different editors for submissions from North America and for those from "the rest of the world." And some journals receive unusually large shares of submissions from certain regions of the world or experience major trends in those submissions. For example, over several decades, the share of submissions to *History of Political Economy* from U.S. authors has fallen from over

75 percent to about 15 percent. Barnett (chapter 10) points out that journals and editors may also face political (and even politically correct) arguments for having editors and editorial boards reflect various types of diversity, including geographical, national, racial, ethnic, gender, political, and methodological. Zilibotti (chapter 6) notes that the *Review of Economic Studies* scrapped a British quota on its editorial board in about 2002 and moved to a "pan-European" governing structure.

In recent decades, advances in empirical work and methods in economics have arguably far outpaced developments in theory, to the point that Bromley (chapter 14) claims that "economics is an empirical science, and any field within economics that persists in offering untestable empirical claims cannot be taken seriously." The subfields represented in some of the chapters in this volume that feature empirical studies on a more regular or even near-exclusive basis have been more widely accepted in the discipline on several counts, including citations to work in these subfields by articles published in top-tier journals. Data and findings from many journals—journals on behavioral and experimental economics; management strategy and decision making; money, banking, and credit; industrial organization; economic development; natural resources; sports economics (where unique data on performance, incentives, and financial incentives are sometimes available for journeymen, superstars, managers, or franchises); and regional (domestic or international) general-interest journals—are regularly cited in the top-tier journals, and some empirical articles from these subfields are published in the top-tier journals.

A large share of articles published in the *History of Political Economy*, the *Journal of Economic Education*, and the *Journal of Economic Issues* are not empirical studies, which affects their position in the discipline and the likelihood of citations in journals from other subfields and general-interest journals. Craufurd Goodwin (chapter 7) writes that although it was once common for the leading economists in the world (including Paul Samuelson and George Stigler) to write about earlier economists and the history of thought, in recent decades "Even parts of the mother discipline that had traditionally welcomed some attention to [the history of economic thought] now turned their backs on anything 'literary.' Economic historians at their meetings and in their journals celebrated their newfound cliometrics and seemed embarrassed by [the history of economic thought]."

Goodwin goes on to note that one option for historians of economic thought is moving to history or philosophy departments, where they

could "become more appropriately voyeurs of economics than participants in it." In fact, there are faculty members in history, philosophy, and
English departments who specialize in economic issues and topics and
regularly draw from at least some historical writings by "literary" economists. My own impression is that more of these scholars espouse heterodox views than do those with the same areas of specialization who are
employed in economics departments. Economic education and the economics of education specialists are often found in schools of education,
in some cases holding doctorate or at least master's degrees in economics
or economic policy.

The *Journal of Economic Education* (*JEE*) features formal empirical
studies and papers with survey results in some of its sections. In addition,
it has sections devoted to pedagogical papers featuring innovative teaching methods for both new and old topics as well as "content" articles
designed to summarize recent developments and findings on topics and
subfields for economics instructors who do not specialize in those areas.
Occasionally, articles appear based on new theories of learning from the
general education literature or new assessment methods developed by
psychometricians or other education specialists. Some articles deal with
precollege (K–12) education. Most articles that do not feature formal
empirical analysis or feature a cross-disciplinary outlook may well underlie, at least in part, Becker and Becker's (chapter 18) discussion concerning reports from the Association to Advance Collegiate Schools of
Business (AACSB) claiming that pedagogical research in economics and
other business areas cannot be as rigorous as research in other business
subfields. Whether or not the rigor claim is true, even in the first volume
of *JEE*, published in 1969–70, George Stigler and Kenneth Boulding
recognized that economic education would struggle for acceptance in the
discipline: Stigler titled his article "The Case, If Any, for Economic Literacy" (1970), and Boulding titled his "Economic Education: The Stepchild, Too, Is Father to the Man" (1969). Education was seen as a
stepchild by academics in many disciplines long before there was a field
of economic education.

With few exceptions, as Becker and Becker point out, the response to
economic education from schools of education has not been overwhelm-
ingly positive. This is in line with the tendency of many educators, including many who are most active with recent developments in the scholarship
of teaching and learning (SOTL) initiatives first launched by the Carnegie
Academy for the Scholarship of Teaching and Learning (CASTL),
to "marginalize" (Shulman 2004, 20) discipline-specific educational

research and journals. Part of this problem probably arises because some leading field-specific journals—including those in economics, physics, math and statistics education, and several business areas—regularly publish empirical studies featuring current methodologies for empirical work in their respective disciplines. That analysis goes well beyond the training of a large share of education professors, many of whom work in curriculum and instruction areas rather than in assessment and psychometrics.

Some subfields eschew mainstream economics or do not limit publications based on the methods and general findings of orthodox economics. Instead, they feature radical, Marxian, or "traditional" institutional economics and other perspectives discussed by Richard V. Adkisson (chapter 11), Steven Pressman (chapter 20), and Hodgson (chapter 19). These journals struggle with maintaining status and respect in the profession. One problem that they face is that journal rankings are based largely on citations in other journals, weighted to reflect the rankings of those journals.

Adkisson's chapter is a plea for tolerating dissenting opinions, for encouraging pluralism in the discipline, and for valuing the work of economists who publish only rarely and who teach in lower-tier departments and schools—not just the contributions of the "big lizard" economists and departments. He claims "pluralism in theory and method can only enrich the economics method." He also criticizes studies that characterize published articles that are never cited as "dry holes" or "useless papers," arguing that many of these papers have value for the authors, readers, and other economics instructors that is not captured by citation counts. Adkisson does not cite a recent study by Howard Wall (2009) that shows that many articles in the highest-ranked economics journals are cited less frequently than typical articles in much lower ranked journals and raises other questions about the value and appropriate use of journal rankings.

Hodgson makes the case for emphasizing the key role that is played by institutions in determining economic outcomes, endorsing both traditional and newer frameworks (including behavioral models of individual, agent, and group actions) for analyzing these effects. Although he feels that it is easier to publish work in institutional and evolutionary economics today than it was thirty years ago, he believes that a mainstream bias still favors standard theoretical frameworks that value technical elegance and mathematical rigor, while often ignoring or slighting real-world problems. He argues that "the turn toward institutions requires a broadening of economics to embrace history, social theory, the methodology of economics, evolutionary theory, and much else," which creates a place for journals that "span multiple disciplines in pursuit of the common understanding of economically vital phenomena."

A basic question that this raises is whether there is a conspiracy or "tyranny of the status quo" to favor big lizards and keep little lizards tucked away in their assigned, marginalized departments and journals. I address that question, in a somewhat larger context, in the next and last major section of this introduction, while considering the first overarching question posed by the collection of chapters in this volume.

Broader Questions and Issues, with Some Suggested Answers and Assessments

This section examines three overarching questions that are addressed by virtually all of the chapter authors:

• Is the system of journals in economics underachieving?

• What can editors do to make the journal system in economics work better?

• What characteristics are most important for a good editor?

The contributors often raise and answer the first two questions in the chapters, but the third question is different. Only a few contributors raise it directly, but as they recount their own experiences, trials, achievements, and frustrations as editors, they indirectly offer important insights into the question.

Is the system of journals in economics underachieving?

In 2006, Derek Bok viewed U.S. colleges and universities as generally doing a good job, but he noted areas where improvement was not only possible but widely recognized as needed and had enough empirical research available to identify some reasonably clear paths toward improvement. For editors and journals in economics, this is perhaps a case of viewing a glass as part empty or part full. Reasonable people can argue the case for improvements, while others may conclude that editors are doing the best they can in a difficult job with compensation ranging from moderate to zero. These perspectives may relate to where the observer stands (and works) in the profession, and the overall "good but far from perfect" assessment found in this volume is undoubtedly affected by the selection process for contributors. But as a group and in virtually all of the individual chapters, the contributors candidly raise and discuss a wide range of problems with the journal review and publication process and take those problems and allegations of other problems seriously.

First and foremost, there is widespread recognition of both type 1 errors and type 2 errors at journals—that is, in this setting, rejecting articles that should have been accepted or accepting articles that should have been rejected. No editors suggest that all errors can be eliminated. Harvey (chapter 4) says that they are inevitable and warns "After you realize you made a mistake, you need to move on. If it eats you up, then this is the wrong job for you." Almost half of the chapters cite Joshua Gans and George Shepherd's (1994) *Journal of Economic Perspectives* article about classic articles by leading economists that were initially rejected. There are also many references to studies of the articles characterized by some (e.g., Laband and Tollison 2003) as "dry holes" or "useless papers" because they were never cited in later works. Many of the editors express regrets about some of the papers they published or did not publish, with more frequent angst about publishing weak papers. At new and lower-tier journals, some of this is tied to the pressure of filling four or more issues each year. There are relatively few cases in which the editors feel that they rejected strong papers that should have been published. McAfee (chapter 3) quantifies this as only three articles out of 2,500 rejections during his time at the *American Economic Review*.

The slow pace of reviews, revisions, and publication of articles that are eventually accepted is noted by most of the editors. Several cite and commend Glenn Ellison's (2002) study, which investigated the growing lag times and tried to determine its fundamental cause. Response (and no response) times from referees and with authors' revisions were major factors but did not seem to be increasing over time. What has almost doubled over a thirty-year period is the number of rounds of revisions required before publication.

Many other issues with the referee process are also noted, including referees who suggest revisions that represent a radically and essentially different paper rather than a revision of the original paper. In some ways, this type of reviewer becomes more of an anonymous coauthor than a true referee and may establish a personal interest or even a sense of obligation in accepting revisions that do what the referee suggested, even if the paper has become weaker in other ways. This also leads to claims that some authors game the system by submitting papers designed to maximize invitations to revise and resubmit (see Friberg, chapter 2, on this), in part because the odds of an outright acceptance have become so low. Authors may pursue revise and resubmit invitations by hedging their claims, suggesting multiple interpretations of results, or targeting the editor's assignments of certain referees with citations and the ways that results are presented. Then authors may "prostitute" (Frey 2003) themselves by slavishly following recommended revisions, even if they disagree with what is suggested.

Several editors say the blind referee process sometimes makes papers worse instead of better, and others note that papers accepted by one group of referees might well be rejected by others. Pressman (chapter 20) cites a study from psychology (Peters and Ceci 1985) in which twelve published papers were resubmitted to the prominent journals in which they were originally published. Only three of the thirty-eight editors and referees who handled the resubmitted papers recognized that the papers had already been published, and of the nine papers that were rereviewed, eight were rejected, mostly for "methodological flaws."

Adkisson (chapter 11) quotes David Laband (1990, 343), who writes that "editors have proven credentials in most cases, whereas referees do not necessarily, or even probably, come from that end of the talent distribution." Adkisson also cites Daniel Hamermesh (1994), who notes concerns about long lags and especially "lost" reviews, but he does not report Hamermesh's (1994, 162) overall and key conclusions on these points: "It is very likely that the person refereeing a paper is better-known than the author. Referees tend to be economists whose work is cited widely and who are near the peak of their career. Most of these high-quality referees either accomplish the task or refuse the assignment very rapidly. Only a small fraction of refereeing requests are handled slowly."

Hamermesh reported that 5 percent of referees never submit a report and that 20 percent who are asked to do reports decline to do so. Pressman says that those numbers are close to his experience but that things have gotten worse over time.

Several of the editors note concerns about referee biases against papers that are innovative but also biases in favor of papers in "faddish" areas. These faddish areas may be subfields that have been accepted relatively recently, newer methodologies that are used by more economists, or more established areas that deal with specific topics that become "hot." Recent examples include experimental and behavioral economics and empirical papers from many areas that are reviewed and accepted more because of their technical methods and strengths than economics content. Ramrattan and Szenberg (chapter 24) extend this discussion into three broad areas of criteria for evaluating articles: "positive (science), normative (belief), and art (practical)."

Bromley (chapter 14) discusses a specific example of a hot topic in an established field—contingent valuation methods for evaluating the effects of the *Exxon Valdez* oil spill—that made it difficult for him to find unbiased referees because many referees and potential referees had been hired as expert witnesses on either side of the lawsuits. In time, this "changed" journals in the field and led Bromley "for the first time in twenty years . . . to entertain doubts about the fairness of the review process." More generally, he sees the continuing overemphasis on technical strengths rather than the overall pertinence and effect of papers as a kind of "safety first" policy for referees and journals, which ultimately leads to the implicit adoption of a "standard format" for most submitted and accepted papers. Pencavel (chapter 5) echoes this by noting a bias for referees and journals to "play it safe" by rejecting controversial papers, papers with mixed reviews, and those out of the mainstream.

The overall effectiveness of the journals in the search for truth that is, ideally, empirically testable and replicable is also open to question based on problems with attempts to conduct direct replications using data sets and statistical programs provided by the authors of papers submitted to the *Journal of Money, Credit, and Banking*, discussed earlier. The major paper on this project and the problems it identified is William Dewald, Jerry Thursby, and Richard Anderson (1986), updated here in the chapter by Dewald and Anderson (chapter 13).

Conspiracy theories circulate among contributors to economics journals. McAfee (chapter 3) notes that several authors whose papers he accepted at the *American Economic Review* thanked him for "breaking the conspiracy of journal editors to favor the top ten departments." But he says that he is confident there is not a conspiracy because, if there were, he would never have been chosen as an *AER* coeditor. Pencavel (chapter 5) says that editors of the top journals receive rents—financial and nonfinancial—that could be exploited because the top journals are downward immobile, making it possible for editors at the top journals to see their job as only arbitrating between authors and referees, with the goal of maintaining the quality and ranking of the journal. This goes back to the question of whether editors serve only as gate keepers or whether they are also expected to devote their time and other resources to developmental and even copyediting functions. At the *Journal of Economic Literature*, Pencavel spent a lot of time improving the clarity of organization and language in the articles he published, but that journal, like the *Journal of Economic Perspectives*, has a specialized role and publishes articles that are usually invited.

McAfee (chapter 3) endorses the exclusively gate-keeper role for editors and also cites David Laband and Michael Piette (1994), who argue that favoritism at top journals exists and is efficient. But more editors who raise the issue seem to side with Spulber (chapter 8), who writes, "We have tried to give fair readings without imposing orthodoxy based on who you know, where you teach, or what the latest hot topic or technique is." Instead, he notes that the *Journal of Economics and Management Strategy* challenged orthodoxy in its choice of topics, taking articles on any industry and on business and management topics and not just standard economics. Zilibotti (chapter 6) points out that the *Review of Economic Studies* has a long history of appointing young editors (including him) and that the stated reason for that policy is "to preserve its independence from the more established senior core of the profession."

Other arguments for rejecting or at least questioning the conspiracy theory reflect rejection patterns at journals. The article by Joshua Gans and George Shepherd (1994) that is cited in many of the chapters in this volume notes that some articles that later turned out to be classic articles were initially rejected. Those rejected articles were written by prominent economists, including Gary Becker, Fischer Black and Myron Scholes, James M. Buchanan, Paul Krugman, Robert Lucas Jr., Franco Modigliani, Paul Samuelson, James Tobin, and Gordon Tullock. This inconsistency in acceptance and rejection decisions is inherent in the "luck of the draw" nature of the referee process, but it certainly raises questions related to efficiency and objectivity of the process for any individual decision. Even so, there are a reasonably large number of general-interest and field journals, which provides some assurance that, in time, most good papers can eventually find an outlet.

What can editors do to make the journal system in economics work better?

Relevant parts of the response to the question of what editors can do to make the journal system in economics work better were discussed in the earlier discussion of the special initiatives already enacted by the contributors to this volume. Some of those initiatives were remarkably successful, some had little notable effect, and most were only partial solutions to problems that are entrenched, stubborn, and sometimes endemic. Dewald and Anderson (chapter 13) summarize why this is so:

Because authors understand that their career prospects are related to the number of articles they publish and the number of citations to their work, incentives with respect to any individual manuscript are in conflict. The paper should be of sufficient quality to gain attention, but time spent polishing, revising, and documenting should be minimized because the profession does not highly value such attributes. Referees want accepted papers to be clear and well documented because the costs of revising them does not fall on them. Editors wish to publish only the highest-quality papers, thereby attracting readers, citations, and ever higher-quality papers (as well as enhancing their own professional stature), but they also must fill the pages of the journal to meet publication deadlines. Eventually, . . . some weaker papers slip through.

Editors can address some of the problems noted in these chapters, for example, by overriding mixed or even negative reviews on an innovative paper that may turn out to be a classic paper in a discipline or subfield. One such case occurred with Vernon Smith's first paper on experimental economics (1962), which was published in the *Journal of Political Economy* after Harry Johnson made the decision to publish the paper, as recounted in Smith (1981). Whenever an editor deals with problems in ways that go outside a journal's usual methods of operation, however, there usually are additional costs to face.

McAfee (chapter 3) and Friberg (chapter 2) suggest exploring some level of coordination across journals, either to encourage a different format for dividing basic text and technical details of articles more along the lines featured in some natural science areas (Friberg) or to reduce the number of times the same article is refereed when it is sequentially rejected by several journals and resubmitted to others (McAfee). Coordination would be difficult to establish and maintain, partly because of the routine turnover of editors. It would also be controversial on some fronts, especially in the case of sharing referee reports, given the "luck of the draw" issues and the conspiracy charges that are already often lodged against the top-tier journals, as noted earlier.

What characteristics are most important for a good editor?

This section does not necessarily list the most important characteristics of good editors in rank order, in part because different characteristics are more important at some kinds of journals than others. Some great editors come up short on one or more of these traits, but in an ideal world, editors of economics journals would probably have the following qualities:

Decisive

McAfee (chapter 3) calls it "opinionated," and Timothy Taylor (chapter 23) writes, "I have opinions to burn." But the essential aspect seems to be decisiveness—being ready, after due consideration, to pull the trigger in dealing with submissions, revisions, requests, and responses from authors, referees, associate editors, members of editorial boards, and other stakeholders. In other areas of journal business, some of the editors argue against an activist practice of pushing for articles on specific topics, and others encourage this practice with special issues, invited articles, and sponsored conferences. Once again, this disagreement sometimes reflects differences at top-tier general-interest journals and lower-tier or subfield journals. But in any case, someone who suffers from decision paralysis is not a good candidate for an editor's position at any journal that deals with hundreds of submissions a year.

Hard Working and Prompt

Editors should be hard working and prompt, especially in the sense of being diligent and well organized, perhaps to the point of being compulsive (McAfee says "obsessive"), especially in the routine business of dealing with articles, referee reports, and other correspondence. Harvey (chapter 4) notes that the median turnaround time at the *Journal of Finance* near the end of his term had been cut down to forty-two days—attributable in part to keeping good records about referee response times (and quality of reports) and making more extensive use of desk rejections. But he stresses the importance of deciding quickly: "Once you have the referee and associate editor reports, there is no reason to sit on a paper and wait to make a decision. Time is not your friend." Similarly, Zilibotti (chapter 6) says that "The first rule for good editorship is 'Never accumulate large delays and backlogs'" and that "No matter how hard-pressed editors are, they can [assign papers to referees] speedily if they take their job as a priority. Those who cannot spare a few minutes every other day for these tasks should not accept editorial responsibilities."

Direct

Editors need to be direct, for example, when they tell authors why an article is rejected or which referee comments to focus on during revisions. Also, as Zilibotti (chapter 6) notes, in the relatively unusual cases of whether to consider a new submission from an author on the same topic that was addressed in a rejected paper, editors should note whether the new submission might be sent to new referees, who are more likely to review the paper using different criteria than referees who saw the earlier version.

Personal and Polite

The traits of being personal and polite shine through in many of the chapters in this book, but especially in the discussions by Pencavel (chapter 5) and Spulber (chapter 8) about how they deal with authors and referees. I was impressed by Pencavel's personal and remarkably extensive thank-you notes for referee reports, which I remembered warmly when reading his chapter.

Ethical

Although the trait of being ethical is not surprising, it struck me as more important after reading the chapters and moved up on my personal ranking of the most important characteristics for editors of journals. It stands out in the many discussions plagiarism. But treating authors, referees, and other editorial staff members fairly and effectively is crucial, too, and in most of these dealings, the editor is in the position of making the final decision, so Acton's warning that power corrupts is in play. Bromley (chapter 14) notes that other economists have incentives to flatter and ingratiate themselves with editors, at least until the editor rejects one or more of their articles, at which time candor may be reestablished with bias in the opposite direction. Harvey (chapter 4) extends this discussion by ruling out any sense of quid pro quo in accepting or rejecting submissions and by avoiding conflicts of interests in assigning referees and in assigning papers to associate editors—if necessary, using an acting editor to deal with a paper. Hodgson (chapter 19) calls for journals to develop and publish policies on potential conflicts of interest by, for example, identifying referees' and editors' past relationships with authors of submitted papers and revealing sources of any funding that the authors of papers have received to conduct that research. Selecting editors who are known for personal and professional integrity can help in all of these settings and may not be as widely recognized and appreciated as a criterion for editorships as it should be.

Entrepreneurial

Being entrepreneurial in fundraising and securing financial support is perhaps less in demand at the established and more prominent journals, but new and struggling journals sometimes require these skills as a necessary condition for survival. In most cases, though, entrepreneurship at journals also entails strategies for attracting better papers and referees and building a strong editorial board with strong associate editors. At least at some journals, this involves invited articles, special issues, and clearly defined sections for different kinds of papers that help to develop and direct a subfield.

Open Minded

Editors need to be open minded, especially about innovative and otherwise unusual articles, so long as they are up to usual publication standards or are capable of being brought up to that standard with a revision. There is even some consensus about "cutting a little slack" to innovative articles, at least in letting them through to the revise-and-resubmit level. Harvey (chapter 4) simply says "take risks" as a purely editorial form of entrepreneurial behavior.

Thick Skinned

Editors need to be thick skinned. McAfee (chapter 3) provides an example of dealing with an author who claimed that he would lose his job and that his family, including young children, would suffer if his paper was rejected. Bromley (chapter 14) and Goodwin (chapter 7) make the same general point, and given acceptance rates, the odds are heavily stacked against making most authors happy. In some cases, another way of describing this trait is "having a sense of humor," which several of the contributors note as being important for an editor's personal sanity and effectiveness. But humor is only partly related to being able to laugh at situations or statements that would otherwise make most people cry and may play a role in other journal decisions, too—for example, in being willing to publish occasionally a humorous or entertaining article.

Altruistic

On several dimensions, editors need to be altruistic, including taking satisfaction from the service role of overseeing what the journal publishes and how it works with modest or often no financial compensation, influencing the direction of the discipline or especially a subfield, and helping some young authors and more experienced economists who are new to editing and refereeing roles, often paying forward a debt felt to those who promoted the editors' own careers. Pencavel (chapter 5) calls editing a "labor of love." Pressman (chapter 20) views the primary roles of referees and editors as being "mentors" to authors. Zilibotti (chapter 6) writes that the most important reason for the success of the *Review of Economic Studies* is "the devotion and intrinsic motivation of its associates." McAfee (chapter 3) says that "Being an editor has not made me a more effective author" but feels that it has made him more effective in providing advice to colleagues and allowed him to reference a broader literature. Harvey (chapter 4) also notes that learning about areas outside his own specialization has been an unexpected bonus of editing a general-purpose journal. In the subfield journals, Goodwin (chapter 7) presents a common sentiment in writing that "There is a real sense of accomplishment in bringing out those four issues a year and feeling that you have contributed to the welfare, or in this case survival, of your field."

In some ways, this discussion of editors' altruistic motives and behavior echoes a line from William H. Shughart II's chapter (chapter 15), in which he discusses claims of altruistic behavior in the government sector: "Prior to the public-choice revolution . . . the 'prevailing view of political scientists was that government is generally benevolent, often benign, and seldom dangerous.'" The irony, at least in my view, becomes most apparent when Shughart goes on to say that "Helping to supply a collective good to my colleagues . . . , which is transformed partly into a private good for the authors of the papers the journal publishes, is, despite inevitable free-riding on my editorial contributions, why I edit." Journals are key institutions in the overall "governance" of academic fields, but they certainly have less monopoly power and far fewer resources and deal with less basic and less sweeping issues than the government sector.

Has this altruistic view of editors become the consensus view of the role of editors of economics journals, at least among the editors themselves if not among other economists who are more cynical because of rejections? Whatever the answer may be, based on this sample of editors, some level of altruism is an important trait to bring to the job and is key to remaining happy and willing to continue to do the job.

Married without Children(?)

Bill Becker (chapter 18) and Spulber (chapter 8) confess that they exploited their wives to provide editing and other services for their journals over periods of many years, which means that at least some editor appointments have something in common with congregations making decisions about hiring ministers and spouses, even if the spouses are unpaid or at least greatly undercompensated for the work they do. Spouses influence the editorial decision in other ways, too. Friberg (chapter 2) says that his wife often complains that he is an individualist who does little to contribute to society, so agreeing to be an editor was "a tangible way to demonstrate my pro-sociality." Zilibotti (chapter 6) notes that he accepted the position at the *Review of Economic Studies* even though his wife recommended against it after she learned that the departing editor, Hyun Song Shin, warned that "it is about like to have another child." In considering the position at the *Journal of Finance*, Harvey (chapter 4) negotiated arrangements to share the work with a coeditor and an enlarged group of associate editors because he wanted to spend his free time with his three teenage children. The costs are clearly substantial and should be considered carefully and addressed before taking the job.

Conclusions

Asking a group of prominent journal editors to contribute these articles was, in many respects, an audacious idea. The final product indicates that the efforts of the volume editors and contributors were valuable for what can be drawn from individual chapters as well as from the collection of chapters. Experienced and novice authors, referees, and editors can find important information and insights in the editors' reflections— sometimes confirmatory, sometimes surprising, and almost always from the perspective of successful economists who became successful journal editors and served in that role for many years.

Some contributors ask what kind of training would better prepare economists to be editors and where and how that training might take place. This would certainly not be an easy thing to do, given the range of skills and traits involved, the comments by Shughart (chapter 15) and others about the learning curve that starts after editors take the job, and Barnett's (chapter 10) succinct summary of some of the special and general issues that he faced: "Did I expect any of this when I agreed to start up *Macroeconomic Dynamics*? Not at all." Technical skills are reasonably well covered in graduate programs. But writing, revising, and reviewing other people's writing are skills that are not taught or well developed in most programs in economics, except perhaps at strong liberal arts schools, where, as Taylor (chapter 23) points out, the number of students going on to graduate programs in economics has fallen sharply over recent decades. It is tempting to use a screening model in considering the selection process for journal editors rather than ideas of formal training and developing human capital. But the many testimonials to mentors who guided these editors into those roles support the idea that training and experience are usually important, too.

After reading all of the chapters, it is easy to compile a lengthy list of problems at journals that the editors recognize but also want others to know are not their fault. The list includes general concerns, such as lag times for authors who are revising articles and for referees whose reviews are delayed well beyond deadlines or never are delivered even after repeated promises. At some journals, lags are also blamed on the electronic review system that is imposed on journals by publishers. Several editors say that it is not their fault that many authors do not write well, do not polish manuscripts and edit well or hire editing help from "cheap" English majors, do not proofread manuscripts or galley proofs carefully, or write multiple papers featuring the same models and data, at times to the point of self-plagiarism. One editor (Wahid, chapter 17) discusses authors who do not catch mistakes in galley proofs but still complain after the mistakes are published—including one case in which an author did not see that his own first name on the article was not correct.

Today, virtually all academic economists have a stake in the process of journals' reviews of manuscripts and therefore in the process of how editors are selected and in the work that falls within or outside the editors' purview. Bromley (chapter 14) notes that journals play several key roles in an epistemic community, including signaling the most recent developments (and fads) in research, validating the credibility of young scholars, and establishing enduring standards by which scholars are measured and ranked in the competition for high status.

The chapters in this volume examine those roles and others and summarize how that work is being carried out at over twenty journals. Some of that information is fairly well known, at least by economists who have worked within the system for a period of years—say, long enough to earn tenure. But as always, God and the devil are in the details, and at least some of the details reported here are likely to be new to most readers. Collecting the reflections from this many editors in one place, even with the selection issues that the process inevitably entails, provides a clearer picture of both the central tendencies and variances across the journals. And far from least important, some reassurance comes from hearing the editors describe and explain how they care about and put effort into their work and how much they think about the difficult problems and issues facing journals, editorial staffs, authors, and referees.

Acknowledgments

I thank Paul Grimes, Bill Becker, and Michael Szenberg for encouraging me to write this chapter and for their helpful comments on earlier versions. I am at least primarily responsible for any remaining errors of commission and omission.

References

Berrett, Dan. 2012. Scholarly Groups' Choices Yield Diverging Fortunes. *Chronicle of Higher Education*, April 1.

Bok, Derek. 2006. *Our Underachieving Colleges: A Candid Look at How Much Students Learn and Why They Should Be Learning More*. Princeton, NJ: Princeton University.

Boulding, Kenneth. 1969. Economic Education: The Stepchild Too Is Father of the Man. *Journal of Economic Education* 1 (1):7–11.

Dewald, William, Jerry Thursby, and Richard Anderson. 1986. Replication in Empirical Economics: The *Journal of Money, Credit, and Banking* Project. *American Economic Review* 76 (4):587–603.

Ellison, Glenn. 2002. The Slowdown of the Economics Publishing Process. *Journal of Political Economy* 110 (5):947–993.

Enders, Walter, and Gary A. Hoover. 2004. Whose Line Is It? Plagiarism in Economics. *Journal of Economic Literature* 42:487–493.

Frey, Bruno. 2003. Publishing as Prostitution? Choosing between One's Own Ideas and Academic Success. *Public Choice* 116:205–223.

Gans, Joshua, and George Shepherd. 1994. How the Mighty Are Fallen: Rejected Classic Articles by Leading Economists. *Journal of Economic Perspectives* 8 (1):165–179.

Hamermesh, Daniel. 1994. Facts and Myths about Refereeing. *Journal of Economic Perspectives* 8:153–163.

Laband, David. 1990. Is There Value-Added from the Review Process in Economics? Preliminary Evidence from Authors. *Quarterly Journal of Economics* 105 (2):341–352.

Laband, David, and Michael Piette. 1994. The Relative Impact of Economics Journals. *Journal of Economic Literature* 32 (2):640–666.

Laband, David, and Robert Tollison. 2003. Dry Holes in Economic Research. *Kyklos* 56 (2): 161–173.

Peters, Douglas, and Stephen Ceci. 1985. Peer-Review Practices of Psychology Journals: The Fate of Published Articles, Submitted Again. *Behavioral and Brain Sciences* 5:187–255.

Shulman, Lee S. 2004. Visions of the Possible: Models for Campus Support of the Scholarship of Teaching and Learning. In *The Scholarship of Teaching and*

Learning in Higher Education: Contributions of Research Universities, ed. W. Becker and M. Andrews, 9–24. Bloomington: Indiana University Press.

Smith, Vernon. 1962. An Experimental Study of Competitive Market Behavior. *Journal of Political Economy* 70 (2):111–137.

Smith, Vernon. 1981. Experimental Economics at Purdue. In *Essays in Contemporary Fields of Economics in Honor of Emanuel T. Weiler*, ed. George Horwich and James Quirk, 369–374. West Lafayette, IN: Purdue University Press.

Stigler, George. 1970. The Case, If Any, for Economic Literacy. *Journal of Economic Education* 1 (2):77–84.

Wall, Howard. 2009. Journal Rankings in Economics: Handle with Care. Working Paper 2009-014A, Federal Reserve Bank of St. Louis.

Economic Theory and Finance

1

A Decade of Editing the *European Economic Review*

Zvi Eckstein, Esther Gal-Or, Thorvaldur Gylfason, Jürgen von Hagen, and Gerard Pfann

The *European Economic Review* (*EER*) was launched 1969 as the first research journal that aimed to contribute to the development and application of economics as a science in Europe. As a broad-based professional and international journal, the *EER* welcomes submissions of applied and theoretical research papers in all fields of economics. Its aim is to contribute to the development of the science of economics and its applications and to improve communication among academic researchers, teachers, and policy makers across the European continent and beyond. The *EER* encourages young researchers to submit their work.

In late 2002, we were called on to edit the *EER*. We are a team of five editors who live in the United States, Iceland, Germany, Israel, and Holland. In our ten years as editors, we accepted articles from all over the world but mainly from European and American economists in roughly similar numbers. This is not surprising as European economics is not different from American economics. There are preferences, tendencies, and market phenomena that economists residing in different countries try to explain. The editing of a scientific journal is a ceaseless search for new and exciting ideas. This chapter tells the story of our expedition that started over a decade ago. What unites us is the love for the scientific approach to economic discovery. What we have in common is the determination to help economists—especially young economists—to communicate their findings and share new ideas with other economists. A wonderful byproduct of our joint effort has been the close friendships we developed over a decade of working together. We are grateful for having had the opportunity to assist in the dissemination of new ideas and methodologies to the research community. We hope that some of these ideas will help in overcoming the hard economic times the world is currently facing.

This story describes the circumstances that led all five of us to start working as editors at the same time, the unexpected things we have found, the unanticipated reactions we have encountered, the ways that we have worked as an editorial team, the central role played by the editorial office manager, the ways we managed to work with five different publishers in ten years, the various initiatives we have developed to involve associate editors and referees, the early electronic editing system, and the creation of an essential database of potential referees. We also describe the difficulties we encountered in reaching one of our early goals to reduce the median time of first response to less than four months. Along the way, we also share a few anecdotes that illustrate the work of an academic journal editor.

How It Started

In the summer of 2002, the entire board of editors of the *EER* stepped down as the result of actions that the European Economic Association (EEA) took to cut all ties with the journal's publishing company, Elsevier, apparently with the intention of cutting ties with the *EER*. The dispute was about Elsevier's pricing policy, and this later was transformed into a fight about the journal's authority and ownership. The EEA, founded in 1986, had been granted an option to use the *EER* as the association's signature journal. The EEA's success grew over the seventeen years of its existence, and the association claimed ownership of the *EER*, a claim that Elsevier denied.

At the time, Joop Dirkmaat was the publisher at Elsevier who was responsible for the *EER*. For Joop, the potential separation was like a bad dream because the *EER* was Elsevier's flagship journal for the publisher's continuously growing portfolio of economics journals. He contacted Gerard Pfann to gauge his interest in helping save the journal from demise. Joop had known Gerard from the time they had success-fully cofounded the *Journal of Empirical Finance* in 1993. The situation was made more complicated when the EEA announced the founding of a new journal that would compete with the *EER*. Gerard saw at least two reasons to accept Joop's request. First, the reputation of the *EER* was already well established prior to the founding of the association, and in this respect, it had the first-mover advantage. Second, although facing competition in continental Europe was a new experience for the *EER*, most economists agreed that such competition was healthy and likely to improve the performance of both journals.

Moreover, Joop was determined to continue publishing the journal at whatever the cost.

Gerard had only one fundamental request—that the whole operation must be electronic so that no paper printouts of articles would need to be delivered by the postal service. Elsevier had just purchased a software program by Aries Systems Corp. called Editorial Manager (EM) for the development of electronic editing. Initially, the program was available only for the medical sciences, and its format at the time was not suitable for the completely different editorial culture in economics. Together, Joop and Gerard decided to adjust Editorial Manager to the demands of economics editing. They also agreed to establish an editorial office run by someone in Gerard's vicinity who knew the culture of academic publishing, was an excellent and respectful communicator, was computer literate, and was fluent in English. Finally, they identified the fields of expertise that needed to be covered by different editors. The expectation was that the market for academic articles would continue to grow for some years. In 2002, the number of submissions received by the *EER* each year was around 350, but the expectation was that the ongoing revolution in electronic publishing would lead to a substantial increase of this number to roughly 500 to 600 per year. Given this forecast, Joop and Gerard decided to recruit a total of five to six editors. Thorvaldur Gylfason (growth and development) and Jürgen von Hagen (money and banking, international macro, international finance, exchange rates) were the first to join the editorial team, followed by Esther Gal-Or (economic theory, industrial organization, experimental economics, behavioral economics), and Zvi Eckstein (macro economics, search models, education, immigration, history, empirical industrial organization). Gerard (labor, investment, finance, econometrics) assumed the role of managing editor.

In January 2003, the electronic Editorial Manager was up and running. This was mainly due to the efforts of Carina Furnée, the new editorial office manager, and Ruud Meesters from Elsevier, who was responsible for Editorial Manager and its relationship with Elsevier. Together they adjusted and redesigned the entire electronic routing and communication systems of Editorial Manager to make it suitable for economics editing. The *EER* became the first journal in economics that was run entirely electronically. Being first implied that we had to deal with quirks in the system that seem ridiculous by today's standards of electronic systems. Take, for instance, the processing of the submission fees that potential contributes were required to include with their articles. Over time, an increasing number of submissions came with handwritten forms that contained wrong or unidentifiable credit card details. From time to time, Carina received an envelope from Elsevier with large amounts of these forms. Even though the submissions were already in process, the envelopes came with the request to contact each of the corresponding authors personally to keep open the possibility of collecting the fees. This meant a huge amount of rather unpleasant work on top of the editorial office's regular workload. Because the envelopes arrived after long delays, many of the papers concerned had already been dealt with. Authors whose papers had been rejected had naturally very little incentive to pay the submission fees in spite of repeated calls and email messages.

Boxes Full of Manuscripts and Referee Reports

Between the summer of 2002 and spring 2003, about half a dozen cardboard boxes filled with paper files arrived at the editorial office. Most of the boxes came from Paris on behalf of Xavier Vives, *EER*'s former managing editor. After a rather slow start, Xavier helped to solve the problem of the large number of manuscripts that already were under consideration and urgently needed to be dealt with. In addition, the four other former editors sent 118 unfinished files separately to our office. Many long nights were spent sorting out the paper files, tying up loose ends, and corresponding with authors who had been waiting for updates on the status of their papers.

We faced a backlog of papers so large that after a paper was accepted for publication, authors had to wait at least eighteen months before seeing their papers in print. Our first goal was to shorten this waiting time to six months. With the help of Elsevier, which allowed a temporary increase in the journal's pages from 1,200 in 2002 to 2,100 in 2005, 2006, and 2007, we achieved our first goal in 2009. In that same year, a new page layout was introduced for the *EER* with a larger page surface, so that each page contains 25 percent more information than in the previous layout (figure 1.1).

The First Meetings of the Editorial Board in 2003

The first strategic discussions of the new editorial board took place during the 2003 meetings of the Allied Social Science Association (ASSA) in Washington, D.C. We discussed the fields of expertise covered by the people who had expressed their willingness to join the *EER* as associate

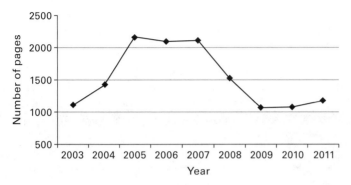

Figure 1.1
Number of pages published by the *EER* between 2003 and 2010

editors, and it was agreed that every editor would find ten AEs in non-overlapping specialized fields. This would translate to a group of about fifty AEs covering a wide range of fields. The hope was that this group would gain access to a large network of expert reviewers. We concluded that it would be important to schedule another meeting of the new editors to continue formulating the strategic direction of journal. The first editorial meeting took place in Maastricht on Friday, April 11, 2003. In addition to the five new editors, Joop and Carina were also in attendance.

At first, we thought that two editorial meetings per year would be necessary as we set the new strategic direction for the journal and that after a couple of years we would shift to one annual meeting. But throughout our ten-year period as editors, we continued to meet twice yearly, in the spring and fall. The advantages of meeting often were numerous. We found that sharing information about difficulties we encountered with the new electronic system, with grievances from authors, and with the ongoing organizational changes at Elsevier helped us run the journal more smoothly. There were frequent changes of staff at Elsevier's publishing department throughout our tenure as editors. During this period, we worked with five different publishers with increasingly less freedom to navigate the direction of the journal. Joop was succeeded by David Clark in 2005. In 2007, the position of senior vice president was introduced at Elsevier, and when David moved to a senior vice president position in another discipline, Valerie Teng took over the *EER* with Diane Cogan becoming her superior officer. In 2009, Diane left Elsevier, and her responsibilities with respect to the *EER* were taken

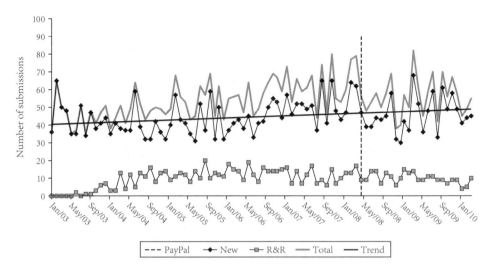

Figure 1.2
EER submissions and papers revised and resubmitted per month

over by Patrick Jackson as senior vice president. When Valerie left Elsevier shortly thereafter, she was temporarily replaced by Jenny Henzen,
and in the summer of 2010, Daniela Georgescu became the next publisher responsible for the *EER*, while Patrick as senior vice president
remained in control in the background. Organizational memory is not
long, and it took much effort on our part to maintain the general direction that we had forged for the journal. Thankfully, there are some
indications that we were successful. The changes that took place in 2002
did not lead to a reduction in the number of submissions. In fact, the
number of submissions increased by almost a quarter in comparison with
2002 (figure 1.2). Moreover, in spite of the larger number of extra papers
published between 2005 and 2007, Thomson's impact factor did not
suffer either (figure 1.3).

Incentives for Associate Editors

Fifty is a large number of associate editors. With half of the submissions
distributed uniformly among associate editors, an associate editor
received an average 3.5 papers in 2003 and six papers in 2010. With
the increase in the number of submissions, the demand on an associate
editor's time has almost doubled over the past decade. Sending out an

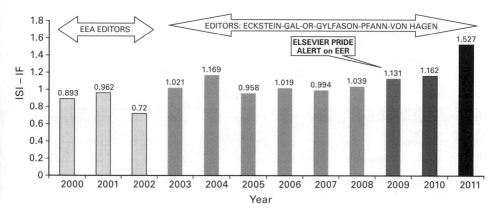

Figure 1.3
EER-Thomson impact factor

invitation to an associate editor to handle papers is asking a favor, and we do not like to ask our friends and colleagues for too many favors. We realized that we had to offer the associate editors something in return for their efforts on behalf of the journal. The role of associate editors was discussed at every editorial board meeting from the outset. Paying associate editors or reviewers for the time that they spent on a paper was not an option because it was considered too costly, both financially and administratively. So we had to come up with alternative tokens of appreciation. Here is a list of five things that we could offer them.

Invitations to Dinners at the Annual ASSA and EEA Meetings

All associate editors received invitations to dinners during the annual meetings of the European Economic Association meetings in August and the Allied Social Sciences Association meetings in January. This was a way to create two opportunities per year for social interaction between the editors and associate editors. Two especially memorable dinners were given at the Everest in the Chicago Stock Exchange and the Puerta de Atocha in Madrid's central railway station. Over time, the number of associate editors attending the meetings or the time available during the meetings decreased. In 2007, David Clark asked us to reconsider the dinners, and we agreed to discontinue this activity given the low attendance rate of associate editors. Associate editors have continued to receive invitations from Elsevier to join the annual cocktail party during the ASSA meetings since 2009.

Organizing Workshops on Original and New Topics in Economics
Joop and Gerard agreed that Elsevier should allocate some resources for the organization of one workshop per year on a new topic in economics. The objective was that an associate editor would initiate the idea for the workshop and organize it in conjunction with one of the five editors. Each workshop was held for at most two conference days and included ten to fifteen papers. Two expert reviewers were also invited to each workshop with the intent that they help the associate editors to select four or five papers to be considered for publication in a special section (a symposium) of the *European Economic Review*. This special section was guaranteed fast publication in a future issue of the *EER*, and the authors of the selected papers had the opportunity to publish their contributions to the workshop in a volume of conference proceedings. Elsevier agreed to publish the proceedings in its prestigious Green Series under the title of "Contributions to Economic Analysis." The associate editor who initiated the idea for the workshop together with one of the editors formed the editorial team for the special section and the proceedings. We decided to take turns in organizing these conferences. In 2005, for instance, we included a special section on "The Economics of Time Use" with associate editor Daniel Hamermesh, and in 2010, Tom Gresik helped us edit a special section on "Multinational Taxation and Tax Competition."

Acting as a Reviewer
We have extended to the associate editors the option of acting as reviewers for papers assigned to them and therefore the opportunity of being eligible for the reward offered to reviewers for timely completion of their reports. The reward comprised of a voucher worth €125, which allowed reviewers to purchase any Elsevier product. The vouchers were used mostly to buy selected copies from Elsevier's Handbooks in Economics series. In 2009, Elsevier handed over the entire handbook operation to an independent subsidiary within its own company, and we were informed that the review voucher could no longer be used to buy handbooks. Since then, vouchers have mostly been used as waivers for submission fees to the *EER*. Associate editors were already exempted from paying submission fees, so we lost this valuable incentive for associate editors.

Access to *ScienceDirect* and *SciVerse SCOPUS*
Editors and associate editors received free access to Elsevier's electronic database called *ScienceDirect*. In 2010, the complete Handbooks in

Economics Series became available from *ScienceDirect*, and associate editors therefore had free electronic access to articles published in these handbooks. In addition, in 2010 a new electronic database, *SciVerse SCOPUS*, became available, and it is comparable to the *Web of Science* and *Google Scholar*. It included a search engine that is useful for finding referees and viewing articles related to submitted papers. Valerie and Gerard agreed that editors and associate editors would obtain free access to this new platform as well because of its likely usefulness in the review process. For associate editors who were affiliated with organizations that had institutional subscriptions to these products, the value of this free access was rather limited.

European Economic Review Talented Economists Clinic

The dwindling amenities available to associate editors encouraged us to seek new alternatives. In 2008, we started a new initiative that we named the *European Economic Review* Talented Economists Clinic (*EER* TEC). Our objective was to use the submission fees paid to the journal for the benefit of young academic economists, who formed a segment of the community that had been of interest to us from the start. The idea was for each editor to identify one of the best-performing associate editors in a given year and invite the associate editors to select two young and promising economists in their fields of expertise. The selected economists were invited to present their work at the yearly *EER* TEC meeting to be attended also by the five associate editors and all five editors. The meeting created the opportunity for the young academic economists to receive comments from the different editors and be introduced to the publishing culture at top-tier economics journals. The *EER* TEC meeting was also an excellent vehicle for invitees to network with other talented peers and to establish first roots for future possible collaborations. We did not try to sway the authors to submit their work to the *EER*. We advised them that gaining exposure by publishing at the very top outlets might actually serve their professional careers. However, we suggested that if at some point in the future they did decide to submit their work to the *EER*, they would be exempted from paying the submission fee. The first three meetings were organized in collaboration with the European University Institute in Florence in cooperation with Luigi Guiso, one of our associate editors. The fourth meeting took place at the Institute for the Study of Labor (IZA) in Bonn. All expenses for the authors and associate editors were covered using submission fees.

Special Initiatives and Commissioned Papers

In addition to the special sections that were initiated by associate editors, we decided to publish sections to commemorate special occasions or to cover new fields of research in economics. For instance, in 2005, Zvi added a series of papers from the conference in honor of Dale Mortensen's sixtieth birthday. Together Zvi and Dale edited a special section on "Labor Search" that we published in 2006. In 2008, we commemorated the fiftieth anniversary of the Phillips curve in conjunction with the Kiel Institute for the World Economy. In early 2011, we published, in two symposiums, papers from workshops organized in the summer and fall of 2010 dealing with different aspects of the international financial crisis that started in 2008. This gave the *EER* a head start among economics journals engaging in the academic debate over the causes of the crisis and the policies dealing with it. We decided not to publish one of the special sections early on, for which we received nine papers from the organizer of the workshop, because eight of the papers of the workshop were coauthored by this organizer. Finally, in 2012, we published our last special section, titled "Green Building, the Economy, and Public Policy." In addition to special sections, we commissioned survey articles on hot topics in economics, including "The Returns to Schooling in Structural Dynamic Models" by Christian Belzil (2007), "Search in Cities" by Yves Zenou (2009), "Field Experiments in Economics" by Steve Levitt and John List (2009), and "Myopia, Redistribution, and Pensions" by Helmuth Cremer and Pierre Pestieau (2011).

Why We Could Not Get the Time to First Response down to Four Months

Long delays between the submission of a paper and the time when an author receives an editorial decision are a problem in today's culture of economics journals. From the start, we tried to work against this problem with various measures. One of the first we took was to introduce turbo rejects—rejecting papers without giving them to reviewers. The idea was that if we editors thought that a paper had little chance of making it through the reviewing process successfully, we would return it immediately to the author. In this way, we would save authors unnecessary waiting times and economize on the valuable time of our potential reviewers. Authors have generally been happy with this idea, which nowadays seems to have become a standard practice for economics journals.

One thing that we regret deeply is our failure to achieve our goal of four months as the median response time between a complete submission and first decision on a paper. We set out this objective early in our term for papers that were not turbo-rejected. There were multiple reasons for our inability to achieve this goal. Some had to do with the shortcomings of Elsevier's electronic system, others with the increase in the number of submissions that we experienced over time, and still others with the slowness of the review process itself.

Elsevier's electronic system—first Editorial Manager (EM) and then Elsevier Editorial System (EES)—did not include a feature that allowed editors to monitor the elapsed time in the various stages of the review process of papers assigned to them. In particular, the efficiency measure pertaining to the duration of the period to first response did not separate turbo-rejected papers from other submissions and did not provide individualized measures for the different editors. With turbo-rejected papers included, our efficiency measure appeared much more favorable than it really was. Moreover, because we did not obtain individualized performance measures, we could not share information about processes and techniques that were helpful in hastening the review process. In spite of repeated requests, Elsevier did not include the above-mentioned two features in its electronic system.

With regard to the number of submissions, the increase from around 350 to 550 per year with a steady number of associate editors implied that we had to assume the role of associate editors on more manuscripts. This meant that we had to identify referees for more submitted papers. Finally, in spite of incentives offered for timely reports, we encountered great difficulties with some reviewers. It was not uncommon for the editorial office to find it necessary to send second and third reminders to reviewers who promised reports but never delivered. There was, for instance, a referee who on being reminded for the fourth time that his promised report was long overdue, responded by saying that we could not imagine the disruptions created by the recent earthquake close to his hometown and, by the way, we might find his three recent papers (attached) interesting.

Conclusion

The decade that we have spent together as editors has been a great experience. Although we were not able to accomplish all of our goals, we hope that we were successful in contributing to the advancement and dissemination of knowledge in economics. We derived great pleasure from interacting with authors, referees, and associate editors from all over the world. Among them was the author who thanked us for having accepted his paper for publication (against the rather hostile advice of one of the referees) and who went on to win a prestigious prize for the published paper. We got a kick out of that. An author of a turbo-rejected paper contacted us one year after the rejection to thank us for the quick review process and recommendation for the alternative outlet for publication. His paper had just been accepted in this alternative outlet. But all good things must come to an end. It is time for us now to step down and allow a new team of editors to bring new ideas and approaches to running the *EER*. We wish them all the best and good luck in advancing the reputation of the journal.

2

The Wish List of an Editor: Some Reflections on Editing the *Scandinavian Journal of Economics*

Richard Friberg

The *Scandinavian Journal of Economics* (*SJE*) was started in 1899. It has gone through a couple of name changes and switched from Swedish to English, but its tradition is unbroken and has been nicely summarized by Mats Persson (1998). About two years ago, Persson called me to discuss something that was too important to deal with over the phone. There was a sense of cloak and dagger, but after we finally found a time to meet, we ended up doing things over the phone after all. Persson asked me if I would be willing to serve as one of three editors at the *SJE*. My wife frequently complains that, apart from a monthly financial contribution to Médecins sans Frontières, I am an individualist who does little to contribute to society. I do not agree, and here was a tangible way to demonstrate my prosociality. I also figured that I would learn something in the process because several of the people that I admire the most in the profession have served as editors. Correlation is not causation, but I have always liked a good correlation, so I was happy to accept Persson's offer of much work for low pay.

In his 1998 article, Persson discusses the question "what is the role of journals?," and I build my reflections in this chapter on that question. Given that many people now have homepages and post manuscripts on the Web, journals' role of disseminating knowledge has become less valuable than it was in earlier eras. The more important role for journals nowadays is as a quality-controlled repository. After going through the editorial process, a paper is presumed to provide new knowledge with a scientific basis. Its calculations are correct, its empirical methods are applied according to current best practices, and arguments have a solid foundation. This quality-controlled version also is one single, final version, making future references easy. We can refer to one article—Danny Quah (1993), for example, or Ernst Fehr and Klaus M. Schmidt (2004)—and do not need to go on archeological expeditions for different versions. Finally, and this was not mentioned in Persson (1998), publications serve as a measure of an individual's scholarly output: how many papers in different types of journals does person A have? This matters for tenure, promotions, research grants, and inter-group prestige. Gossip of the style "Did you hear that her *Econometrica* went straight in?" is eerily reminiscent of how a front flip 720 is assessed at a ski resorts.

What motivates me as an editor is providing a quality-controlled repository. However, an unattractive shadow is sometimes cast by the fact that the number of publications serve as a measure of scholarly output. At times it seems as though some authors are trying to maximize the number of their published articles.

There are many ways to sort the steady inflow of papers that I see as an editor. Some papers (according to me) are interesting to a broad audience and are well executed. They pose few problems. I can easily ask people at the top of the field to act as referees, and the whole review process is rather straightforward. At the other end of the spectrum, papers can fail because they are poorly written, use data that are inappropriate for the question posed, or consider an artificially contrived theoretical twist. We receive few such papers, and they present few problems for me as an editor. I do a summary reject after reading and supporting my decision. This work is straightforward. The tough part of the job comes from some of the papers in between these two ends of the spectrum. A paper can be competently executed but make a contribution that is hard to judge. An empirical paper, for example, might use appropriate data but be one of several papers that examine similar issues. Some papers I find rather boring, but my editorial arrogance has not yet reached the level where I can give my boredom as an argument for rejecting a paper. Other papers that I do find interesting might not be making a contribution that is as new and important as the authors claim that it is.

How can we make the handling of these intermediate cases as smooth and accurate as possible? I have organized my discussion in this chapter around a set of suggestions for how referees, editors, and authors should behave. Although practices can take generations to evolve, writing wish lists can be a worthy activity in its own. My son, for example, has written *a dog* 250 times on his birthday wish list. My list begins with my wishes for referees.

Wish List for Referees

Please give me a quick short review that honestly evaluates the contribution rather than spending a long time to list marginal improvements.

For papers of what might be called intermediate quality, finding referees that I trust can be time consuming. I need people who are likely to catch any omissions or errors. The level of commentary provided by referees varies hugely, but as a general rule I am impressed with their ability to find omissions and errors. As a rule, I receive careful and precise evaluations of the technical level of a paper. Where I often receive less aid is in judging the contribution.

Here is a hypothetical example. In long-distance running, "rabbits" or pace setters set a fast pace early in a race and then drop out part-way through the race after exhausting themselves. Consider a literature that examines the effect of rabbits on finish times and on the identity of the winner in long-distance races. In terms of policy, this may matter. The New York City marathon banned the use of rabbits in 2007, but other marathon races allow them. This is not a huge issue, perhaps, but it might say something fundamental about the ways that humans respond to incentives and the things that make us competitive. As I sit and look through this paper that examines the causal effect of pace keepers on finishing times in marathon races, I might find that the paper is well written, the authors argue that they have a particularly clean identification strategy.

If I deem that this topic is too narrow for the *SJE*, I do a summary reject even if the paper is well written. But the authors emphasize that this is a fundamental contribution to the link between incentives and competition in sports, and while my judgment indicates that they overstate their case, I can't rule out that they are right. Instead, I ask for the opinions of some referees who have published in top journals that are in a somewhat broader field (say, sport economics). But they politely decline. Some introspection suggests that they do so after a brief look at the paper: even if pressed for time, I will say yes to a request to referee a paper that I find really interesting after having glanced at it. I take it as a negative signal if I have trouble finding referees to accept. A three-line evaluation would be very helpful for me. Is it that the potential referees lack time, or do they feel that the contribution is too narrow? In the end, I find referees with a list of publications in what feels like a very narrow subfield (economics of marathon running). In my experience, such referees often deliver a careful check of correctness and suggest improvements. When I receive reports back in these cases, they often suggest that the author revise and resubmit the paper. I then give the paper a more careful reading and may check some central reference. If I am not convinced, I turn to associate editors to get a second opinion. This is one of the reasons that we have associate editors for, but they are a limited set of people who to some extent face the same problem that I do, which is that they are too far removed to judge the contribution. So quick evaluations from people within the field as it is broadly defined would be lovely.

Keep to deadlines, and if you can't, communicate with us.
I have not done the statistics on this one, but it certainly feels like most referees wait until after a deadline before they send in their reports. Some wait quite a bit, and we do not know if it is because they are running late or if they have forgotten. Automatic reminders are sent out, which would be a great time for referees to let us know why they have not sent in the report. Something like "Been swamped, sorry. You'll have it by May 5" would be helpful. Although response rates to automatic reminders are close to zero, most people respond quickly to personal communication, frequently with a note saying that "I'll get it done by next week." In practice, this means more like three weeks after perhaps another nudge. Almost all referees provide important services, and sometimes they just need to shut out the world and focus on research, but ignoring deadlines generates more, rather than less, email clutter. It is preferable to set a longer, realistic time horizon and keep it than be overly optimistic. Most papers receive a first decision within three months, but it takes considerable work to maintain this schedule.

Some people say, "Don't send in your referee report too quickly. You'll have to do too many reports." Although people who never respond or who break deadlines in a notable way are unlikely to be asked again, those who send in reports may be invited to review again at some point in the future regardless of how quickly they returned their reviews. The system that we use to handle papers shows us the history of our referees. We wait at least a year before asking again and avoid overusing the services provided by referees.

Apart from the above two points, keep doing what you do.
The previous remarks should not overshadow that we typically get careful reports within reasonable time which serve as a quality check and improve the papers. We are grateful for that.

Wish List for Editors

Before turning to my wish list for authors, let me also make a wish for the work of other editors.

Cut innovative work a bit of slack.
Subfields tend to develop standard ways of proceeding, and failing to follow a particular procedure sometimes is criticized by the elders (the referees, in this case). After microfoundations were introduced, macroeconomics was supposed to be microfounded, which was good in principle but forced us to work with complex models when sometimes striking simplifications are more useful. In the structural models that are used in empirical industrial organization, some short cuts and omissions are acceptable, whereas others invite a recommendation of reject. We should do all the loops and tricks to solve some problems that we know how to tackle, whereas other problems are perfectly fine to sweep under the rug. For really innovative work, some of these check lists can add a lot of complexity. It is part of the referees' work to point out these possible omissions. Part of my work as editor is to prioritize the referees' comments—by indicating which concerns are crucial and which concerns can be addressed with a bit of explaining and discussion. Ideally, referees also rank the relative importance of their concerns in their letter to the editor, but if they do not, the editor needs to take this into account.

Similar concerns arise in also in microeconometric work. If I am producing the umpteenth paper on the effect of rabbits on finishing times in marathon races, the quality of the paper's data and identification need to be outstanding to make a contribution in an area where much is already known. If referees coming from this mind frame are confronted with new data and a new question, they may be unduly critical. Again, the role of editors is to provide a check on this. However, authors' expectations regarding the likely demands placed on various types of projects affect the questions that researchers pose. Some of the papers in microeconometrics that examine "new" questions are very weak in the handling of the data and the description and analysis of identification. Maybe skilled researchers, in a rational response to the editorial process, are excessively playing it safe?

Wish List for Authors

Finally, I turn to my wish list regarding authors. One set of wishes concern the crafting of papers.

Be careful to place your paper in the literature, and take the time to polish your paper.
These demands are placed on all authors, and many meet them the first time around. Surprisingly, however, many authors are sloppy about these requirements. When junior faculty members see some of the "big names" publishing rather homely ideas in good journals, one reason is their craftsmanship in expressing their ideas.

Maximizing the number of papers should not be the goal.
Further wishes of mine border on somewhat presumptuous advice about how one should conduct research. This little branch of the philosophy of science (and of life) usually surfaces in the wee hours after a number of beers in a conference setting, but given the invitation to share thoughts on editing I might as well take the opportunity to vent some ideas. I claim no originality here, but some questions need to be ever repeated.

In my ideal world, a paper summarizes something that the writer is really dying to share with the world. It is not primarily a publication. Some people are amazingly productive and generate that kind of idea all the time. Others may generate a lot of publications by making slight variations on previous papers and sending them to different journals. The incentives early in a career are to publish papers and do so quickly, but after tenure, I wish that many of us could slow down. The opportunity cost of writing another variation on a common theme is that it may crowd out more fundamental work.

A highlight of the year in Stockholm is seeing the Nobel laureates in early December. In 2005, Thomas Schelling was one of the laureates, and in his after-dinner speech, he made this point: get tenure, and then use that freedom to do what you really want to do (research, not surfing). Not all of us can be a Coase or a Schelling, but I think our long-run impact would be higher with fewer rather than more papers. Andrew Wiles's withdrawal to prove Fermat's last theorem is perhaps an extreme example, but I think we would be better economists if we to a greater extent dug down to create a new data set or new theory or paid our dues to implement a market design. I have heard at least one very smart guy in his fifties regretting that he did not devote more time to fundamental issues.

One common piece of advice is that there should be one idea per paper. If you have three ideas that come out of the same model, make each of them into a paper. One argument is career-focused: this approach gives you more publications. Another motivation is that this makes an idea more accessible for other researchers. If I am looking for information about how pace setters affect the results in marathon races, maybe it is more useful to find it in a focused paper rather than in a paper that examines the effect of pace setters in a number of different competition formats. But papers in economics often bury the contribution deep in the paper. There are often many similar papers circulating with connections between them that are far from clear. Rather than stressing that one paper makes a small (but interesting) twist to a previous model, many authors try to portray each work as more different from previous papers than it actually is. I have had a handful of cases where a paper borders on plagiarizing the author's own work. A paper's reference to Cat (2004), for example, might note that the two papers study a similar problem but might give readers the impression that its model is new. But when I check Cat (2004), I find that the same model is there. This is bad form and results in a sharply worded rejection.

If authors have a model and think that one interesting implication is worth working out, I do not suggest that they never should do so. My wish is simply that they clearly state that a paper is a spinoff of another. I have nothing against saying that "We use the model of Pheidippides (2010) to study the effect of payout structure on finishing times in marathons" and then moving directly into action or stating that "Using the data and econometric model from Radcliffe (2003), this paper simulates the effect of extreme heat on marathon dropout rates." I am more inclined to accept such a paper than one that uses text that is similar to another paper but strives to differentiate itself from the first paper. Papers in some of the natural sciences are short and place much background information in appendixes. Perhaps this could be a useful model for economics as well, but it is hard for only one journal to change practices.

Look at problems that are close to your heart or experience.
I often hear that economists need to work with U.S. data or U.S. policy issues to publish well. It may be true that if you send papers to, for instance, the *American Economic Review* that are based on data from Sweden, then your contribution needs to be based on exceptional data or a compelling identification strategy. If writers are working with data from smaller countries or on policy issues of particular relevance to such countries, they need to be careful to establish the need for the work and place it in the literature. But good work should do this in any case, and

contributions are more meaning if writers have a deep knowledge of the institutional setting for the issues that they study. The likelihood that they will produce something really interesting is then much greater, and we may learn that similar issues are faced by many others. The Nobel Foundation publishes autobiographies of the laureates on its Web site (http://www.nobelprize.org), and laureates often say that their ground-breaking ideas have been shaped by personal experiences. A good example is George Akerlof's experiences in India, which bolstered his interest in why and when markets fail. It is impossible to read works like John Maynard Keynes's *The Economic Consequences of the Peace* (1920) and Albert O. Hirschman's *National Power and the Structure of Foreign Trade* (1945) without sensing the passion that these authors felt for their subjects. That makes them interesting to read nearly a hundred years after World War I ended or seventy years after Nazi foreign policy attempted to dominate Europe. No one can make contributions at this level all of the time, but even in our run-of-the-mill work, we need to stay close to our passions. Most of us could earn higher wages in other lines of work, so why should we stay in academia if not we are not following our passions? If nothing else, this pursuit makes my life as an editor more stimulating.

References

Fehr, Ernst, and Klaus M. Schmidt. 2004. Fairness and Incentives in a Multi-Task Principal-Agent Model. *Scandinavian Journal of Economics* 106 (3):453–474.

Hirschman, Albert O. 1945. *National Power and the Structure of Foreign Trade.* Berkeley: University of California Press.

Keynes, John Maynard. 1920. *The Economic Consequences of the Peace.* New York: Harcourt, Brace, and Howe.

Persson, Mats. 1998. The First Century of *The Scandinavian Journal of Economics. Scandinavian Journal of Economics* 100 (1):1–9.

Quah, Danny. 1993. Galton's Fallacy and Tests of the Convergence Hypothesis. *Scandinavian Journal of Economics* 95 (4):427–443.

3

Edifying Editing

R. Preston McAfee

I have spent a considerable amount of time as an editor. I have rejected about 2,500 papers and accepted 200. No one likes a rejection, and fewer than 1 percent of authors consider it justified. Fortunately, there is some duplication across authors, so I have made only around 1,800 enemies.

The purpose of this chapter is to answer in print the questions I frequently am asked in person. These are my answers, but they may not apply to you.

Who Makes a Good Editor?

When Paul Milgrom recommended me as his replacement as a coeditor of the *American Economic Review*, a post I held for over nine years, one justification for the recommendation was that I am opinionated. At the time, I considered *opinionated* to mean "holding opinions without regard to the facts," and one dictionary definition suggests "stubbornly adhering to preconceived notions." But another side to *opinionated* means "having a view." It is a management truism that having a vision based on false hypotheses is better than a lack of vision, and like all truisms it is probably false some of the time, but the same feature holds true in editing: the editor's main job is to decide what to publish and what not to publish. Having some basis for deciding definitely is better than not having a basis for deciding. Even though I do not think of myself as obstinate, stubborn, or bigoted, editors find it valuable to have an opinion about everything.

Perhaps the most important attributes of an editor are obsessive organization and the ability to process work unrelentingly until it is done. The *AER* is a fire hose. In my first year, I handled 275 manuscripts. In my first year at *Economic Inquiry*, I processed 225 manuscripts to completion. I typically write referee reports on the same day that they are requested, which has helped me keep my inbox clear (even in the days before electronic inboxes). This "clear the inbox" strategy may not be a good strategy for success in life but it is a valuable characteristic in editors. Otherwise, after returning from a couple of weeks of vacation, there will be a mountain of manuscripts visible on satellite photos awaiting processing.

Another characteristic of successful editors is a lack of personal agenda. If you think that papers on, say, the economics of penguins are extraordinarily important, you risk filling the journal with second-rate penguin papers. A personal agenda is a bias, and biases lead to bad decisions. Although everyone has biases, if your reaction is "But it isn't a bias; I'm just right," you have a strong personal agenda.

Finally, a good editor is a very thick skin. One well-known irate author received a rejection and wrote to me, "Who are you to reject my paper?" The answer (which I did not send) is, "I'm the editor." Some authors write over and over again asking about their papers and complaining about decisions. If you lose sleep over decisions, wring your hands in anguish, or take every disagreement as a personal affront, you probably should decline any offers to edit a journal. One author wrote me, with no evidence of a sense of humor, that if I rejected his paper, he would be denied tenure, and his three children would go hungry. My response (which I did not send) was, "Good luck in your next career." There are papers I wish I had accepted—three of them, to be exact. Not bad for 2,500 rejections.

How Do I Become an Editor?

One of the surprises of being an *AER* coeditor was the number of people who believe that journals are controlled by the highest-ranking economics departments for the benefit of those departments. A conspiracy theory has been the prevailing belief of authors in spite of the wide editorial net cast by the *AER*. After I accepted papers from three different authors (from economics departments without graduate programs), they thanked me for breaking the conspiracy of journal editors to favor the top ten economics departments.

I am confident that there is no conspiracy, for if there were, I would not have been chosen as a coeditor. The causality actually runs the opposite direction: people who publish a lot are hired by top departments. Nevertheless, the papers in the *American Economics Review: Papers and*

Proceedings issues are selected by the *AEA* president who organizes it, and thus those issues represent a conspiracy.[1]

Anyone can become an editor by being n extraordinary referee. Referees who respond quickly with thoughtful reports are appointed as associate editors after half a dozen years or so, and after that, they soon become coeditors.

What Editorial Strategies and Tricks Can You Share?

In the past, the *Journal of Economic Theory* communicated its decisions with a form letter that listed possible decisions. When an article was accepted, the form letter had a box with a checkmark next to the word "Accept." Although everyone prefers an acceptance to the alternatives, this was a quite hideous notification method. Consequently, I decided to write what my assistant called the gush letter, in which I explained to authors why I was enthusiastic about publishing their papers and why they should be especially proud of the contribution. Many authors have told me that my personalized acceptance letters were the only the positive feedback that they ever received from a journal. But these letters served an additional role. If as an editor you cannot easily explain why you are excited to publish a paper, then you probably should reject it. If you can easily explain your reasons, then do so for the good of humanity. It creates a lot of social value at very low personal cost.

A great efficiency is gained when I look at reviews as they arrive. About half the time, I feel comfortable rejecting a paper on the basis of a single negative review. Because the waiting time for the second review is often two or three months, this procedure cuts down the waiting time substantially, as well as saving the time of a second reviewer.

When I am having trouble making a decision on a paper, one strategy is to talk it over with a group of colleagues at lunch. I provide a description of the issue and see where the conversation goes, peppering the discussion with the author's contribution. Whether a few economists do or do not find the results intriguing is useful data on whether the paper will be well received.

In his study of refereeing, Daniel Hamermesh (1994) discovered that if a report is not received within three months, then the expected waiting time was a year. Economists often make promises that they do not fulfill, which is a grim fact of editing. When one author wrote to chastise me for making him wait four months for a response to his submission, I politely responded that I had been waiting over five months for a referee's report from him. As a result, I often request more than the standard two referee reports. At the *AER*, more than two thirds of those who are asked agree to review manuscripts, and at *Economic Inquiry*, that proportion is below half. To get two, I now need to request four. Finding referees used to be much more challenging, and I assiduously kept track of the fields of expertise of everyone I encountered at conferences (which made me quite unpopular), but the Social Science Research Network (SSRN) makes finding reviewers much more straightforward since it is now easy to identify people with recent working papers on any topic.

I reject 10 to 15 percent of papers without refereeing. This type of desk rejection prompts some complaints (such as "I paid for those reviews with my submission fee"), but when it is appropriate, a desk rejection is also the kind thing to do. If there is no chance that I am going to publish a paper, why should I waste the referees' time and make the author wait? Not all authors agree, but in my view, journals are in the business of evaluating papers, not improving papers. If you want to improve your paper, ask your colleagues for advice. When you know what you want to say and how to say it, submit it to a journal.

Although some authors are irate about desk rejections on the principle that their submission fee pays for refereeing or that they deserve refereeing, the editor, not the referees, makes the decisions, and I generally spend a significant amount of time making a desk rejection. I think of a desk rejection as a circumstance where the editor does not feel that refereeing advice is warranted.

Some authors attempt to annoy the editor, and their reasons for considering this to be a good strategy are not clear. In my own journal dealings, I attempt to be professional, and this is what I seek in editors handling my own submissions. When I had a journal assistant (before everything began to be handled electronically), I asked her to impose a twenty-four-hour cooling off period whenever I wrote something that seemed emotional or unprofessional. I still delay sending emails when I feel at all peevish or irritated.

In their attempt to irritate the editor, some authors will ask "Have you even read my paper?" This is a more subtle question than it first appears, for the word *read* has a somewhat elastic meaning. Establishing beyond a reasonable doubt that a paper is not suitable for a journal can take from a few minutes (when the paper's summary of its findings is incomprehensible or not ambitious) to many hours. With experience, the amount of time that an editor spends on the bottom half of a paper goes to about zero (except for the desk rejections, which get a bit more), and most of their time is devoted to papers that are close to the acceptable versus unacceptable line.

Joshua S. Gans and George B. Shepherd's article on "How Are the Mighty Fallen: Rejected Classic Articles by Leading Economists" (1994) created among editors what I think of as the fear of rejecting "The Market for 'Lemons.'" George A. Akerlof's paper on "The Market for 'Lemons': Quality Uncertainty and the Market Mechanism" (1970) was rejected by three prominent journals, including the *AER*. No one wants to go down in history as the editor who rejected a paper that subsequently contributed greatly to the writer's winning of a Nobel Prize. However, I eventually came to the conclusion that the fear is overblown. There are type 1 and type 2 errors, and any procedure that never rejects "The Market for 'Lemons'" produces a low average quality. One lesson is to be open to the new and different. I use a higher bar for topics that generate a lot of current excitement and hence may be a fad. (At the time of this writing, behavioral economics is such a topic.) A second lesson from Akerlof's experience is to be careful in crafting rejection letters. The letters that Akerlof received, with their smug acceptance of general equilibrium as the end state of economics, look pathetic today. Finally, Akerlof's experience was unusual in that his rejection was not one of the many papers rejected by Lord Keynes, who was said to have suffered mightily from the personal agenda problem discussed above, and who rejected about half of the great rejected papers.

What Are Some Common Problems with Manuscripts?

Around 25 percent of the submissions to the *AER*, in my experience, are rejected due to poor execution. The papers made a good start on an article-worthy topic, but they provided too little substance for the audience.

Most of my experience is in editing general-interest journals, and my number one reason for rejection is that the paper is too specialized for the audience. When the interest in the paper is limited to a specific field, the paper belongs in a field journal, not in the *AER* or even *Economic Inquiry*. I expect submissions to make the case that the paper is of interest beyond the specific field and often ask, "Why should a labor or public finance economist want to read this paper?" A good strategy is to identify the audience and then submit to a journal that reaches that audience.

A surprising number of papers provide no meaningful conclusion. I consider these papers to be fatally incomplete. I have seen one that had a heading "Conclusion" with only one sentence: "See the introduction." Opinions vary, but I consider a serious conclusion section to be essential. After going through the body of the paper—which usually is hard work—it is time to get a payoff, which is delivered in the conclusion. In an introduction, the writer establishes the importance of a problem and summarizes the findings—and a conclusion is that the reader has actually gone through the body of the paper at the point where they encounter the conclusion. Thus, the kinds of points you can make are different. If, after finishing the body of the paper, a writer really has nothing more to say, then it is not clear why anyone should read the paper. The conclusion should be more than just a summary of the paper.

Paul Milgrom is fond of saying that theory papers can be evaluated based on generality and simplicity and that it is important to remember that both are goods. I think Milgrom's insight is similar to what is sometimes known as the "bang for the buck" evaluation: how much work do I have to do, and how much time do I have to spend for the amount of insight I receive? Being clear about the contribution and relating it accurately to other papers makes the paper simpler to understand and more likely to be accepted.

Do You Have Any Amusing Anecdotes to Share with Us?

There is a lot of heartbreak in journal editing since most of the job is rejecting papers. If you are looking for amusing anecdotes, subscribe to *Readers' Digest*.

The job of theory editor at the *AER* is unique in one way. There are thousands of people who believe that they have a great economic idea that economists desperately need to hear. Let us agree to call these people kooks for want of a better term. Pretty much 100 percent of kooks are theorists. You will not meet, say, a physicist or physician with a great economic idea that involves running regressions or doing lab experiments, although occasionally a table might illustrate a correlation between some economic variable like lawyers or fluoridated water and per capita gross domestic product.

An illustration of the great economic idea is the value of time. A paper was submitted pointing out that the order of consumption of goods may matter (for example, Alka-Seltzer should be consumed after a large meal, not before). The paper computes the number of orders in which one can consume a given number of goods, but it does not explain why the number of orders is interesting. One inessential and unsurprising detail is that the author has never heard of multinomials and manages to get the formula slightly wrong. The important thing is that he submitted two papers, both identical except that the second paper replaces the word *consumption* with *production*. Both papers have no references but state that the paper is so novel that there are no appropriate references. I received these papers prior to instituting desk rejections and sent both papers to one referee. To counter the author's assertion that economists have never considered the timing of consumption, the referee wrote a one sentence report: "Arrow-Debreu commodities are time-dated." The referee also provided two references and wrote in the letter to me that "the *AER* refereeing fee is just enough to buy a bottle of scotch, which helps me forget these miserable papers."

Another paper began with the memorable sentence "An economic system is like an electric power plant." The paper analyzed electric power generation in great detail. It included diagrams of power plants and discussed Kirchoff's laws and other essential ingredients of electrical engineering. Not present, however, was anything recognizable as economics, like prices, demand, or even cost. There was no attempt to explain in what way a power plant was like an economic system. I rejected this paper, which prompted an unending series of irate complaints, including a claim that John von Neumann worked on and was unable to solve the problem that the author had solved. No reference was given to demonstrate von Neumann's interest in the problem. The generous interpretation is that von Neumann would publish only when he actually solved the problem. After more than a dozen letters, I informed him that I would no longer open his letters. They kept coming for months.

The essential mystery of editing is why the reports that I receive as an editor are so much better than the reports that I receive as an author. Reading thousands of referees' reports has changed my perspective on reports. Editors may wait a long time for referee reports, but they are generally serious, thoughtful, and insightful. Authors who complain about referees usually focus on inessential details rather than the main substance of the review. Virtually all reviewers understand papers well enough to evaluate them, and when they do not, it is usually because the author failed to communicate well. Moreover, referees offer good advice about how to improve the paper and take the research to the next level. It is worth remembering that the referee's task is to give advice to the editor, not to the author.

Many people write to me saying that they refereed a manuscript for another journal and want to give the author a new chance. I see this response as wildly inefficient. First, the referee has a good idea of what the author has accomplished and can quickly review the current draft. Second, if the author has ignored serious issues that were pointed out previously, this deficiency is important information about the quality of scholarship that I really want to receive. Third, the fact that another editor selected the same referee is a confirmation that we have selected well; papers should pass muster with experts in the field. The only circumstance where I do not want to hear from a repeat referee is when the referee recommended rejection for personal, unprofessional reasons, which is precisely the set of the circumstances where they will not tell me that they reviewed the paper for another journal.

At a conference, I overheard one author tell another economist that an idiotic referee reviewed his *AER* submission. He detailed all the stupid things that the referee said, and the economist listening to the story commiserated and wholeheartedly agreed with the author, even though the commiserator was the referee in question. This referee had written a thoughtful and serious report on the paper of a friend, but the author did not appreciate the insights in the report.

As a final anecdote, I received a referee report from a respected economist, who said in the letter to me: "I have written a gentle report because the author is obviously inexperienced and very junior and I don't want to discourage him. But make no mistake: this paper makes no contribution, and you should not encourage a revision." The author of that paper, which I rejected, had already won a Nobel Prize in economics.

What's Up with *Economic Inquiry*?

I strongly recommend Glenn Ellison's 2002 paper on journal publishing. This paper changed my perspective on problems with economics journal editing. Ellison finds that the profession has slowed down and that the "submission to print" time at major journals has doubled. Surprisingly, most of the slowdown is in the number of revisions, not the "within-round cycle time." It turns out that the interminable wait for a response was common twenty-five years ago. What has changed, Ellison shows, is that the number of rounds has nearly doubled. I had thought it was deficiencies in my own papers that caused me to revise three, four, or even five times, but it is a professionwide phenomenon.

Like most economists, I am obsessed with efficiency, and wasted resources offend me in an irrational way. The way that economists operate journals is perhaps the most inefficient operation that I encounter on a regular basis. It is a fabulous irony that a profession obsessed with efficiency operates its core business in an inefficient manner. How long do you spend refereeing a paper? Many hours are devoted to reviewing papers. This would be socially efficient if the paper was improved in a way that is commensurate with the time spent, but revising papers using blind referees often makes papers worse. Referees offer specific advice that push papers away from the author's intent. It is one thing for a referee to say, "I do not find this paper compelling because of X," and another thing entirely to say that the referee would rather see a different paper on the same general topic and try to get the author to write it. The latter is all too common. Gradually, like a lobster in a pot slowly warming to a boil, we have transformed the business of refereeing from the evaluation of contributions with a little grammatical help into an elaborate system of glacier-paced anonymous coauthorship. This system encourages authors to submit papers that are crafted not for publication but for survival in the revision process. Why fix an issue when referees are going to force a rewrite of a paper anyway?[2] My sense is that the first revision of papers generally improves them and that it is downhill from there.

The "anonymous coauthorship" problem has an insidious aspect: having encouraged a revision, referees often feel obliged to recommend acceptance even if the paper has gotten worse. Referees become psychologically tied to the outcome because they caused it. I once directed an author to return a paper to an earlier state because a referee encouraged the author to make a mess of what had been a clean, insightful analysis.

When I was asked to recommend an editor for *Economic Inquiry*, it occurred to me that *EI* was ideally positioned for an experiment. Experimenting with extremely successful journals like the *AER* or *Journal of Political Economy* has a large potential downside, and it also is not very useful to experiment with a brand-new journal. New journals are not on anyone's radar screen, and attracting high-quality papers to a new journal is challenging. Successful new journals tend to be run in an autocratic way by a committed and talented editor, and policies play a small role in the operation. As a result, the ideal experiment is a journal like *EI*, which has a decent but not stellar history.

I offered to serve as editor, provided that I was given a free hand to experiment with policies, including the no-revisions option. The no-revisions option is a commitment by the journal to say yes or no to a submission and thereby prevent the endless rounds of revision that are common at other journals and at *EI* itself. No revisions is an option for the author, not a requirement. I implemented no revisions when I assumed editorship in July 2007, and about 35 percent of the papers were now submitted under this option in 2012.

When I started at *Economic Inquiry*, Steve Levitt mentioned the no-revisions policy in his popular Freakonomics blog, and I was surprised by the comments that he received. Most anonymous commentators were negative. They (1) did not think that it was necessary, (2) did not think that I could commit to it, or (3) ignored the fact that it was optional and considered whether it would be socially optimal for all journals to impose it.

The decision to agree to no revisions is and should remain optional. Inexperienced authors are ill advised to choose it. Authors with a novel, difficult thesis will often need a conversation with referees to convince them that the paper is worth publishing. The no-revisions option works best with experienced authors who know what they want to say and how to say it and who want a forum to broadcast that to the profession. The option removes the journal from the business of rewriting papers and increases the importance of evaluating them. Speculation about what would happen if all journals forced all papers through the no-revisions process is misguided. It is like saying that Taco Bell should not exist because it would be a bad thing if Taco Bell were the only restaurant.

Some commentators seem to think that *EI* cannot commit and that papers will be submitted that deserve revision but are too flawed to publish as is. But this is not a problem unless the journal is desperate for manuscripts. Many other journals are available to take the author's revised paper. At least a dozen rejected manuscripts would have been clear candidates for revise and resubmit absent the no-revisions policy. That is a risk the authors take when they choose the option. Half a dozen would have received a recommendation to revise and resubmit but instead were accepted.

Finally, is the no-revisions policy socially useful? No one is required to use this option, but about 35 percent of submissions come in this form, which suggests that some authors think it is a useful experiment. Only one journal has copied the policy to date, but the sensible thing is to wait and see if *Economic Inquiry* improves.

A no-revisions policy does not prohibit an author from benefitting from advice. At this time, 100 percent of the authors who received acceptances under this policy actually revised their manuscripts in light of referees' comments. The difference is that these revisions were voluntary, not coerced. That is, the referees and editor say, "This paper meets our standards as is but would be even better if . . . ," and the author is then free to improve the paper.

I have spent a lot of time thinking about the coeditor process. At the *Journal of Economic Theory*, associate editors are de facto coeditors in the sense that they send papers to referees for review and make recommended decisions that almost always stick. There are about forty associate editors, which ensures that there are always a couple of bad ones. Bad coeditors pollute journals by preventing the journal from having consistent standards and responses, and the more coeditors there are, then the more likely there will be a problem of conflicting standards and expectations. While I was an associate editor at *JET*, some papers on auction theory were published that were not as good as papers I rejected, which is a frustrating experience for an associate editor and more so for a rejected author. However, employing only a few coeditors makes the job larger than most would accept. So what is the right organizational form?

Empirically, the top journals are run with four to six coeditors who are distinguished by field. However, being an editor at this rarefied level is strongly rewarded by the profession; at lesser journals, the professional benefits are much smaller. Consequently, it is much more difficult to find people who are willing to take a quarter of *EI* than, say, a sixth of the *AER*, even though a sixth of the *AER* represents handling more manuscripts per year. Moreover, the top journals require an editor to be a jack of all trades who can handle papers in a diverse set of areas. As an *AER* coeditor, I had to handle theory papers on trade, finance, and environmental economics, fields in which I had never read a paper when I started. The broad general coeditor is hard to find, even for the top journals.

The strategy I have adopted is a hybrid scheme. Like the top journals, *EI* has general coeditors for applied microeconomic theory, empirical microeconomics, and macroeconomics. In addition, we have specialized coeditors for two kinds of subfields. First, in subfields where we receive more than ten papers per year (like sports, defense, experimental, and health), we have specialized coeditors who handle all the papers. Second, in fields where I would like to send a signal of interest (like neuroeconomics or algorithmic game theory) because I think the field is likely to boom in future years, I also have specialized coeditors. Thus, unlike *JET*, responsibility among the specialized coeditors is clear. This hybrid scheme is an experiment to see if it makes evaluating manuscripts more efficient.

The *JPE* has a history of publishing entertaining articles in a column called "Miscellany," but this tradition began to lapse with George J. Stigler's death. As the publisher of Axel Leijonhufvud's classic humor article "Life among the Econ" (1973) (*EI* used to be called *Western Economic Journal*, and it remains a journal of the Western Economic Association), *EI* has a venerable history in this area. I would like to acknowledge Yoram Bauman for his work as a specialized coeditor for *EI's* "Miscellany" column. I think that the profession needs an outlet for this kind of thing, and I am gratified to see that two of the forthcoming papers for "Miscellany" are by Nobel laureates.

It is too early to tell whether these experiments have made the journal sustainably better, but the rate of submissions has more than doubled.

Do You Have Anything Else to Say, or Are You Finally Done?

Authors of articles expend a great deal of effort in trying to determine what editors are interested in, and they tailor their papers toward a specific editor's interests. They devote similar efforts to figuring out what topics journals seek. I do not think that journals really have favorites, and patterns are more a consequence of the pattern of submissions. Editors, however, do have favorites (it is unavoidable), but the papers accepted are not strong evidence of what those favorites are. When I accepted a paper for the *AER*, I usually raised the bar a bit for papers on the same topic, and in a close decision, it could matter. I did not want a single area to dominate the journal. So topics in the journal, for me, were actually slightly negatively correlated with the likelihood of acceptance, although such a correlation was weak.

I use higher standards in my own research area than in other areas because it is harder to impress me. In areas with which I am unfamiliar, a paper benefits from educating me about basic insights available in other papers. This is also a small effect because such benefits will be experienced only in my reading and will not be experienced by the referees, who have substantial expertise. Nevertheless, in a close decision, it could make a difference. Overall, I think submitting a paper where the editor has deep expertise usually produces a higher bar but less variance in the evaluation.

Being an editor has not made me a more effective author, or it has improved me much less than I anticipated. It has, however, made me much more critical of my own work and much more effective at providing advice to colleagues. I can reference a broader literature. Being an editor at a major journal is a great way to keep abreast of new developments because even if a particular paper is not submitted to one's own journal, it is usually discussed in some submissions to the journal. But overall, it probably is not a good strategy to be an editor for the sake of being a more effective author.

In this chapter, I have talked mostly about the challenging aspects of being an editor. But the great thing about editing a journal is reading terrific manuscripts that one would not have otherwise encountered. This happens just often enough to make me glad to serve and keep me gushing.

Acknowledgments

I thank Kristin McAfee, Dan Hamermesh, and Glenn Ellison for very useful comments.

Notes

1. David N. Laband and Michael J. Piette (1994) argue that the journal conspiracies are efficient.

2. I am not going to comment here on two other major inefficiencies. First, after a journal publishes the paper, which was freely provided, as a profession we lose general access to it because of monopoly pricing by journals. Monopoly pricing of economics journals represents also an appalling state of affairs or a delicious irony, depending on your perspective (see Bergstrom 2001). Second, a huge number of papers are being refereed many times, which is one of the dramatic costs of not coordinating across journals.

References

Akerlof, George A. 1970. The Market for "Lemons": Quality Uncertainty and the Market Mechanism. *Quarterly Journal of Economics* 84 (3):488–500.

Bergstrom, Ted. 2001. Free Labor for Costly Journals. *Journal of Economic Perspectives* 15 (3):183–198.

Ellison, Glenn. 2002. The Slowdown of the Economics Publishing Process. *Journal of Political Economy* 105 (5):947–993.

Gans, Joshua S., and George B. Shepherd. 1994. How Are the Mighty Fallen: Rejected Classic Articles by Leading Economists. *Journal of Economic Perspectives* 8 (1):165–179.

Hamermesh, Daniel. 1994. Facts and Myths about Refereeing. *Journal of Economic Perspectives* 8 (1):153–163.

Laband, David N., and Michael J. Piette. 1994. Favoritism versus Search for Good Papers: Empirical Evidence Regarding the Behavior of Journal Editors. *Journal of Political Economy* 102:194–203.

Leijonhufvud, Axel. 1973. Life among the Econ. *Western Economic Journal* 11:327–337.

4

Reflections on Editing the *Journal of Finance*, 2006 to 2012

Campbell R. Harvey

The *AER* is a fire hose. In my first year, I handled 275 manuscripts.
—R. Preston McAfee (chapter 3 in this volume)

If the *American Economic Review* is a fire hose, then the *Journal of Finance* is a tsunami. In my first year as editor of the *Journal*, I handled 1,275 manuscripts. If one takes into account papers that are revised and resubmitted, that figure is even larger. Over my six years (2006 to 2012) as editor, I handled approximately 7,500 submissions. Even at the point of my so-called retirement on July 1, 2012, I still had more than five hundred manuscripts under my control. The job does not go away until these manuscripts are settled.

The *Journal of Finance* was founded in 1946 and is the official journal of the American Finance Association (AFA). Among economics journals, the *Journal of Finance* ranks third in total citations (behind *American Economic Review* and *Econometrica*) and fourth in terms of five-year impact factors (behind *Journal of Economic Literature*, *Quarterly Journal of Economics*, and *Journal of Political Economy*). In 2011, the acceptance rate was 5.4 percent, and the median turnaround time was forty-two days.

The Invitation

In September 2005, I received a telephone call from René Stulz of the Ohio State University. I was not sure why he was calling. I initially thought he was going to invite me to a seminar. He then said that he was the chairperson of the AFA's editorial search committee and that the association wanted to offer me the job of editor of the *Journal of Finance*.

I was speechless.

I had no idea that René was leading the search committee. Indeed, I had learned only a week before that the association was searching for a new editor. I was tipped off by an email that was mistakenly sent to me instead of John Campbell (AFA president) of Harvard University. The email was a long treatise by another finance person who was nominating himself for the job. I deleted the email and did not think of the matter any further.

During the long pause that followed Rene's offer, a number of things went through my mind. First, René, who served as editor from 1988 to 2000, was not just the chair of the search committee. René is arguably the most successful editor in the history of the *Journal of Finance*. When he took over the *Journal*, it was not known as the top journal in the field of finance. The *Journal of Financial Economics*, which began in 1974, had overtaken the *Journal of Finance*. In addition, a new journal in finance, the *Review of Financial Studies*, debuted with its first issue in the spring of 1988 and was instantly an A-level journal. René's leadership, however, led to a renaissance that elevated the status of the association's journal to the number one position in the field. This legacy continues. The revealed preference of authors submitting to finance journals shows that among the three A-level journals in the field today—the *Journal of Finance*, the *Journal of Financial Economics*, and the *Review of Financial Studies*—the *Journal of Finance* is generally considered the top journal.

Second, in 1994 René made me an associate editor of the *Journal of Finance* at a relatively young age (I graduated from the University of Chicago in 1986). I served as associate editor of the *Journal* until 2000. René had also taken some risk in publishing my paper "The World Price of Covariance Risk" in the *Journal* in 1991. His detailed comments on the manuscript moved the paper from making a marginal contribution to making a significant contribution to international finance.

All of this was going through my head over the long pause after he popped the question. I wanted to say "Yes!" However, the opportunity required careful consideration, so I thanked René and said that I needed to talk with a few people first. I was particularly interested in talking with the outgoing editor as well as my dean. I received Rene's permission to discuss the offer with these individuals.

Due Diligence

René served as editor for twelve years. The next editor, Rick Green of Carnegie Mellon University, served only three years (2000 to 2003). Robert Stambaugh of Wharton also served only three years (2003 to 2006). Because the AFA requires an editor to give at least one year's notice before leaving the job, both of these editors provided notice after serving for two years on the job. It was therefore unlikely that any paper published in the *Journal* would have these individuals' name on it as editor. This raised some questions: Why only three years? Had the number of submissions exploded, making it impossible to do the job?

I raised this concern with Rob, the outgoing editor. Rob was on my dissertation committee at the University of Chicago. I have a great memory of pitching my dissertation to him in his office in 1985. He thought it was very good work. It was surely publishable in the *Journal of Financial Economics* or the *Journal of Finance*. However, he was unsure it was good enough for a Chicago dissertation!

With regard to the *Journal of Finance*, Rob said something very important. In particular, he said that his own research went best when he could find a week or so to devote much of his attention to it. That was a challenge at the *Journal*, where new papers arrive every day. When Rob said this, I realized that I might be able to do the job because my research style is different. I tend to work on multiple projects at the same time, switching back and forth with little or no set-up time. I could thus envision doing some journal work and then some research work, switching back and forth without affecting my ability to conduct research.

Next I spoke with my dean at Duke University, Doug Breeden. When Doug heard of the offer, his response was "Take it!" Duke's young business school had yet to have an editorship of such a premier journal. Doug made it easy for me. He offered (1) no teaching for $N + 1$ years, where N was the number of years I was editor; (2) no chairing of any committees and only light committee work at the school in general; (3) an administrative assistant; and (4) course relief for a coeditor if I decided to choose one from Duke. This was an extremely generous offer.

The Western Finance Association

There was a complication, however—the Western Finance Association (WFA). In the field of finance, there are two main meetings: the American

Finance Meetings, which are part of the Allied Social Science Association (ASSA) meetings, are held in January, and the WFA meetings are held in June.

The AFA/ASSA meetings are mainly for recruiting, and much time is spent in hotel rooms interviewing candidates. The AFA/ASSA meetings are huge, and people attend from many fields.

In contrast, the WFA meetings are for those in the field of finance. There is no recruiting and no advertising. The WFA meetings are often held in remote locations, and attendees spend three days attending sessions and talking to colleagues. The meetings are very competitive: about 1,400 papers are submitted to the conference, and 144 are selected to be on the program. Each paper is reviewed by two referees. Most papers on the program end up in A-level journals.

I had previously agreed to be program chair for the 2007 meetings. This meant that in the fall of 2006 (during my first six months as editor of the *Journal of Finance*), I would have to handle 1,400 WFA papers as well as the onslaught of *Journal of Finance* papers.

In an effort to spread the load, I asked the WFA if there was any possibility of deferring the program chair job. The answer was no. However, in the back of my mind, I was thinking that we had seen this before. Rick Green, editor of the *Journal* from 2000 to 2003, was WFA president in 2000 and served as program chair the year before.

The Review of Financial Studies

Over the 1999 to 2005 period, I served as coeditor of the *Review of Financial Studies* (*RFS*). The structure of the *RFS* is different. There is an executive editor (who was Maureen O'Hara of Cornell University) and usually four coeditors, with papers essentially divided up among the coeditors and editor. Although I managed more than my one-fifth or one-quarter share of the papers, the flow of papers was very small compared to that of the *Journal of Finance*. In my busiest year at the *Review*, I probably oversaw four hundred papers. The *Journal of Finance* would triple that load.

The Dilemma

The dilemma that I faced was as follows. I wanted to accept the *Journal of Finance* job, but I wanted to serve for two terms (that is, six years). This raised the question of how I would manage the *Journal of Finance* job (and the WFA job), maintain my research, and still have time for my family (at that time, my three children were age nine, eleven, and fourteen).

The Solution

Substantially Reduce My Time Commitment for the WFA

Much of the time of the program chair was devoted to making 2,800 referee assignments. I decided to automate this process. I sketched out an algorithm whereby authors submitting papers would categorize their papers. The algorithm also relied on information from the program committee so that each member provided areas of expertise. We needed filters for conflicts of interest (like home institutions). The algorithm was coded up by then Duke University Ph.D. student Jules van Binsbergen. I also appointed three of my colleagues at Duke as coprogram chairs. This made meeting my responsibilities to both the *Journal of Finance* and the *Review of Financial Studies* feasible.

Take Advantage of Duke University Relief

Actually, I did not take advantage of all of the Duke relief. I told the dean that it would be a mistake to set the precedent of buying off all my courses. Doing so would run the risk that others in some other area within the school might get an editorship and demand "the Harvey deal" (even though their journal might have only a quarter of the submissions that the *Journal of Finance* has). I suggested that Duke pay for two courses off and ask the AFA to buy out the rest. The AFA agreed to this arrangement.

Appoint a Duke-Based Coeditor

My long-term coauthor and colleague, John Graham, agreed to be coeditor. At the same time, he had an offer to be coeditor for the *Review of Financial Studies*, which he turned down when he accepted the job with the *Journal*. He substantially helped with decisions on empirical corporate finance papers and also determined paper order and interface with the publisher. We met at least weekly to discuss papers in progress and assign both associate editors and referees.

Substantially Step Up Desk Rejections

At the *Review of Financial Studies*, I was not allowed to desk-reject, which was frustrating to me. At the *Journal*, I aimed to desk-reject 30 percent of submissions. If I could manage to reduce effective new submissions to approximately eight hundred papers after the desk rejects, this would put me in the ballpark of the volume of papers that René Stulz handled as editor.

Change the Role of the Associate Editor

In the previous editor's regime, associate editors mainly suggested referees. I developed a new protocol whereby associate editors (1) gave a more detailed preliminary judgment of the paper in addition to suggesting referees, (2) got the paper back if either they initially liked the paper or the referee liked the paper so they could give more detailed comments, and (3) shepherded the paper through the process conditional on a revise and resubmit.

Change the Number of Associate Editors

The idea here was that by increasing the size of the board, I could ask for more time (but less frequently) from the associate editors. In addition, with an expanded board, the associate editors would generally be assigned papers directly in their areas of expertise, making it easier for them to give their own evaluation of the papers.

Know the Referee Pool

One factor that I did not fully appreciate at the outset was that I knew the referee pool. Over my six years at the *Review of Financial Studies*, I had used probably a thousand referees and developed a knowledge of who was good and who was not. I knew the people who were chronically late. I generally knew who to go to. This knowledge was fresh because my term with the *Review of Financial Studies* ended in 2005 and my term with the *Journal* was set to begin in 2006.

With the above in place, I accepted a three-year term as editor with an option to extend it to a six-year term after the first year. After one year, I exercised this option and extended my contract through 2012.

Key Insights

You Are Going to Make Mistakes

You are going to accept papers that you should have rejected and reject papers that you should have accepted. There is no way to eliminate this risk. After you realize you have made a mistake, you need to move on. If it eats you up, then this is the wrong job for you.

Maintain a No Quid Pro Quo Policy

You routinely receive papers from both former journal editors (who might have accepted your papers) or current journal editors (who might be considering your papers). You must treat these papers as you would any paper. In rejecting a paper at the *Journal of Finance*, editors may fear that doing so could negatively affect their chances at the other journal. Too bad. That is part of the job.

Have Authors Undercite Your Own Work

John Campbell, president of the AFA, gave me this wise advice. Authors sometimes think that their chance of a revise and resubmit will go up if they include twelve cites of the editor's work. At least for me, this strategy had the opposite effect on the probabilities. On papers that did get a request to revise and resubmit, I often struck references to my own work. Optics are important, and readers of a journal should not get the impression that the editor is using the editorship to increase citations to his or her own work.

More Readers Are Better Than Fewer

The norm in the field of finance is generally one referee. It is impossible for the editor to read all 1,300 *Journal of Finance* submissions each year. Under my system, an associate editor and a referee read the paper. The associate editor also had the option of assigning two or more referees. Multiple referees were usually assigned to controversial papers or to papers that we had favorable prior on. I carefully read and marked up every paper whose author was asked to revise and resubmit, about 120 in most years. Many papers in the empirical corporate finance area were also read by the coeditor. Hence, even with a single referee, each paper was read by a minimum of three readers and potentially many more. In my calculus, the more readers, the less noise in the decision making.

Be Aggressive on Conflicts of Interest

There were many levels of recusal.

• Part of the associate editor's job was to suggest a referee who had no conflicts of interest with the paper that was being evaluated. Sometimes a paper had to be sent to a referee with whom there would be a conflict (for example, a paper criticizing the referee's own work), but in those situations, multiple referees were assigned.

• The associate editors had to reveal if they had any conflict of interest with the author of the submitting paper or a competing paper.

• I assigned an acting editor if the author was (1) a Duke faculty member, (2) a current Duke Ph.D. student, (3) one of my former students, or (4) one of my coauthors. In addition, I assigned acting editors for (5) papers that competed with or criticized my papers and (6) papers that competed with or criticized papers by other Duke faculty. Acting editors were drawn from a pool of senior people in the finance profession as well as associate editors. The acting editor chose the referees and wrote the decision letter. This was not an anonymous job. The initial letter to the referee did not have my name on it. I had no input in the process (other than choosing the acting editor). If the paper is published, the initial footnote will include a credit to the acting editor.

Be Especially Diligent in Your Own Research Area

Not all mistakes are equal. In particular, publishing a paper that is (ex post) below the margin paper in your own research area is far worse than publishing a paper that is below the margin in an area that you are not known for. I therefore routinely assigned extra referees if the paper was in one of my areas. Again, optics are important, and it is damaging to a journal for readers to perceive that the editor is simply promoting his or her own research agenda.

Use External Advisers

In situations in which a paper was a close call, I appointed an advisory editor. The advisory editor might give a high-level opinion. The advisory editor might also review the entire file (referee and associate editor correspondence and reports).

Recognize That Impact Factor Is an Imperfect Measure of Quality

It is short-sighted to make decisions simply based on the expected number of citations. For example, I doubled the number of theory papers in the *Journal of Finance*. I did this knowing that such papers gather far fewer citations than some other areas.

Do Not Fixate on Turnaround Time

If you doubt the quality of the review and the paper is at the margin, get another review. Turnaround time in finance averages below two months for each of the top three journals, so a little extra time is not a big deal.

Decide Quickly

After you have the referee and associate editor reports, there is no reason to sit on a paper and wait to make a decision. Time is not your friend because there are set-up costs, such as refamiliarizing yourself with the paper. Also, authors want quick resolution. You cannot stall on rejections. Yes, it is true that receiving rejections is painful, but as editor you need to be able to hit the reject button and move on. You cannot let it get to you. If you do, you are in the wrong job. I found it much easier to reject papers at the *Journal of Finance* than at the *Review of Financial Studies* because getting rejected at the *Journal* was not the end of the line for a paper. Authors received excellent feedback and with a solid revision had a much greater probability of placing the paper at the *Journal of Financial Economics* or the *Review of Financial Studies*.

Work Hard on the First Revision: Up and Out

As an author, I was always frustrated with multiple rounds of refereeing. Sometimes new issues came up on the revision, and sometimes some of the rounds seemed trivial. At the *Journal of Finance*, I instituted a system whereby most of the work is done in the initial report. In addition, speculative requests to revise and resubmit were not issued (that is, papers were rejected). Hence, the author would have a lot of work to do after receiving the first report. By 2011, the probability that a paper (that would eventually be published) would be accepted after just one revision was greater than 50 percent. After the second revision, the cumulative probability was 95 percent. When I took over, the cumulative probability on the second revision was only 40 percent.

Aggressively Desk-Reject

Sometimes you know by the title of a paper that it is not appropriate for the top general-purpose journal in your field—for example, "Tests of the CAPM in Morocco." Many authors submit papers to the *Journal of Finance* knowing that their paper has zero chance of getting a revise-and-resubmit recommendation. They simply intend to use the referee report as input for a revision and then submit the paper to a B- or C-level journal. Indeed, some authors submit a first draft of a paper with potentially no one reading it before the referee gets it. Given the $100 submission fee and the less than two-month turnaround, this was a good deal for the submitting author. However, I ended this practice through an aggressive desk-reject policy. The *Journal* asks a lot from the referees, and it is not fair to make them readers of papers that have no chance of appearing in a top journal. The one exception that I made to the desk-rejection rule pertained to papers submit by newly minted Ph.D.s. In such cases, I usually sent the paper to referees. If the paper was clearly below the bar, however, I sometimes asked rookie faculty members to withdraw the paper but provided some feedback and allowed them to submit the paper again in the future.

Track Late Referees and Referees to Be Avoided

I created a Google document that listed late referees. Some of these referees are highly valued. The document helped allocate these high-quality but late referees to papers for which their advice would be particularly important. The document also included a list of referees to be avoided (that is, blacklisted) due to poor reviews in the past.

Beware Referee and Area Fixed Effects

As I said earlier, knowledge of the referee pool was one of the key reasons that I could do the *Journal of Finance* job efficiently. Knowing the referee pool means that as editor you can apply fixed effects: some referees are too tough, and some are too easy. Both of these categories of referees can be excellent reviewers, but it is their recommendation that needs adjusting. There also exist area fixed effects. In particular, I found that referees in the areas of asset pricing theory and corporate finance theory tend to be tougher than referees in some other areas. Again, benefiting from my time at the *Review of Financial Studies* (where I handled both empirical and theory papers across the spectrum of finance topics), I was able to make some adjustments.

Mitigate Appeals

Appeals are a nightmare. Over my six years, I handled 210 appeals. Most of these appeals came in the first three years. At that point, we altered the policy such that authors were allowed one appeal every three years. This applied to all authors on the appealed paper. The tipping point was a paper for which the associate editor recommended desk rejection. The author of this particular paper had appealed multiple times in the past. I decided to send the paper to two reviewers. The first reviewer said that it was the worst paper he had ever reviewed—not just for the *Journal of Finance* but any top finance journal. The second review was highly negative. With three highly negative assessments of the paper, I rejected the paper. Shortly thereafter the author appealed the decision. I had had enough. I went to the AFA and asked for a new policy. The once-every-three-years rule greatly decreased the number of appeals.

Guide Authors to Spend Extra Effort on the Abstract and Introduction

The abstract and introduction are key elements to marketing a paper. I therefore recommended that authors spend a lot of time rewriting their abstract and introduction. A successful abstract and introduction should clearly state the paper's new economic insight and also make the case that the new economic insight is big enough for the flagship journal in our field. Further, the abstract and introduction need to be pitched to the general reader, not to a specialist in the sub-area of the article. The abstract and introduction also need to be engaging so that the general reader is interested in exploring the rest of the paper.

Be Willing to Learn about Other Areas

One unexpected bonus of editing a general-purpose journal is that the editor gets to learn about other areas. I most looked forward to reading papers outside my areas of specialization. Although I was not an expert in these areas, I always felt that I could contribute to the paper. At minimum, the editor needs to understand what the paper is doing and why it is important. Authors need to make that clear.

Take Risk

You don't want to be the editor that rejects a soon to be classic paper, like Fischer Black and Myron Scholes's paper on option pricing. This paper, which appeared in the *Journal of Political Economy* in 1973, is one of the most-cited papers in finance and economics. Scholes went on to win the Nobel Prize for the paper (Black would have won too, but he passed away at an early age). I did not want to be the editor who rejected the next Black and Scholes paper. Consistent with my first point on making mistakes, it is better to take some risk with papers, knowing that some of them will be mistakes. To illustrate some risk taking, in the October 2010 issue of the *Journal of Finance*, I published a paper in the emerging area of neurofinance. The article includes color images from f-MRI brain scans. I also published papers dealing with genetics and finance. As a third example, the *Journal* published an ingenious paper where the authors used audio recordings of chief executive officers at quarterly conference calls and ran the audio through a computer program to assess the probability that they were telling the truth.

Advice for Authors

• The paper should be read and commented on by colleagues before it is submitted.

• Ideally, the paper has been presented at seminars and conferences.

• Treat any comment received at a seminar or conference as you would treat a referee comment. Address these comments, and when appropriate, email the commenter to explain how you addressed the suggestions.

• In your paper, make it very clear what the new economic insight is and why it is important.

• Theory papers should (1) explain why the model is useful, (2) make clear where the paper deviates from past models, (3) offer new testable implications and not merely fit a known fact, and (4) include a discussion of both the strengths and the weaknesses of the approach.

• Empirical papers should (1) explain why the finding is important, (2) clearly differentiate the paper's approach from past approaches, (3) not be shackled by past methods (we do X because another did X in the past), (4) present a clear economic justification for the empirical examination, (5) convince the reader that there has been minimal data mining, (6) check for robustness and influential observations, and (7) use state-of-the-art econometrics.

Advice for Referees

• Be efficient. If the paper is clearly below the bar, you do not need to write a long report.

• Be clear in your advice in the cover letter. The editor wants to know your opinion. The editor does not want to read, "It is a tough call that I will defer to your editorial judgment."

• The key question to consider is whether the contribution is big enough for the top journal in the field.

• It is not your job to rewrite the paper.

Other Initiatives

As editor of the *Journal of Finance*, I had many aspirations. However, with approximately 1,300 manuscripts to oversee each year, most of these initiatives had to be put aside. Here are two examples of projects that were not fully implemented.

Replication Policy

Along with the editor of the *Journal of Financial Economics*, Bill Schwert of the University of Rochester, and the editor of the *Review of Financial Studies*, Matt Spiegel of Yale University, I drafted a detailed replication policy. The idea was that all three top finance journals would have the same policy. A number of top economic journals have already implemented replication policies. We circulated the draft policy among the boards of the associate and advisory editors. It is an understatement to say that there was a furor. More than half of the associate editors and advisers had strong negative opinions on the replication policy. Their arguments comprised three main points. First, the policy would impose a large burden on authors. In addition, there were fears that authors would have to provide programming support to the many faculty and students around the world who tried to replicate. Second, finance, in contrast to general economics, makes extensive use of proprietary data. There was a concern that even with exemptions to the replication policy, researchers would be discouraged from using proprietary data. Third, the one economics journal that did not have a replication policy, the *Quarterly Journal of Economics*, had seemingly pulled ahead of the other top economics journals. Following a lively online debate about the policy, in the end it was shelved.

Digital Publishing

I had a grand vision of a different delivery system and enhanced functionality for the *Journal of Finance*. However, I did not have the time to spearhead this effort because of the large number of papers that I had to manage each year. The AFA searched for an Internet editor but never found the right candidate. Nevertheless, I did make some changes. First, I made sure that the historical backfile was complete. Certain pages were missing from older issues of the *Journal*. Second, I had both *JSTOR* and Wiley (publisher of the *Journal of Finance*) insert hyperlinks in the PDFs of the historical articles. The hyperlinks make it easier to move from one article to another and hence make research more efficient.

New Initiatives

Shortly after I retired, I accepted a new position with the AFA as editor of the AFA Digital Publishing Initiatives. This position allows me to complete the unfinished business related to bringing the *Journal* into a new digital era. There are three prongs in the strategy.

Enhanced Functionality of *Journal of Finance* Articles

Most people have probably accessed HTML versions of journal articles. Although there is some increased functionality, these versions are often clunky, and thus a flat PDF is still generally preferred to the HTML version. The idea of enhanced functionality is to maintain the clean appearance of a print-published article (using reflowable HTML5) while adding new features. The result is similar to an e-reader. The article looks like a page from the *Journal* but with a few differences. For instance, there is a left-hand side bar in which full references to any paper cited in an article pops up. Click on a citation, and you are taken immediately to that paper, no matter where it is published. Unfortunately, only Journal articles from 2004 (which are coded in XML) are easily converted to the new functionality. We face the challenge of fully digitizing the entire backfile from 1946 to 2003. This involves not simply scanning historical files to PDF but providing full searchability and potentially retypesetting the entire backfile.

Mobile Delivery

There will be two mobile delivery models.

HTML5 Version of the Journal

With this version, readers with an Internet connection will be able to access the *Journal* with a smart phone or tablet. This delivery mechanism will provide the enhanced functionality described above.

iOS Version of the Journal

This version will work directly with Apple products (iPad, iPhone). Essentially, this version will allow readers to download a *Journal of Finance* application that contains the complete history of the *Journal of Finance*. The articles will look like the original articles and have increased functionality but not at the same level as the HTML5 version that is available through an Internet connection. For instance, links will exist between *Journal of Finance* articles but not to articles published by other journals—unless an Internet connection is active.

New Website for the *Journal of Finance*

The *Journal of Finance* Web site had not been touched in ten years. It was embarrassing. The new site was launched in December 2012.

Conclusions

The *Journal of Finance* is impossibly large for only one person to manage. It exists thanks to the cooperation of many people. I was very lucky to have a coeditor, John Graham, who sat two offices down the hall and who provided an amazing amount of help. Our excellent assistant editor, Wendy Washburn, shielded me from most of the administrative burdens of the job. Our expert copyeditor, Brenda Priebe, polished every article published under my editorship. AFA Executive Secretary and Treasurer David Pyle has a deep knowledge of the journal's history and was always available for advice. The associate editors and referees were thoughtful and exemplified a culture of extraordinarily prompt turnaround. For instance, while the turnaround time is bimodal (due to desk rejections), 83 percent of manuscripts were processed in less than a hundred days in 2011. In addition, many of the papers that went more than a hundred days involved a second referee, which was to play in the authors' favor. Here is the statistic I like the best: on December 31, 2011, the longest that any paper had been in review was only 160 days. So of the 1,300 papers, not a single paper was in review for more than six months.

For me, editing the *Journal of Finance* was the greatest challenge of my career. I learned so much from it. And I will miss it.

Fortunately, the *Journal of Finance* is in good hands with its new editor, Ken Singleton of Stanford University.

5

Journals, Editors, Referees, and Authors: Experiences at the *Journal of Economic Literature*

John Pencavel

I have been invited to write about my experiences as editor of the *Journal of Economic Literature* (*JEL*) and to reflect on what these experiences may mean for the status of journals in intellectual inquiry. I was editor of the *JEL* for thirteen years from 1986 to 1998. Before becoming editor, for four years, I served as associate editor under the editorial supervision of Moses Abramovitz. After stepping down as editor, I was a member of the board of editors of the *JEL* until 2006. Therefore, I was associated with the administration of the *Journal* for almost twenty-five years— from 1982 to 2006.

What I write here focuses on my years as editor. However, as associate editor, I learned a great deal from Moe Abramovitz, and I am indebted to him for the model he provided me of a conscientious and active journal editor. In effect, my years as an associate editor were something of an apprenticeship to an eminent and honorable scholar, and I benefitted greatly from the training and education I received from Moe.

The *JEL* Survey Articles

First and foremost, I must write that the editorship of the *JEL* was largely a labor of love. No doubt, I worked hard at the position. I took a deep personal interest in the well-being of the journal and invested much effort in it. However, this was not selfless. There were substantial private returns. Although my department at Stanford had kindly assigned me to teach a graduate microeconomic theory class, I felt that my knowledge of economics was becoming increasingly specialized. I knew more and more about a narrower scope of economics. The editorship of the *JEL* represented an opportunity to counter this professional imperative toward specialization. As editor of *JEL*, I invited articles on topics that I knew little about and that I wanted to become much better informed of. This required a prior investment in reading about these topics so I could identify the appropriate people to approach and perhaps to write these articles. My board of editors was often very helpful in proposing particular people or in guiding me away from unsuitable writers. The board consisted of economists whom I had selected and who were approved by the American Economic Association's executive. The members of the board had different specialties, and they shared with me the goal of publishing articles that informed nonspecialist economists about important research in particular fields of economics.

I would approach a potential author and declare my interest in an accessible survey paper directed to nonspecialist economists. I encouraged the likely author to sketch an outline of the paper that he or she would deliver. I asked that the paper not be organized around names and particular papers as if it were a string of abstracts pieced together, such as "X (1980) claimed this, Y (1984) argued that, and Z (1989) responded in this way." This is tedious to read, if not to write. I asked for a selective and synthetic review of a major research effort in which a necessary ingredient would be the evaluation of this research endeavor: What have been the successes and the failures in this line of research? How much confidence can be placed in the literature's findings? What do we think we know, and what do we believe we do not know? Where should future research efforts be directed? This element of evaluation ought to be of value to the specialists. Here was an opportunity to step back from the research frontier, take stock of a significant intellectual enterprise, and pass judgment on it. In this way, a successful *JEL* article would speak both to the specialist and nonspecialist economists.

Because the paper was designed for the nonspecialist, if it were appropriate, I did not hesitate to scrawl across the page of a submitted draft, "I don't follow this." For a paper in labor economics, my area of expertise, I would be more likely to scrawl, "This won't be understood by the nonspecialist." This insistence on a paper that was accessible to the nonspecialist and the many drafts that some papers went through to satisfy my requests for expository clarity did not endear me to certain authors, some of whom gave up and took their work product elsewhere. However, in most cases and for those papers that were ultimately published in the *JEL*, this concern with expository clarity enhanced the paper's readership and influence. I have always believed that exposition matters, even in the most technical of articles, and it is surely no coincidence that the discipline's unquestioned intellectual giants of the past fifty years or so have been very effective expositors.

One quality lauded in the academic community is the ability to analyze arguments and propositions in a detached and dispassionate manner. However, it is unusual for authors of a manuscript to show the necessary detachment and disinterest in their own papers. I have found that, at the stage of floating arguments and testing chains of thought in discussion, scholars are often quite disinterested and detached. But after scholars put down these arguments and claims in writing, they often become attached to their papers almost as parents are to their babies. It is as if the act of expressing these arguments and claims in the written word elevates the papers to a position calling for deference and respect. For the editor, this means that suggestions for changes in papers are best couched to authors gently, respectfully, and perhaps indirectly. The most effective way to induce changes in a submitted manuscript was to treat all papers with deep respect and high regard, even if this sometimes required me to shed my personal beliefs and prejudices and adopt a more neutral stand.

Under my editorship, some weak articles probably were published, and some very good articles probably were omitted. These are the errors that any editor makes. I think that these two types of errors do not operate on editors with equal force. Because the error of publishing an inadequate or poor article is much more visible and conspicuous than the error of failing to publish an excellent article, editors (and even referees) tend to play it safe. They are inclined to turn away potentially controversial papers, those that receive mixed reviews, and those that are out of the mainstream. This asymmetry in potential losses helps to account for the famous journal rejections of what, in retrospect, turned out to be seminal pieces of work (Gans and Shepherd 1994). I was aware of this asymmetry and tried to lean against it, but nevertheless it would be remarkable if I never turned away what would have been excellent publications.

After the *Journal of Economic Perspectives* (*JEP*) was established, I was often asked how the ideal *JEL* article differed from that of its sister journal, the *JEP*. I thought of the prototypical *JEL* article as a thorough review of a class of research and one that articulated different points of view. The author of this article was encouraged to come down on one side or the other of a controversy, but this judgment should be expressed after a fair and balanced characterization of other points of view. By contrast, I saw the prototype *JEP* article as one in which the author was encouraged to advance his or her perspective on a research venture. Balance was achieved in the *JEP* by having several articles by various authors on a given topic, not by one article describing and assessing different judgments. Indeed, several *JEP* editors expressed this same goal for their articles.

The Referees

The process of scientific inquiry is, above all, a social activity. Each of us may sit isolated for years developing an argument. But ultimately, to constitute a recognized contribution to knowledge, the argument has to meet a social test—to be evaluated and critically examined by others in the intellectual community. It is here where the journals perform an essential function of review and information dissemination.[1] The *JEL*'s role is not so much that of publishing articles containing original frontier research but that of communicating an important class of scholarship to a wider intellectual community and of providing dispassionate assessment of that scholarship. The *JEL* stands as an attempt to keep our horizons broad and, in this way, strengthen the bonds of the economics community by sharing knowledge among its members.

I owe a deep debt to the many referees that I called on for advice. A number of referees wrote remarkably thorough and discerning reports. Their anonymous contributions to many published papers were often substantial. My practice was to invite the referees into the paper-writing process early. I sent referees the outlines of proposed papers and sought their assessments of the projected article. When suitable drafts of the paper were delivered, I went back to the same referees for their assistance, which was usually provided very generously. My practice was to speak to each referee on the telephone before sending the draft to him or her. At that time, I asked for a delivery date for the report and telephoned if the report was not delivered by the referee's chosen date. In this way, referee reports were garnered in a few months, and no author ever waited more than twelve weeks for a referee-evaluated response to a submitted *JEL* paper. Most authors heard from me within two months of the submission of their papers.

This turnaround time may have been shorter than many other journals but not significantly so for a leading journal in the 1980s. However, this turnaround time seems to have become increasingly rare and editorial practices are far less conscientious today. In part this is because of the increase in volume of manuscripts that these journals now handle, but this helps explain why referees may be more tardy; it doesn't account for why editors are willing to allow their authors to hang on in ignorance of what is going on.

I myself submitted a paper to a respectable journal within the past two years. I received no word from the editorial office that the paper had arrived nor any word of the disposition of my paper. Exactly one year after submitting the paper, I wrote to the journal seeking confirmation that the paper had been received and asking what had happened to my submission. The identity of the coeditor who was handling my manuscript was revealed to me, but when I contacted him, he simply ignored my request for information. Then, after sixteen months, I received two referee reports (until that time, I did not know if my paper had been sent to referees) and an apology from the coeditor for the referees' tardiness. Of course, I had not been writing about the referees' tardiness; I was complaining about the coeditor who lacked the professional courtesy to inform me of the status of my paper.

Colleagues have described some comparable, if less extreme, cases with other journals, which leads me to conjecture that occurrences that were unusual twenty years ago are commonplace today. Why? I suspect that one important reason is that editors today are less inclined to see their professional standing tied to the success or failure of the journal they edit. Nowadays, a journal editorship is one job among many, and inefficient practices and discourteous treatment of the authors of submitted papers constitute the necessary by-product of the modern scholar who juggles many different activities. The number of journal editors and coeditors seems to have increased, although I do not know whether the ratio of the number of journal editors and coeditors to submitted papers has increased. Twenty years ago, the editorship of a major journal in economics was an honor, but today my conversations with some journal editors lead me to wonder whether the honorific quality of the job has tarnished. In many cases, an editorship appears to be viewed primarily as a burden, and under these circumstances, it seems that authors must tolerate whatever little courtesy that an editor may allot to them.

I have often said that my experience as editor convinced me that "the referee is always right." This is a remarkable claim, and many examples can be found that prove this statement false. What I mean by this somewhat extreme aphorism is that after a reputable referee has spent a considerable amount of time and effort in understanding a paper, if he asserts that the paper is arguing one thing whereas the author insists that she has written something else, then the author has failed to persuade a skeptical yet serious colleague—the referee—of the soundness of the argument. This calls for a better and more effective exposition by the author. In other words, it is not a bad rule of thumb for an editor to act as if the referee's claims are correct and to ask the author of the paper to explain the argument more carefully so that a diligent referee will not draw the wrong inference.

The *JEL*'s Bibliographic Activities

Of course, the *JEL* is known not only for its authoritative survey articles but also for its bibliographic activities such as book reviews, periodical abstracts, and the contents of major journals. Indeed, some of my most important decisions as editor involved keeping *EconLit*, the bibliographic reference source, within the ownership of a professional association, the American Economic Association, rather than selling the rights to a for-profit company such as Elsevier. Who knows what the prices of *EconLit* would be today if it were not owned and managed by the AEA but owned and managed by Elsevier?

The information contained in *EconLit* was ideal for distribution through the Internet and, indeed, this became the source of considerable revenues for the American Economic Association. Our first step was to license CD-Roms of *EconLit* by Silver Platter and these licensing agreements not only distributed a useful resource to economists but also generated substantial income for the AEA.[2] The subsequent development of on-line access to *EconLit* has provided more largesse for the Association. The revenues generated from *EconLit* have been used to keep the prices of the flagship journals relatively low and to embark on the production of both the *Journal of Economic Perspectives* and, more recently, of the AEA-sponsored field-specific journals. When I encouraged the development of *EconLit* on CD-Rom, I did not realize how fruitful for the Association it would become. Both because *EconLit* is a monopoly of information about Economics literature and it has public goods features, I always had the firm belief that it should remain the property of the not-for-profit AEA and not of a for-profit commercial venture.[3]

One aspect of the bibliographic arm of *JEL* concerned the classification by subject matter of books and articles in economics. When I became editor, the classification system was several decades old, and because I felt it was not well suited to contemporary economics, I embarked on designing a new classification system. Initially, I proposed an overarching classification that distinguished the major fields within economics, such as international economics, public economics, and economic history. Within each of these major fields, I enlisted the assistance of specialists to propose a finer classification system, and I distributed widely the various proposals that I received. Many people were involved, and I received constructive contributions. Perhaps the involvement of so many scholars explains why the new system (launched in 1992) took over so quickly and why, except for modifications here and there to accommodate the shifting boundaries and expansion of the discipline, the basic structure remains in effect today. It is used by other economics associations as the basis for their own classifications, and more often than not, the classification system introduced in 1992 finds wide international application.

The Contents of Current Periodicals

When I was editor and before the widespread use of the Internet to convey large quantities of information, the hard copy of the *JEL* contained sections titled "The Contents of Current Periodicals" and "Abstracts of Selected Articles." Nowadays, these sections appear only online and not in the hard-copy version. These sections of the *JEL* contained the titles of the major journals of economics (organized alphabetically) and listed the articles that were published in each recent issue. In the early 1990s, we listed the contents of about 330 journals, and for a subset of these journals, we also published abstracts of the published papers. My job involved, in part, the responsibility of determining those periodicals selected for listing and, from these listed periodicals, those selected for abstracting. This task of selection probably induced more outrage from certain journal editors than anything else I did as *JEL* editor. This is because each journal sought to be included in the list of major journals; a listing in the *JEL* became the mark of approval that the *Journal of Economic Nonsense* had attained the ranks of the premier periodicals in economics. In this period, the number of journals was growing, and I often received requests from editors for their journals to be listed in "The Contents of Current Periodicals." In earlier days before I became editor, *JEL* board of editors meetings were taken up with long discussions over the merits of various journals—or so I was told. I felt that I needed some mechanical procedure or dispassionate rule to determine which journals ought to have their contents listed and which ought not. The criterion I developed was a measure of the citations that a journal's articles were receiving from other journals' articles.

When I became editor, I initiated a thorough review of our procedures both for listing and for abstracting. It was clear that some journals were included in our lists simply because they had qualified for inclusion back in the 1960s when the *Journal of Economic Literature* started publication and that there had not been a serious reevaluation of their contents. In other cases, I wondered whether a journal's inclusion reflected some favor to a friend or the personal predilections of members of the *Journal of Economic Literature*'s board of editors. The reevaluation of the journals involved computing many different citation indicators to measure the impact of each and every journal.[4] This was completed by the early 1990s, and it led to changes in the *JEL*'s procedures. This work led me to address the sort of questions that were characteristic of industrial organization. Viewing each journal as if it were a firm's product and defining the industry as the set of all such firms (journals), we may ask a few questions:

Is the industry competitive?

Is the industry concentrated in a few firms?

Are there barriers to entry?

How profitable are the firms?

Has innovation affected the structure of the industry?

Competition?

The opportunities for scholars to publish and the opportunities for economists to read about research are tremendous. Not merely is every specialty and style represented in these journals, but even within specialties there are many different outlets for research. If each journal is a product type, then economics journals satisfy the first requirement of a highly competitive industry: there are many products. These products are not the same, but there are sufficiently close substitutes in the market for the industry to be described as highly competitive.

Concentration?

At the same time, along some dimensions, the market for economics articles can be said to be highly concentrated. In what sense is this true? In my analysis of various citation indices, I found that a relatively small set of journals provides most of the citations. Many journals publish articles that are barely cited at all. Indeed, many journals have issues in which none of the published articles is ever cited by articles published in other journals.

At the other end of the spectrum, using one such citation index, the top 10 percent of journals account for 88 percent of all citations, and the top nine journals account for half of all citations. In other words, a very large fraction of all citations are concentrated in a small number of journals, and it is in this respect that the market for economics journals may be said to be concentrated. In this sense, concentration is fully compatible with competition. Although most citations are to articles in a small number of journals, there is keen competition among these quality journals for articles that are potential candidates for publication in a number of them.

Barriers to Entry?
If citations are concentrated in a few high-quality journals, has the composition of the quality journals changed over time? I do not know the answer to this because the citation analysis that I undertook was restricted to the 1980s. However, let me offer a conjecture: there has been a certain asymmetry such that it has been easier for journals to enter the class of high-quality journals than for journals to fall out of that class. Most would classify *Econometrica* and the *Journal of Political Economy* as top tier journals today and, indeed, they would have been so judged fifty years ago also. However, other journals that would be judged today as quality journals were not in operation fifty years ago including the *Journal of Economic Perspectives* and *the Journal of Economic Literature*. As the profession has grown in size so more quality journals can be supported. Hence, while it might be argued that no journal classified as a quality journal fifty years ago has fallen from that status, other journals have joined that exclusive club.

Of course, some journals are recognized as being important producers of information within particular specialties. Indeed, there are obviously few barriers to the mere publication of journals—I wish there were more!—and it has not been difficult for some journals to establish a very high reputation within specialties. This has surely been the big change over fifty years: the growth in the number of specialty journals which testifies to Adam Smith's maxim that specialization increases with the size of the market.

With respect to the top-quality, general-interest journals, it is noteworthy that none of those that would be classified as top quality fifty years ago has dropped out of that class. This development might be portrayed as the extension of the aristocracy. The class system of journals is characterized by downward immobility out of the aristocracy but upward mobility into the aristocracy!

Advantages of Incumbency?

This downward immobility out of the aristocracy suggests to me that there are genuine advantages attached to incumbency. It might be true that reckless editors who hold views that are unrepresentative of the profession and that they impose on the articles they publish have the power to ruin the aristocratic status of a quality journal. In general, however, after an aristocratic journal has attained that state, it appears to require the editor to behave simply as an arbitrator between authors of submitted papers and referees so that the quality of the journal is preserved.

I hasten to add that a good editor does act as more than a plain arbitrator. However, the fact that mere arbitration is sufficient to preserve the status of an aristocratic journal indicates there are considerable advantages to incumbency. When the journal has attained that aristocratic status, it is largely sheltered from challenges that will cause its demotion. The journal's status earned over many years of publication is something that cannot be captured by a new entrant. Such advantages constitute a rent.

What are the forms of these rents, and who enjoys them? The rents may consist in part of monetary returns (salaries to the editors and staff, payments to referees or authors). The fact that profit-seeking publishing companies seem eager to introduce new journals suggests that they see monetary returns in the activity. But at least among the high-quality journals, the rents are not entirely monetary. Some of these rents are nonmonetary, particularly the satisfaction of being involved in the distribution of information that is highly regarded by peers within your profession.

Innovation?

Finally, let us note how, in many activities over the past century or so, a radical innovation (either in production technologies or in types of products manufactured and sold) has converted a competitive industry into a monopoly. So production methods and the type of products produced have changed immeasurably in the last hundred years. What is remarkable is that this is not true of Economics journals. Yes, the process of going from accepted manuscript to published copy has been transformed in the past fifteen years or so by the use of computerized technology.

However, the editorial process is largely the same as that operating a century ago: manuscripts are submitted, reviewed by the editor and his referees, and, if deemed suitable, an iterative process converges on a publishable article that is printed in hard copy form. If there has been innovation, it has taken the form of the type of articles that Economics journals are publishing today: the range of subjects that the editors of the quality journals are willing to consider seriously for publication is considerably wider than it was fifty years ago. But this merely reflects the changes that have taken place within the profession and the journals cannot be said to have lead the profession in this.[5]

It is often forecast that in the future, there will be drastic changes in the manner in which information is conveyed to scholars. Some predict that the current printed and bound journals will be not be supplemented but replaced entirely by information that can be retrieved electronically and printed at the wish of the reader. The journal system as we have known it for over a hundred years will cease. It would be foolhardy to deny that possibility, but at the same time I am not confident of this outcome. Although these other methods of information retrieval may well partially replace the hard copy, I also see enduring advantages for the conventional form of journal so that the industry we are observing will retain its current features for many years.

Appendix

This appendix documents the statement in the text about the pattern of citations. Inferences from the citation indices about the impact of journals differ from index to index, but for the points that I want to make, these differences are for the most part of second order of importance. I prefer to concentrate here on one such index and discuss it rather than cloud the discussion with several such indices. The work described here was undertaken in the early 1990s.

The citation index I present here was constructed as follows. I arbitrarily selected eleven principal economics journals. I label these the gold-medal journals. Although the choice is somewhat arbitrary, I think there would be wide agreement among economists about the inclusion of most of these journals in the set of gold-medal journals.[6] For each and every journal—not just the gold-medal journals but all journals whose contents were listed in the *Journal of Economic Literature*—we counted the number of times that articles published in the gold-medal journals in 1988 cited articles published in each other journal over the previous four years.

Consider the *Journal of Industrial Economics* as an example. We counted the number of times that articles published in the gold-medal journals in 1988 cited articles published in the *Journal of Industrial Economics* in the years from 1984 to 1987. The answer is twenty-six.

We then expressed this number as a percentage of the number of articles published annually by the journal under consideration. Thus, if the *Journal of Industrial Economics* published thirty articles per year, the citation index would be 87 (that is, 100(26/30)). This is a measure of the impact of the *Journal of Industrial Economics* per article that it publishes.

We constructed the values of this index for each of the 320 journals that were established before 1987 and whose contents were listed in the *Journal of Economic Literature*. The mean value of this index was 12.15 with a standard deviation of 43.16. Its minimum value was zero, and 74 percent of the 320 journals had a value of zero. Its maximum value was 402 (*Econometrica*).

What is remarkable is the degree of inequality in citations. A common graphical representation of this is the Lorenz curve. Suppose that we order the journals from lowest in the rankings of citations to highest and then plot the cumulative percentage of journals on the horizontal axis (ranging from zero to 100 percent) and the cumulative percentage of citations on the vertical axis. If each journal had the same number of citations, the Lorenz curve would simply be the diagonal line running from the bottom left-hand corner to the upper right-hand corner. This would be the representation corresponding to complete equality. But if the bottom-ranked journals receive fewer citations while the top-ranked journals receive a disproportionate share of citations, then the Lorenz curve will lie below the diagonal. Such is the case, in fact, and its departure from complete equality is marked. Some points along the curve might be instructive.

Denote by y the cumulative percentage share of citations (the vertical axis of the graph) and by x the percentage share of the population of journals (the horizontal axis). Then some points on the Lorenz curve are as shown in table 5.1.

In other words, 74 percent of the journals contributed zero percent of all the citations, 80 percent of the journals contributed 1.5 percent of all the citations, and 99 percent of the journals contributed almost 73

Table 5.1

x	74	75	80	85	90	95	99	100
y	0	0.2	1.5	4.8	12.7	29.8	72.9	100

percent of the citations. Expressed differently, 26 percent (100 minus 74) of the journals contributed 100 percent of the citations, 10 percent of the journals contributed 87.3 percent of the citations, 1 percent of the journals contributed 27.1 percent of the citations. This gives the impression of substantial inequality among the journals in citations.[7] If a Lorenz curve with the appearance of that graphed applied to the distribution of incomes in a society (the use to which the Lorenz curve is often put), then that society would be regarded as deeply inegalitarian.

However, to illustrate Disraeli's maxim, suppose these same data are used to construct another measure of concentration—namely, the Herfindahl index. Let s_j be journal j's citations expressed as a fraction of all the journals' citations. The Herfindahl index, H, is defined as $\Sigma_i(s_i)^2$. Clearly, H ranges from zero to unity. The minimum value of H is $1/n$, where n is the number of journals—here, 320. The maximum value of H is unity when one journal accounts for all the publications, a monopoly of citations. Larger values of H indicate greater concentration of citations among fewer journals. George J. Stigler (1966) reported values of H of 0.331 for the auto industry in 1964, 0.221 for the cigarette industry in 1963, 0.253 for the soap industry in 1958, and 0.019 for the fire and casualty insurance companies in 1963. For this sample of 320 journals, I calculate the Herfindahl index to be 0.044. I am assured that a value of the Herfindahl index of 0.044 would not prompt litigation by the Antitrust Division of the U.S. Justice Department. However, note that Stigler's indices relate to the production of U.S. firms only. The Herfindahl index that I computed for economics citations embraces the production of citations internationally. This issue of inequality in the impact of economics journals merits further analysis.

Notes

1. Publication in the major journals does not mean that the scholar's argument is valid. It means that the article has survived the reviewers' skeptical examination and deserves to be the subject of critical assessment by a wider audience.

2. The *JEL* was the first major economics journal that subscribers could choose to receive as a CD-ROM rather than in printed, hard-copy form. I started this CD-ROM version of the *Journal* in March 1995.

3. The day-to-day administration of *EconLit* was overseen in the Pittsburgh office of the *JEL* by Drucilla Ekwurzel, who does a splendid job sustaining and nurturing *EconLit*.

4. I relegate to an appendix the technical aspects of one such index.

5. Perhaps a qualification is in order here with regard to the *Journal of Political Economy*. It has been willing to publish articles on unconventional research topics although these articles have used highly conventional research methods.

6. These eleven journals were as follows: *American Economic Review, Econometrica, Economica, Economic Journal, International Economic Review, Journal of Economic Literature, Journal of Economic Theory, Journal of Political Economy, Quarterly Journal of Economics, Review of Economics and Statistics,* and *Review of Economic Studies.*

7. Eugene Garfield of the Institute for Scientific Information has shown me comparable degrees of inequality in other disciplines. Such inequality in economics is also suggested by Arthur M. Diamond's 1989 analysis.

References

Diamond, Arthur M. 1989. The Core Journals of Economics. *Journal of Citation Studies* 50 (1):2–9.

Gans, Joshua S., and George B. Shepherd. 1994. How Are the Mighty Fallen: Rejected Classic Articles by Leading Economists. *Journal of Economic Perspectives* 8 (1):165–179.

Stigler, George J. 1966. The Economic Effects of the Antitrust Laws. *Journal of Law & Economics* 9:225–258.

6

Memoirs of an Editor

Fabrizio Zilibotti

I was a managing editor of the *Review of Economic Studies* (*ReStud*) from 2002 to 2006. Since 2009, I have been the chief editor of the *Journal of European Economic Association* (*JEEA*). Both the *ReStud* and *JEEA* are nonprofit journals, and they are owned, respectively, by an independent society and by the European Economic Association. In this chapter, I describe some salient aspects of my editorial experiences.

The Review of Economic Studies

The invitation to become an editor at the *Review of Economic Studies* came largely as a surprise. I had no record of previous editorial experience, had been invited to join the board of associate editors of the *ReStud* only one year earlier, and therefore was not especially familiar with the procedures of the journal. At the time, the *ReStud* was generally perceived as a journal that specialized in economic and econometric theory. I am a macroeconomist with an applied focus on growth and political economy, and there had been no editor with a profile similar to mine in the recent history of the journal. Finally, the journal had a strong British identity, with all previous managing editors being based in UK institutions. When I was approached, I was a professor at the Institute of International Economic Studies of Stockholm, although I was considering an offer from University College London that I eventually accepted.

As I soon learned, the appointment of young editors was not unusual at the *ReStud*. The journal has a long-standing tradition of assigning editorial and governance responsibility to young scholars. The stated reason is to preserve its independence from the more established senior core of the profession. The roots of this tradition lie in the history of the journal, which was founded in 1933 by a group of young British and American economists as a sort of antimainstream voice.

I joined the editorial team at a turning point of the journal's identity. Its progressive detachment from a strong British base became clear after my appointment, first with the appointment of Bernard Salanie and Juuso Välimäki (who were not based in Britain), and then with the decision to eliminate the British quota in the editorial board, paving the way for a pan-European governance of the journal. The choice of applied researchers as editors was an indication that the journal was moving in the direction of a general audience.

ReStud is a very independent journal. It is governed by its editorial team, board of directors, and board of associate editors. The board of directors is an executive body consisting of former editors or relatively senior researchers. The board of associate editors is responsible for the strategic choices of the journals, including the appointment of new managing and associate editors. In other words, the current owners of the journal appoint the future ones by a secret ballot vote. Associate editors play a dual role of governance and support of editorial activities. Those who underperform in refereeing tasks come to public attention in board meetings and may not be reelected. Given its minimal governance and the young age of its members, the *ReStud* management runs remarkably smoothly. If some may criticize it on the ground of a certain clubbish culture, yet the journal owes its success mostly to the devotion and intrinsic motivation of its associates.

The main premonitory sign of my appointment as managing editor was my receipt of an anomalous number of requests to referee papers. I initially had some mixed feelings about accepting the invitation. Seven years after receiving my Ph.D., my priority was to push my research agenda rather than to become an expert in deciding the fate of other people's research. When Hyun Song Shin called me, I was both puzzled and flattered. I did not have a clear idea of what an editorial job would imply or of how much time this would require. Hyun did not make my choice simpler by stating candidly that, in terms of commitment, "it is about like to have another child," especially since I had experienced fatherhood a few years earlier in 1999. Hyun's forecast proved to be an overstatement, but I appreciated his effort not to understate the size of the commitment. New editors who accept the task without much concern about its burden are strong candidates for failure. Following Hyun's recommendation, I contacted Orazio Attanasio, whom I was supposed to succeed to as managing editor. Orazio said that being an editor was not as bad as one might fear and that, in any case, this was the classical proposition that one cannot refuse. Not everyone that I consulted advised me to accept. A senior colleague was skeptical that I would benefit from taking up such a large task at an early stage of my career. My wife (also an academic economist) strongly recommended against accepting a commitment that promised to be as onerous as having a second child. Eventually, a mixture of ambition, curiosity, and sense of duty prevailed. So when I moved from Stockholm to London in July 2002, I was a managing editor *in pectore*. The appointment would start in the following September.

At the time, I did not know yet that within a few weeks I would also become the manager of the editorial office. It was not an easy additional task, partly due to the very diverse personalities of the two office employees. Jane Martin, who sadly passed away in 2009, was the chief administrator and production editor. She was a great person, wholeheartedly dedicated to the journal, and everybody who has worked with her remembers her with great affection. The second employee, the information technology administrator, was in charge of managing the database and sending reminders to referees. He liked to work remotely, mostly at night, and the vigorous style of his reminders to unresponsive referees was notorious, raising frequent PR crises with the more sensitive referees. In spite of everybody's good will, the primitive nature of the database of the time and the fact that papers were handled essentially manually caused submission to fall occasionally into "black holes", our jargon for situations in which papers failed to be assigned and to have a recognizable destination. I remember a horror story during the early stage of my tenure, where I found out that a paper written by renowned senior authors, of good quality, but too narrow to be suitable for a general audience journal such as the *ReStud*, had been left unattended for almost a full year. It did not fall into any editor's area of knowledge, and finding competent referees who were prepared to review it swiftly proved difficult. Eventually, I rejected the paper on the basis of fairly mediocre reports. For once, the (civilized) complaints of the authors attracted my genuine sympathy.

When I joined the editorial team, the business was being run collegially. Since all editors lived in the London-Oxford area, we could meet physically every fortnight. I benefited greatly from the advice of the senior editors at the time, Mark Armstrong, Orazio Attanasio, and James Dow.

My experience at the *ReStud* was not free of turbulence. Troubles surfaced periodically about the manual management of the database, the editorial office, and editorial process. The overall management became more problematic as the editorial team got scattered around the world, raising unavoidable coordination problems. I remember the difficult transition to a new online software system (Editorial Express), in the middle of a temporary collapse of the editorial office. In the end, everything worked out well, but at the time, I sensed the fear of an unrecoverable breakdown.

Concerns eased up as time went by. In 2006, when I passed the baton to Kjetil Storesletten, I was relieved that no major disaster had occurred. To the opposite, the journal was sailing along quite well. Seven years after my departure, the journal is as buoyant as ever and enjoys a growing impact and booming submissions. In September 2006, I felt happy to have concluded my experience of managing editor, and looked forward to the time when I would finally focus on my own research (well, except for the final group of papers that I would continue to handle throughout 2007, when my duties would definitely be over). I promised my family that a long time would elapse before I would consider accepting another editorial experience. After declining two offers, however, in the summer 2008, I accepted the offer to become the chief editor of the *Journal of the European Economic Association*. On January 1, 2009, I was again an editor.

The Journal of the European Economic Association

The *Journal of the European Economic Association* (*JEEA*) is a young journal that was established in 2003 after a tumultuous divorce between the European Economic Association (EEA) and Elsevier, the publisher that owned (and owns) the *European Economic Review*, which at the time was the journal of the association. The conflict stemmed from the pricing policy practiced by Elsevier, which the association judged to be exploitative of both the libraries paying very high subscription fees and the unrewarded work of referees. Since then, the *JEEA*, originally published by MIT Press and now by Wiley-Blackwell, has been a core constituent of the mission of the EEA. The journal was placed initially in the hands of an experienced editorial team which was led by Xavier Vives and which included, in addition, Patrick Bolton, Jordi Gali, Alan Krueger, and Roberto Perotti. Orazio Attanasio joined the team few years later. Establishing new journals is a difficult endeavor, and the funding team did a terrific job. In 2013, the journal celebrated its tenth anniversary with pride and a sense of a mission by and large accomplished.

Once again, I took over as chief editor of the *Journal of the European Economic Association* in a time of transition. Two coeditors, Marios Angeletos and Fabio Canova, had been appointed shortly before me. Six months after I started, Orazio Attanasio stepped down and was replaced by Stefano Della Vigna. In September 2011, Dirk Bergemann also joined the team.

The structure of the *JEEA* is different from that of the *ReStud*: the *JEEA* chief editor fulfills a more direct governance role. The editors are responsible to the board and executive committee of the EEA rather than to the board of associate editors of the journal. By its constitutional rules, the direction of the EEA is volatile because a new president is elected every year. Contrary to the *ReStud*, which is an established top-five journal, the *JEEA* has to fight to attract good papers, in competition with the best field journals. The coeditors and I made a major investment in increasing the efficiency of the editorial process, which I discuss in detail below. The submission flow, which had been stationary since the inception of JEEA, increased by 75 percent between 2009 and 2012. Another important reform was the suppression of the *Journal of European Economic Association: Papers and Proceedings* special issue, which collected the main lectures delivered at the annual congress of the EEA and some short papers written out of the invited sessions of the congress. Such short papers, which accounted for over 50 percent of the total articles published by the *JEEA*, were on average of lower quality and of less impact than regular submissions. Without them, the *JEEA* is a more ambitious journal.

The average paper received by the *JEEA* is less technical than those I used to handle at the *ReStud*. There is a stronger correlation between the editors' research identity and the field in which the journal receives its submissions. In practice, this means that editors tend to receive more papers close to their area of interest. In a sense, editorship is more active: we solicit contributions and shape the development path of the journal. All of this makes the editorial activity somehow more fun.

Editorial Responsibility

The golden rule for good editorship is "Never accumulate large delays and backlogs." Once this happens, it is difficult to catch up: As the number of pending papers increases, the editor procrastinates and eventually feels overwhelmed. Another lesson is that an editor must take responsibility. When a decision is uncertain, it is better to break the tie soon (most likely, in a negative direction) than wait. Talking to another editor about difficult cases can help tremendously. Rejecting papers makes one unpopular, but straight rejections account for 95 percent of the decisions. One must resist the temptation to keep alive papers (for example, by inviting speculative resubmissions) if they hold only a dubious promise of eventual acceptance. Rejecting a paper in the second or third round is trickier than declining a first submission because authors often work hard on solicited revisions to please editors and referees. An acknowledgment such as "Thanks to the precious help of the editor and of the referees, the paper has improved immensely" may be in part a formality, but often it reflects the genuine conviction of the authors that, after months of hard work, the paper is a winner. At the first round, the editor can get away with a cheap "Sorry, I am not convinced" or "It is a good paper but not top journal material." In the second round, such a criticism becomes unacceptable to authors. The editor already knows what the paper tries to achieve and has asked the authors to work in some particular direction. Thus, a rejection must be motivated on the ground that the authors have failed to address comments or that they could not deliver the paper that the editor had hoped to publish. This is a slippery terrain and is fertile ground for dispute, frustration, and grievance.

I remember an episode involving me as a coauthor rather than as the editor. Our paper was rejected, but the editor left the door ajar for a new submission if my coauthors and I could address some of the referees' major comments. The editor wrote that this might be beyond feasibility but that we could try to deal with the task. Although the paper had been formally rejected, the editor's indication was specific, and we remained hopeful. The revision took us about one year of hard work. When we submitted the new paper, the editor probably forgot the history of the submission, and sent it to new referees who were completely unimpressed by our effort to address the points raised by different referees in the previous round. They ended up recommending rejection for totally different reasons. The editorial decision caused us great frustration. How do I see this episode, after having been an editor? The editor was actually perfectly entitled to seek advice from new referees (perhaps his hesitation in the first round originated from not being convinced by the original reports). His mistake was not to announce the procedure that he would follow in the case of a new submission. Had we known, we would have followed a different, more appropriate strategy. Moreover, we wouldn't have felt so surprised and frustrated after a negative decision.

With the memory of this episode, I try to follow a systematic approach. When I solicit a revision, I outline a clear path for a successful resubmission: "I can accept the paper if you do this or that." In the rare cases in which I formally reject a paper but allow the authors to submit a "new" paper based on the original submission, I keep my promises vague. I provide some broad indications, but I am clear that the paper will undergo a fresh evaluation that may include new referees and new criteria. The reason for such a fresh submission to be eventually rejected can be "anything".

All in all, revise-and-resubmit papers and reject-and-resubmit papers make up less than ten percent of the decisions on new submissions. The most common outcome is a straight rejection. I follow a policy of not reconsidering negative decisions unless they turn out to be based on factual mistakes (an event that rarely occurs). Currently, I make a significant number of negative decisions without consulting any referee (desk rejections). In an earlier stage of my editorial career, I was shier about using this procedure, fearing that I might offend some authors. Back then, I would desk-reject only unprofessionally written papers. Today, I desk reject one third of the first submissions. As I try to explain to authors, these include many serious papers, including interesting ones that are, in my view, better suited for field journals. These might be competent extensions, narrow or very technical contributions, articles providing limiting value added on a well-exploited topic, or studies analyzing questions that I simply do not find sufficiently exciting for the journal. There may be an element of subjectivity in such evaluations. When authors say this, I reply they may be right and that there are other journals that might be able to fix idiosyncratic editorial decisions. I am confident, however, that most such papers would not pass the referees' filter. Even if they partially did, positive reports would not change my prior opinion. So why should I ask referees to work and authors to wait? Authors of desk-rejected papers rarely complain. One of the rare objections is "How can the editor decide on a topic that he is not familiar with without hearing expert referees?" The answer is simple: even if I have only a limited familiarity with what is going on in a certain area of research, I am confident that the question the paper addresses is not sufficiently interesting. Another objection I have heard is that "I hoped that I would get detailed comments from expert referees instead of a useless one-paragraph letter." This argument stems from the confused idea that referees provide their services to authors. In fact, they provide services to the journal and should not be asked to waste their valuable time on unpromising submissions. I always recommend my (best) Ph.D. students who are entrusted to write a report for a journal not to spend much time on weak papers. A clear (yet motivated) negative signal is useful to editors. To put it differently, referees are not Ph.D. advisers. They are expert scholars who help the editor decide whether a paper is suitable for publication. If the editor already knows the answer, then the referees are not useful. Even so, too many desk rejections may harm a good decision process by possibly discriminating against less established authors. For this reason, I do not expect my rate of desk rejection to increase in the future.

Disappointed Authors

The list of people that an editor annoys during her or his tenure is long and includes senior people with a high visibility in the profession and serious researchers that the editor holds in high esteem. My experience suggests that civilized norms prevail in the profession. Many people have probably expressed their dislike of my decisions in private, but only a tiny minority of them has taken the pain of writing back in aggressive terms. Who are the authors who take the uncivil path? In my experience, there is only one clear pattern: they usually belong to fields that are far from my own research interests. The typical case is a paper of which I am in charge because the "natural coeditor" (i.e., the coeditor who would normally be treating papers in the respective domain), has a conflict of interest due to personal or institutional connections with one of the authors. Although I might know little about fractional cointegration (an example with no reference to any real event), I may happen to handle papers in that area. The author may well be an authority in the field and believe that he or she is submitting a major contribution. Rejections hurt, and many people are naturally predisposed to blame them on a poor editorial process rather than on intrinsic weaknesses of the research. This can be even more likely to happen when the rejection letter is signed by an editor who is not a bona fide celebrity in the field. Another relevant factor in these kinds of situations is that the repeated-game nature of the editor-author interaction tends to discourage emotional reactions. Because an author's relationship with an out-of-field editor is often perceived as of the one-shot game type of situation, the outraged author sees little cost in annoying the editor. Finally, some authors adhere quickly to colorful conspiracy theories. They might tell their friends, "Surely the fact that my paper has been assigned to an incompetent editor reflects a conscious policy choice of the journal, which is turning against our field." Often, the truth is that the editor that they would have liked has declined to handle their paper. The reason may be that the expert editor knew well both the authors and the paper, disliked the latter, and preferred not to be involved in a reject decision.

Some important misunderstandings drive this behavior. First, editors understand their limitations when they do not have technical competence in a specific area, but good journals have access to a large pool of expertise in these cases (for example, via associate editors). I may not be an expert of time-series econometrics, but I know many experts, and when necessary, I can cry for help. Most of the times in which I have approached a Nobel Prize winner or a field leader with a request such as "This paper is not in my garden, and I want to ensure the author a competent and fair editorial process," I have received support. Therefore, the angry authors are often dealing, without realizing, with a field leader who is sitting in the shadows. When they yell at the rejection letter written by an "incompetent editor" based on the opinion of "ignorant referees," they may be addressing their anger at somebody much more famous than they may think. Short reports with sharp messages are especially dangerous targets of outbursts because they often are the sign of very senior referees. Needless to say, the spicy correspondence sometimes flows back and forth with the expert in the shadows, exposing the intemperance of the complainer. Everything is also shared with the rest of the editorial teams because transparency is the best tool to ensure that hot feelings do not affect the editor's impartiality. It is rare that an angry reply catalyzes approval or high esteem. Uncivil behavior does not pay, but it is also infrequent. In four years at the *ReStud*, I can remember no more than four or five cases of authors who lost their self-control and good manners. At the *JEEA*, it has happened only once so far (for once, it was an author I knew well . . .). Snappy feedbacks signaling dissatisfaction against this or that referee are a little more frequent but also easier to forgive and forget.

Some authors follow a subtler strategy by trying to initiate a discussion about the content of each report. Sometimes they argue that referees have made excellent points but are wrong in thinking that their comments cannot be addressed in a revision. In these cases, I tend to say "Great. I am happy to hear that the reviews were useful. I am confident that they will help you write a better paper to submit to another journal. For that, I wish you all the best."

Referees

Appointing good referees is a crucial task. The prerequisite of a good choice is a broad knowledge of the contributors to the different streams of literature that an editor is supposed to cover—which typically exceeds her or his core research area. For this reason, a good editor is a well-rounded economist rather than a narrow specialist (a rule that is unfortunately often forgotten by associations and publishers appointing editors, resulting in general audience journals turning periodically mono-thematic . . .). It is not sufficient to know the names of field leaders. Senior people can be called to help occasionally, but most referee reports are provided by relatively young scholars. In this perspective, my experiences as a serial recruitment officer, first at Universitat Pompeu Fabra and then in Stockholm, has helped me tremendously. The exposure to the junior international job market (especially its higher end) gives an editor the opportunity to know what young people in the best graduate schools are doing with their research.

Over time, editors learn about the personality and taste of different referees. Some people (including excellent referees who write great reports) are hypercritical, and would never recommend any paper for publication. Their recommendations range between flat and borderline negative recommendations. The editor must carefully read all nuances in these reports and letters, not just the summary assessment. There are as well "soft" referees who view all papers as interesting and worthy of publication. This set of people includes careless reviewers and researchers who are genuinely positively inclined toward other people. There is an asymmetry between a quick negative report and a quick positive one. The former conveys the impression that, according to the referee, the paper was not worth writing a careful report. So there is signal in such a response. An enthusiastic but sloppy positive report, however, is practically useless. It delivers a contradictory message: the referee claims to like the paper, recommends it for publication almost as it is, but did not feel that it was worth spending a few hours in building a convincing case. How carefully did she or he read it? Such reports are typically dismissed as uninformative.

There is also an age effect. Not surprisingly, young researchers tend to be more critical, and more mature researchers are more supportive. The positive letter of a young person typically reads like this: "This is an interesting paper dealing with an interesting question and proposing, potentially, a novel answer. However, the paper is far from being publishable in your journal. I would either reject the paper or offer an opportunity of revision, making clear that it is unlikely that this will be successful." Guessing referee personalities from general traits is less easy than one might expect. Some people who are hypercritical in seminars and have a mixed reputation in terms of social skills are very constructive referees, and some friendly, soft-spoken researchers turn cruel when acting as anonymous referees.

Some people write mediocre or idiosyncratic reports. Although the correlation is far from perfect, it goes in the expected direction: good researchers are on average better referees. For this reason, doing a good job as a referee is a valuable investment for building a good professional reputation. An invitation to join a good editorial board is a tangible measure of success. Such a reputation does not necessarily help to get papers accepted with a particular journal but is important when it comes to tenure letters, letters of reference, and grants. Thus, I am puzzled when I see some young researchers (including former graduate students in institutions where I have been) who systematically decline requests to referee papers. This kind of behavior leads to a bad reputation. Moving up in age, some respected researchers in my own age group have sent me a number of submissions over my editorial tenure but have never sent me a single referee report. They respond to my requests to referee a paper with these kinds of comments: "I am sorry, Fabrizio, but as you can well understand my multiple commitments do not leave me time to write reports in this period. As you know, I direct a very large research group, and I have an intense teaching schedule. But you can contact one of my Ph.D. students. And by the way, do you have any news about the paper I submitted almost two months ago? I know you do a terrific job, but I often wonder why the editorial process in economics is so painfully slow." These messages are supposed to impress me making me feel ashamed of disturbing such a busy and prominent person. Instead, they intrigue me, especially when the list of competing commitments that the author invokes consists of the standard tasks of every researcher. Another common noncooperative attitude is to accept a request to referee a paper but then shift the proposed deadline ahead by three or more months: "I am sorry, but I cannot do this before I complete my teaching duties." This attitude is especially annoying when it comes from people who have agreed to act as an associate editor of the journal. Declining an offer to join the board entails no stigma, and I am fully sympathetic with people who do not want to take such a commitment. It is different when a researcher sends an enthusiastic letter of acceptance ("I am very honored . . .") and then, few weeks later, declines the first referee request, blaming it on teaching obligations or too many competing refereeing commitments. These people seem to confuse an invitation to join an editorial board with an award or a medal to mention in their curriculum vitae. Once again, this is not a representative behavior but applies to a few deviant types. Most associate editors at the *ReStud* and the *JEEA* perform a terrific service to those journals.

A critical choice for an editor is the referees' fields. Editors should not restrict their attention to researchers in the narrow area of the submission. I usually involve at least one referee who is a generalist. Such a referee plays an important role and should be especially trustworthy because she or he is expected to give me the representative reaction of a mature general reader. There are other reasons not to restrict oneself to the inner circle of experts. Deep expertise is often associated with vested interests that are for or against a certain paper, author, or methodology. Some referees are enthusiastic about anything that is written in their field, especially if it cites extensively their work. Others are hypercritical, either because they can figure out any possible dinky objection or, worse, because they are dogmatic and take the conventional way of doing things as the only acceptable one. Some people, in addition, play repeated games. In some fields, especially narrow ones, scratching each other's back is much too common. People in these fields typically support any papers that follow the methodology that they like and behave in a sectarian fashion against the rest of the profession. Sometimes authors want to have exclusive rights to some niches, and they block any entrant. This attitude is funny to me because leadership in a small pond is no sign of great success. I take it as a sign of insecurity. There are a number of renowned authors whom I never ask to write a report for this reason.

Then there are cross-field disputes. In some fields, I had to avoid some researchers who potentially could have given me helpful suggestions. Instead, they would make comments such as "This paper proposes a calibration exercise, but calibration is not a useful methodology for making progress in understanding labor markets." Ideology is a broad issue that influences editors' choices, too. Editor are entitled to give some direction to the journal that they lead, but the first question I ask myself when I consider a paper and read the referees' reactions is, "Does this paper make progress when judged by the standards of its own literature?" In my view, ideological editors are never good editors. Many people in the profession disagree with this eclectic approach and think, instead, that good editors must hold strong views, especially as long as they share their specific ideology.

Authors often complain about referees' alleged errors and say things such as, "I would like you to reconsider the decision because it is based on the misunderstanding of a referee." Sometimes authors accept part of the blame in a dubiously sincere exercise of modesty: "The referee's mistake is entirely our fault because we did not spell out the argument and its intuition sufficiently clearly. We will do a better job and convince the referee if you allow us to submit a revision." I have then to remind the authors that all of this is great, but they should not overlook the fact that I decided to reject the paper, so the revision must be sent to another journal.

It is relatively rare that a rejection hinges on a technical mistake. When it does happen, the editor should feel accountable: if the editor's objection is proven wrong, then the author is entitled to ask that the paper be reconsidered. However, the more common reason for a negative decision is an evaluation of the overall contribution. A casual remark in the editorial letter, such as "In addition, referee R1 has some quibbles about a specific technical issue," does not mean that the issue was pivotal to the decision. I often intercept dubious or clearly wrong remarks from referees. If they have no bearing on the final decision, it may be costly, for an editor, to expose loyal referees who have generously spent time helping the journal. Usually, if the case for a rejection is straightforward, I make no comment. Sometimes, I insert a brief comment in the editorial letter to help the author understand what the referee meant. When a paper is not rejected, the editor must identify the comments that need to be addressed, and this may require some diplomacy. It is useful to note, nevertheless, that a confused remark from an expert referee (or from the editor himself) often indicates that the paper was unclear in the first place.

A good presentation and a clear message are important. People often criticize the excessive role of marketing in the publication process. Well-polished but dull papers should not be published by the best journals, as they sometimes are, but authors should never submit arcane papers that are written in bad English, poorly reasoned or scantly motivated. Equations and regressions alone do not make a paper. Economics is a social science, and a key task of a study is to show that its findings are interesting for economists. Because editors and referees are overloaded by demands on their time, they might overlook papers with an unfocused introduction or weak and confused motivation. Here the role of graduate schools is important. In Europe, for instance, far too many schools offer Ph.D. programs that do not teach students even the basic rules for writing papers.

Young authors are not the only problem. I once heard a senior author say that he does not put much effort into refining his first submission because the writing can be revised after the editor and referees have signaled their interest. I would not recommend this strategy. Seldom (possibly, too seldom) does the editorial process spot diamonds in the rough. Good presentation and sharp reasoning are important for a successful publication strategy and even more so for its subsequent impact.

Is the Editorial Process Biased?

There are reasons to believe that the peer-review process is biased in favor of established authors. The first is statistical discrimination. Because established authors have proved that they are capable of writing good papers, it therefore is more likely that they submit interesting papers. This can make both editors and referees better predisposed when they review the work of these authors. Although individual authors may feel that this is unfair, statistical discrimination may be in the best interests of the journal. The obsession of publishers and associations with objective impact factors reinforces such a bias. I recently made a list of the three *JEEA*-published papers that were most cited by Google Scholar each year. The period covered was from the *JEEA*'s start in 2003 to 2012. All except two have at least a well-established coauthor. If statistical discrimination is regarded as unethical, then journals could take measures to offset it. These might include quotas in favor of young authors and special awards for the best paper published by authors within three years after receiving their Ph.D. I am not aware of any discussion in this direction, probably because it may not be in the interest of any single journal to deviate from the equilibrium.

The second issue is that experienced authors do on average a better job at packaging their work. Although a good presentation is an important part of a good paper, some may feel that journals should devote more attention to the core contribution.

The third (in my view, very relevant) issue is that established authors have better access to high-quality seminars and other networks to disseminate their work. Good referees attend those seminars and are impressed by a successful presentation, especially if it takes place in front of a highly reputed audience.

The fourth potential source of bias is explicitly corrupt behavior, such as editors and referees who misrepresent their views to favor established colleagues. They generally are driven by *do ut des* (I scratch your back, and you scratch mine) considerations. Even though they know that it is taboo, referees may deliberately reveal their identity or let the author know about their role through subtle strategic comments in their review. Editors themselves may seek the favor of people who can affect positively their career. I am in no good position to dismiss such a malignant theory. The optimist view would say that such opportunistic behavior may eventually backfire. Some editors build a solid reputation for their integrity, and others do not. I have received some nice words from senior authors whose paper I had rejected, along the lines of "I was, of course, disappointed by the outcome, but I want to thank you and the referees for handling the submission professionally." Well, this kind of response was nice and unexpected.

To reduce the pro-establishment bias, some journals have implemented a double-blind referee process. In the Google era, this is a hopeless route.

Although young and less established authors must fight against the indifference and disregard of editors and referees, fame has its drawbacks as well. Renowned authors are more likely to suffer from an unfair peer-review process due to intellectual disputes and personal feuds. To mitigate the risk of biased reviews, some colleagues argue that authors should be allowed to rule out referees they dislike. This is already possible in some journals, like the *American Political Science Review*. I have seen instances of reviews that were influenced by negative prejudice, but I am skeptical about the proposed remedy. First, some fields are already so narrow that restricting further the range of referees risks limiting the set of potential referees to the author's friends. Second, some conflicts of interest are informative. Sometimes, biased referees have a competing paper. Although conflicts of interest should be revealed to the editor, it is not obvious to me that silencing such information would be good for the process. Sometimes, two papers written simultaneously are so close to each other that an informed editor may decide to ask the authors to merge efforts into a single paper. Third, a potential reviewer may be ruled out only for having raised legitimate objections in some seminars or conferences. Finally, established authors may be better placed to know which referees would dislike an article.

Another concern is whether the process is biased in a conformist direction. Anticonformist papers may be written by both young and established authors. Smooth mainstream papers tend to generate less variance in their reviews than do novel approaches. Bold papers may hit the imagination of one referee but rarely generate consensus. Here it is up to editors to make the right call and pick winners. Some of the most frequently cited papers that I have published received conflicting reports, including sometimes strongly hostile referees. Once again, I believe that the process may exhibit some excess of conformism, but I doubt that important innovative contributions can be blocked forever. At most, they may be delayed, or if the importance of a seminal contribution is not recognized, then another researcher might claim credit for the idea at a later stage. This is a problem in all sciences, not just in economics.

I should add that many authors confound anticonformism and imagination with the relaxation of sound methodology. Writing a paper with an unconventional message is no excuse for low standards. Yet some people find consolation for their professional frustration in depicting themselves as idealists in a corrupted world, saying things like "My papers do not make their way into top journals because they are controlled by orthodox economists."

Speed of Decision

The editorial process in economics is slow. This has negative consequences on the diffusion of new ideas and on the fairness of promotion decisions concerning young researchers. After working as an editor at two journals, I believe that editors can do a lot to speed up the process substantially. As an author, I have waited for over a year on several occasions before getting a decision on a submission to other journals. This can be avoided. Good editorship starts as soon as a paper is received. There is no reason to wait for a couple of weeks before assigning papers to referees. No matter how hard-pressed editors are, they can deal with this task speedily if they take their job as a priority. Those who cannot spare a few minutes every other day for these tasks should not accept editorial responsibilities.

The next task is to make sure that all invitations to act as a referee are accepted. Nowadays, there are software programs that can chase referees automatically, but automatic reminders often are ignored. So the editor or an editorial assistant should promptly contact unresponsive referees. It is annoying when a colleague does not find the time to send a quick email answer saying, "Sorry, I don't have time." Yet it happens.

The next step involves monitoring incoming reports. A well-argued timely negative report should trigger action. Most frequently, the case is straightforward ("This paper does this and that. Its contribution is clearly not at the level of a general-audience journal"), so it makes no sense to wait for more reports.

Finally, there is the issue of delayed and delinquent referees. My strategy is to establish a contact line with slow referees as early as possible. This work takes some time, and one must overcome the psychological temptation to "wait and see." Unfortunately, some referees have a strong procrastination bias, and unless they are chased aggressively, they never write back.

As I mentioned above, during my tenure at the *ReStud*, an editorial assistant used to send aggressive reminders, but the effect was mixed. One referee might respond apologetically, and others would be annoyed and either complain or stop accepting tasks in future. I now prefer a more gentle approach: "I have now received all other reports, but your opinion is still very important to me. When can I expect to receive your report?" If this is not enough, I move to a slightly more confrontational message: "At this point, if you cannot send me a report within X days, I prefer to come to a decision without your input." Most referees take action at this point. Sometimes there are credible personal circumstances delaying the delivery, and in these cases the editor wants to be patient. If such a problem is detected two to three months after the submission, even some additional delay would not prompt disaster. The most unfortunate case is the rare case in which a referee defaults and writes that she or he is no longer willing to write a report. Once again, if this anomaly case is detected early, the editor can still take measures that prevent a major delay. Help messages to associate editors or loyal referees usually work. Occasionally, delinquent referees turn quiet and stop answering emails. In these cases, there is little one can do other than appoint another referee and make a note in the dataset (accessible to all current and future coeditors) describing the behavior. The good news for this severely delinquent referee is that she or he will soon stop receiving papers to referee. The bad news is that her misbehavior does not pass unnoticed and is highly stigmatized. Even under the worst personal situation, a referee's report should not take longer than six months.

Some people, including notoriously slow and uncooperative referees, hold strong views about the inefficient editorial process in economics and compare economics with other disciplines. For these people, the remedy is straightforward: give referees a two-week deadline, and stick to it. These colleagues fail to acknowledge that the typical paper in economics requires more editorial work than do papers in many other disciplines. For instance, a plain in-or-out approach may be feasible in purely experimental disciplines, where the experiment but not its description is the major task. The typical paper in economics is more demanding to write. A theory of a social phenomenon must clarify the nexus between the real-world phenomenon and its model, and this nexus is often not obvious. A mathematical model does not live its autonomous life without a convincing connection between a theory and its empirical test, but this connection is often controversial. I am convinced that most papers improve significantly over the referee process. Some editors and referees are prepared to make endless iterations, although the marginal value of making authors work on a certain project becomes at some point negligible or even negative. The editor has a responsibility to stop the process at the right point. Some fellow editors seem to view complete consensus as a necessary condition for publishing a paper, and even though the thinking of most referees tends to converge over several iterations, it is sometimes impossible to placate a negative referee. Insisting on asking authors to please skeptical referees may actually become counterproductive for the quality of the final product. Sometimes, negative referees grow increasingly aggressive as the process goes by (saying things like "I cannot even understand why the paper has reached such an advanced stage of the refereeing process. I never would have recommended it to any respected field journals"). Whenever I have challenged such catastrophic claims and made a positive decision, I am not aware of any subsequent damage to the journal's reputation.

Many journals today see opportunities in establishing a reputation for having an efficient editorial process. At the *JEEA*, we have made a big investment in this direction since 2009. The results are tangible. In 2008, it took an average of four months for a new submission to receive a decision. In 2012, it took two months. I am a great fan of this approach, but I acknowledge the possibility of detrimental general equilibrium effects. The *JEEA* is not the only journal that is putting more emphasis on editorial turnaround times. Many journals have worked hard to become more efficient. In response to our improvements, the number of submissions to the *JEEA* increased from 400 per year in 2009 to 700 per year in 2012. This jump in numbers is exceptional, but other journals face submission booms, and there are several new journals in the profession. I suspect that authors may respond to these increased editorial efforts by making a larger number of submissions. If journals reply within a couple of months, why not try a more ambitious sequence? The result may be more pressure and demands on referees' and editors' time, a sort of tournament curse.

Plagiarism

Plagiarism and self-plagiarism are taken seriously in the profession. Ruling on accusations of plagiarism is, for many reasons, a nightmare for editors. Thankfully, I have faced no major serious allegation of plagiarism during my editorial tenure. Sometimes, authors have asked me to remedy presumed previous injustices, which were difficult to verify. In such cases, I had to explain to submitters that I could only evaluate the novelty of a piece of research relative to the existing research (by the same and by other authors). Irrespective of my own convictions (in some cases, I suspected that the submitters had a point), I cannot restore justice by publishing ideas or material that have already appeared elsewhere— even if the previously published piece involved some fraudulent action. On a few occasions, I have faced bizarre requests. One author asked me not to publish a paper (which had been accepted by another coeditor) because the working paper version of the submitted work contained an extension (that was not accepted for publication in our journal) that allegedly stole ideas from the complaining author's work.

When serious and well-documented plagiarism is exposed, editors need to behave responsibly and not cowardly. I once observed (without being a party to) a controversial case. A colleague discovered that the theory presented in one of her papers, which was published few years earlier in a top theory journal, had been reproduced almost literally in an article published by a minor British journal with only insignificant changes in the interpretation of some variables. Her article was not even cited. When the case—which was clear fraud—was denounced, the journal editor's sole concern was to escape responsibility. The plagiarists were asked to write a note, later published in the journal, where they listed a few references, including one to the work of the plagiarized authors. The original authors had no opportunity to defend their case in the pages of the journal, and the editor dismissed their further complaints as a nuisance. The plagiarists enjoy a positive (albeit small) number of citations of their "contribution." This sad case of bad editorship reminds me of the recent episode involving the captain of a capsized Italian cruise ship, the *Costa Concordia*. Although the captain was directly responsible for the disaster, he left the ship and swam ashore, abandoning the many passengers who were trapped on the ship.

Thankfully, plagiarists cannot always count on the connivance of editors. Recently, the *Journal of Economic Perspectives* publicly rebuked three authors for publishing some material in multiple journals in violation of the agreement with the journal. This attention triggered a look at a number of other cases of dubious publication strategy involving the same authors, which cost them a sad fall into disrepute.

The Future of Publishing in Economics

Academic publishing is at a turning point. Today's journals are a legacy of a pre-Internet model where many copies of each journal were printed and journal space was limited due to printing costs. Today, few hard copies are sold and distributed around the world, and it would be relatively easy to expand the size of journals. In fact, the role of publications is no longer so much about the circulation of ideas but rather about quality certification. Papers begin to be cited long before their publication, and most research is read in its mimeo and working paper versions. The argument against expanding the journal is that it would water down the reputation and quality-control role of the journal. However, it remains unclear why, in spite of the major increase in size of the economics profession, we continue to have a rating system based on rigid top-five criteria. Evidently, there is a strong hysteresis. The American Economic Association has seized the opportunity by introducing (high-quality) B journals. Many journals (including the *JEEA*) are working hard to qualify themselves as the best non-top-five journals. Yet publishing a paper in a top-five journal has an immense premium in the career process.

Traditionally, the cost of producing a journal and paying editors was covered by individuals and institutions that subscribed to the journal. However, the number of both types of subscriptions has declined sharply. In earlier days, universities bought several copies of each journal to satisfy the local demand of simultaneous readers. Nowadays, few researchers read hard copies, and most universities have gone to a single subscription. Unauthorized access to electronic copies is common in many parts of the world. Individual subscriptions are irrelevant sources of income for journals because most readers access the journals through electronic institutional subscriptions. The declining trend in subscriptions is an irreversible process. Yet there is a bottleneck: production costs have also declined, but journals must continue to pay their editors. Submission fees could be an alternative source of revenue. However, there are contraindications to doing this, such as their discriminatory effect against low-income researchers (a system of targeted fee exemptions is in principle possible but somewhat costly to administer).

I believe that it will not be long before entirely new models will emerge. Future journals will be entirely online, and this move will likely be combined with some deeper innovations. For instance, clickable executable links could give interested readers the opportunity to reproduce econometric results on the spot. Technical proofs could be accompanied by a dynamic model that takes the reader through the formal steps of the analysis interactively or provides additional intuition through an online link to a video explanation provided by the authors. Material that today is buried in remote online appendixes could be made accessible by similar methods. Paradoxically, this process seems to be moving slowly, and the first few innovative attempts have so far ended in failure. An important issue is that unlimited space at publication outlets is not the right way to go. It will continue to be important for both print and online journals to be rated and for the seal of quality to be granted to only a limited number of articles. The exact form in which this should happen is unclear. Perhaps the shift will occur only when one of the incumbent leaders (a top-five journal) takes the initiative. There may be a hanging fruit for these journals.

History of Economics

7

On Editing the *History of Political Economy*

Craufurd Goodwin

Some general-interest journals in economics (such as the *American Economic Review, Southern Economic Journal,* and *Economic Journal*) were established by professional associations, and others by prominent universities (for example, the *Journal of Political Economy,* the *Quarterly Journal of Economics,* and *Economica*). Field journals have emerged typically because specialists believed that their subdisciplines were not getting enough space in the general-interest journals. The journal that I edited from its inception in 1969 until 2010, *History of Political Economy,* came into existence not for these reasons but to become a hearth around which the beleaguered members of a new subdiscipline, the history of economic thought (het), could gather to resist the possibility that their field might die aborning. By the late 1960s, scholars in this field, of which I was then a young member, concluded from the evidence that they were, indeed, faced with extinction. The situation seemed dire. For most of the twentieth century, the subject of the history of economic thought had been dominated by magisterial figures whose courses were well attended by undergraduates and postgraduates, whose publications were welcomed by mainstream journals, and whose professional and departmental positions were secure. Among the most prominent of these figures were Joseph Schumpeter, John Maynard Keynes, Jacob Viner, Lionel Robbins, Joseph Spengler, Wesley Mitchell, John R. Commons, Frank Knight, John Kenneth Galbraith, and George Stigler. None of these giants was historian first and economist second; it was always the other way round. History was not exactly their hobby, but to their colleagues it looked that way, and it was easy to think of closing down the "history of doctrines," as the field was called, when the old men died and space was needed in the curriculum for new, more technical or more empirical material. The old lions departed the field increasingly during the 1960s, leaving their less prominent colleagues especially vulnerable. The next generation of scholars in het was respected for its published work, but its members typically did not have the same high status in the profession or the clout at their universities as had their mentors. Some of these were A. W. (Bob) Coats, Ronald Meek, Donald Winch, R. D. C. (Bob) Black, Mark Blaug, Joseph Dorfman, Bob Eagly, Warren Samuels, Frank Fetter Jr., William Jaffe, Denis O'Brien, William Allen, William Grampp, Vincent Tarascio, and Samuel Hollander. Evidence of the crisis was that their courses in het were regularly canceled, especially at the graduate level, and rejected manuscripts were returned to authors from general-interest journals by return mail. Even parts of the mother discipline that had traditionally welcomed some attention to het now turned their backs on anything "literary." Economic historians at their meetings and in their journals celebrated their newfound cliometrics and seemed embarrassed by het.

Beyond the discipline of economics, important changes also were occurring in the 1960s, a decade that began with high optimism and ended in war. The expectation was that economists could lead the war on poverty, save the environment, maintain full employment and price stability, and demonstrate how wars could be fought most efficiently. Who needed history of economic thought for all that? Not many, it seemed.

So what was to be done? Three paths seemed open, and each had reasonable arguments for and against. The first was for historians of economics to continue as before, pleading with the mainstream for a little space, even if just a small eddy, resisting the temptation to set their own course. This path was advocated vigorously by Lionel Robbins at a conference at Sussex University in 1968, the first of its kind to focus seriously on the existential problems of het. A second path, contemplated by some, was for historians of economics to secede from the economics profession and set up their own tent, perhaps in history, history of science, or philosophy. There, it was suggested, they could become more appropriately voyeurs of economics than participants in it. Two serious obstacles lay in this second path. First, most historians of economics were trained as economists and not in these other disciplines, and second, the occupants of these potential new homes did not come forth enthusiastically with welcoming hands. They too had problems. The third path was to develop het as a proper new subdiscipline of economics, like labor economics or money and banking, with all the paraphernalia that this involved. But to do this, the historians of economics would have to create their own institutions, the first of which should be a journal.

The Birth of *HOPE*

The third path was preferred by most of the younger scholars in the field, and plans were laid and several meetings held during the 1960s to explore ways to move in that direction. A proposal for a journal in Great Britain to be edited by Mark Blaug and Bernard Corry went nowhere. Duke University's department of economics seemed another place to try. In addition to three specialists, the department then and later contained champions of the subject who resisted effectively the disciplinary cleansing that was occurring elsewhere. Some of the most helpful included Bill Yohe, Ed Tower, Vladimir Treml, Jack Blackburn, Dave Davies, Frank de Vyver, Charlie Ferguson, Tom Nechyba, and George Tauchen. Without their quiet support, the journal idea never would have taken off and thrived. When at the end of the 1960s two members of the het troika at Duke (Spengler and Smith) departed the scene, the department agreed with alacrity to the appointment of Neil de Marchi, just finishing his Ph.D. at the Australian National University, and it accepted the lateral movement into het of Roy Weintraub, who began academic life as a theorist. The Duke University Press, although doubtful about the future prospects for a journal, agreed to be the publisher so long as the deal involved no financial risk. By this time, I had become an experienced academic fund raiser and collected enough funds to cover the probable losses of the journal during the first five years, a reasonable trial period. A conference was held at Duke in 1968 to make sure that we had enough good material for the first issue, and we were on our way. We decided to start with two issues a year (soon increased to four) and to signal through our name (*History of Political Economy*) that we intended to be eclectic and reach across disciplinary boundaries and into policy discussions. We did not appreciate for a while after settling on the name that we had a felicitous acronym appropriate for the time.

The community that gathered around and supported this fragile infant journal in the early years was made up of various parts. There were a few of the old lions. Joe Spengler served as chair of the editorial board (which never met), and George Stigler became an indefatigable referee, helping to maintain the highest standards and to give an aura of respectability during the crucial early years. Second, a few specialists who had been laboring for years in comparative obscurity and isolation were delighted to join a community that brought them together through the refereeing process. These included William Jaffe, Frank Fetter Jr., William Barber, Carl Uhr, Henry Spiegel, Terence Hutcheson, Ronald Meek, and

Geoff Harcourt. Third, some important leaders of the profession who were not themselves primarily historians believed in retaining an historical dimension to the discipline and volunteered their services when needed. These included Paul Samuelson, Harry Johnson, Martin Bronfenbrenner, and Don Patinkin, to mention only four. It was encouraging when Arthur Burns, soon to become chair of the Federal Reserve Board, became one of our first subscribers. Fourth, *HOPE* became a surrogate home for a variety of heterodox economists, from the ideological right and left and from diverse methodologies, who had shared the cold shoulder extended by the profession to the historians. Because some of these refugees often had limited historical skills, they presented special challenges in the editorial process. The momentum of teaching het in the main postgraduate programs and serious undergraduate programs begun by the old lions in the golden age before 1960 continued for a while under their students and successors, at least through the 1970s, and *HOPE* was sustained by this younger generation of authors, referees, and advisers—Sam Hollander, Mark Blaug, Jeff Biddle, Evelyn Forget, Wade Hands, Phil Mirowski, Steve Medema, Margaret Schabas, John Davis, Karen Vaughn, Mary Morgan, Kevin Hoover, Bruce Caldwell, Ross Emmet, and Robert Leonard. Since that time, the teaching of het at a higher level and especially to graduate students has steadily declined, but this community of teachers still seems to thrive.

One consequence of the circumstances in which *HOPE* was born was that this heterogeneous community of supporters became exceptionally cooperative and responsible referees. They were well aware that they were part of a struggle for subdisciplinary survival, and through refereeing they might offer postdoctoral guidance, especially to the younger survivors. Often senior scholars devoted extraordinary amounts of time and effort to preparing referee reports and, through *HOPE*, engaged with younger scholars to guide their research. In some of these cases, the quality of the referee reports was substantially higher than the original submission, and in some cases, the reports were even longer. Over the years, the community around *HOPE* has continued to see its editorial role as sustaining and reinvigorating het and also as providing assistance to a publication medium. *HOPE* was deeply engaged in the formation of the History of Economics Society and for some years collected the dues of members at the same time as subscription fees. It has warmly welcomed the growth of a newsletter of the society into a sister journal, the *Journal of the History of Economic Thought*. Special programs and conferences were begun after a decade or so of initial consolidation of the journal, and ultimately an annual series of spring conferences led to the publication of a fifth special issue intended to help invigorate the field with new ideas and new approaches. Minisymposia under Roy Weintraub's direction and ad hoc special issues were also introduced as a form of publication between conventional articles and books.

When *HOPE* was contemplated in 1968, I was half-time teaching (not only het but several other courses as well) and half-time vice-provost of the university. There was no third half available for the journal. The plan was that Robert S. Smith, a specialist in Spanish and Latin American economic thought who was just entering retirement, would become the editor. I would be the associate editor and would be responsible mainly for fund raising, relations with the university administration, and encouragement of the various efforts to strengthen the subdiscipline. However, tragedy struck before the first issue could go to press. Bob Smith died unexpectedly, and I took over by default simply because there was no one else. Like most of the other editors in this series, I had no editorial experience, but unlike them I had no editorial mentor. I did, however, have a splendid colleague in Neil De Marchi, who arrived in 1971 and did many things, including taking over the reins when I was away from the Duke campus for extended periods.

I continued to edit *HOPE* because there never seemed to be anyone at Duke (where we thought the journal should remain) to take over. And after a while, inertia took over. The editorial duties were minimized by the local community that formed around the journal. These were mainly the associate editors—Neil De Marchi, Roy Weintraub, Bob Coats (when he taught at Duke), Kevin Hoover, and Bruce Caldwell. Exceptional managing editors (the people who do the heavy lifting of copyediting and dealing with the production process)—initially an excellent classicist John Dowling and currently Paul Dudenhefer, a scholar of English literature—made the job of editor less irksome and more fun. It seems miraculous that over more than four decades there have been no serious disagreements among the editorial team. But there has been an abundance of rollicking good humor. Kevin Hoover took over as editor in 2010, presumably with a sentence of less than forty-two years and time off for good behavior.

Some Questions to Be Addressed

Over the first few years at *HOPE*, we found that a number of significant policy questions had to be answered. I do not suggest that these were all answered "the right way" or that we would answer them the same way today, with hindsight. Because these have relevance beyond *HOPE*, I describe several of them briefly, with our answers.

1. Should we be open-minded in considering manuscripts, or should we have explicit or implicit priorities and seek to guide the field in various ways? Should we have a view toward rational reconstruction, biography, early non-Western thought, writings with a strong political commitment, or other segments of the literature? In practical terms, should we as much as possible send manuscripts to referees that we know are sympathetic to a particular kind of work (on Marx to Marxists and on Sraffa to Sraffians)? Or should we confront authors with referees who are likely to be deeply skeptical of their project? Despite what some authors may think, we chose the first path of sending papers to potentially friendly readers and have encouraged eclecticism from the beginning. We look for high quality but recognize that quality can be defined in various ways. We appreciate that there is a case on the other side of this answer and accept the charge that we may be weak kneed and lily livered. Our decision is conditioned in part on our lack of certainty that we knew where the field should be going. In some cases, we have acted as an incubator for subsubdisciplines (like the philosophy of economics) until they have reached their own economies of scale and start their own journals. The appearance of new journals in het, beginning in the 1970s, posed a challenge and an opportunity for *HOPE*. Now we had competition for the best manuscripts, but we also could issue rejections knowing that if (as many authors asserted) our referees were incompetent and not doing their job, then this proposition could be tested through submission to other journals.

2. Who should be the real gatekeepers to publication—the editor, the editor in conjunction with the associate editors, or the referees? Technically, the answer is the first, but for *HOPE*, we have made it effectively the third. We seldom overturn the recommendations of the referees, except in the exceptional case of blatant irresponsibility of a referee. We have concluded that the field is so broad and deep that it is seldom possible for the editor to second-guess two skilled experts, and indeed to do so is contrary to the spirit of peer review. For those who call for editorial overruling of referees, we respond with humility that we do not usually have the confidence to do so. This being said, we soon discovered a continuing problem in our peer review with heavy dependence on a few referees for advice. In this disparate field of het with relatively few

qualified scholars on highly specialized topics, often there are not many options in the selection of referees. When some referee candidates are unwilling, unreliable, or in other ways unsuitable for duty, the result may be overuse of the relatively few scholars who are thorough, timely, balanced, and constructive, and there is a danger that their personal predilections and prejudices may come to influence the field. This is a danger to which an editor must remain constantly alert.

3. How do you provide for the financial survival of a journal that is not attached to a membership society? The economics of journal publishing are complex and ever-changing. When we began, we knew we had a five-year window to prove our viability. The challenge was to build up the subscriber base quickly. There are two kinds of subscriber. Individuals pay relatively low fees and are notoriously feckless. A rule of thumb is that it takes the revenue from a one-year subscription spent on advertising to attract a new individual subscriber, and it can be predicted that a significant proportion of new subscribers will soon drift away. The institutional subscribers must be counted on to pay the freight, and they do. Their fees are much higher than those for individuals, and if they hang on for several years, they are likely to become effectively permanent and unwilling to face the costs and objections from users that result from terminating subscriptions. *HOPE*, however, began at a time of relative abundance in higher education, and libraries were willing to entertain new subscriptions. We began with a part-time secretary, and when she was not engaged with editorial matters, she typed up personal letters for my signature to department chairs in economics around the world, urging them to subscribe to *HOPE* and even providing a draft letter to send to their librarians. This did the job, and by the end of the first decade, we began to be perceived by the Duke University Press as, if not quite yet a cash cow, at least a promising heifer. By now, the heifer has grown into a splendid cow, and we face the specter of our publisher extracting the consumer surplus from the libraries and their other subscribers and cross-subsidizing their book publication from the journals. Are these matters about which an editor should worry?

4. How can the culture of publishing be improved, sustained, and passed on among authors, referees, and others? This is a question facing not just *HOPE* but all journals. At the moment, rules of behavior involving publication are picked up on the job by newcomers. There are no mechanisms through which good behavior can be inculcated for those writing articles and submitting to periodicals, reading manuscripts as referees,

or editing journals and book series. Unlike most other aspects of professional life, these behaviors are not taught. The expectation is that they will be picked up by osmosis, and the result is that an editor is likely to receive a report from an inexperienced referee that says in its entirety, "This is rubbish," and a message from a rejected author that says, "You are not an editor, you are a sadist, and I will never darken your door again." Both messages are unhelpful. Publication is one aspect of academic life where scholars have not been trained to control their emotions, and the publication process is more painful as a result. After encountering many such comments, a seasoned editor will have developed a thick skin. Sadly, it is the unskilled authors who suffer the most from their inexperience. They do not appreciate that something can be learned from even the harshest commentary (we never rewrite referee reports to dull the sharp edges). In the same way, an unsophisticated referee with an unsubstantiated dismissal of a manuscript loses an opportunity to aid in the growth of another, perhaps younger, scholar. Hoping to improve the culture of scholarly publishing a little, we published an *Academic's Handbook* (3rd edition, Duke University Press) with chapters on book and journal publication.

5. Should we employ double-blind refereeing as standard practice? This question was put to our editorial board early on, and the consensus was decidedly in the negative. The principal argument in favor of the practice is that it protects authors from potential discrimination by age, sex, nationality, or some other illegitimate criterion. The argument against is that an author's prior publications can be a significant consideration in reaching a recommendation about a new publication. Is the author perhaps just recycling? Our decision was to use double-blind refereeing only when an author insisted on it. One board member said that he would resign if required to use it. My observations are that in a field as small as het and with the Internet steadily increasing transparency, anonymity is exceptionally difficult to preserve despite the best efforts. Even though some authors think otherwise, prejudice and discrimination are extremely rare, and when observed, they are typically the opposite of what is feared. Prominent authors receive tougher handling from referees than do tyros. The sense of referees is that distinguished writers should be held to the highest standards from the start but that younger or more isolated authors should be helped to reach these standards with constructive suggestions for revision.

6. Can higher quality in a journal be achieved by commissioning articles as well as by waiting to see what comes in over the transom? In principle, one might think so, but in practice, we have found that this does not happen. In the early years, we tried several experiments with unhappy results. Sometimes the commissions were simply late in arriving, and in most cases they were a disappointment. When commissions were bad, they were hard to reject; we did it and lost some friends. In one painful incident, we invited three distinguished economists to present accounts of their early accomplishments as a panel at the annual meeting of the American Economic Association. All three papers were boastful, self-serving, inaccurate, and unacceptable. We did not repeat the experiment, except with conferences and symposia where the circumstances are quite different.

7. Should we charge a submission fee and remunerate referees? There are strong market-based arguments for both practices, in particular that they might cut down frivolous and "unripe" submissions and reduce the time lag in reaching a judgment by providing a financial incentive for referees to be punctual. But we have always felt that the transactions costs would be too high. It would be necessary to employ an accountant and to enter into far more correspondence with authors than is required now.

8. Is it possible for a journal such as *HOPE* to survive for long if it serves a subdiscipline of economics that, in North America at least, makes virtually no provision for specialized postgraduate training? Can the lateral flow of new entrants into this field from other fields sustain the cadre of research scholars forever? Thus far, the raw numbers in het, as evidenced by members of the History of Economics Society, have kept up remarkably well. But one ominous sign of the times may be a steady increase in the proportion of *HOPE* authors who are resident in countries where the elimination of het from graduate education is less advanced. The proportion of American authors in *HOPE* has declined steadily over four decades: in volume 1 (1969), it was over 75 percent American; in volume 20 (1988), it had fallen almost to one half; by volume 41 (2009), the percentage of Americans had fallen to about 15 percent of *HOPE* authors. What could *HOPE* do to increase the participation of American scholars?? For a start, we have created a collection of archives of significant economists called the Economists' Papers Project in our university library. This has served as a magnet for historians of

economics who pursue serious manuscript research. Most recently, Duke has established a Center for the History of Political Economy that is devoted to research and teaching in the subject.

9. From the earliest discussions in the 1960s, as befits our calling, we have kept almost every scrap of paper that came out of the activities of *HOPE*. All of that material is now with the Economists' Papers Project at Duke. We have processed well over four thousand submissions, and we have retained referee correspondence, early drafts, correspondence with the authors, and everything else about papers that have been accepted and rejected. This is a treasure trove for the history of economics and for the history of the history of economics. For example, the more than a hundred referee reports by George Stigler over many years give an important perspective on this major scholar. But should these archives be opened generally for researchers? And if so, under what restrictions and after what interval? We have moved cautiously on this question and have not reached any definitive position.

10. What is the best way to organize the editorial team at *HOPE*? Many of the large journals in economics assign to associate editors segments of their fields. We have not done so, fearing that this would reduce uniformity and equal treatment in different parts of the subject. Instead, associate editors are called on generally for policy guidance and for specific guidance on difficult cases—marginal cases or cases where the author is enraged for some reason. This device reduces substantially the demands on the editor.

Conclusion

A question asked and answered by other editors in this series has been something like, "Is it worthwhile becoming an editor of a journal in economics, and if you had the choice, would you do it again or advise someone you care about to do it?" The answer must depend on the opportunity cost of the person in question. For me, the benefits have substantially outweighed the costs. There is a real sense of accomplishment in bringing out four issues a year and feeling that you have contributed to the welfare or, in this case, survival of your field. You have a unique opportunity as editor of seeing where the good work (and bad) is being done and where the field is moving. The amount of time that the job takes depends very much on your own personality and work style. There are innumerable small decisions to be made constantly, and if you tend to obsess over such things, this is not the job for you. Here you need to move on quickly and not worry very long over whether you made the right move. As other editors in this series have noted, with all the paper that accumulates in this job, you want to keep an empty inbox. The demands of the job also depend on the community in which you are embedded. I have been exceptionally fortunate at Duke in having marvelous and supportive colleagues who have included the editorial team, the managing editor, the department chair, and the publisher. It would not be worthwhile doing this job if you had to fight any of these worthies. This is not a job through which you will make many friends and admirers. It is a cliché that authors who are accepted and published think that it was entirely their own exclusive accomplishment and that there is no need for gratitude. Those who are rejected, on the other hand (more than 80 percent, in our case), invariably think that the decision was wrong and a result of the malfeasance or bad judgment of others. Because the referees are anonymous, the editor becomes the surrogate other and the target for the anger and sometimes real fury that come forth. But sooner rather than later, you become inured to the slings and arrows. The comment I received from a disgruntled author that I treasure most after forty-two years with *HOPE* is this: "I have observed that since you became editor the quality of the journal has steadily declined."

Acknowledgments

I am grateful to the history of political economy group at Duke University for helpful comments on this chapter.

Microeconomics and Industrial Organization

8

On Turning Twenty: The *Journal of Economics & Management Strategy* Comes of Age

Daniel F. Spulber

As I write this reminiscence, the *Journal of Economics & Management Strategy* (*JEMS*) is reaching a milestone: it is turning twenty. It has been a terrific journey thus far, and yet I feel that it is only just beginning. I have had occasion to think about the journal's beginnings, the many events that have happened over the last two decades, and the things that might lie ahead for the journal.

Today, *JEMS* is a leader at the intersection of economics and management. It is widely read around the world. Although it started as a specialty journal, it is becoming a general-interest journal by addressing a wide range of topics of that are of interest to both economics departments and business schools. The journal is present in most academic libraries and continues to climb the journal rankings.

How *JEMS* Got Started

I joined the Kellogg School of Management at Northwestern University in the summer of 1990 and was soon swept into a transformation of my academic department, which is another story in itself. The basic idea of the change was to integrate economics into teaching and research on management strategy. One of the first steps in the transformation of the department was a name change from policy and environment to management and strategy. In addition, new faculty members were hired, new courses were developed, and new directions in research were charted.

I thought that starting a journal devoted to the application of economics to management strategy would be a contribution to the department's efforts. I also thought that starting such a journal had the potential to achieve two important objectives: to encourage more economists to work in the field of management strategy and interest management-strategy scholars in economic approaches to the field.

When the journal started, submissions were immediately of high quality, and the coeditors and referees did a lot of great work for the journal. That continues to be true today. The journal has always been highly international, and part of the journal's contributions was attracting great researchers from around the world. International scholars contributed to the journal's growth and quality of research.

The early years were difficult for a number of reasons. I am grateful to my wife, Sue, who handled assistant editor duties for a number of years while raising our three children. It helped that Sue had a Ph.D. in geology from Brown University. Without her hard work, *JEMS* would never have gotten off the ground. For a number of years, *JEMS* lacked proper office space to run the journal, and we ended up doing a lot of the work at home. As our children grew older, it became more difficult to juggle their activities with the journal, and we had to put the journal on a more permanent footing. The initial years were complicated further because we did everything by regular mail and used only hard copies of manuscripts and referee reports. I remember using many large manila envelopes to deliver multiple copies of articles to the coeditors for sending to reviewers. Eventually, I began to hire work-study students to help with the journal. Finally, the school provided office space and staff support.

The Idea of *JEMS*

When I was around age twelve, my family spent a year in New York City. We often listened to classical music on WQXR 105.9 FM. After an especially wonderful piece of music, usually Mozart, the host would say that it was an "OTW (out of this world) gem." This term sounded just right to me. Eventually, I thought that a journal called *JEMS* would have great articles—each one a gem—which has proven to be true.

Another early thought was that *JEMS* should be fun for its readers, authors, and editors. Although that goal might seem to be at odds with an academic journal, people have often told me that they enjoy reading *JEMS*. For one thing, we did not impose any strict length guidelines, so that authors could produce long papers to explain their ideas and give more real-world examples. The editorial process was rigorous but somehow less formal. Coeditors and referees emphasized motivation and applications as well as rigorous analysis. Many coeditors have stuck with *JEMS* since the beginning, and their contributions to the journal have been essential.

One thing that has not changed is that every author receives a personal letter from me with the final decision on their paper. We also try to give each author a coeditor's report and two referee reports. Not every author is happy, but we have tried to give fair readings without imposing orthodoxy based on who you know, where you teach, or what the latest hot topic or technique is.

As the number of economists in business schools has increased, many have published their work in *JEMS*, particularly when writing on business-related topics. *JEMS* has proven to be an important resource for researchers in economics departments and in business schools, including departments of finance, managerial economics, accounting, marketing, organization behavior, and management strategy. In addition, the journal has served as a resource for managers and managerial consultants who are seeking up-to-date research on management strategy and provided practitioners with a means of access to innovative economic research.

The first issue was the first of many blockbusters, with a great range of topics and high-quality research that would be sustained in future issues. The first issue contained important contributions in organization economics, finance, industrial organization, regulation, transaction costs, and management:

Margaret Meyer, Paul Milgrom, and John Roberts, "Organizational Prospects, Influence Costs, and Ownership Changes"

Bengt Holmstrom and Barry Nalebuff, "To the Raider Goes the Surplus? A Reexamination of the Free-Rider Problem"

Beth Allen and Jacques-Francois Thisse, "Price Equilibria in Pure Strategies for Homogeneous Oligopoly"

Timothy J. Muris, David T Scheffman, and Pablo T. Spiller, "Strategy and Transaction Costs: The Organization of Distribution in the Carbonated Soft Drink Industry"

Richard J. Gilbert, and David M. Newbery, "Alternative Entry Paths: The Build or Buy Decision"

Kyle Bagwell, "Pricing to Signal Product Line Quality"

Eric Rasmusen, "Managerial Conservatism and Rational Information Acquisition"

Jeffrey S. Banks, "Monopoly Pricing and Regulatory Oversight"

Shortly after establishing the journal, which launched in 1992, I wrote two survey pieces to explain my ideas about the field of management strategy (Spulber 1992, 1994). This was a way of priming the pump for potential authors who were seeking to develop research in the field of economics and management strategy. The first survey was an attempt to survey how economists viewed the firm, with a suggestion that much more needed to be known about management strategy. The survey classifies economic theories of the firm into four categories based on the level of aggregation in economic models:—neoclassical, industrial organization, contractual, and organizational incentive. Economic theories of the firm are evaluated on the basis of their potential application to problems of management decision making. The survey suggests that a management perspective can be useful in developing an integrated theoretical analysis of the firm that addresses both competitive strategy and organizational design.

The second survey attempted to cover the field of management strategy in a way that would provide an introduction to the area for economists. Management strategy was closely tied to the field of management, with roots in psychology and sociology. The survey examined organizational design, competitive strategy, and public-policy considerations. In addition, I offered some suggestions on how economic analysis can be applied in unifying and developing management strategy as a field of study. From its inception, *JEMS* has explored applications of economics to management strategy and a broad range of business issues.

JEMS continues to influence research and other journals in microeconomics, industrial organization, and management strategy. Early on, an article in *Fortune* magazine called the journal a "showcase for the new research." Various economics journals have issued special issues on similar topics to those pioneered in *JEMS*. More economics journals are considering management topics that have appeared in *JEMS*, and the journal's articles are included in tenure decisions at leading institutions. *JEMS* is highly ranked in both the economics and the management lists based on its impact factor score. Additionally, *JEMS* has emerged as a leading journal in the field of strategic management according to a recent citation-based study (Azar and Brock 2008).

The Evolution of *JEMS*

An essential aspect of *JEMS* has been to cover many different aspects of economics and management strategy. The journal has challenged orthodoxy in the choice of topics that are considered appropriate for economics journals. Business and management topics were important from the outset, and this has influenced other economics journals. *JEMS* has always viewed any industry as being of interest for economists, whether that industry is agriculture, health care, sports, airlines, telecommunications, retail, or e-commerce. Economics journals have tended to designate particular industries as topics more suited for special-interest journals.

Perhaps the most interesting aspect of editing *JEMS* has been the special issues. These have been highly influential in terms of charting new areas of research and developing the connections between economics and management strategy. The journal put out five special issues on the industrial organization of health care, which affected the field as well as other journals. The idea was to show that high-quality empirical and theoretical research could be applied to an industry, and in this case, health care, the research looked at institutions in the health care industry, including firms, market institutions, and regulatory agencies.

JEMS also published special issues on

- Tournaments, contests, and relative performance evaluation
- The Federal Communication Commission's spectrum auctions
- Management strategy and the environment
- Nonmarket strategy and social responsibility
- International business
- Empirical studies in marketing
- Industrial organization of the food industry

The journal published three special issues on economics and strategy of entrepreneurship. Although entrepreneurship has been neglected within the economics literature, there is a rapidly growing amount of high-quality research in this area. The articles in these special issues are contributing to the development of the field of entrepreneurship in economics. The work breaks new ground in theoretical and empirical approaches to modeling the strategic decisions of entrepreneurs. The first special issue on this topic, edited by Thomas Hellmann and Scott Stern, included the following articles:

Edward L. Glaeser and William R. Kerr, "Local Industrial Conditions and Entrepreneurship: How Much of the Spatial Distribution Can We Explain?"

Mariassunta Giannetti and Andrei Simonov, "Social Interactions and Entrepreneurial Activity"

William J. Baumol, Melissa A. Schilling, and Edward N. Wolff, "The Superstar Inventors and Entrepreneurs: How Were They Educated?"

Iain M. Cockburn and Megan J. MacGarvie, "Patents, Thickets and the Financing of Early-Stage Firms: Evidence from the Software Industry"

Timothy S. Simcoe, Stuart J. H. Graham, and Maryann P. Feldman, "Competing on Standards? Entrepreneurship, Intellectual Property, and Platform Technologies"

Paul Gompers, Anna Kovner, and Josh Lerner, "Specialization and Success: Evidence from Venture Capital"

Roland Strausz, "Entrepreneurial Financing, Advice, and Agency Costs"

Andres Almazan, Javier Suarez, and Sheridan Titman, "Firms' Stakeholders and the Costs of Transparency"

Andrew F. Daughety and Jennifer F. Reinganum, "Hidden Talents: Entrepreneurship and Pareto-Improving Private Information"

JEMS continues to publish high-quality articles in entrepreneurship and related topics. The interaction between innovation and entrepreneurship is an important area for *JEMS*.

A highlight of working on *JEMS* was publishing an article by Nobel Prize–winner Ronald Coase titled "The Conduct of Economics: The Example of Fisher Body and General Motors." In it, Coase addresses general issues in applied economic research, and his insightful and compelling article reflects his research interests as well as his experiences as a journal editor. Coase urges economists to be careful and unbiased in describing institutions and conducting empirical work, citing the inaccuracies in the frequently used story of Fisher Body.

The Editorial Process

JEMS delegates most of the review process to its coeditors. Although coeditor decisions are advisory to the editor, their recommendations are almost always followed by the journal. Occasional exceptions to this rule occur when authors of a rejected paper can resolve problems that are identified by reviewers.

JEMS has been lucky in having highly talented coeditors. The *JEMS* coeditor group provides important leadership in the many research areas covered by the journal. One of the most important indicators of the success of the journal is the large number of editors of leading journals who are *JEMS* alumni. In fact, one interesting aspect of running the journal is the constant stream of invitations to the journal's coeditors to work on other journals or at least on more than one editorial board. This is evidence of the coeditors' important research contributions, and it also is a compliment to the journal itself that its coeditors are viewed as attractive candidates by other journals.

JEMS has also been lucky to have had many highly effective and professional reviewers who use their expertise to provide careful and extensive reviews without compensation. The journal realizes that reviewers make time in their busy academic schedules of teaching and research. Reviewers receive a signed letter thanking them for their contribution to the journal at each stage of the review process.

The Internet has been responsible for major changes in the editorial process. For the first ten years or so, *JEMS* was run entirely by traditional mail, which meant that each stage of the editorial process involved preparing and sending envelopes by mail. A submission included four hard copies of the manuscript—one for the journal, one for the coeditor, and one each for the two referees. The same process was repeated for revisions. For the journal's second decade, the use of e-mail considerably improved and speeded the editorial process, displacing snail mail.

One major change occurred just shy of the journal's twentieth birthday when *JEMS* went online with a software program called ScholarOne. This program automated many of the nuts and bolts of the editorial process, including sending routine letters, keeping track of the status of the manuscripts under review, and reminding coeditors and referees of upcoming deadlines. With an online system, editors can work remotely, which is helpful for busy academics. Surprisingly, going online boosted submissions because authors have found it easier or more appealing to submit online.

The *Journal's* Mission

The articles in *JEMS* apply economic analysis to the study of the competitive strategies and the organizational design of firms. The journal is based on the proposition that economics has much to contribute to the study of business decision making and that microeconomics can be greatly strengthened by the consideration of practical issues in management strategy.

The journal emphasizes rigorous modeling using economic theory and econometric analysis. The journal is a complement to management journals that take a more applied approach or, in some cases, a more traditional view of management strategy. Articles in *JEMS* include intuitive explanations and examples applied to specific industries that broaden the potential audience. *JEMS* provides a research forum that helps to promote interaction among social scientists in economics, business, and law.

JEMS publishes articles in such economic areas as the theory of the firm, industrial organization, organization theory, game theory, health economics, international trade, labor, law and economics, and regulation. In addition, the journal publishes papers on economic analysis in cognate areas of management including accounting, finance, marketing, and organization behavior. A connecting link between these diverse subject areas is the development of the economic theory of the firm.

JEMS publishes work on economic institutions. Ronald Coase provided the insight that the scope of the firm's activities depends to a great extent on the comparison of transaction costs of market exchange versus the costs of governance within the firm. Coase's path-breaking work led to the development of a theory of transaction costs and organizations, with particular emphasis on vertical integration and the structure of the firm. A large body of subsequent research examines how transaction costs affect the design and performance of market institutions.

The theory of the firm is an important foundation for the economics of management strategy. Elsewhere, I develop an analysis of the theory of the firm that was motivated by the study of economic institutions (Spulber 2009). Individual agents establish institutions based on their preferences, endowments, and other characteristics. Individuals acting as entrepreneurs establish firms, and firms create and manage markets and organizations. Firms play an economic role when intermediated exchange (transactions between consumers that go through firms) is more efficient than direct exchange (transactions between consumers that do not involve firms). Consumers can engage in transactions with each other, either in the form of spot transactions or contracts, and can form various organizations to coordinate their transactions, including clubs, cooperatives, associations, nonprofits, and partnerships. The critical difference between firms and direct exchange among individual agents is the separation of the firm's objectives from those of its consumer-owners. Extending the Fisher separation theorem of neoclassical economics, a transaction institution is defined to be a firm if its objectives can be separated financially from those of its owners. Organizations such as clubs, consumer cooperatives, worker cooperatives, and basic partnerships have objectives that cannot be separated financially from those of their owners so that they are not firms. For example, clubs maximize the consumption benefits of their members. There are economic benefits to establishing firms when they improve efficiency in comparison to direct exchange (Spulber 2009).

Important advances in industrial organization have enhanced our understanding of how firms select optimal competitive strategies in equilibrium. This has been made possible in large part through the application of game theory to the study of competition. The types of strategic actions studied in industrial organization include pricing policies, output levels, contract terms, product quality and durability, investment dynamics, and research and development. Progress in analyzing competition has been made using models in which consumers and firms possess asymmetric information about costs or demand such as nonlinear pricing models or signaling models of limit pricing. In addition, dynamic games have allowed important extension of static pricing, investment, and entry models. Significant developments have also occurred in the application of econometrics to test models of industrial organization, particularly in industry studies. *JEMS* publishes both theoretical papers in industrial organization and also empirical analyses of the competitive behavior and equilibrium strategies of firms in particular industries.

The economic theory of organizations examines the determinants of vertical integration, including imperfect competition, incomplete contracts, uncertainty, and incomplete information. Work on the economics of information has examined the consequences of moral hazard in market contracts and within organizations. Communication in organizations and also the design of incentives are being examined using game theory. The principal-agent model has been developed and extended in a variety of ways, including multiple agents, multiple principals, long-term relationships, and the principal-supervisor-agent model. These extensions provide powerful new approaches to addressing difficult questions in management. *JEMS* publishes theoretical and empirical papers on organizational structure and design and the practical implications for management.

New approaches to international trade include many elements of industrial organization, particularly in the analysis of imperfect competition, intermediation, and innovation in international markets. The competitive strategies of firms now play an important role in the economic theory of international trade. This research has been stimulated by the growing intensity of international competition and its consequences for the performance of established firms. There is growing interest in the strategic decision making of international business. *JEMS* publishes research on competitive strategy in international business.

Managers often are concerned with the implications of legal restrictions on economic activity. Contract rules affect the nature of interactions between the firm and its suppliers, thus affecting decisions about vertical integration. Contract rules also affect the firm's transactions with customers, including decisions about performance and investment in reliance. The many developments in the theory of transactions and contracts have far-reaching consequences for the study of firms. *JEMS* publishes work on legal and market institutions and their effects on the decisions and organizational structure of firms.

Antitrust law and enforcement place important restrictions on the competitive strategies of firms. Restrictions on monopolization and collusion affect pricing and marketing actions, customer contracts, the formation of joint ventures, and the exchange of information between firms. Rules on price discrimination can affect the pricing policies of firms including quantity discounts, targeted discounts, product bundling, and market segmentation. Marketing plans are influenced by antitrust rules regarding exclusive dealing, tying contracts, resale price maintenance, territorial restrictions, and other trade practices. The evolution and scope of firms often are affected by antitrust policies toward horizontal, vertical, and conglomerate mergers. *JEMS* publishes papers on antitrust law and its consequences for management strategy. Emphasis is placed on the equilibrium effects of antitrust on the strategies of firms and on the endogenous determination of public policy in equilibrium. Econometric studies of the effects of antitrust law and enforcement on competitive strategies are also of particular interest.

Government regulation creates many constraints and opportunities for firms. Every industry is subject to a wide variety of regulations, including price controls, entry restrictions, licensing and patent requirements, product quality and safety regulations, workplace health and safety regulations, and environmental pollution regulations. These regulations restrict the actions of firms, can entail high compliance costs, and sometimes create competitive opportunities. For example, firms can gain competitive advantage from the imposition of some regulation by the government if their costs of compliance are below those of rival firms. In addition, firms may differentiate their products by noting their qualities in relation to regulatory standards. For example, firms have achieved enhanced sales and increased financial backing by advertising their product's benign effects on the environment (through "green marketing" and "green investing"). Firms can also benefit from changes in market demand that are induced by regulation (for example, by changing the characteristics of products in response to labeling requirements). *JEMS* encourages theoretical and empirical papers that examine the economic effects of government regulation. The endogenous determination of firm strategies and regulatory policies within equilibrium market models is of particular interest. The discussion should provide some analysis of the effects of regulation on the equilibrium strategies of firms rather than just providing a social welfare analysis of public policy.

Management strategy is concerned with practical decisions faced by the managers of companies as they seek competitive advantage over rival firms. In association with profit maximization, the goals of the firm might include entry into new markets, increase in market share, growth or survival of the firm, or vertical expansion. Strategies for achieving these goals include pricing policies, investment expenditures, new product innovation, enhanced product quality, cost reduction and process innovation, supplier contracts, marketing plans, and financing methods. In addition, the managers of the firm may seek to change its internal organization and incentive structure to attain particular objectives. Finally, the managers of the firms may make detailed plans to implement the chosen strategies over time.

The study of management strategy can contribute to managerial decision making by presenting alternative policy options, examining the expected consequences of alternative competitive strategies using market models, and recommending particular strategies based on their efficacy in achieving the firm's goals at the market equilibrium. Therefore, management strategy has a crucial normative component.

There is a long tradition in economics of advising public policy makers. Indeed, for most economists, the word *policy* is synonymous with *public policy*. Thus, each area of economics has an important public-policy component. Economists have devoted considerable attention to international trade policy, fiscal policy, monetary policy, and employment policy. Public finance and economic development are generally directed toward government policy. The economic analysis of law is concerned with comparing alternative legal institutions from the point of view of aggregate efficiency. The economic analysis of regulation and antitrust apply theories of industrial organization. It is standard for economic research papers to conclude with an analysis of the social welfare implications of firm behavior, market institutions, or government policy. Economists have devoted considerably less attention to the problems that must be solved by managers of firms. However, there is significant scope for economists to contribute to business policy making with the same vigor and insight that they have applied to public policy making. *JEMS* publishes public policy studies, particularly those emphasizing the effects of given policies on the strategy of the firm.

The managers of firms must decide the quantity and variety of goods to produce, thus determining the scale and scope of the firm. In addition, managers select product characteristics, the production technology to be used, and the mix of capital, labor, and productive inputs. Further, managers establish or modify the organizational structure of the firm, choosing lines of authority and communication, incentives, accounting methods, and other rules. The firm's managers seek out sources of financing in capital markets, specialized personnel in labor markets, and resources, services, and equipment in factor markets. Finally, the firm's managers identify potential customers and communicate with them through pricing, sales efforts, and marketing channels.

Management strategy is often interdisciplinary because the manager is responsible for coordinating the functional areas of the firm, which are generally studied by specialists in accounting, finance, marketing, and organization behavior. Economic theory and econometric analysis of the firm can provide a unifying set of approaches and research methods or at least a common language. The investigation of applied strategy problems faced by managers can provide a common purpose. Management strategy as a field of study is characterized by a unique set of questions on how firms compete and how managers design organizations. *JEMS* articles help to define and extend the field of management strategy.

Important Changes and the Road Ahead

The Internet has changed the publishing process for most journals. Until recently, I kept hard copies of all of the major journals, and I well remember the day that I threw out most of them. University libraries provide researchers with online access to journals, and the connection between search engines and online academic journals allows researchers to use their computers to make a rapid search through many journals and archive articles. Hard copies are no longer necessary, and library access often displaces individual subscriptions. Physical trips to the library also are replaced by virtual visits to online journals.

For *JEMS*, online access has meant a much wider readership, and downloads and citations to *JEMS* articles have increased substantially. John Wiley & Sons' massive Wiley Online Library, with over 1,500 journals and greater online access to content, helps to showcase the journal Thanks to the efforts of Wiley-Blackwell, *JEMS* is in practically every academic library. Generally, online publishing has generated significant benefits from ease of access to electronic data bases and the use of search engines. Online publishing is not without its critics, however. Publishers bundle journals and charge libraries based on usage. There are concerns that electronic publishing results in market concentration in publishing and narrows the range of journals that are available through libraries (Jeon and Menicucci 2006, 2009). In addition, online searching may encourage scientific consensus, with fewer authors being cited and older articles being neglected (Evans 2008). Trends in citation patterns coincide with the rise of online publishing and need not be caused by search engines. Some of these effects may be due to other factors, such as an absence of the history of economic thought in graduate programs and a growing tendency to cite the most recent article in a stream of literature.

At the same time that the *JEMS* submission process went online with ScholarOne, the journal introduced its new Web site at http://www.kellogg.northwestern.edu/research/journals/jems/index.htm. The Web site introduces prospective readers and authors to *JEMS*'s distinguished editorial board and the journal's conference activities. *JEMS* will continue to introduce new topics and break new ground. There are many issues and questions to explore at the intersection between economics and business. As *JEMS* comes of age, the journal is still very young with much more to learn and discover.

References

Azar, Ofer H., and David M. Brock. 2008. A Citation-Based Ranking of Strategic Management Journals. *Journal of Economics & Management Strategy* 17 (3):781–802.

Coase, Ronald. 2006. The Conduct of Economics: The Example of Fisher Body and General Motors. *Journal of Economics & Management Strategy* 15 (2):255–278.

Evans, James A. 2008. Electronic Publication and the Narrowing of Science and Scholarship. *Science* 321 (5887):395–399.

Jeon, Doh-Shin, and Domenico Menicucci. 2006. Bundling Electronic Journals and Competition among Publishers. *Journal of the European Economic Association* 4 (5):1038–1083.

Jeon, Doh-Shin, and Domenico Menicucci. 2009. Interconnection among Academic Journal Websites: Multilateral versus Bilateral Interconnection. Working paper, Toulouse School of Economics.

Spulber, Daniel F. 1992. Economic Analysis and Management Strategy: A Survey. *Journal of Economics & Management Strategy* 1 (3):535–574.

Spulber, Daniel F. 1994. Economic Analysis and Management Strategy: A Survey Continued. *Journal of Economics & Management Strategy* 3 (2):355–406.

Spulber, Daniel F. 2009. *The Theory of the Firm: Microeconomics with Endogenous Entrepreneurs, Firms, Markets and Organizations.* Cambridge: Cambridge University Press.

9

Reflections on Being a Journal Editor

Lawrence J. White

Journal editors serve as gate keepers for any academic discipline because journals are important vehicles for the spreading of ideas and information within the discipline. For many disciplines, they provide indicia of the professional standing of faculty at colleges and universities. These characteristics of journals are probably more important for the economics discipline than for some other disciplines because books are less important for economics than for some other disciplines.

So what does it take to be an editor of an economics journal? What do editors do, and how do they do it? What do they think and feel? What philosophy guides them?

After reading all of the chapters in this book, the reader should have a better idea of the answers to these questions. In this chapter, I offer my take on them.

My Background and My Editorships

My Background
I was trained as an industrial organization (IO) economist, receiving my Ph.D. from Harvard University in 1969. I spent fifteen months working abroad in Pakistan and Indonesia and then taught as an assistant professor in Princeton University's economics department from 1970 to 1976. In the fall of 1976, I moved to New York University's Graduate School of Business Administration (now the Stern School of Business) and its economics department, where I have been ever since.

During my years at NYU, I have been fortunate to have had the opportunity to have served in the U.S. government three times. From 1978 to 1979, I served on the senior staff of the President's Council of Economic Advisers, where my responsibility was primarily in the environmental and other microeconomics-oriented regulatory area. From

1982 to 1983, I served as the chief economist of the Antitrust Division of the U.S. Department of Justice, where I managed a staff of forty economists, who provided the economics input into the division's investigations and prosecutions of antitrust cases.

Finally, from November 1986 through August 1989, I was one of three board members on the Federal Home Loan Bank Board (FHLBB), which was the agency that regulated the savings and loan (S&L) industry and that also provided deposit insurance for S&Ls. At that time, the S&L industry was recognized as facing severe financial difficulties, so I received a quick, firsthand immersion in the nuances and difficulties of financial regulation and in the realities of asymmetric information in financial services and financial regulation. The FHLBB position led me to a new field of research—financial services regulation—that I have continued to pursue, alongside my older interests in IO and its policy applications in antitrust and other regulatory areas.

My Editorships

At various times in my professional career, I have served as a journal editor. From 1984 to 1987 and again from 1990 to 1995, I was the North American Editor of the *Journal of Industrial Economics*. In the summer of 2004, I began serving as the General Editor of the *Review of Industrial Organization*, a position that (as of the summer of 2013) I still hold.

In the fall of 1983, just after I had returned to NYU from the Justice Department's Antitrust Division, a friend asked me whether I might be interested in joining with another friend to enter a bid to take over the editorial responsibilities of the *Bell Journal of Economics* (*BJE*), which had been a product of the Bell Laboratories economics group since 1970. In the wake of the antitrust division's 1982 consent decree with American Telephone and Telegraph Company (AT&T) to break up the company, the journal would be transferred to the RAND Corporation in 1984. This transfer had the collateral consequences of greatly reducing the support for economists and economics at AT&T (and the Bell Labs).

After some thought, I decided not to explore the possibilities of proceeding further. I did not have a strong vision of how to run a journal, and the magnitude of the *BJE*'s operations seemed daunting.[1]

In the spring of 1984, however, I was approached by the North American editorial board of the *Journal of Industrial Economics* to find out whether I would be interested in taking the position of Managing

Editor (U.S.) of the *JIE*. The previous Managing Editor, H. Michael Mann, had recently died, and a replacement was needed (and no one on the editorial board apparently wanted the full responsibility).

The *JIE* position seemed more manageable to me. The *JIE* had been published since 1952 with a British General Editor,[2] but it had had a strong North American presence on its editorial board from the beginning.[3] This presence was converted into the managing editor position in the early 1970s, with a great deal of autonomy with respect to editorial decisions concerning the approximately one hundred annual submissions (about half of the overall flow of submissions to the *JIE*) that came from authors in North America. The British General Editor, Donald Hay, was supportive and seemed like a good man to work with. The members of the North American board—Morris Adelman, Richard Caves, F. M. Scherer, and Richard Schmalensee—were a first-class group and promised their strong support.

I accepted the offer of a five-year term (with a changed title to North American Editor so that Canadians would not feel excluded) that would start in the summer of 1984. My one proviso was that I could accept future government positions. Because I had recently served in two positions in the U.S. government that were immensely interesting and productive for my academic career, I wanted the flexibility to be able to accept any future government position that might (albeit, with an extremely low probability) be offered to me, without anyone's feeling that I had reneged on my commitment to the *JIE*.

That opportunity did indeed arise in the fall of 1986 when I was asked to take the position as a board member on the FHLBB. I continued as North American Editor for the *JIE* into early 1987 but asked Almarin Phillips if he would be interested in taking the position. Fortunately, he agreed.

After leaving the FHLBB in August 1989, I returned to NYU. I felt a continuing loyalty and obligation to the *JIE* and also saw the editorship as a way of keeping abreast of developments in the IO discipline. When I asked Al Phillips and Stephen Davies (the General Editor who had succeeded Donald Hay) if I could reclaim the North American editorship, they both agreed, and I served a five-year term, from the summer of 1990 to the summer of 1995. Severin Borenstein and Joseph Farrell succeeded me.

My current stint as General Editor of the *Review of Industrial Organization* (*RIO*) began in the summer of 2004, after the previous General Editor (John Kwoka)[4] and the leadership of the Industrial Organization

Society (for which the *RIO* is the official journal) asked if I would be interested.

What I Do, How I Do It, and Why I Do It

One of the goals of every journal editor is to publish good, informative, thought-provoking papers that cause members of the profession to read the journal's articles on a regular basis and to submit their best papers for publication in that journal. Equivalently, the goal is for one's journal to be perceived by the profession as a top-tier journal. I am no exception in that regard.

But how does one do that? Especially puzzling, at least for me, is how an editor changes a profession's perceptions if a journal is not already perceived as a top-tier journal.

When a journal is starting, everyone involved with it wants to start as strongly as possible with an editor who is recognized to be an intellectual leader in the field, an editorial board that includes leading members of the field, and a set of articles in the initial issue or two that meet the above criteria.[5] But what happens when an editor is managing a journal that has been around for decades and is generally perceived as not being top-tier? That is the position in which I found myself at the *JIE* and again at the *RIO*.

At both journals, my major strategy has been to put myself in the shoes of a submitting author (a role that I have played many times in my professional career) and ask, "What do authors want (short of an acceptance at a top-tier journal)?" It has always seemed to me that authors want a reasonably rapid initial editorial decision from a journal; if the initial decision is negative, a clear explanation why and helpful comments for improvement from referees; if the initial decision is positive (an invitation to revise and resubmit), clear instructions from the editor as to what is expected and how to interpret the referee reports; and a high probability that the revise-and-resubmit process will involve only a few rounds and will have a favorable ultimate outcome.

Accordingly, a great deal of my journal-focused efforts have involved trying to satisfy these concerns with the hope that the word will spread throughout the profession that the journal of which I am the editor has these favorable characteristics—and that this will lead better authors to send better papers to the journal.[6] In addition, I have encouraged the members of the journal's editorial board to organize symposia on specific topics within IO. Interesting topics may attract more attention to the journal (by readers and authors), and the symposia are a potential vehicle for attracting higher-quality authors who might not otherwise submit articles to the journal.

But underlying all of this has to be an editorial viewpoint on my part—a statement of what I am looking for and why. I start there and then proceed to how I try to implement that viewpoint.

What I Am Looking For
I start with an advantage. For both of my editorial positions, I have edited an industrial organization (IO) journal. Given my graduate training and professional research, this means that I am reasonably familiar with the major topics in the field and the interesting questions that are worth exploring.[7] Further, I am willing to define IO fairly broadly (even if it takes me beyond the traditional IO areas with which I am the most familiar).

Throughout my professional career, I have been more interested in empirical research and in policy applications than in theory developments, and I carry those interests—some might say biases—into my editorial perspective. In the language of international trade, my comparative advantage is in understanding empirical testing and policy applications and the ways that articles in these areas can be made better and clearer.

I understand and appreciate the role and value that good creative theory can play in helping the profession develop and expand its horizons. The developments in asymmetric information (in the 1970s and 1980s) and the developments in auction theory (more recently) both come to mind as theories that expand economists' horizons and help us understand the world around us. Especially with respect to asymmetric information, they also help to refute the claim that economists' models assume that markets work perfectly and do not reflect real-world imperfections. I am interested in fresh theory that can help shape intuitions (as well as policy) with respect to how the world works.

Nevertheless, much theory leaves me cold. For example, most efforts to apply Cournot models to various market situations leave me with the impression that the Cournot assumption was chosen because of its mathematical tractability and not because the author believed that it provided a good reflection of how real-world firms actually react to each other. I have even less patience when authors use these Cournot models to offer antitrust policy recommendations. Further, the demonstration that the introduction of asymmetric information into some aspect of a competitive market may cause welfare to worsen is by now not a cutting-edge or earth-shaking result, and I am loathe to consider such an article seriously for publication.

Although that does leave me leaning more toward empirically oriented articles, some categories of empirical articles try my patience as well. Sometimes authors are sloppy in their use of data. They address too few issues about weaknesses or ambiguities in their data. They do not examine extreme data points and ask themselves whether those values are realistic or whether they represent an error somewhere along the way. Sometimes they do not describe or explain their data in ways that would help the reader understand what they have done and why. In the words of a colleague, such authors "don't respect the data."

Another problematic category of empirical articles is the effort to estimate production functions or cost functions (or to estimate measures of productivity that are based on underlying production or cost functions) where the author is using a broad array of heterogeneous firms. The first problem is that the author is forcing a single set of parameters on a set of firms that are highly likely to have diverse production technologies (and thus have substantially differing parameters). The next problem is that the author is forced to use either a firm's sales or its value added as the measure of output. Both measures pose obvious problems as representations of output, which few such authors seem prepared to acknowledge. Finally, the input variables for these efforts are usually just broad measures of employees (with no efforts to measure human capital) and accounting-based measures of physical capital and (where sales is the output measure) aggregate purchased materials. Again, the problems are almost always too severe.

When such a paper is submitted (and my initial scan of the paper indicates that it is in one of these categories),[8] I have come to the conclusion that a desk rejection is the best course of action. The probability that I will publish the paper is so remote that I do not want to waste the time and efforts of referees and delay unnecessarily my editorial response to the author.[9] My rejection letter to the author explains why I have found the paper to be unsuitable for publication in the journal.

What I Do[10]

At the top of my list of job responsibilities has been an effort to reach initial editorial decisions and transmit them to authors in a timely (relatively rapid) fashion. My resolve has been strengthened by hearing many stories of authors (especially young authors, for whom the tenure clock is ticking) who wait for inordinately long periods for an initial decision from a journal. My goal is to have a mean and median elapsed time of two or three months from the date of initial receipt of a manuscript to the first editorial response to the author, with no author ever waiting longer than six months to receive an initial editorial decision.[11]

Next, I want authors to feel that they are getting clear messages from me. When authors receive a rejection letter, I want them to know why I rejected their manuscript. When I do a desk rejection, I explain my reasons. When I reject on the basis of unenthusiastic or negative referee reports, I rely on those reports but may add a few additional comments of my own, based on my quick read of the paper (which is motivated partly to make sure that the referees have not missed anything important and partly to see if I can add anything to help the author).

When the authors receive a revise-and-resubmit letter, I want them to have a clear idea of what they need to do. Some referees' reports are clear about the revisions that are needed, but sometimes the reports are unclear and even mutually contradictory. In any event, I read the manuscript sufficiently to form my own impressions of what needs to be done—which may reinforce the recommendations of the referees, add to those of the referees, or contradict those of the referees. My letter includes my own instructions in addition to the referees' reports. And I always ask the author to send the revised submission with a letter that addresses all of the points that the referees and I have raised.

Finally, I want the referees to feel a further involvement with the journal that goes beyond the submission of their reports. Accordingly, the referees receive a copy of the letter that I send to the author (which indicates my decision, reasoning, and suggestions) and (anonymous) copies of both referees' reports. I also want the referees to feel assured that their anonymity has been protected.[12] Whenever possible, I copy and paste the text of their reports into the body of the electronic message that I send to authors, which removes the potential fingerprints of a referee's document so that their identity cannot be discovered. In the few instances where the text of the report cannot be copied and pasted into the message to the author but instead must be attached, I remove any identifying fingerprints in the background of the file.[13]

I try to do an immediate triage when an article is submitted. When it is an article that I think does not have a reasonable chance of being published, I exercise the desk-reject option described above. My ideal is to email the appropriate letter to authors within a few days of receipt of their manuscript submissions. More likely, because of backlogs, other deadlines, teaching, research, and writing obligations, the letter may take a few weeks or even a few months to be sent.

When I believe that an article has sufficient potential merit that it does not qualify for a desk rejection, I send it out to two referees who I usually select from three pools—authors of recent relevant articles that are cited in the references, authors who have recently published on the same topic in the *RIO*, or authors who I know have expertise in this article's area. I ask referees to provide a report within six weeks.[14] Not all requests are immediately acknowledged, which requires follow-up. If a prospective referee responds negatively (or never answers at all), then I have to start all over again. And not all referees who initially agree to write a report actually follow through (despite repeated email nudges from me at seven weeks and again in the subsequent few weeks). If a referee has not delivered a promised report by the tenth or eleventh week, I face the dilemma of whether to start over or to rely on the single report that arrived on time. My decision to find a new referee usually depends on the quality of the single report in hand and the proximity of my self-imposed six-month requirement to deliver an editorial decision to authors.

I generally send a revise-and-resubmit decision to an author only if I believe that there is a fairly high probability that the revision is going to be publishable (perhaps with an additional round or two to clean up some matters that I did not notice in the initial draft and for some overall clarification and polishing). This high standard is another response to the stories of authors (and my own personal experiences) who have gone through three or four rounds of revisions with a journal editor and still received an eventual rejection letter. In the few instances where I think that the success of the revision is considerably more risky (but the value of the successful revision is sufficiently high), I try to convey that added riskiness to the author in my initial R&R letter.

Because my R&R letter states clearly what I expect to be accomplished in the revision, I usually do not send the revised manuscript back to referees. This feels to me to be the counterpart to the desk-reject issue: I do not want to waste referees' time and efforts on refinements when I already have a clear idea of what is needed.

Putting Principles into Practice

I have been the general editor of the *Review of Industrial Organization* for nine years, since the summer of 2004. The annual flow of over-the-transom submissions[15] is approximately 200 to 250 per year, so I have had to make editorial decisions on about 2,000 manuscripts. After a year of transition, I have kept the mean and median times of first editorial response to authors within my goal of two to three months, and only a (literal) handful of elapsed response times have exceeded six months. The percentage of R&R editorial responses has been in the 15 to 20 percent range.

I am always looking for ways to make the *RIO* better and to attract better articles from better authors. I like to think that there has been an overall improvement in the quality of papers during my eight years, but I am an interested party.

Notes

1. In 1982, the *Bell Journal of Economics* published fifty-one articles plus two major book reviews. It probably received about three hundred manuscripts a year. In a relatively short time—since it began in 1970 under the editorship of Paul MacAvoy—it had acquired an excellent reputation as a first-line place for industrial organization articles.

2. The first General Editor was P. W. S. Andrews, who was at Oxford University.

3. Of the five members of the initial editorial board at the *Journal of Industrial Economics*, three—Joel Dean, Robert Heflebower, and Edward Mason—were based in the United States.

4. Before him, the *Review of Industrial Organization* had been under the long-standing General Editorship of William G. Shepherd. The origins of the *RIO* go back to 1984, when Stanley Boyle was the Editor for volume 1, number 1. Boyle was the General Editor for an earlier journal, the *Industrial Organization Review*, which began publishing in 1973 (and ceased publishing in 1980) and might be considered a predecessor to the *RIO*.

5. That, at least, is the way that I perceive the recipe for the launching of the *Bell Journal of Economics and Management Science* in 1970. The *BJEMS* soon became recognized as the leading journal in IO, and it has maintained that position through its transition into the *RAND Journal of Economics*.

6. This reputation may also lead not-so-good authors to send more not-so-good papers to the journal. But I am willing to accept this increased manuscript flow as the price for getting better manuscripts.

7. Ultimately, these matters are subjective, especially at the margin. I take comfort in the fact that there are a number of IO and related journals in existence, and if I make some type 2 errors (that is, I reject a few articles that objectively have merit), then authors can turn to other journals.

8. An additional category is a paper that does not really address IO issues and is better suited for the audiences of a journal in other fields. For example, a paper might really be more about labor economics or international trade than IO.

9. At an annual conference of the European Association for Research in Industrial Economics (EARIE) a few years ago, I participated on a panel of editors of IO journals who discussed their editorial practices. One editor expressed concern that desk rejections, although important and necessary, were nevertheless unfair to authors and should be used only sparingly. My memory is that I offered a defense of desk rejections at the time but that I subsequently wished that my defense had been stronger, along the following lines. Desk rejections by editors economize on referees' time and efforts and provide faster editorial responses to authors. There are numerous alternative journals—general-interest journals, IO journals, theory-specialization journals, empirical specialization journals—to which a desk-rejected author can turn. And if the editors of multiple journals independently reach desk-rejection decisions on a manuscript, perhaps those decisions can tell the author something important.

10. Although most of the things that I do at the *RIO* were also my practices at the *JIE*, here I describe my operations as I currently conduct them at the *RIO*. One big change initially was the use of email and attachments for all author submissions (and subsequent resubmissions), author-related communications, referee requests, and referee reports. Starting in 2010, the *RIO* (at the request of Springer, its publisher) converted to a system of online submissions. All of this has substantially sped all of the steps in the editorial process. I sometimes think back to my days as North American editor of the *JIE* in the mid-1980s and again in the early 1990s, when everything was done through the physical mail and wonder, "How did we do it?"

11. The "time to first editorial response" is the most interesting and most important data that I collect and report to my board of editors. The other interesting statistic is the percentage of manuscripts for which that first editorial response is a revise-and-resubmit letter. Any other statistic is largely uninteresting (at least, as a measure of editorial activity). The length of time from the R&R letter to eventual publication is as much a function of how long authors take in their revisions as it is a function of the editor's delay. The number of additional R&R rounds is also a function of the authors' efforts as well as the editor's, and the same is true for the percentage of R&R manuscripts that are eventually published.

12. I have never tried to double-blind the process, which would block the name of the author from the referees. In the world of easy Internet searches, the referees can probably find the author's identity by searching on the title of the paper. Even before Internet searches, references to working papers and other unpublished documents were clues as to an author's identity.

13. Occasionally, when referees have (apparently) inadvertently identified themselves in the report (for example, by referring in the first person to one of their own studies), I ask them if this was intentional or whether they would like to modify the report to remove the identification.

14. Anything shorter than six weeks feels too short and an undue burden on the prospective referee. (The *RIO* does not have a payment system for referees.) But the difference between anything longer and six weeks feels small, so providing any longer turnaround period (say, eight weeks or even three months) would be

unlikely to improve the likelihood that the prospective referee will agree to provide a report.

15. In addition, there are invited papers, which can arise through a number of routes. In the annual "Antitrust and Regulatory Roundup" (which was initiated by my predecessor, John Kwoka), the chief economists of the three major antitrust and regulatory agencies in the United States and of the antitrust authority for the European Union write essays about the important issues that their agencies' economists have faced. Other sources include special symposia that are arranged by or at the suggestion of a member of the editorial board (with editorial selection and supervision exercised by the special editor(s) for those symposia), a collection of papers from a conference on an IO-related topic (with the conference organizer exercising editorial selection), and the keynote address at the annual International Industrial Organization Conference.

Macroeconomics

10

The Internal Politics of Journal Editing

William A. Barnett

I have been invited to write an essay on my experiences as founder and editor of the Cambridge University Press journal *Macroeconomic Dynamics*. I have decided to focus the essay on my experiences in starting up the journal. Few economists who have not themselves started a new journal are aware of the nature of the process and its sometimes complicated academic politics.

The Conflict

As is known to many economists, there was a conflict between another well-known journal and its society at around the time that I started up *Macroeconomic Dynamics* (MD) in 1996 and 1997. The journal was the *Journal of Economic Dynamics and Control* (JEDC). The society was called the Society for Economic Dynamics and Control (SEDC). I was a member of the society and knew people involved on both sides of the conflict. The society wanted to be able to select that journal's editorial board, which presumably meant changing existing members. But the society did not own the journal. Elsevier owned the journal and wanted to retain control of the editorial board membership. Consequently, the society approached Academic Press with a proposal to start up a new journal, with the society being authorized to appoint the editorial board. Tom Cooley was to be the managing editor, and there was to be a heavier emphasis on real business-cycle theory than was the case with the *JEDC*. Academic Press turned down the proposal.

There were bad feelings about this conflict, both within the society and on the journal's editorial board. I called an eminent officer of the society regarding the society's concerns, and I also called Steve Turnovsky, one of the *JEDC* journal's editors at the time, regarding the journal's concerns. I explained that I could start up a new journal that would be purely scientific and neutral regarding the differences of opinion between the society and the journal. I explained that I could propose the new journal to Cambridge University Press, with which I had good relations as editor of one of that publisher's monograph series. I was advised by the society's officer and by Steve that it would be a good idea and that I should do it as a possible means of solving the problem. I was concerned about how much of a commitment of my time would be required and whether that commitment was justified. As a result, I asked the society's officer whether the plans to try to start up another new journal by the society would stop if I produced a neutral scientific macroeconomic journal with the name *Macroeconomic Dynamics*. He said that, yes, it would stop and that the plans were only talk.

First New Journal

I proposed the new journal to Cambridge University Press, which accepted the proposal. Next, I needed to select a board of editors. I selected a group of advisory editors and associate editors with the intent of spanning all areas of good macroeconomic science without any prejudice or identifiable agenda in methodology, geography, or politics. Then the problems began. I was lobbied by various advisory editors and associate editors to make changes in the editorial board. The degree of factionalism surprised me. There were attempts to change the balance toward a particular methodological or political view and also to change the balance geographically, nationalistically, regionally, racially, or ethnically. There also were gender-based pressures. Sometimes the lobbying was directed at perceived underrepresentation of a particular group. When I found that the criticism was justified, I asked for suggestions of economists to be added and invited additional board members from that group. More disturbing were pressures to eliminate a minority from representation so that the journal would represent solely the interests of a particular group, as is the case with many other journals, such as the *Journal of Post Keynesian Economics*, the *Quarterly Journal of Austrian Economics*, and various regional economics journals (such as those published in languages other than English). I was particularly surprised by the lobbying from some of the European board members to discredit and thereby eliminate board members from other European countries. Because a fundamental purpose of this journal was to avoid becoming identified with any such faction or group, I often did the exact opposite by increasing the size of the minority so that the minority no longer could be marginalized or ignored. After it became clear that attempts to eliminate a minority were counterproductive, that kind of lobbying ended. As a result, the editorial board became very large and very diverse, with only the sophistication and high-tech competency of all members holding them together. To this day, the editorial board of *Macroeconomic Dynamics* is unusually large and diverse.[1]

Editorial Board Selection Problems

All seemed to be peaceful, and the journal startup was successful. I then was informed by SEDC's officer, during a telephone call, that he objected to having econometricians on the board of advisory editors. He did not object to having associate editors who were econometricians but felt that I should not be listening to the advice of econometricians on the board of advisory editors. The advisory editors included a minority of econometricians, such as Peter Phillips and Ron Gallant, who are among the world's most important econometricians. The SEDC's officer and one of his coauthors also were among the advisory editors of *Macroeconomic Dynamics*. At the same time, Cambridge University Press told me that the board of advisory editors was too large. Based on the pressure from Cambridge University Press and my deep respect for the SEDC officer's contributions to the field of macroeconomics, I removed from the board of advisory editors all of the econometricians except for Mark Watson and Adrian Pagan, whose contributions to macroeconomics have been major. Evidently, that was not good enough for the SEDC officer, who resigned from the board. His coauthor did not resign and is on the journal's board to the present day. The SEDC began again to plan for its own new journal.

Second New Journal

The SEDC revised its proposal to Academic Press for a new journal. Instead of proposing only one editor, Tom Cooley, the society proposed a board of coeditors, including all of the present and recent past presidents of the society, such as Ed Prescott and Tom Sargent, along with Tom Cooley. Although most of the coeditors were largely window dressing and Tom Cooley was to be the managing editor, Academic

Press accepted the new proposal. The title of the new journal was to be *Economic Dynamics*, and the society was to change its name to the Society for Economic Dynamics (SED), removing the words "and Control." But Steve Turnovsky, who had close ties with the *JEDC*, told me that the proposed title of the new SED journal was objectionable to the *JEDC* and in particular to its publisher. At the time, the *JEDC* was divided into two sections, one of which was named "Economic Dynamics." As a result, Elsevier, the publisher of the *JEDC*, had its attorneys contact Academic Press with objections to the proposed title for the new journal. A few weeks later, Steve called me to say that Academic Press had decided to change the name of the new journal to *Dynamic Macroeconomics*. I was under the impression that the information about the new title came from one of Tom Cooley's students. Steve suggested that I inform Cambridge University Press about the new title, so I called and explained that Academic Press was planning to start a new journal with the name *Dynamic Macroeconomics* and that I was editor for Cambridge University Press of the journal *Macroeconomic Dynamics*.

Resolution of the Journal Title-Selection Conflict

Following the call by the Cambridge University Press attorneys to Academic Press about objections to the name *Dynamic Macroeconomics*, Steve unexpectedly received a phone call from Academic Press asking him for a suggestion for the new journal's title. He suggested the title *Review of Economic Dynamics*. In making this suggestion, he had in mind a somewhat parallel (and harmonious) situation by which the *Journal of International Economics* was published by Elsevier and the *Review of International Economics* was published by Blackwell (now part of Wiley). Academic Press accepted that suggestion, and the journal *Review of Economic Dynamics* (*RED*) was born and has subsequently evolved into a fine journal. There now were three journals with related objectives—the *JEDC*, *RED*, and *MD*. All that had transpired had its origins in research on the time inconsistency of optimal control policy. That research had motivated much of the former SEDC's objections to the *JEDC*'s publication of papers on optimal control policy and to the role of optimal control theorists, such as David Kendrick and Steve Turnovsky, in founding and editing the *JEDC*. Paradoxically, both *RED* and the *JEDC* now are published by Elsevier, which has bought Academic Press.

Interviews Series

At the time I started *MD*, I had to select the sections (such as book reviews, surveys, and notes) that would be included in the journal. I observed that no peer-reviewed professional journal was publishing interviews with macroeconomists or microeconomists, although *Econometric Theory* was occasionally publishing interviews with econometricians, and the *American Statistician* was publishing interviews with statisticians. I decided to add an interviews section, which occasionally published interviews with important macroeconomists and with famous microeconomists whose work has been influential in macroeconomics. The choice of those to be interviewed was to depend on support of the journal's advisory editors.

Problems arose immediately. It was proposed that the first economist to be interviewed should be Wassily Leontief because he was at an advanced age and his health was failing. When I proposed interviewing Leontief to the advisory editors, there was much opposition to the invitation on the grounds that he was primarily a microeconomist. With little time left to debate the matter and because of his importance in the profession, I decided to adopt a very broad definition of macroeconomics as aggregated microeconomics. There was no other outlet for publication of interviews of famous microeconomists. Leontief's interview was the first we published.

Another microeconomist who was interviewed early in the evolution of the interviews series was David Cass at the University of Pennsylvania. His interview included use of a four-letter word in a hostile statement about a former dean at Carnegie Mellon University. The dean's name was mentioned. Cambridge University Press called me and asked if I could get David to tone down his language. He refused and demanded publication of the word exactly as included, on the grounds that the interview was a quotation that could not be changed by the editor, copyeditor, or publisher. Cambridge University did not like the explanation but agreed that it had to be accepted. The controversial words were typeset in the interview as "f--- you."

From then on, when I invited anyone to be interviewed, I explained the Cass precedent and said that the people who were interviewed for the journal could say whatever they wanted in a peer-reviewed journal without any peer review at all. Subsequently, everyone who has been invited to be interviewed has accepted, except for Jean-Michel Grandmont. He complained that the interviews included too many Americans and not enough Europeans. I pointed out that a large percentage of those we had interviewed were born in Europe and moved to America before winning their Nobel Prizes (for example, Leontief and Modigliani). I did not understand how Jean-Michel's refusal to be interviewed in France was in the best interests of increasing the number of Europeans interviewed within Europe.

The interview series turned into a collection of interviews of many of the stars of the profession. As a result of popular demand, Paul Samuelson and I subsequently collected some of the most interesting of those interviews in a book called *Inside the Economist's Mind* (Barnett and Samuelson 2007). Translations of that book have been published in Korean, Russian, Chinese, and German, and the book has its own blog.[2]

In addition to the *MD* interviews section, which is unusual among economics journals, *Macroeconomic Dynamics* includes one other unusual section—the *MD* vintage articles section, which publishes old unpublished papers that have become citation classics and heavily cited working papers. Such papers often no longer can meet normal peer review in comparably high-quality journals because they tend to overlook more recent research. But because of their established importance, reflected in heavy citations to them, they are viewed by *Macroeconomic Dynamics* as meriting easy access in the public domain. The resulting *MD* vintage articles section appears infrequently but is very successful and provides a public service that is much appreciated by the authors who cite those important papers.

The Present and Future

Although the morphing of one journal into three had its origins in an internal conflict within the profession, the driving force for growth of all three journals since then has been the explosive growth in high-quality scientific research in macroeconomics throughout the world, including mainland China, Taiwan, Singapore, and Hong Kong. All three journals have continued growing rapidly and harmoniously and playing key roles in disseminating high-quality research in macroeconomic dynamics.

Did I expect any of this when I agreed to start up *Macroeconomic Dynamics*? Not at all.

Notes

1. See http://econ.tepper.cmu.edu/barnett/MDboard.html.
2. See http://economistmind.blogspot.com.

References

Barnett, William A., and Paul A. Samuelson, eds. 2007. *Inside the Economist's Mind: Conversations with Eminent Economists.* Hoboken, NJ: Wiley-Blackwell.

Methodology of Economics

11

Reptilian Economists of the World Unite: A Tolerance Manifesto

Richard V. Adkisson

Lizards, lizards, large and small:
The Econ tribe needs one and all.

A graduate school colleague, Les Manns, was prone to refer to certain others in the economics profession as big lizards. We never really discussed the definition of *big lizard*, but the term seemed to refer to economists who were regularly published, held offices in professional organizations, had a reputation beyond the department, and were actively engaged in a community of scholarship. From our graduate student perspective, almost everyone looked like a big lizard. Now that many of us have met the minimal graduate school standards of lizardness, we have seen that whatever our own degree of lizardness, there are always bigger lizards scampering around the academic terrarium.

There is a hierarchy in the economics profession—degrees of lizardness, if you please. The big lizards are graduates of the top programs, publish in the top journals, and work in the top departments. Likewise, paradigms and methodological approaches are measured by their distance from mainstream conventions. However, it is less clear that being a big lizard equates with having significant social impact. I argue below that smaller lizards are often more influential and have greater social impact than would be suggested by standard measures of economic lizardness.

My intent is not to ridicule the big lizards. The profession needs them. Rather, the points I hope to make are that small to medium-size lizards often play important roles and that pluralism in theory and method enriches the economics profession.

The chapter begins by looking at the tendency to define quality and influence in a way that overvalues the economics of the top levels of the economic hierarchy and discounts the value of the lower levels. Then I reflect on my experiences as a professional economist and journal editor to argue that placement below the top does not doom one to a meaningless, unfruitful, and uninfluential career. A career in the lower levels of the hierarchy can be as, or more, influential as a career at the top.

Status and Attitudes at the Top of the Economics Hierarchy

Publications in top journals and high citation counts lead to high rankings for individual economists and for economics departments (Rupp and McKinney 2002; Davis, Huston, and Patterson 2001; Dusansky and Vernon 1998). Graduate students in the top economics programs are socialized to aspire to publication in top journals (Colander and Klamer 1987; Colander 2005). The strong emphasis on "topness" brings at least three unintended consequences. First, many departments tie promotion and tenure decisions to publication in the top ten, twenty, or thirty journals, leaving many supplicants unsatisfied (Mixon and Sawyer 2005; Fender, Taylor, and Burke 2005). Second, the quality of an article is often judged by where it is published or who the author is as much as by the content and usefulness of the article (Beed and Beed 1996). Third, and the one of primary interest here, is to draw distinctions, often invidious, between those who do and those who do not publish in top journals and graduate from or work in top departments.

(No) Room for All

The rank order of the top journals varies from analysis to analysis, but the topmost group almost always includes the *American Economic Review*, the *Journal of Political Economy*, *Econometrica*, the *Quarterly Journal of Economics*, and the *Review of Economics and Statistics* (Axarloglou and Theoharakis 2003). A search of the contents of these five journals reveals that they published 224 articles in 2007.[1] On average, that is about ten full articles per issue. Based on this average, even expanding the list to the top twenty journals would only leave nine hundred or so annual spots for articles in top journals.

Perhaps nine hundred or even 224 articles are more than enough to disseminate the true advances in economic knowledge in one year. Still, this volume would leave most economists with no outlet for their work. Stephen A. Woodbury (2000) showed that 60 percent of Ph.D.-level economists were employed in academia. In 1995, that 60 percent represented over eleven thousand Ph.D. economists with academic employment.[2] Granted, not all academic economists have active research agendas, but thousands of them regularly attend and present papers at the annual meeting of the Allied Social Science Association in January, and many others participate in various association and regional meetings throughout the year. This seems to indicate a high if not universal level of scholarly engagement. Not all active researchers can publish in the top journals, and most of them do not.

Top Quality?

Focus on the top journals sometimes presumes that the highest-quality, highest-impact articles are published in the top journals. This may often be the case, but there is evidence suggesting that it is not always so (Axarloglou and Theoharakis 2003; Beed and Beed 1996; Smyth 1999). Many articles that have proven that some seminal and other highly cited articles were rejected by one or more top journals (Gans and Shepherd 1994, Simonovits 2005). Some report empirical results that cannot stand the scrutiny of replication (Dewald, Thursby, and Anderson 1986). Geoffrey M. Hodgson and Harry Rothman (1999) suggest that the system of top journals may actually retard innovation and pluralism in economics. Others show concern for the usefulness and fairness of the refereeing process (Laband 1990; Hamermesh 1994; Laband and Piette 1994; Azar 2006). Some are concerned about favoritism in the selection process (Medoff 2003; Mixon 1998). Much, though not all, of this criticism and suspicion is directed at the top journals. With a certain cynicism arising around the editorial process, it seems no wonder that the publishing process has begun to be discussed as a game between authors and editors (Faria 2005).

Invidious Distinctions?

Studies of the sociology of economics often focus on what distinguishes the top journals, top economists, and top departments from the pack. This is not unusual. In almost any venture—sports, movies, politics—those who are perceived to be at the top of their game receive disproportionate attention. However, as with some athletic, movie, or political stars, excessive attention can distort one's world view and may lead to a sense of entitlement if not disdain for the great unwashed masses. For example, in discussing the relative value of editorial versus reviewer comments, David N. Laband (1990, 343) writes "editors have proven credentials in most cases, whereas referees do not necessarily, or even probably, come from that end of the talent distribution in economics." Similarly, graduate students at top departments are quietly pressured to suppress their interests in policy work or undergraduate teaching (Colander and Klamer 1987; Colander 2005). Some researchers refer to papers with no subsequent citations (dry holes) as "useless papers" and suggest that an abundance of such papers can be found in the "lesser journals" (Laband, Tollison, and Karahan 2002, 315, 331; Laband and Tollison 2003). The view that uncited papers or papers with few citations are worthless, led David N. Laband, Robert D. Tollison, and Gokhan R. Karahan (2002, 331) to the following conclusion:

There is a huge, albeit implicit, public subsidy for academic research in America—every faculty member employed by a public college or university with a research mission is supported salary-wise by state and/or federal tax dollars. These faculty received course reductions in otherwise required teaching each year in order to promote research. But if much, if not most, of the research produced has little or no impact whatsoever, the implication is both clear and of substantial import: the enormous social investment in research is, by and large, wasted and comes at the expense of time and effort that could have been devoted to providing education.[3]

The tens of thousands of economists who have had rich, fulfilling, and fruitful careers without being published in the top journals and while producing a few dry holes would beg to differ. Many big lizards might disagree as well. References to ends of the talent spectrum, lesser journals, useless research, and forcing students to keep their true career interests in the closet may serve to draw lines of demarcation through the community of economic scholars but seem hardly to serve the instrumental purpose of advancing economic knowledge and applying it in useful ways. In his tongue-in-cheek examination of the econ tribe, Axel Leijonhufvud (1973, 328) noted the following:

Members of high castes are not infrequently found to peck those of lower castes. While such behavior is regarded as in questionable taste, it carries no formal sanctions. A member of a low caste who attempts to peck someone in a higher caste runs more concrete risks—at the extreme, he may be ostracized and lose the privilege of being heard at the tribal midwinter councils.

For an account of life in the lower castes, see Frederic S. Lee (2004).

Economics for the Rest of Us

The case made above may overstate the attitudes of many highly ranked economists, and many economists lower on the hierarchy also have disparaging things to say about the upper crust. Still, as the Leijonhufvud (1973) quote suggests, the upward pecks are easier to ignore than the nagging pecks from above. In what follows, I try to make a case based on evidence, experience, and anecdote that there is plenty of room at the table (or in the terrarium) of economics. Rather than drawing invidious distinctions among economists, journals, and departments, it seems more useful to recognize and respect the fact that there are a variety of important roles to be played in the profession and that professional quality has many dimensions. I provide some examples and arguments to make the case for a pluralistic attitude among economists.

Departmental Variety and Departmental Fit

The economics department at the State University of New York at Albany publishes a directory of 190 departments that offer the Ph.D. in economics or agricultural economics.[4] This directory includes only U.S. and Canadian universities. The economics department of the University of Victoria, Canada, lists an even longer list of non-U.S. departments.[5] Neither list includes the thousands of economics departments that offer only lower degrees. Even if the thirty, forty, or fifty top departments are counted, only a small portion of the world's economists work under top-level conditions, as normally defined. Unless one assumes that all economists in nonranked departments are at the lower end of the talent spectrum, one must conclude that many, if not most, of the talented economists are placed outside the top departments. Likewise, it seems safe to assume great heterogeneity across these many departments (because the University of Chicago, the Massachusetts Institute of Technology, and Harvard University are heterogeneous).

The best new economists might be assumed to go to top departments, but they go elsewhere, too. With respect to departmental placement of talented people and their subsequent career outcomes, Paul Oyer (2006) found evidence that initial placement tended to affect career paths of graduates from top departments. Top researchers in top departments typically begin their careers in top research departments. However, given variations in labor-market conditions, there are times when top graduates are placed in lower-ranked departments than might have been the case in better times. After this happens, their skills tend to evolve to match the needs of their institution, making it difficult or undesirable to move up to more research-oriented, highly ranked departments.

Similarly, the top programs face capacity constraints, meaning that many highly talented students receive their training in lesser-ranked programs. There are also talented people who for reasons of limited geographic mobility, finances, or similar constraints choose to study in lower-ranked programs even when they might qualify for the top programs. Thus, at any given time, there is a cadre of bright and talented graduates who have the skills and desires of the best of the best but not their shiny credentials. Variety in graduate programs generates variety in graduates, even if the graduates are of equal innate ability, background, and desire. I turn to my own department's experience for examples.

I work in a nonelite department. Research is expected, but other demands are strong. We teach a lot, and most of our teaching serves the undergraduate business program (although our graduate programs are growing). We also have substantial demands for service placed on us, and many on the faculty are diverted to applied policy work rather than purely academic research. Our salaries are relatively low. Several on our faculty graduated from programs ranked in the top fifty by Richard Dusansky and Clayton J. Vernon (1998). Several have degrees from nonranked institutions. In spite of heterogeneity in training, all are bright, competent people who have adjusted to the environment in which they were placed. No two are the same. Most are excellent teachers. Many have substantial publication records. Some have substantial local, state, and national policy influence. All work hard and have a role to play in the department. In spite of many differences, the atmosphere is highly collegial. Meanwhile, few have been published on the pages of the top journals, and the Nobel selection committee has yet to call.[6] Many of my professional acquaintances around the world work in similar circumstances.

An anecdote might serve to drive home the importance of departmental fit. The anecdote relates to Paul Oyer's 2006 work and a search process that we conducted in the 1990s. One might assume that any department, perhaps especially a lowly unranked department, would desire to hire as high on the hierarchy as possible. This is not always the case. We advertised for a new assistant professor and had an abundance of applicants. We chose three candidates from the pool for on-campus interviews. Each of the three candidates had freshly minted degrees—two from top-ten departments and one from a department ranked in the thirties range (using Dusansky and Vernon's 1998 rankings). All were talented and well trained. All were decent human beings. On any given day, any of the three could hold their own against any random gathering of top candidates. The one who was hired was the one who best fit our program. In this case, the degree of fit was inversely related to the rankings of the degree granting departments. We often find this to be the case. Our most successful faculty members often come from nonranked departments. I suspect that many economics departments have had similar experiences.

My point is not that top graduates are always a bad fit for lower-ranked departments but that matching people with departments involves more than simply looking at a graduate's credentials. Sometimes it is important who one studied under. Sometimes it is important where one graduated. Sometimes it is important what school of thought a candidate adheres to. More often, matching people to departments requires paying attention to qualities such as teaching ability and experience, personality, interest in living in the area, and ability to relate to local students. When narrow standards for a top economist (and subsequently for appropriate training) are set, we risk molding young economic scholars into a shape that simply does not fit the larger environment of economics.

Journals, Citations, and Impact

The American Economic Association indicates that over six hundred journals are indexed in its *EconLit* database. A quick search of *EconLit* showed 41,045 entries with a 2007 publication date. Included in this number are refereed articles, notes and comments, books, working papers, and book reviews, and some items are listed more than once, reflecting multiple authorships. The numbers indicate that most of academic discourse is carried on outside of the top journals. In addition, economists produce thousands of policy reports, impact studies, and other writings that are never published in the traditional sense, which is evidence that research production outpaces the capacity of the top journals. David N. Laband, Robert D. Tollison, and Gokhan R. Karahan (2002) seem to suggest that all or most of the research published in the many lesser journals should not have been published and constitutes a waste of taxpayer money. I respectfully disagree and appeal to my experiences to make my argument.

For the moment, I focus on the process of academic research results in publication in academic journals. Several studies are cited above, and many others have been published that attempt to measure the quality of journals. Sometimes opinion surveys are taken, but more often citation counts are used to judge the influence (and therefore presumed quality) of articles and journals. In turn, economists who produce highly cited articles and the departments that employ them are deemed to be of high quality. Although there are many reasons to question citations as a measure of quality and influence, the process seems well intended and perhaps as good as any other single criterion. Still, to focus exclusively on citation counts is to overestimate the influence of some research while ignoring other important research outcomes.

I am honored to be the editor of the *Journal of Economic Issues* (*JEI*). The *JEI* has been published by the Association for Evolutionary Economics (AFEE) since 1967 and focuses primarily on research with original insititutionalist foundations. It is not a mainstream journal and does not rank among the top journals ranked by the typical standards discussed above. On the other hand, when the *JEI* is ranked, it achieves at least midlevel status, and many authors are proud to have their work published on its pages (see Barrett, Olia, and Von Bailey 2000; Mason, Steagall, and Fabritius 1997; Kalaitzidakis, Mamuneas, and Stengos 2003; Axarloglou and Theoharakis 2003). As Laband et al. (2002) suggest of the lesser journals, the *JEI* has published many "dry holes." On the other hand, many *JEI* articles have citation counts that can compete with the best. Four Nobel laureates have published in the *JEI*.[7] Four American Economic Association distinguished fellows[8] have work in the *JEI* as have two John Bates Clark Medal winners[9] and two members of the President's Council of Economic Advisers.[10] The *JEI* regularly receives submissions from across the world.[11]

The above paragraph suggests that the *JEI* has had and continues to have some substantial, if not universal, influence in the economics profession. It is long lived and anchors a widespread community of scholars whose careers have been closely tied to AFEE and the *JEI*. In the bigger picture, as painted by the various rankers of journals, the *JEI* is one of the lesser journals that publishes the inconsequential research that Laband et al. (2002) claim have wasted the taxpayers money. I have used the *JEI* as an example, but it is not an isolated example. There are hundreds of journals that are important to a subset of the profession but largely disregarded by those at the top.

Building on the *JEI* example, I would like to argue two points. One is that a lesser journal can be important if the emphasis is taken off citation counts. The other is that dry holes may have more influence than they are credited with having.

Think about what would be lost if only the top few economics journals were allowed to survive. Only the ideas of the top economists would find an outlet for their scholarly activities. Only the ideas that were deemed most important (at the moment) would be discussed. Past ideas that do not fit current ideology or conditions would be lost. New ideas that challenge mainstream thought would not find expression, at least by traditional means. The Soviet experiment appears for now to have failed. Does that make Karl Marx's critique any less insightful? For several decades, the mainstream decided to assume away the most important motivators of human behavior. Does that make Thorstein Veblen's insights less important? The business cycle smoothed out for a while. Does that mean we should toss out what is known about discretionary macroeconomic policies? Should John Maynard Keynes be forgotten simply because fiscal policy solutions happen to be out of vogue? One important role of the lesser journals is building on good old ideas that happen to be out of style and allowing new ideas to percolate until their time comes.[12]

Another important role that the lesser journals play is keeping science and the scientific approach alive among the masses. Perhaps not every research project leads to profound knowledge (presumably measured by citations). Still, what if thousands of bright, well-trained economists become frustrated by the lack of publishing outlets and give up the idea of searching for new knowledge and understanding and telling others what they find. Would they simply have to accept the knowledge created from above (top economists in top journals) and passively deliver this knowledge to their students? Rather than participating in the scientific quest and encouraging their students to do the same, would they simply become the mouthpiece of the elite? Enquiring minds want to know.

Finally, perfect economic knowledge does not exist. Theory evolves. Models come and go. New problems of all shapes and sizes arise. Economics needs to be flexible enough to respond. Just as economists work better when they fit their department, economics works better when it fits the problem: "economists are expected to provide a persuasive description of economic phenomena that makes sense of our current and past economic life-experience as individuals and communities" (Heilbroner and Milberg 1995, 94). Heterogeneity in economic problems calls for heterogeneity in economic solutions, and heterogeneity is well served by variety in research. In turn, variety in research is well served by variety in research outlets.

Turning again to the *JEI* example, I can say with great confidence that few if any of the articles published in the *JEI* over the years would ever have found their way to the pages of the top few journals. I can say with equal confidence that few if any of the articles published in the top few journals would pass muster at the *JEI*. As with departments, it is a matter of fit. The *JEI* and many other nonelite journals simply do something different. As we have learned in other venues, being different does not justify sterilization, discrimination, or termination.

But what about the dry holes, you might ask. The term *dry holes* refers to published journal articles that are not subsequently cited in other writers' work (Laband et al. 2002; Laband and Tollison 2003). In this discussion, I also include damp holes (papers with only a few citations) in my references to dry holes. Dry holes can be important in more ways than one might suspect. As mentioned already, researchers remain engaged in the scientific process even if they leave behind a trail of dry holes. In addition, one has to risk drilling a few dry holes if one is to find a gusher. Finally, the lack of citations understates the real-world importance of some research.

When will we witness the next great breakthrough in economics? I don't know either. I do know that we will probably see many mediocre ideas before we see another great one. I provide one example that makes this point. Anyone who has studied public finance will be familiar with Charles M. Tiebout's 1956 article "A Pure Theory of Public Expenditures." He demonstrated that, with perfect mobility, local public expenditures would be allocated efficiently because people would vote with their feet, moving to the jurisdiction that provided the mix of local public services and taxes that matched their preferences. A search of Google Scholar indicated that this article had been cited 3,166 times, so it is not a dry hole. I mention this because Tiebout was not a prolific writer, and his other works received far less attention than this seminal article. In a way, he might be compared to a one-hit wonder, but it was a very important hit. What if in our anxiousness to avoid dry holes, we had stifled Tiebout's research efforts?

I turn again to my personal experiences to argue that some dry holes are more important than they seem. I provide three examples.

Our (now former) university president was trained as an economist. Being thus influenced, he proposed that we reduce the university's nonresident tuition to the same level as in-state tuition to attract more out-of-state students. A colleague, Jim Peach, and I were asked to analyze the impact of this proposed policy. Using the same methods that we would use for nearly any project, we read the literature, gathered some data, did some statistical analysis, and concluded that the university should not lower nonresident tuition if its goal is to attract out-of-state students. The policy proposal was dropped, and the university avoided a substantial (and fruitless) decrease in tuition revenue. We also published our study (Adkisson and Peach 2008). To date, the article is a dry hole, and although it may eventually be cited, we do not expect it to be heavily cited. And yet this article has value. First, the fact that the paper is a dry hole hides the fact that the research reported in the paper had a significant (university-level) policy impact. Second, the act of subjecting the research to academic scrutiny kept us honest. The review process ensured that our analysis met high standards regardless of the fact that our original purpose was to shed light on a local issue. Finally, as did the literature we reviewed for our paper, our findings may help other universities facing similar decisions.[13]

The second example relates to work published in the *Journal of Economic Issues* (Hayden and Fullwiler 2001; Hayden 2002; Hayden, Wood, and Kaya 2002) and in Gregory F. Hayden and Steven R. Bolduc (2000). These authors looked at various issues related to the proposed location of a low-level radioactive waste dump in north central Nebraska. In the end, the effort to locate the dump was abandoned largely because this line of research showed that the cost-plus contracts governing the process (and largely incomprehensible to most decision makers) were going to push the cost far beyond any of the previous estimates and that the dump was not anywhere near financially viable. This contribution was so important that in her account of the waste-dump drama, Susan Cragin (2007) referred to 1996 as "the Hayden year." According to the *Social Science Citation Index*, the three journal articles have netted a total of three citations to date. One of them is a self-citation. This work cannot be said to be uninfluential simply because it created a dry hole.

The third point is that many sparsely cited articles are useful for teaching purposes. These dry holes can substantially influence the thinking of the next generation of economists. Particularly important are articles that present important economic issues and ideas in understandable ways. Can first-year graduate students really be expected to learn effectively from articles that only a few highly specialized economists have the ability to write and understand without massive effort? Perhaps by the time that they are writing their dissertations, they are prepared to do so, but they certainly cannot begin there.

Finally, thousands of economists work outside the walls of academia. One brief example comes from the state of New Mexico. New Mexico relies heavily on energy taxes for its public revenue. Recent high energy prices have been a boon to the public coffers of the state. During the summer of 2008, the state's governor, Bill Richardson, called a special session of the legislature to consider policies to return some funds to New Mexico's citizens, including a possible a tax rebate. Between the decision to call the session and the actual session, energy prices, which by nature are volatile, began to fall. Legislative economists have the duty to forecast revenues. Immediately before the session, they still were struggling to provide a consensus revenue forecast. In the face of price volatility, the forecast of the one-time surplus was lowered from $400 million to $225 million, and the programs proposed by the governor were scaled back substantially (Massey 2008). None of the work of these economists will ever be cited in a journal, but who would argue that they (and thousands like them) have no important influence?

Conclusion

Many tasks are undertaken by academic (and other) economists. We teach at all levels and to students with wide variation in talent and preparation. We conduct policy analyses at all levels, from institutional and local to national and international. We develop theories of economic behavior. We test our theories against empirical evidence. We seek empirical answers where theory has yet to tread. We delve into the most fundamental human motivations. We help govern our departments, colleges, and universities. We advise governments and businesses. Is there any reason to think that any one ideal top economist is capable of fulfilling all these roles? Is there any reason to think that any one ideal top department can adequately train economists to fulfill all these roles? Should we not express our appreciation for the plurality of roles and ideas in our profession and avoid making narrowly defined distinctions between top economists and the rest of us?

Allow me to return once more to the topic of lizardness. I live in the desert. On any given day when it is warm, I can step outside my house and see lizards scurrying about doing lizard stuff. I have visited Costa Rica and seen iguanas at every turn. The iguanas are much larger than the small lizards in my yard, but I doubt that they could survive in my back yard, at least not without substantial intervention on my part. It is probably too dry, and there is certainly too little to eat (and someone would probably chase them away with a stick). It also is not clear that my little desert lizards could survive in Costa Rica. Does this reality mean that one lizard is more or less valuable or necessary than the other? By now, it should be obvious that I do not think so. Each has its place, and each should be given the space it needs to thrive. So it is with the lizards of economics. We need them all.

Notes

1. The 224 articles did not include things otherwise distinguished as notes, comments, or shorter papers, nor did it include the *American Economic Review* proceedings issue.

2. In recent years, the American Economic Association has maintained regular paid memberships at around seventeen hundred (Siegfried 2007).

3. A *Social Science Citation Index* search conducted in August 2008 revealed that this 2002 article had been cited nine times, including two self-citations. The Laband (1990) paper yielded thirty citations, including one self-citation. The Laband and Tollison (2003) paper had ten citations.

4. See http://www.albany.edu/economics/undergraduate/eco_phds.shtml.

5. This list was originally provided at http://web.uric.ca/econ/depts_Uvic.html. The link has since gone inactive. See http://econlinks.com/economics_departments.php for similar information.

6. Blakely Fox Fender, Susan Washburn Taylor, and Kimberly Gladden Burke (2005) showed that higher teaching loads and service requirements have a significantly negative impact on the probability that a person will publish in the top journals.

7. Jan Tinbergen, Gunnar Myrdal, James Tobin, and James M. Buchanan.

8. Nicholas Georgescu-Roegen, James M. Buchanan, Martin Brofenbrenner, and Geoffrey Moore (note that Nobel laureate Buchanan has been double counted.

9. Kenneth E. Boulding and James Tobin.

10. Murray Weidenbaum and Henry C. Wallich.

11. Credit for any success the *JEI* has had must go to previous editors, editorial board members, authors, and other supporters. My tenure has been too short to take any credit.

12. For example, several recent books have presented as new ideas that have been alive in institutional and evolutionary economics circles for a century (see Beinhocker 2006; Thaler and Sunstein 2008; Levitt and Dubner 2005; and Ariely 2008.

13. Our department is regularly called on to do policy analysis. Much of it is highly influential even if not widely cited. I suspect that many other similar departments have the same experience.

References

Adkisson, Richard V., and James T. Peach. 2008. Non-resident Enrollment and Non-resident Tuition at Land Grant Colleges and Universities. *Education Economics* 16 (1):75–88.

Ariely, Dan. 2008. *Predictably Irrational: The Hidden Forces That Shape Our Decisions*. New York: HarperCollins.

Azar, Ofer H. 2006. The Academic Review Process: How Can We Make It More Efficient? *American Economist* 50 (1):37–50.

Axarloglou, Kostas, and Vasilis Theoharakis. 2003. Diversity in Economics: An Analysis of Journal Quality Perceptions. *Journal of the European Economic Association* 1 (6):1402–1423.

Barrett, Christopher B., Aliakbar Olia, and Dee Von Bailey. 2000. Subdiscipline-Specific Journal Rankings: Whither Applied Economics? *Applied Economics* 32:239–252.

Beed, Clive, and Cara Beed. 1996. Measuring the Quality of Academic Journals: The Case of Economics. *Journal of Post Keynesian Economics* 18 (3):369–396.

Beinhocker, Eric D. 2006. *The Origin of Wealth: Evolution, Complexity, and the Radical Remaking of Economics*. Boston: Harvard Business School Press.

Colander, David. 2005. The Making of an Economist Redux. *Journal of Economic Perspectives* 19 (1):175–198.

Colander, David, and Arjo Klamer. 1987. The Making of an Economist. *Journal of Economic Perspectives* 1 (2):95–111.

Cragin, Susan. 2007. *Nuclear Nebraska: The Remarkable Story of the Little County That Couldn't Be Bought*. New York: Amacom.

Davis, Joe C., John H. Huston, and Debra Moore Patterson. 2001. The Scholarly Output of Economists: A Description of Publishing Patterns. *Atlantic Economic Journal* 29 (3):341–349.

Dewald, William G., Jery G. Thursby, and Richard G. Anderson. 1986. Replication in Empirical Economics: The *Journal of Money, Credit, and Banking* Project. *American Economic Review* 76 (4):587–603.

Dusansky, Richard, and Clayton J. Vernon. 1998. Rankings of U.S. Economics Departments. *Journal of Economic Perspectives* 12 (1):157–170.

Faria, Joao Ricardo. 2005. The Game Academics Play: Editors versus Authors. *Bulletin of Economic Research* 57 (1):1–12.

Fender, Blakely Fox, Susan Washburn Taylor, and Kimberly Gladden Burke. 2005. Making the Big Leagues: Factors Contributing to Publication in Elite Economics Journals. *Atlantic Economic Journal* 33 (1):93–103.

Gans, Joshua S., and George B. Shepherd. 1994. How Are the Mighty Fallen: Rejected Classic Articles by Leading Economists. *Journal of Economic Perspectives* 8 (1):165–179.

Hamermesh, Daniel S. 1994. Facts and Myths about Refereeing. *Journal of Economic Perspectives* 8 (1):153–163.

Hayden, F. Gregory. 2002.Policymaking Network of the Iron-Triangle Subgovernment for Licensing Hazardous Waste Facilities. *Journal of Economic Issues* 36 (2):477–484.

Hayden, F. Gregory and Steven R. Bolduc. 2000. Contracts and Costs in a Corporate/Government System Dynamics Model: A United States Case. In *Industrial Policies after 2000*, ed. Wolfram Elsner and John Groenewegen, 235–284. Boston: Kluwer.

Hayden, F. Gregory, and Scott T. Fullwiler. 2001. Analysis of the Financial Assurance Plan in the License Application for a Low-Level Radioactive Waste Disposal Facility. *Journal of Economic Issues* 35 (2):373–383.

Hayden, F. Gregory, Kellee R. Wood, and Asuman Kaya. 2002. The Use of Power Blocs of Integrated Corporate Directorships to Articulate a Power Structure: Case Study and Research Recommendations. *Journal of Economic Issues* 36 (3):617–705.

Heilbroner, Robert, and William Milberg. 1995. *The Crisis of Vision in Modern Economic Thought*. Cambridge: Cambridge University Press.

Hodgson, Geoffrey M., and Harry Rothman. 1999. The Editors and Authors of Economics Journals: A Case of Institutional Oligopoly? *Economic Journal* 109 (453):F165–F186.

Kalaitzidakis, Pantelis, Theofanis P. Mamuneas, and Thanasis Stengos. 2003. Rankings of Academic Journals and Institutions in Economics. *Journal of the European Economic Association* 1 (6):1346–1366.

Laband, David N. 1990. Is There Value-Added from the Review Process in Economics? Preliminary Evidence from Authors. *Quarterly Journal of Economics* 105 (2):341–352.

Laband, David N., and Michael J. Piette. 1994. Does the "Blindness" of Peer Review Influence Manuscript Selection Efficiency? *Southern Economic Journal* 60 (4):896–906.

Laband, David N., and Robert D. Tollison. 2003. Dry Holes in Economic Research. *Kyklos* 56 (2):161–173.

Laband, David N., Robert D. Tollison, and Gokhan R. Karahan. 2002. Quality Control in Economics. *Kyklos* 55 (3):315–334.

Lee, Frederic S. 2004. To Be a Heterodox Economist: The Contested Landscape of American Economics, 1960s and 1970s. *Journal of Economic Issues* 38 (3):747–763.

Leijonhufvud, Axel. 1973. Life among the Econ. *Western Economic Journal* 11:327–337.

Levitt, Steven D., and Stephen J. Dubner. 2005. *Freakonomics: A Rogue Economist Explores the Hidden Side of Everything*. New York: Harper Collins.

Mason, Paul M., Jeffrey W. Steagall, and Michael M. Fabritius. 1997. Economics Journal Rankings by Type of School: Perceptions versus Citations. *Quarterly Journal of Business and Economics*. 36 (1):69–79.

Massey, Barry. 2008. New Forecast: NM has $225 Million Revenue Windfall. *Las Cruces Sun News*, August 12.

Medoff, Marshall H. 2003. Editorial Favoritism in Economics? *Southern Economic Journal* 70 (2):425–434.

Mixon, Franklin G., Jr. 1998. Favoritism or Showcasing High-Impact Papers? Modeling Editorial Placement of Journal Articles in Economics. *RISEC: International Review of Economics and Business* 45 (2):327–340.

Mixon, Franklin G., Jr., and W. Charles Sawyer. 2005. Contribution, Attribution and the Assignment of Intellectual Property Rights in Economics. *Journal of Economic Studies* (Glasgow, Scotland) 32 (5–6):382–386.

Oyer, Paul. 2006. Initial Labor Market Conditions and Long-Term Outcomes for Economists. *Journal of Economic Perspectives* 20 (3):143–160.

Rupp, Nicholas G., and Carl Nicholas McKinney, Jr. 2002. The Publication Patterns of the Elite Economics Departments: 1995–2000. *Eastern Economic Journal* 28 (4):523–538.

Siegfried, John J. 2007. Report of the Secretary for 2007. *American Economic Review* 98 (2):573–576.

Simonovits, András. 2005. Selection by Publication in Economics. *Acta Oeconomica* 55 (3):255–269.

Smyth, David J. 1999. The Determinants of the Reputations of Economics Departments: Pages Published, Citations and the Andy Rooney Effect. *American Economist* 43 (2):49–58.

Thaler, Richard H., and Cass R. Sunstein. 2008. *Nudge: Improving Decisions about Health, Wealth, and Happiness*. New Haven, CT: Yale University Press.

Tiebout, Charles M. 1956. A Pure Theory of Public Expenditures. *Journal of Political Economy* 64 (5):416–424.

Woodbury, Stephen A. 2000. Economics, Economists, and Public Policy. *Quarterly Review of Economics and Finance* 40:417–430.

Managerial Economics

12

Notes from a Second-Line Journal: Suggestions for Authors

Paul H. Rubin and Antony W. Dnes

One of us has been editor in chief of *Managerial and Decision Economics (MDE)* since 1994, and the other has been European coeditor since 2000. It is a fact of life that most of the papers that we receive have been rejected elsewhere. Because the mainline journals in economics and business have very low acceptance rates, on the order of 10 percent or less, many perfectly good papers are rejected, and we know more generally that many truly great papers have been rejected one or more times before being published (Gans and Shepherd 1994). Most of us will spend much of our careers resubmitting papers until we find the correct home for them. Few of us are able to make careers publishing only in the top few journals. Here we provide some suggestions for authors for resubmitting papers (and for writing them in the first place), based on our experiences as editors at *MDE* and as authors. They are relevant for any journal.

The publishing process is a matching market: the author wants the paper published as quickly as possible in the best journal, and the editor wants to publish the best-quality papers that are available to the journal. Like any market, functioning can be improved if transactions costs are reduced. In recent years, these costs (particularly the costs of delays) have been increasing (Ellison 2002). Here we have some suggestions for authors that can reduce these costs and improve the process for both sides of the market. Basically, these suggestions will help the editor make a quicker decision, and a quicker decision is better, even if it is a rejection.

Get the English Right

More and more academicians are not native English speakers. If you are not a native speaker, then it is possible that your English is weak. Every year we reject many papers simply because the grammar or usage is incorrect. Before submitting a paper, you should be sure that the language is correct. This may mean finding a native English coauthor, or it may mean hiring an editor. But either way, when the journal editor cannot understand the point that you are trying to make, then he or she will reject the paper without even sending it to a referee. If the editor slips up and does send it to a referee, the rejection process is delayed because the referee will write back and say that the paper is unintelligible. Our experience suggests that many authors struggle with this issue, apparently checking their work against less demanding nonnative standards of English. We do not mind if the article is in American or British English, but it does need to be accurately written, and this is the author's responsibility.

Update Your References

Updating references is one of the most important simple things that should be done to a paper before it is submitted to a journal. The editorial process is slow. This means that if you have submitted the paper elsewhere and gone through the review process, the paper may be over a year old before you resubmit it. There is nothing wrong with this. But it often means that the references in the paper are out of date. Before resubmitting after a rejection, do a literature search (this is easy to do with Google Scholar), modify the paper to reflect any new literature, and add references to this more recent literature. We often tell authors, "Your most recent reference is several years old. This indicates either that you have not kept up with the literature or that the profession is no longer interested in your topic." We will generally allow a resubmission, but other editors may not be so candid or so forgiving. There is no excuse for submitting a paper with outdated references. If there are no more recent references, then maybe the profession really is not interested in your topic. In this case, you must explain why they should be. There is another advantage to updating references, discussed in the next point.

Help the Editor Find Referees

The worst aspect of publishing (from the perspective of both authors and editors) is getting relevant timely referee reports. In spite of what authors may think, editors hate delay and would like the editorial process to be quicker. Editors are frustrated when refereeing takes too long, and one of the most unpleasant aspects of editing is sending a paper out several times in search of a willing referee. For authors, careers authors may be harmed by delay (especially when one is seeking tenure). So anything that an author can do to help the editor find referees is a good thing for everyone—a genuine Pareto improvement. There are two sources of delay. First, an editor must find a referee who is willing to read a paper. We sometimes send a paper out to five or more referees to find two who are willing to read it, and sometimes we are forced to rely on only one referee. Each time that we send it out, there is a delay. Second, even when someone agrees to referee the paper, the actual time from receiving the paper to reading and writing a report can take a long time. Both of these delays can be reduced if the editor can find someone who is interested in the topic and is willing to read the paper and read it quickly.

MDE is a general journal. It covers many subfields of business and economics. That means that we as editors will generally not be familiar with all of the literatures involved in editing the journal. We do not always know who the appropriate referees are. We are forced to search for referees. (This generally is true of editors of all but the most highly specialized journals.) The easiest and most appropriate place for an editor to look for referees is in the references to the paper. It is here that the author can help. The author should cite authorities who would be appropriate referees for the paper. We do not mean that the author should try to game or manipulate the citing process to bias the result but that the author should cite people who are appropriate for refereeing. These are the natural authorities to cite.

One advantage of updating references is that it makes this referee search process easier. If we send the paper to a referee who has not written on the topic for several years, it is likely that the potential referee is no longer interested in the issue. This is one reason that current references are important. Additionally, the most important scholars in the field are not likely to want to referee every paper that cites them. Nobel Prize winners do not make good referees. Although it is important to cite leading authorities, it is also important to cite younger or more specialized scholars who are currently working in the field, whose work may be more directly relevant for your paper, and who are more likely to respond quickly to a request for refereeing.

It is also useful to look at back issues of the journal to which you are submitting and try to find something relevant to cite from that journal. Authors who have published in a journal are more likely to want to be helpful to the editor by refereeing, and this pattern of citation also indicates that the journal is more likely to be a good fit for the paper. Following these suggestions will give the editor a broader range of potential interested referees and with any luck will speed up the process. In our case, *MDE* is a fast-turnaround journal so that finding referees quickly is important, but no editor wants long delays.

Don't Be Negative

Some scholars feel obligated to criticize the literature to which they are contributing (with comments like "Jones's paper is deeply flawed because he ignored obvious feedback effects"). There is no need for this, and it is counterproductive. You have identified a gap in the literature (or you would not be writing the article), but that does not mean that your predecessors were foolish. It is possible to highlight your contribution without tearing down previous contributors ("We can generalize Jones's important result by considering feedback effects"). Moreover, because the editor is likely to pick referees from the papers cited, if you are too negative, you will just antagonize the potential referee, which is why this approach is counterproductive. (Jones will be happier with the second statement than with the first.)

Pay Attention to Referees

If a paper is rejected, the editor will generally send you the referee's comments and perhaps his or her own comments. Some authors ignore these comments for rejected papers and resubmit the paper elsewhere without rewriting. This is both a scientific error and a strategic error. From a scientific perspective, the referee may have had valid criticisms, and it is improper to ignore these criticisms and not to correct errors. The referee may suggest extensions that are not feasible ("The paper should be extended beyond 2000"). Indicating in the resubmission why you have limited the paper as you have may help in the next round ("Data are available only up to 2000"). If the extensions are feasible, you might think about doing them or at least listing them in the conclusion as suggestions for future research. If one referee thought that they were relevant, others may think so as well.

It may also be that the referee simply did not understand the paper. If so, then your first response as an author is to get really mad. This is a correct and wholly proper response. However, it should not be your final response. The referee is someone who was chosen by the editor because the editor thinks that the referee has expertise in understanding the paper. Also, the referee has probably spent more time reading the article than most readers will. If the referee does not understand the paper, you should ask yourself why. You should read your paper carefully to see what gave the reader a misleading impression and rewrite the paper so that other readers will not make the same error. Even if the error was due to quick and careless reading (as such errors always are), you can put in a sentence or two indicating that this particular reading is inappropriate so that future quick and careless readers will not be misled in that exact way.

From a strategic perspective, remember that the pool of potential referees for a given paper is limited and that the second editor may well send the paper back to the same referee. Editors differ in their reactions to hearing that the referee has already seen the paper, but we generally ask for comments with a proviso that the referee point out that he has seen the paper previously. If the author has not changed the paper, this will bias the referee against it. So for strategic reasons, it is also important to respond in some way to referees' comments, even from referees who rejected the paper, however adverse these may be and regardless of misunderstandings that may be apparent.

Be Sure the Journal Is Correct for the Paper

MDE is a very broad journal. We publish papers in virtually all areas of business as long as they have some connection to economics, and conversely. Even so, we often get papers that are outside the scope of the journal. Some are pure business with no economics, some are pure economics with no managerial implications, and some are based on sociological or other noneconomic theories. We try to catch these papers before sending them for refereeing, but we are not always successful. This means that the author may have a long wait to learn that the paper never should have been submitted. Everyone's time could be saved if the author looks at the journal to see what sorts of papers the journal publishes. Even, better, if you look for a paper in the journal that is relevant to your paper, you can help the editor find a referee and also determine if the paper is suitable for the journal. (If you cannot find any, it may not be the best home for the paper.)

Moreover, sometimes a paper can be made relevant. For example, we sometimes get a theoretical paper in economics and ask the author to include some managerial implications. If there are any, then the paper can be made relevant. An author can save time by doing this sort of doctoring before submission. Moreover, from the perspective of the editors, citation to the journal improves placement in rankings and is always welcome.

There is a particular type of inappropriate submission that we often see at *MDE* but that probably is seen at other journals as well. Being a practically focused economics journal, *MDE* receives a number of articles each year from individuals who are keen to expound on a pet project to improve management and industry, often using the buzz words of the day. An example would be an article that emphasizes a nebulous holistic approach to the complexity of business management in which the writer has no real means for deciding when problems become too complex for established decision making to handle. Sometimes these articles are dense with references, but they never go beyond restating these references. It is important to ensure that the article is linked to a current significant problem (in our case, in the field of business and management) and that the article goes beyond restating (in however glorious terms) the current literature.

Following these suggestions will not guarantee that your articles will be published or that you will obtain tenure at your university, but you will speed up the publication process, and you can make your career better and your life less stressful. You also will have the satisfaction of contributing in a professional manner to the incremental growth of economic science and, in the case of *MDE*, to management practice.

References

Ellison, Glenn. 2002. The Slowdown of the Economics Publishing Process. *Journal of Political Economy* 110 (5):947.

Gans, Joshua S., and George B. Shepherd. 1994. How Are the Mighty Fallen: Rejected Classic Articles by Leading Economists. *Journal of Economic Perspectives* 8 (1):165–179.

Money and Banking

13

Replication and Reflection: A Decade at the *Journal of Money, Credit, and Banking*

William G. Dewald and Richard G. Anderson*

Why Edit a Professional Journal?

In 1975, with reluctance, I accepted the editorship of the *Journal of Money, Credit, and Banking* (*JMCB*), which at the time was the flagship journal in monetary economics and banking. It was founded by Karl Brunner in 1969.[1]

Let me recount how the editorship was offered to me. Karl wanted to take the journal with him to Rochester University when he resigned his Everett D. Reese Chair in Economics and Finance at the Ohio State University, the school's first endowed chair. I had played a major role in recruiting Karl for that position, and that appointment marked a major turning point for the better in economics and finance at Ohio State and perhaps the university as whole. He was already something of an economics conference impresario, and he blossomed in such activities at Ohio State. He had a view that there was a lot of good research on topics covered in standard money and banking textbooks that was not getting published in the prestigious journals of the day, and he wanted to create a new money and banking journal to accommodate that work. Perhaps my most lasting contribution was to suggest that the word *credit* be added to the name of his proposed journal.[2] Karl connected with the managers of the Ohio State University Press, and the journal came to be. He made me a member of the *JMCB* advisory board and asked me to publish in the journal from time to time. When Karl resigned to accept a position at Rochester University, I felt that because he had created the *JMCB*, he was entitled to take it with him. More powerful interests than mine prevailed, and Ohio State kept the journal. I resigned from the advisory board in protest, and many other members did as well. I played an active role in the search for a new Reese Professor, and the search committee, which included representatives from both economics and finance, expected that the new Reese Professor would also become the *JMCB* editor. The search led to the appointment of Edward J. Kane, who in recruitment discussions stated that he did not want to be obligated to edit the *JMCB*. Nonetheless, we all thought that he would. We were wrong, and thus the position remained unfilled. I was again involved in the search for an editor. We offered the job to Robert Barro, but it remained open. The journal went editorless for several quarterly issues beginning in 1974, essentially being pasted together by the Ohio State University Press with remnants of submitted articles that Karl had not taken with him to Rochester. I was on leave in Washington, D.C., in 1974 and was cornered at a meeting at the Brookings Institution by Franco Modigliani and James Tobin, both members of the *JMCB* advisory board who had not resigned, and they expressed their concerns about an editorless *JMCB*. Back at Ohio State in 1975, my colleagues Ernst Baltensperger and William Oakland and I cobbled together a couple of issues with even slimmer leavings than had been available the previous year. At this point, being persuaded that Ohio State was not going to give up the *JMCB*, I accepted the editorship when it was offered to me. So why did I want to be an economics journal editor? Thirty odd years later, I'm still not sure. I had had the temerity to offer the advice to my colleague Karl Brunner that all of the conference organizing and journalizing that he was undertaking was keeping him from generating more of his own research. He obviously ignored my advice. And as editor, as noted below, I was drawn into a similar pattern in trying to enhance the reputation and prestige of the *JMCB* in publishing sound empirical and theoretical research about money, credit, and banking.

At the *JMCB*, my goal was to increase the reputation and ranking of the journal, and Ohio State administrations considered it to be a vehicle for enhancing the university's reputation as a consequence. To do so, I strove to keep high editorial standards. It is difficult to define precisely what this means. Editors have the right to reject a submitted manuscript without sending it to referees; they also reserve the right to reject referee reports. Editors also choose the referees and are aware of the likes and dislikes of prospective reviewers. In short, an editor can have life-and-death authority over papers submitted to the journal up to the limits of forbearance of the journal's owners and editorial advisory board. At the *JMCB*, I always had large group of associate editors who were chosen to reflect the major subspecialties and positions. But I also commissioned papers and refereed some myself.

One of my first acts as editor was to pay homage to Karl Brunner. Despite the circumstances—the Ohio State University Press management had been left in the lurch by Karl's resignation, and the university did not accede to his demand that he be allowed to take the *JMCB* to Rochester University—I did it with the financial and editorial support of Allan Meltzer and many of Karl's colleagues and students from Ohio State and UCLA, where he was before he came to Ohio State. Included in those essays in Karl's honor was Armen Alchian's brilliant exposition of the essence of money, an exposition that he indicated grew out of many discussions on the subject with Karl. Allan and I and others presented the published volume to Karl (and Rosemarie) at their home in Rochester (Dewald and Meltzer 1977). He was genuinely surprised and delighted, and I was pleased to have organized the festschrift for such a master of doing that same sort of thing for others.

The editorship of a professional journal is an entrepreneurial position if the incumbent wishes it to be, albeit in part at the expense of the editor's own research. The journal provides a platform to assist in organizing conferences and the like, not the least of which is the ability to commit to publishing the conference papers. Karl Brunner had started such a tradition,[3] and I continued it.[4] Conferences published by a professional journal have the potential to increase its professional prominence by increasing its value to readers (and subscribers).[5] My position as editor of a prominent journal in monetary economics allowed me to offer the *JMCB* as an outlet for conferences organized by others on relevant topics and to organize conferences using the leverage of a commitment (subject to quality) to publish the papers. I do not doubt that my ability to ensure publication in the *JMCB* eased soliciting papers for the conferences.[6] In 1979, I obtained papers for the conference on "Financial Market Behavior, Capital Formation, and Economic Performance" that was sponsored by the National Science Foundation. The conference was organized by Benjamin M. Friedman of Harvard University and held May 14, 1979, at the Brookings Institution in Washington, D.C. The papers appeared as a special issue in May 1980 (volume 12, number 2). In 1980, I obtained the papers presented at the "American Enterprise Institute Seminar on Rational Expectations" that was organized by Bennett McCallum and sponsored by the AEI. It was held on February 1, 1980, in Washington, D.C. Those papers appeared as a special issue in November 1980 (volume 12, number 4, part 2). In 1982, I organized (with Phillip Cagan) and obtained for the journal a second AEI-sponsored conference, "Current Issues in the Conduct of U.S. Monetary

Policy," held in Washington, D.C., on February 4 and 5, 1982. The papers appeared as a special issue in November 1982 (volume 14, number 4, part 2). In 1983, I organized (with R. Alton Gilbert) the Federal Reserve Bank of St. Louis's eighth annual economic policy conference on banking market studies, which was held on November 4 and 5, 1983, in St. Louis. The papers appeared in November 1984 (volume 16, number 4, part 2). The final conference was another organized with Phillip Cagan and sponsored by the AEI. It was held on February 8, 1985, in Washington, D.C., and entitled "Monetary Policy in a Changing Financial Environment." These papers appeared in November 1985 (volume 17, number 4, part 2), after I had retired from Ohio State.

Conferences are not the sole entrepreneurial opportunity available to an editor. In 1981, I organized a "Money, Credit, and Banking Debate," which was held at Ohio State on April 30, 1981, and its papers were published in the *JMCB* in February 1982. Its motivation was the Federal Reserve's October 6, 1979, announcement that henceforth open-market operations would focus on controlling the quantity of nonborrowed bank reserves rather than the federal funds rate. Subsequently, the economy experienced increased volatility in both interest rates and money growth. The debate topic was stated as "Is the Federal Reserve's Monetary Control Policy Misdirected?" Two academics argued the affirmative (Robert Rasche of Michigan State University and Allan Meltzer of Carnegie-Mellon University), and the negative was argued by the Federal Reserve's two most senior staffers for monetary policy (Peter Sternlight, manager of the New York Fed's Open Market Desk, and Stephen Axilrod, staff director for monetary policy at the Federal Reserve Board). History will forever be ambiguous regarding a winner, but the debate succeeded in both bringing a stimulating event to Ohio State's campus and providing thirty pages of spirited text in the *JMCB*. Federal Reserve chair Paul Volcker was unhappy with the prospect of such a debate being staged, which he expressed to me in a face-to-face meeting. Although the event had been heavily publicized, I did withdraw the planned audience vote about the winner of the debate. As it turned out, the Fed speakers were very effective in presenting the Fed's case, and large numbers of Wall Streeters who flew to Columbus to listen heard an in-depth discussion of the vital issues of the day. The debate was reported in major national newspapers and a *Fortune* magazine feature article.

Another entrepreneurial initiative was the "*Journal of Money, Credit, and Banking* Lecture," which was an opportunity to invite a distinguished monetary economist to campus and for the journal to publish the lecture. This lecture series allowed me, with the consent of the journal's advisory board, to invite those monetary economists that I felt were most valuable and, in some cases, to obtain a high-profile paper for the journal. Flexibility was important in recruiting these speakers, and the lectures sometimes were presented at Ohio State in Columbus and sometimes elsewhere. Robert Lucas Jr., for example, presented the 1980 lecture "Economic Policy and the Business Cycle" in Columbus on May 8, 1980; this lecture was never published in the journal. The 1981 lecture, entitled "Monetary Policy: Theory and Practice," was presented by Milton Friedman on July 5, 1981, at the Western Economic Association meetings, and published in the *JMCB* in February 1982 (volume 14, number 1). He had been asked to present the lecture in Columbus but demurred, so I made arrangements with the Western Economic Association to have the lecture presented at their annual meetings in San Francisco, where Milton and Rose Friedman resided. I hired a court reporter to stenotype Friedman's presentation, which he delivered without notes. Amazingly, he made virtually no changes in the oral transcript, and I published it without any further changes.

Book reviews also were a prominent and popular feature of the journal. At times, my more rigorous manuscript policy reduced acceptance rates. In those cases, book reviews filled space in issues when manuscripts were scarce. The November 1981 issue, for example, devoted twenty pages to reviews of more than twenty books by seventeen reviewers. This feature, so far as I am aware, was not duplicated anywhere else among professional journals, except perhaps at the *Journal of Economic Literature*.

The Frustrations of Editors

Other authors in this volume relate stories of conflicts with authors, referees, and, in some cases, other editors. All of these occurred at the *JMCB*, but here I prefer not to discuss individual cases or use this as a forum to settle old grievances.

Economists are trained to conduct analysis in terms of optimizing behavior subject to constraints, but they seldom apply this tool to analyses of their own behavior. Can this framework be applied to the behavior of authors who submit papers to journals? Some parts of the work are straightforward and perhaps tautological. Authors seek to maximize their utility, which usually is measured by academic prestige and income (and income often is related to the academic prestige that attracts competing offers of employment).

Because authors understand that their career prospects are related to the number of articles they publish and the number of citations to their work, incentives with respect to any individual manuscript are in conflict. The paper should be of sufficient quality to gain attention, but time spent polishing, revising, and documenting should be minimized because the profession does not highly value such attributes. Referees want accepted papers to be clear and well documented because the cost of revising them does not fall on them. Editors wish to publish only the highest-quality papers, thereby attracting readers, citations, and ever higher-quality papers (as well as enhancing their own professional stature), but they also must fill the pages of the journal to meet publication deadlines.[7] Eventually, the editor can publish only what is at-hand, and some weaker papers slip through. These conflicting winds wear down editors after a time. I like to think that I balanced these well at the *JMCB*.

Discussions with friends and colleagues about these conflicting motives convinced me that much published empirical work in economics is sloppy and contains errors. Few if any proposed solutions to the constrained-optimization problem described in the previous paragraph include carefully repeating all the empirical analysis and archiving data, programs, and documentation. After a paper is published, the rewards flow to an author through citations to that paper. So long as the published results cannot be shown by another researcher to be erroneous, citations will flow—and the flow of citations is unlikely to be increased if another researcher simply confirms that the published results are correct. This asymmetry suggests that utility-maximizing researchers will neither carefully self-audit nor document empirical work. This view led to the "*JMCB* Project," which dominated several years of my editorship.

The "*JMCB* Project"

In July 1982, with the collaboration of two colleagues (Jerry G. Thursby and Richard G. Anderson), I started the "*Journal of Money, Credit, and Banking* Data Storage and Evaluation Project" with little financial but substantial moral support from the economics division of the National Science Foundation. The first two goals for the project were to collect from authors and make available to readers the programs and data that were used in empirical *JMCB* articles and to attempt to replicate the results in a sample of published articles. The second two goals were to increase the value of published articles for readers, thereby enhancing the reputations of both the articles' authors and the journal, and to determine whether published articles contained inaccuracies or errors that called into question the research results. The project ended in 1984.

We used the *JMCB* as a vehicle to request, store, and distribute programs and data. As economists, we focused on the costs of replicating published empirical results.[8] In our enthusiasm (or hubris), we assumed that a significant reduction in these costs would stimulate a significant increase in replication activity. Perhaps the largest cost of replication, to prospective replicators, is triggering a suspicion in authors that the replicator suspects, seeks, or has discovered a flaw in the published work that will cause the number of future citations to decrease. Using the journal as the intermediary protects the anonymity of the would-be replicator.

As was explained in a 1986 article (Dewald, Thursby, and Anderson 1986), the expected benefits of replication to a replicator are modest. At best, the researcher gains a deeper (and perhaps more correct) understanding of the technique that was used in the article. Whether the replication succeeds or fails, the efforts of the replication seldom are publishable. Our own replication efforts suggested that "inadvertent errors in published empirical articles are a common-place rather than a rare occurrence. While correction of the errors did not affect the authors' conclusions in most studies, the errors make independent replication impossible unless the replicator errs in precisely the same way" (Dewald et al. 1986, 587–588).

We do not claim originality for stating that authors should expect to make available the programs and data that underlie their research and that replication using such data is essential for the forward progress of science. Ragnar Frisch, for example, wrote of such expectations in *Econometrica*'s first issue in 1933. We do claim some originality for stressing that the editorial and peer-review processes of professional journals are the appropriate vehicles for handling such data and programs. As we stated in 1986 (Dewald et al. 1986, 588–589):

The frequency and magnitude of errors in empirical articles raise serious questions regarding the integrity of the refereeing process of professional journals. Referees are concerned primarily with methodology, theoretical specification, statistical estimators, and importance of results; an author's programs, data, and calculations are typically assumed to be correct. While our findings suggest that this assumption often is unwarranted, we hesitate to suggest—due to the massive amount of time which would be required—that referees should be required to check an author's computer programs and data. Our findings suggest that the existence of a requirement that authors submit to the journal their programs and data along with each manuscript would significantly reduce the frequency and magnitude of errors. We found that the very process of authors compiling their programs and data for submission reveals to them ambiguities, errors, and oversights which otherwise would be undetected.

But here, too, there is prior art. Edward J. Kane (1984) suggested a similar argument, and Robert A. Mittelstaedt and Thomas S. Zorn (1984) provided a tableau of replication concepts, the most straightforward of which is what we did at the *JMCB*—what Ed Kane labeled "econometric auditing." Simply stated, this approach begins with data and programs that are provided by the author and then asks if the same results included by the author in the published article can be obtained by using these tools.

In the first phase of the *JMCB* Project, we found that many authors could not furnish their data and programs. We initially requested data from the authors of sixty-two articles published from 1980 to 1982, prior to the beginning of the project on July 1, 1982. About a third of the authors did not respond to either a first or second request for data. Among the responding authors, half either could not locate their data or chose not to submit them. Most of these authors said that they could have done so if requested when the manuscript was first submitted to the *JMCB*. Next, we requested data from the authors of papers that either had recently been accepted for publication or were under editorial review. More than three-quarters furnished their data. The most commonly stated reason for not supplying data was that it had been lost. We concluded that it is important for journals to request data from authors when papers are first submitted.

Among these submissions, two were superior. They were clearly documented, and their published results were fully reproducible. One was from future Nobel Prize laureate Robert F. Engle, and the other from Robert H. Rasche. In a number of other datasets, differences between the authors' results and ours were small, although in one manuscript we detected (prior to publication) an error that reversed the results. Overall, we received fifty-four submissions and judged eight as satisfactory and fourteen as valueless in understanding the authors' work. Others were deficient in at least one important respect.

One of our larger subprojects within the *JMCB* Project was perhaps the profession's first real-time data experiment and was the earliest published case of scientific replication in economics of which we are aware.[9] The authors of a published article studying the interaction between bank lending and the macroeconomy submitted their banking data but said that the macrodata had been lost. The authors suggested this loss was insignificant because the data could always be collected from the *Survey of Current Business*, although they did not recall which issues had been used to obtain the data. We collected every observation on the necessary macrovariables that had appeared in all issues of the *Survey* during the period when they conducted their research, reestimated their model for every combination of such data, and displayed in our article densities of the resulting parameter estimates. The authors were greatly displeased with our findings: parameter estimates that were produced using the most recent data in our collection were far from the authors' estimates, and the authors' estimates were far from the central portions of the densities.

It is an old rebuke that practitioners of a profession tend to be better at counseling others than themselves. With respect to journal editing and particularly replicability, this is especially true. Economists have seldom explored the process of producing peer-reviewed journals as a problem in optimization that is subject to constraints, as is commonly done with other topics. What are the objectives and constraints? Journal editors seek to sustain or increase the prestige of their journals by publishing papers that their readers find valuable and, at least as important, come to be cited in articles published in journals of equal or higher stature. But they face the constraints of accepting enough papers to fill the required number of issues and not alienating authors with excessive demands for revision. Authors seek to maximize the quality of each individual article to increase future citations but also to retain intellectual property that will assist the production of future articles—thereby maximizing their lifetime stream of publications and citations. Readers, presumably, wish to read interesting papers that assist their own research and understanding of the field. Most authors produce multiple articles for publication, most editors handle multiple articles (sometimes by the same author), and most readers have a choice of which journals to read and cite. In Richard G. Anderson, William H. Greene, B. D. McCullough, and H. D. Vinod (2008), this interaction (when a journal requests data and program code from an author) is interpreted as a repeated game in intellectual property of the type studied by Vincent P. Crawford and Joel Sobel (1982). Generally, the optimal strategy for most authors is to reveal as little as possible subject to the article being published. Hence, journal requests for data and program code impose a binding constraint on the author and, if possible, are rejected.

The editors who followed me at the *JMCB* did not share my enthusiasm for replication. All the files and data from the project were destroyed.[10] A number of researchers have "constructed formal models that suggest, in equilibrium, the number of successful replications is near zero" (Anderson et al. 2008, 101). Destroying the data tends to make that self-evident. The recent increase in the number of journals that are collecting data is discussed by Daniel S. Hamermesh (2007) and Anderson et al. (2008), but no journal requires data submission as a condition of publication, and few journals require the authors' programs.

In closing this section, I note a small experiment that I conducted at Federal Reserve Bank of St. Louis after I became research director (Anderson and Dewald 1994).[11] In early 1993, without prior warning to the authors, I requested the datasets and programs that were used to produce the papers presented at our October 1992 annual economic policy conference. Authors' responses were similar to those that we had observed at the *JMCB* a decade earlier. Authors who had completed their studies just prior to the conference promptly submitted their data and programs, and those who had completed their research several years earlier found it costly (or impossible) to do so. The following year, I informed participants in our 1993 conference well in advance that their data and programs would be expected at the time of the conference. Authors generally found it imposed little burden to submit data and programs with their manuscripts when they were aware of the requirement in advance.

Legacy

The legacy of my editorship at the *JMCB* undoubtedly is the *JMCB* replication project. Prior to the publication of Dewald et al. (1986), only the *JMCB* had a data and program code archive. Before that article was published, the *American Economic Review* had adopted an editorial policy that required all authors to furnish data to others on request. McCullough and Vinod (2003) requested data files from authors and by using them demonstrated that the *AER* policy was a failure. Hamermesh (2007) presents survey evidence that few *AER* authors received requests for data, which perhaps makes it rational not to prepare datasets and related documentation. In 2004, *AER* editor Ben Bernanke adopted a mandatory data and program code archive. Compliance has been excellent, at least according to the annual reports of the editor.

The *JMCB* Project put to rest the cheap talk that it was easy to replicate a published paper and that a researcher need only ask the author for the programs and data. Our experience confirmed the intuition that arises from any simple model of utility maximization by researchers—to do no more on an individual paper than is necessary to maximize total lifetime publications and citations for all papers. To our surprise, we found that many authors could not (or would not) furnish data and programs, even at the time the paper was submitted to the journal, often arguing that the data had been lost. The situation is little better today. The economics profession seems trapped in a stable bad equilibrium wherein replication is interpreted as an affront to the author and no one questions the quality or accuracy of published results lest he or she also be questioned. Although some journals collect data, none requires its submission as a condition of publication, and few journals collect authors' programs. In closing, I must note that many of the profession's finest researchers now make available on their Web pages the data and programs for their research. This list is long, and I cannot mention more than a few, but notable among such authors is Mark Watson at Princeton University, James Hamilton at the University of California at San Diego, Peter Ireland at Boston College, Ellen McGratten at the Federal Reserve Bank of Minneapolis, and Eric Swanson at the Federal Reserve Bank of San Francisco.

Finally, I believe that the *JMCB* Project stimulated discussion of replication in other fields, including political science (led by Gary King at Harvard) and business management (Hubbard and Vetter 1996; Mezias and Regnier 2007; Evanschitzky, Baumgarth, Hubbard, and Armstrong 2007).

Notes

*William G. Dewald is emeritus professor of economics, the Ohio State University, former editor of the *Journal of Money, Credit, and Banking,* and former director of research at the Federal Reserve Bank of St. Louis. Richard G. Anderson is economist and vice president, Federal Reserve Bank of St. Louis, a former assistant professor at Ohio State. First-person statements herein are those of Dewald.

1. The *Journal of Money, Credit, and Banking*'s masthead page shows Karl Brunner as editor through the August 1974 (the third issue of that year). The final issue of 1974 (November) and the first issue of 1975 (February) show no

editor. The second and third issues of 1975 (May and August) show an editorial triad consisting of three Ohio State faculty—Dewald, Ernst Baltensperger, and William Oakland. The final issue of 1975 (November) shows Dewald as editor.

2. There had been a money and banking textbook with the same title published by a Yale University economist, Westerfield (1938).

3. For example, the "Universities-NBER Conference on Secular Inflation," held on November 5 and 6, 1971, at the University of Chicago and sponsored by the NBER and the University of Rochester, was published in February 1973 as volume 5, number 1, part 2.

4. Before I became *JMCB* editor, I was on leave from Ohio State to head a U.S. Department of Labor office that contracted research on the topic of international trade and employment. I edited the conference papers and comments that were made at a conference on the research results (Dewald 1978).

5. When I became research director at the Federal Reserve Bank of St. Louis in 1992, I ended their practice of placing the bank's annual policy conference with a commercial publisher and published it as an issue of the St. Louis *Review*. At the time, the *Review* was printing six issues per year, and the conference became one of these issues. Circulation for the conference increased from a few thousand copies (sold largely to libraries) to 25,000 copies, the mailing circulation of the *Review*.

6. Karl Brunner left Ohio State for the University of Rochester in 1971, where he started the *Journal of Monetary Economics* (*JME*) and the Carnegie-Rochester Conference Series (originally separate publications but later merged into one under the wing of Elsevier). Karl resigned as *JMCB* editor in 1974, and the first issue of *JME* appeared on January 1, 1975. In its first sentence, Brunner's editorial introducing the new journal includes the phrase "money, credit, and banking" and emphasizes that the *JME* will "cover a range of interest substantially beyond monetary analysis" and will "encourage attention to major issues of monetary, credit, and banking policy." The editorial left no doubt that he intended the *JME* to compete directly with the *JMCB*. The Carnegie-Rochester Conference Series appeared in 1976 as "A supplementary series to the *Journal of Monetary Economics*." The Carnegie-Rochester series was subsumed into the *JME* in 2002 beginning with volume 49, number 1, when the number of issues in each annual volume of the JME increased from three to eight.

7. One of the pet peeves of authors is to have a paper accepted for publication and then remain unpublished for an extended period. I sought to keep a low inventory of accepted papers to avoid this problem, but as a consequence (as noted above), I occasionally had to fill journal pages with book reviews.

8. In the *JMCB* project, we defined *replication* as "obtaining exactly the same numerical results as contained in the published article, preferably by using the authors' data and programs." This has been called "economic auditing" (Kane 1984), "type I" replication (Mittelstaedt and Zorn 1984), and "pure replication" (Hamermesh 2007). We explicitly eschewed the metaanalysis school of replication, which argues the correctness of individual studies matters little because "on

average" important findings will float to the top as does cream on whole milk. This is what Hamermesh (2007) labels "scientific replication." A challenge to this line of argument arises when publication bias is recognized. This is the so-called file cabinet effect: papers with insignificant or outlandish results are tucked inside file cabinets, and only papers with "significant" or "important" results are published (see Anderson et al. 2008). For an interesting case study of this phenomenon, see Arthur M. Diamond Jr. (2009).

9. Dean Croushore (2008) surveys the history of real-time (that is, vintage) data research in economics. Daniel S. Hamermesh (2007) and others define "scientific replication" as bringing the same model to a similar dataset.

10. The *JMCB* started a data and program code archive in 1989. B. D. McCullough, Kerry Anne McGreary, and Teresa D. Harrison (2006) find that fewer than one in ten submitted datasets are capable of being used to reproduce the results in the respective published articles.

11. In a related action, when I became research director, I required that all empirical papers in the Bank's *Review* be accompanied by programs and data that were sufficient to replicate the published figures. Initially, a research analyst was required to replicate each article's results prior to posting the data and program code. Over time, resource pressures caused that requirement to slip, as documented by McCullough et al. (2008, table 1), who found that the supplied data and programs were insufficient to replicate many articles.

References

Anderson, Richard G. 2007.Replicability, Real-Time Data, and the Science of Economic Research: FRED, ALFRED and VDC. *Federal Reserve Bank of St. Louis RE:view* 88 (1):81–93.

Anderson, Richard G., and William G. Dewald. 1994. Replication and Scientific Standards in Applied Economics a Decade after the *Journal of Money, Credit, and Banking* Project. Federal Reserve Bank of St. Louis *RE:view* (November/December):79–83.

Anderson, Richard G., William H. Greene, B. D. McCullough, and H. D. Vinod. 2008. The Role of Data/Code Archives in the Future of Economic Research. *Journal of Economic Methodology* 15 (1):99–119.

Crawford, Vincent P., and Joel Sobel. 1982. Strategic Information Transmission. *Econometrica* 50 (6):1431–1451.

Croushore, Dean. 2008. Frontiers of Real-Time Data Analysis. Working Paper 08-4. Research Department, Federal Reserve Bank of Philadelphia. March.

Dewald, William G. 1978. *The Impact of International Trade and Investment on Employment: A Conference on the Department of Labor Research Results.* Washington, DC: U.S. Government Printing Office.

Dewald, William G., and Allan H. Meltzer, eds. 1977. Essays in Honor of Karl Brunner. *Journal of Money, Credit, and Banking* 9 (1) (pt. 2).

Dewald, William G., Jerry G. Thursby, and Richard G. Anderson. 1986. Replication in Empirical Economics: The *Journal of Money, Credit, and Banking* Project. *American Economic Review* 76 (4):587–603.

Diamond, Arthur J., Jr. 2009. The Career Consequences of a Mistaken Research Project: The Case of Polywater. *American Journal of Economics and Sociology* 68 (2):387–411.

Evanschitzky, Heiner, Carsten Baumgarth, Raymond Hubbard, and J. Scott Armstrong. 2007. Replication Research's Disturbing Trend. *Journal of Business Research* 60 (4):411–415.

Hamermesh, Daniel S. 2007. Viewpoint: Replication in Economics. *Canadian Journal of Economics. Revue Canadienne d'Economique* 40 (3):715–733.

Hubbard, Raymond, and Daniel E. Vetter. 1996. An Empirical Comparison of Published Replication Research in Accounting, Economics, Management and Marketing. *Journal of Business Research* 35 (2):153–164.

Kane, Edward J. 1984. Why Journal Editors Should Encourage the Replication of Applied Econometric Research. *Quarterly Journal of Business and Economics* 23 (1):3–8.

McCullough, B. D., and H. D. Vinod. 2003. Verifying the Solution from a Nonlinear Solver: A Case Study. *American Economic Review* 93 (3):873–892.

McCullough, B. D., Kerry Anne McGeary, and Teresa D. Harrison. 2006. Lessons from the *JMCB* Archive. *Journal of Money, Credit, and Banking* 38 (4):1093–1107.

McCullough, B. D., Kerry Anne McGeary, and Teresa D. Harrison. 2008. Do Economics Journal Archives Promote Replicable Research? *Canadian Journal of Economics. Revue Canadienne d'Economique* 41 (4):1406–1420.

Mezias, Stephen J., and Michael O. Regnier. 2007. Walking the Walk as Well as Talking the Talk: Replication and the Normal Science Paradigm in Strategic Management Research. *Strategic Organization* 5 (3):283–296.

Mittelstaedt, Robert A., and Thomas S. Zorn. 1984. Econometric Replication: Lessons from the Experimental Sciences. *Quarterly Journal of Business and Economics* 23 (1):9–15.

Westerfield, Ray B. 1938. *Money, Credit, and Banking.* New York: Ronald Press.

Urban Economics

14

Epistemic Flagpoles: Economics Journals as Instrumental Rhetoric

Daniel W. Bromley

Instrumental Rhetoric

Deirdre McCloskey (1983) has made a number of profound contributions to economics. Nothing in her prodigious output can match the masterful article offering clarity on the word *rhetoric*. Clarity, however, brought anxiety: "You mean economics is concerned with trying to persuade? Here I thought we were pursuing (and publishing) truth." But as McCloskey taught us, the essential task in science is to offer the more compelling account. The central purpose driving each of us is to bring others to our side. We do that by convincing them that we have the best story to tell about a particular matter.

An academic department is a holding company, and each member of a department can be thought of as a one-person multiproduct firm. Our output is disciplinary literacy among undergraduate students, specialized training for graduate students at some universities, dissertation supervision of graduate students at those universities, and a record of published output. In all of these activities, the "owner" of the firm is intent on imparting his or her particular insights to others. Although academic success is measured across all of these outputs, some outputs carry more weight than others. In economics, journal articles are trumps. Mature scholars soon start to write books, but journal articles establish authors' reputations that books then elaborate. Academics bring others to their side by speaking with clarity and conviction to other members of the same discipline.

A discipline is a self-organizing group of individuals who share a common set of language and concepts, employ compatible empirical protocols, and appeal to rather uniform standards of "truth." The purpose of particular disciplines is to tell others what they would be well advised to believe about the facts and phenomena that fall under the ambit of said disciplines. Are you worried about genetically modified organisms? Ask a geneticist or a plant breeder. Are you worried about the safety of a particular food item? Ask a food scientist or a microbiologist. Are you curious about the probability of rain next Tuesday? Ask a meteorologist. Are you puzzled that share prices rise when a large corporation dismisses thirty thousand of its employees? Ask an economist. Disciplines are epistemic communities. Members of these communities communicate (note the similarity) through a variety of means. Journals play several roles for an epistemic community: (1) they announce the latest research fads, (2) they validate the credibility of fledgling members of that particular community, and (3) they establish the enduring standards by which current and future members of the community shall be judged in the competition for high status within that particular community. Journals are epistemic flagpoles up which ideas are run to see who will and will not salute. Journal editors control the flagpole.

This can be a troublesome calling. In a way that is familiar to the superrich or the beautiful, you can never be sure whether others are nice to you because you are eminently likeable or whether their seeming fondness for you springs from other motives. When they respond with immoderate wrath on receiving a rejection letter, we get a rough indication of their enduring attachment. A sense of humor is an essential prerequisite for this job. I have two rejection letters at the ready. The first is of British origins:

We have received your manuscript "_____." You will be pleased to learn that we find it to be both novel and interesting. Unfortunately, the part that is interesting is not novel, and the part that is novel is not interesting.

The second letter is said to be Chinese in origin:

We have received your manuscript with boundless delight. If we were to publish your paper, it would be impossible for us to publish any work of a lower standard. And as it is unthinkable that in the next thousand years we shall see its equal, we are, to our regret, compelled to return your divine composition and to beg you a thousand times to overlook our short sight and timidity.

I have, on very few occasions, invoked the first letter. The second one will not be used.

I was asked to address the "experiences of journal editors." The interest therefore seems to concern the various perspectives that editors of economics journals bring to their job as keepers of the flagpole.

The Journal *Land Economics*

First, a bit about my particular flagpole, *Land Economics*. It was established by Richard T. Ely in 1924 as the *Journal of Land and Public Utility Economics*. Ely, an eminent economist at the University of Wisconsin, was one of the founders of the American Economic Association. He was also an adherent of the "social gospel" movement and referred to himself as a Christian Socialist. In the waning years of the nineteenth century, the Wisconsin state superintendent of education, an ex officio member of the University of Wisconsin board of regents, grew alarmed at Ely's public positions and launched an aggressive attack against Ely— criticizing both his support of laborers in their quest for improved working conditions and his teaching of "socialism and other dangerous theories." He called for a regent investigation of Ely and his writings. This led to the famous "academic freedom trial" that still stands as a singular moment in defining academic freedom in American higher education. That trial resulted in the famous assertion that "Whatever may be the limitations which trammel inquiry elsewhere, we believe that the great state university of Wisconsin should ever encourage that continual and fearless sifting and winnowing by which the truth alone can be found." The university president, Charles Kendall Adams, wrote that statement in defense of Ely, and it was endorsed by the regents in 1894 (Hansen 1998). *Land Economics*, which has always been published by the University of Wisconsin Press, carried that quote on its cover until 1976.

Quaint as it now seems, we must not overlook the fact that Ely's problem is not that rare. It seems that there will always be instances when particular political and economic interests seek to bully university faculty. Indeed Nobel economist T. W. Schultz, who received his Ph.D. at Wisconsin in 1930, was much influenced by the successors of Ely—John R. Commons, Benjamin Hibbard, Selig Perlman, and George Wehrwein. Schultz himself felt the whip of public outrage. He was chair of the department of economics at Iowa State College when, in 1943, one of his colleagues published a pamphlet announcing that margarine was nutritionally equivalent to butter and that its increased use would liberate scarce resources for the war effort. The president of Iowa State College, under pressure from the dairy industry, insisted that the publication be withdrawn from circulation. As editor, Schultz resisted, and when the original report was reviewed yet again and revised, it made an even stronger case for the advantages of margarine compared to butter. In the immediate aftermath of this event, Schultz soon left Iowa State for the University of Chicago, and the department lost an additional fifteen professors (Beneke 1998).

I have been an editor for over thirty-four years, which means that I had an early start. Indeed, the opportunity came to me shortly after being promoted to the rank of associate professor at the University of Wisconsin at Madison and after just five years as a faculty member.

Land Economics is an applied journal that focuses on environmental economics, pollution regulation and enforcement, endangered species, law and economics, urban and rural land uses, property taxation, various natural resources (oil, fisheries, timber, minerals), and international development as it relates to natural resources. *Land Economics* was the first American journal devoted to this particular range of issues, many of which became prominent in the 1970s. The journal has grown and matured with the field (Roulac, Dotzour, Cheng, and Webb 2005). I have been editor of the journal for approximately 40 percent of its existence, and so I too have evolved along with the journal. In the following pages, I reflect on that coevolutionary process.

The Early Years: Embracing Rigor

A newly minted Ph.D. in economics comes on the job market with assured convictions about an extremely limited set of theoretical concepts and empirical techniques—but with little awareness of or interest in the historical evolution of the discipline. Rather like medical students, most new Ph.D.s have spent approximately three years acquiring a set of skills that are expected to last them for the better part of their professional lives. However, unlike medical students, economists do not spend time under the careful tutelage of established members of the same epistemic community in a structured program whose purpose is to situate their classroom materials in the larger practice of their craft. We do not have internships or residency requirements. Instead, we throw twenty-five-year-olds into the serious business of scholarship.

These days, under the press of yet more econometrics and game theory, these students know little if anything about the origins of their newly acquired craft (Colander 2007). Apparently, they have little interest in it. Nor is the professoriate concerned about history of thought. As a colleague expressed it once in a faculty meeting: "Why should we have our students study the incorrect ideas of our predecessors? I never had a course in the history of economic thought, and it has not held me back." Few instructors seem to assign journal articles that are more than three or four years old. The field moves fast, and young researchers must get to—and remain at—this moving frontier. It cannot be said that new Ph.D.s in economics are well educated in their discipline, nor is their training especially deep or wide—although new Ph.D.s tend to imagine that there is nothing that matters in economics that they do not understand.

And so at the tender age of thirty-four, with training in economics but without an education in the discipline (although in those ancient times, we were required to take one course in the history of economic thought and show passable knowledge of one foreign language), I gained control of a flagpole. Consistent with the dubious convictions of the intellectually presumptuous, I was not in doubt about what the journal needed: it must become more rigorous. And so I set out to make it a more respected academic journal. It took about three years for anyone to notice. Lambda Alpha International, the honorary society for the advancement of land economics, was founded—also by Ely—in 1930. In those days (the 1970s), members of Lambda Alpha International received a copy of the journal as part of their annual membership dues. One day, I received a letter from the officers of Lambda Alpha International suggesting that the new direction of the journal was pulling it too far away from its more practical and historic focus on issues of direct concern to those involved in the real estate business—what the British would call "the property market." My colleagues on the editorial board— mostly faculty members at the University Wisconsin at Madison— supported the new academic emphasis I was pursuing, and we decided that it was time to separate the journal from Lambda Alpha International. The loss in subscribers was substantial, but their special subscription discount meant that our revenue losses were minimal once the size of the print run was adjusted. In the interest of making the journal more academically acceptable, I (we) had willingly shed approximately twelve hundred readers.

The separation was probably inevitable. The 1970s were the glory days of environmental action and legislation. Earth Day, the Clean Air Act, the Clean Water Act, the National Environmental Policy Act, and Rachel Carson's *Silent Spring* were in the news, and it was a propitious time to situate *Land Economics* at the forefront of academic work on the economics of environmental resources. There were other real estate journals, although they too were becoming more formal. The 1980s represented a period of growth and heightened respectability for the journal. Subscriptions held steady despite the appearance of many new journals encroaching on our historic turf. Submissions were up, and acceptance rates plummeted to approximately 23 to 24 percent. As with elite universities, lower acceptance rates suggest superior quality.

And then in March 1989, the *Exxon Valdez* spilled approximately 11 million gallons of crude oil over 11,000 square miles of Prince William Sound in Alaska and out into the Pacific Ocean. This amount of crude oil would have provided fifteen minutes worth of gasoline consumption to U.S. drivers in 2007—so little loss of gasoline and yet so much environmental damage.[1] But there was also profound collateral damage within the field of environmental economics. The litigation associated with the oil spill altered friendships within a rather small field of economics, and it changed the journals pertinent to the field. Prior to that time, the use of contingent (hypothetical) valuation methods (CVMs) for measuring the alleged nonmonetary value of the natural world had been slowly gaining popularity. Suddenly, Exxon, the federal government, and the state of Alaska found themselves in need of environmental economists to discern the monetary value of the damages from the oil spill.

Following 1989, the proportion of published papers on hypothetical valuation increased from its long-term average of 10 to 15 percent to an average of about 25 percent, where it has remained since. With so many papers focused in one area of work—and an area that was not without serious conceptual and empirical disagreements—it was becoming difficult to offer subject-matter variety in each issue. The field of environmental economics had succumbed to a fad. Although the *Exxon Valdez* oil spill expanded the intensity of the fad, it had been started by the federal government.

Recall that the 1980s and 1990s were a period of concern about "excessive regulations" that were thought to hamper the competitiveness of the economy. President George H. W. Bush put Vice President Dan Quayle in charge of a Council on Competitiveness. In 1993, President William J. Clinton issued Executive Order 12866 on "Regulatory Planning and Review." Three years later, the Office of Management and Budget issued new rules about federal action. Its document titled "Economic Analysis of Federal Regulations under Executive Order 12866" declared that the regulatory policies should "maximize net benefits to society." Many government agencies had seen this coming since the late 1980s, and the demand for benefit-cost studies had been growing rapidly. The consulting incomes of environmental economists improved considerably. Grants and contracts multiplied as well, and journals bore the brunt of this new fad.

But there is an additional enduring effect from this era. During the 1990s, a significant number of the established economists who specialized in such valuation studies were under contract either to Exxon, the federal government, or the state of Alaska. It became difficult to find fair and balanced reviews, and it was often impossible to tell which individuals were working for which party in the litigation. For the first time in twenty years, I began to entertain doubts about the fairness of the review process. Blind reviews are of little value in a small field because everyone knows who is doing what. In addition, the skewed mix of papers was a lingering concern. And so I became less open to yet another study of a CVM experiment, and I became weary of yet another axiomatic proof of the validity of some hypothetical valuation exercise. Indeed, I had written several articles that were critical of the technique (Bromley 1990, 1991, 1993, 1995, 1997; Vatn and Bromley 1994).[2] I was not alone in my concern for hypothetical valuation exercises. In 1993, Jerry Hausman (1993) edited a book that was critical of the entire undertaking. In that same year, the National Oceanic and Atmospheric Administration, a major user of contingent valuation studies, released the results of a special panel of experts who had been asked to comment on the conceptual and empirical validity of the method (Arrow, Solow, Portney, Leamer, Radner, and Schuman 1993). Then in 1994, the *Journal of Economic Perspectives* published three papers devoted to the matter. One paper argued that it was important in the policy arena (Portney 1994), one paper offered a theoretical and empirical exploration of the methods (Hanemann 1994), and one paper was critical of much that was being done (Diamond and Hausman 1994).

Rigor had been achieved, but the journal had become more narrow and perhaps less interesting.

The Middle Years: Seeking Creative Thought

As both an author and editor, I realized quite soon that there is a tendency among editors to embrace a policy of safety first. By *safety first*, I mean editors' pervasive fear that they might actually publish a bad paper or a paper in which something is later (soon after publication) found out to be wrong. This fear manifests itself in two ways. First, papers are forced into a standard format—problem, existing literature (where the problem is found to reside), model, estimation, discussion, and, in an applied journal, policy implications. Second, papers are screened aggressively for technical flaws but only indifferently for pertinence, which is more difficult to judge (so this may not be all bad). What does not seem pertinent today may turn out to be highly pertinent in the near future. But journals can indeed be technically sound and of dubious interest.

The journal had arrived at a point in which papers that lacked conceptual rigor stood very little chance of surviving the review process. Even when I would select reviewers who I imagined would be open to innovative and exploratory papers, the reviewers would invariably damn such papers by stating that surely I was not interested in such stuff—even though I did want to publish good papers of that genre. Their concerns implied that the journal's reputation for publishing rigorous work would surely suffer should I weaken my resolve. I soon realized that this dual tendency toward standardization and safety first must surely be precluding important work from serious consideration. Equally important, I worried that there seemed to be little discussion about those issues for which environmental economists had valuable insights. As an experiment I composed the following letter:

From the Editor

Among the things that editors worry about is whether in the review process, we eliminate from broader distribution those articles expressing ideas that, at the moment, may seem a little farfetched. This has another component, which is the failure of a journal to receive such articles if the perception exists that there is little chance of getting them published. The recent increase in the formalistic articulation of economic concepts raises the prospect that the time will come when some economic ideas of great import will not see the light of day because they do not lend themselves to expression in such form. In my discussions with a number of economists, the point is often raised that all journals are becoming more formal (mathematical), and this is a cause for concern on the part of everyone I talk with—including those whose mathematical skills are not only well developed but often on display.

The general concern is that this dominant form of communication precludes the type of thought process that was so much a part of the classical tradition in our discipline. This does not mean that formal models of either a theoretical or an empirical nature are irrelevant to our discourse over economics and natural resource policy. But it does mean that many good ideas and important concepts that do not lend themselves to formalistic expression are being driven out of economics journals into other media where economists have fewer chances to see them.

Having worried about this issue for some time, it seems appropriate to make an effort to test the hypothesis that there are good economic questions and issues that warrant wide circulation but that do not lend themselves to the longer and more detailed articles that we have traditionally published. It is with this in mind that we established a section entitled "Speculations," which is devoted to the publication of brief statements by economists on any topic that has traditionally been relevant to *Land Economics*. I ask only that the statements be less than ten double-spaced pages and that they focus on economic questions of interest to our readers. I hope that authors will consider this an opportunity to raise questions of a constructive nature about economic issues that warrant closer scrutiny.

The submissions are reviewed by me, though I may seek advice from members of the Editorial Board. The intent is to speed up the review process with the idea that extensive revisions and modifications would not be the norm. We are under no need to publish any set number of such submissions and prefer to have the "Speculations" section expand and contract as the supply of accepted articles dictates.

The pertinent question concerns the "supply response" to this invitation. Honesty demands that the response from authors be judged seriously underwhelming. In the ten to fifteen years that this announcement has been inserted in the *Journal* at various frequencies, we have received approximately four to six submissions. Why are policy-oriented economists so little interested in exploring novel ideas? Is the pressure for more and more journal articles now so severe that there is no time to reflect? And even if reflection is possible, is the opportunity cost of time so high that no one can afford to write ten pages? Are we now so competitive that we are afraid to speculate in public out of fear that someone else will hijack our idea and publish a paper thereon? Or, and this is even more serious, have applied economist lost the ability to formulate an economic issue in the absence of a formal model?

The Later Years: Enforcing Hume's Fork

Many economists believe that the economic models that they construct and the empirical claims that are predicated on those models represent objective truth about the world. This position reveals innocence of what philosophers call Hume's fork. Hume's fork tells us that there are two classes of propositions—those concerning relations between ideas and those concerning relations between matters of fact. A continuing problem in economics is that many authors believe that the models they build— relations of ideas—offer a clear and plausibly reliable mapping into propositions about the world of facts that those models presume to depict. Often authors will claim that their structurally dependent model proves certain things about the way that things are in the world. However, models can do so only if they are built to be tested against the world that they presume to replicate.

After a few years of dealing with a plethora of such axiomatic exercises, my tolerance began to diminish. But a qualification is in order. In general, there are two types of axiomatic models. The first type might be called *ontological models*. Here we have models that concern the nature of being, of existence—indeed, of reality. Existence theorems in economics are of this sort. Such models demonstrate possibilities. A second type is what I call *prescriptive models*. Although the terminology is flawed, economists often refer to ontological models as examples of "positive" economics and to prescriptive models as examples of "normative" economics. Indeed, Milton Friedman's *Essays in Positive Economics* (1953) demonstrates the usual confusions about positive. Philosophers, but especially Hilary Putnam, have done much to undermine this flawed positive/normative distinction among economists (Putnam 2002).

If *Land Economics* were a theoretical journal, the ontological models would be quite fine. However, we are an applied journal, which means that prescriptive models are the coin of the realm, and articles that elaborate prescriptive models without any empirical grounding are without redeeming value. These prescriptive models offer up a variety of assertions about efficiency, socially preferred policies, Pareto improving policies, and welfare-enhancing policies. Notice that policy prescriptions are, at the same time, policy predictions. "Efficiency demands that policy X ought to be implemented" simultaneously implies that "policy X will bring about an efficient outcome."

These empirical claims arise from—and are therefore quarantined by—the self-referential models within which they are embedded. Many environmental economists insist that our field is a policy science and that therefore we must offer up policy prescriptions. Such claims are not wrong; they are simply incomplete. Economics is an empirical science, and any field within economics that persists in offering untestable empirical claims cannot be taken seriously. But there was a more serious problem with some of these prescriptive models: they are untestable. When an environmental economist claims that a particular scenic vista is worth some monetary amount and therefore ought to be preserved against the onslaught of some commercial development, an untestable prescriptive empirical claim is on display.

By refining my conception of rigor, I began to worry about such prescriptive assertions emanating from settings in which their plausibility could not be assessed. After crafting too many letters on this matter I finally created a standard one:

Dear _____,

Thank you for submitting your manuscript "_____" for consideration in *Land Economics*. After giving it a preliminary review, we must regretfully conclude that we cannot consider it further.

Land Economics is primarily interested in the policy aspects of land and related natural resources, and we insist that all papers have this as a rather prominent aspect. With this in mind, it is necessary that papers have a strong empirical component. Although one can always derive so-called policy implications from purely axiomatic models, the very generality (universality) of such approaches is also their fatal limitation in a policy sense. Without the necessary applicability theorems that connect purely axiomatic models to some particular policy context, the derived policy implications are entirely self-referential because they are pre-figured by the assumptions on which the analytical model rests. Although there can then be debate about the various assumptions that preordain these alleged policy implications, this is not a subject of interest to the vast majority of our readers.

Thank you for giving us a chance to consider your paper.

Daniel W. Bromley, Editor

A Few Reflections of a Life at the Flagpole

Since Lionel Robbins, most economists claim that "Economics is the science which studies human behaviour as a relationship between ends and scarce means which have alternative uses" (Robbins 1932, 16). Robbins then goes on to claim that "Economics is entirely neutral between ends; that, in so far as the achievement of *any* end is dependent on scarce means, it is germane to the preoccupations of the economist. Economics is not concerned with ends as such" (Robbins 1932, 24). The fundamental problem with this definition is that it fails to call our attention to the origins of—the reasons for—particular scarcities. It is not enough to claim that scarcity is the common element in our discipline without then showing a serious interest in how particular scarcities are often socially constructed. When Robbins and other economists insist that economics is not concerned with ends, the implication is that one can always be clear about the difference between means and ends.

Consider a country in Central America in which six or seven families own all of the agricultural land. The indirect theorem of welfare economics says that given any possible initial endowment of assets, a competitive market will give rise to—and sustain—a Pareto optimal allocation of resources. The economist who is intent on hiding behind Robbins's dictum will be pleased to discuss the efficiency properties of resource allocation in such a setting. And in doing so, this particular economist may well relish the immunity that comes from an assertion that economics is not concerned with ends as such.

But the more pertinent question concerns the recommendatory power of a finding that all resources in such a setting are optimally allocated. Of what interest is it to learn that the very few landowners and the thousands of landless peasants are precariously perched on some Pareto frontier? Recall that Pareto optimality is optimal only with respect to the value judgments that are inherent in the conceptual structure that yields the concept of Pareto optimality. And the single value judgment essential to the present discussion is that economics is neutral between ends. Foreswearing any concern for ends licenses economists to comment blithely on the efficiency attributes of an allocation of land, labor, capital, and management such that some large number of people work very hard for very little while others work hardly at all for handsome rewards. The silence of the ontological economist serves two purposes: it makes it unnecessary ("unscientific") to comment on this situation, and it ratifies (by that silence) the tacit disciplinary legitimacy of a situation that most sentient adults would find morally odious. In this way, economics removes itself from its proper centrality to a long list of profound economic problems (Bromley 2006).

And the prescriptive economist would enter here to announce that rectifying this offensive situation cannot be justified in the absence of a clear showing that the gainers from a thoroughgoing land reform—the current landless peasants—could gain enough through a redistribution program that would produce an economic surplus that would allow the losers (current landowners) to be compensated and still leave a surplus for the peasants to enjoy. In other words, if redistribution would not be Pareto safe, then it is economically irrational to do so.

Other examples could be adduced. Studies will seek to ascertain if poor peasants in Bangladesh who are now drinking poisonous water (because clean water is so scarce as to be unavailable) can muster a sufficient willingness to pay not to be poisoned. If they cannot come up with enough to cover the necessary costs of ridding their water supply of poisons, then they deserve to be poisoned. The Paretian economist can be ruthless. Thomas Carlyle, in 1849, had a similar reaction to economists about slavery in the Caribbean. Carlyle originated the assertion that economics was the "dismal science" (Ogilvie 2007).

Nearly four decades of reading and seeking coherent reviews of such papers (approximately seven thousand of them, by my reckoning) can indeed become tedious. Those of us in control of the flagpole often lament the state of the discipline. We share incredulous anecdotes and smile at the feeble attempts of our contributors to appear as objective analysts. Sometimes it seems hopeless. And then along comes a sparkling paper that makes it all worthwhile. Such papers are produced by economists who understand the fatuousness of the Robbins dictum. These papers adhere to the idea that economics, properly understood, is not the science of choice but the science of choices and their consequences. These papers show us that economics, properly done, is the study of how societies organize themselves for their provisioning.

When those papers arrive on our desk, we are once again proud of our discipline and its better practitioners.

Notes

I am grateful to Lee Hansen for comments on an earlier draft.

1. Almost twenty years later, Exxon has yet to reimburse those fishing families and others whose livelihoods were harmed.

2. After I became editor of *Land Economics*, I no longer submitted articles to it.

References

Arrow, Kenneth, Robert Solow, Paul Portney, Edward E. Leamer, Roy Radner, and Howard Schuman. 1993, January 15. Report of the NOAA Panel on Contingent Valuation. *Federal Register* 58 (10):4602–4614.

Beneke, R. R. 1998. T. W. Schultz and Pamphlet No. 5: The Oleo-Margarine War and Academic Freedom. *Choices* 13 (2):4–8.

Bromley, Daniel W. 1990. The Ideology of Efficiency: Searching for a Theory of Policy Analysis. *Journal of Environmental Economics and Management* 19 (1):86–107.

Bromley, Daniel W. 1991. *Environment and Economy: Property Rights and Public Policy Oxford*. Cambridge, MA: Blackwell.

Bromley, Daniel W. 1993. Regulatory Takings: Coherent Concept or Logical Contradiction? *Vermont Law Review* 17 (3):647–682.

Bromley, Daniel W. 1995. Property Rights and Natural Resource Damage Assessment. *Ecological Economics* 14:129–135.

Bromley, Daniel W. 1997. Rethinking Markets. *American Journal of Agricultural Economics* 79 (5):1383–1393.

Bromley, Daniel W. 2006. *Sufficient Reason: Volitional Pragmatism and the Meaning of Economic Institutions*. Princeton, NJ: Princeton University Press.

Colander, David. 2007. *The Making of an Economist, Redux*. Princeton, NJ: Princeton University Press.

Diamond, Peter A., and Jerry A. Hausman. 1994. Contingent Valuation: Is Some Number Better Than No Number? *Journal of Economic Perspectives* 8 (4):45–64.

Friedman, Milton. 1953. *Essays in Positive Economics*. Chicago: University of Chicago Press.

Hanemann, W. Michael. 1994. Valuing the Environment through Contingent Valuation. *Journal of Economic Perspectives* 8 (4):19–43.

Hansen, W. Lee, ed. 1998. *Academic Freedom on Trial: One Hundred Years of Sifting and Winnowing at the University of Wisconsin–Madison*. Madison: University of Wisconsin Press.

Hausman, Jerry, ed. 1993. *Contingent Valuation: A Critical Assessment*. Amsterdam: North Holland.

McCloskey, Donald [Deirdre]. 1983. The Rhetoric of Economics. *Journal of Economic Literature* 21:481–517.

Ogilvie, Sheilagh. 2007. "Whatever Is, Is Right"? Economic Institutions in Pre-Industrial Europe. *Economic History Review* 60 (4):639–684.

Portney, Paul R. 1994. The Contingent Valuation Debate: Why Economists Should Care. *Journal of Economic Perspectives* 8 (4):3–17.

Putnam, Hilary. 2002. The Entanglement of Fact and Value. In *The Collapse of the Fact/Value Distinction*. Cambridge, MA: Harvard University Press.

Robbins, Lionel. 1932. *An Essay on the Nature and Significance of Economic Science*. London: Macmillan.

Roulac, Stephen E., Mark O. Dotzour, Ping Cheng, and James R. Webb. 2005. Evolving Research Priorities: The Contents of *Land Economics*. *Land Economics* 81 (4):457–476.

Vatn, Arild, and Daniel W. Bromley. 1994. Choices without Prices without Apologies. *Journal of Environmental Economics and Management* 26 (2):129–148.

Economics of Public Choice

15

Supplying Private Goods and Collective Goods at *Public Choice*

William F. Shughart II

You haven't done nearly as bad of a job [as book review editor] as I expected.
—Gordon Tullock to the author, circa 1991[1]

Editors are grossly underpaid for their work, and they are grateful for every bit of help.
—William G. Shepherd (1995, 122)

Public Choice, under the title *Papers on Non-Market Decision Making*, was launched at the University of Virginia (UVA) by Gordon Tullock in 1966 (Rowley and Houser 2012, 16). Apparently at the suggestion of William C. Mitchell (Simmons 2011, xiii), the journal was given its present name in 1969, coincident with the establishment of the Center for Study of Public Choice at Virginia Polytechnic Institute and State University (Virginia Tech), which reassembled from diaspora a group of former UVA faculty members and graduate students who had scattered to the winds after administrators there had denied Tullock promotion to full professor on three separate occasions (Rowley and Houser 2012, 17).

Tullock, who holds—and always will hold—the title of founding editor on the masthead of *Public Choice*, originally planned to publish one volume of articles annually in book form rather than as a more standard academic periodical comprising two or more issues per year (Tullock 1991, 130). He began the journal on a shoestring, after learning to his pleasant surprise that the University of Virginia Press was willing to print his first issue for the modest sum of $700 (130). From then on, supported by small grants from the National Science Foundation, fees collected from authors who bought reprints of their articles, the "free" use of UVA's office facilities and typing services (supplied by the invaluable Betty Tillman), supplemented from time to time by money from his own pocket, Tullock released sequels to the first volume of *Papers on Non-Market Decision Making* over the next two years.[2]

Following its renaming, *Public Choice* attracted a growing number of new manuscript submissions. Faced with an increasingly heavy workload that he could no longer handle himself, Tullock contracted with Martinus Nijhoff in 1978 to publish and distribute the journal (Tullock 1991, 136) and to provide him with periodic but modest compensation. His decision was based on his need for assistance with the business end of journal management (including printing, mailing, and collecting payments from subscribers) and not with his editorial responsibilities. He relished the opportunity to read the manuscripts of contributors to the expanding public-choice literature, especially those of younger scholars whose academic careers he was predisposed to promote by issuing decisions to accept for publication papers that had been rejected elsewhere (Tullock 1991, 135).[3]

After being disappointed by the process of soliciting and reading the reports of external reviewers,[4] Tullock (1991, 132) did "most of the refereeing" of manuscripts submitted to *Public Choice* himself. On the rare occasions when Tullock had a submission in hand about which he was not sure, he typically sought the advice of a colleague down the hallway at the Center for Study of Public Choice, asking that person not for a full referee's report but for a brief written or verbal opinion supporting an up-or-down editorial decision.[5] Thus, until May 1990, when Tullock handed the editorial reins over to Charles Rowley and Robert Tollison, who became joint coeditors for manuscripts submitted from North America, *Public Choice* essentially was a one-man show (Rowley 1991a, 201–202).[6] The journal prospered under Tullock's somewhat idiosyncratic but brilliant editorial regime. As of 1988, *Public Choice* ranked thirty-second on a list of eighty-six economics journals judged on the basis of various metrics, including the impact factor, which was compiled from data published in the *Social Science Citation Index* (Durden, Ellis, and Millsaps 1991, 173–174).

One reason for the journal's success, in my judgment, was that, whether or not he solicited or accepted the advice of other scholars as to a particular manuscript's merits or demerits, Tullock saw every paper submitted to *Public Choice* and made all editorial decisions personally. In actual practice, Tullock stored in separate filing cabinet drawers every manuscript he had accepted, rejected, or returned for revisions. He knew the authors and the topics of current research in public choice and could, by monitoring and managing the queue of submissions directly, guide the field's development.[7]

The editorial process changed in 1990 (Rowley 1991a). Following the appointments of a European editor early that year and then of joint coeditors for North America in May, for reasons that are not entirely clear to me, editorial decisions began to be made separately and independently in Europe and the United States. In the meantime, Martinus Nijhoff had been acquired by Kluwer Academic Publishers, which was headquartered in the Netherlands. Three hard copies of every manuscript submitted to *Public Choice* had to be mailed to Dordrecht, and a desk editor there would assign it, based solely on the corresponding author's geographic location, by mailing one copy to the European or the North American editors.[8] (The second copy was kept in Dordrecht, and the third was sent to the journal's referee after the editors secured the agreement of a scholar to review it.) All subsequent communications between authors, editors, and referees were routed through Dordrecht.

Besides the swaths of forest that had to be cut down to produce hard copies of manuscripts and the excessive delays caused by correspondence on paper passing back and forth across Europe or the Atlantic Ocean, no one person (except for Kluwer's desk editor, who had no authority to issue decisions) oversaw the entire queue of manuscripts. The editors for North America did not know what papers on what topics had been accepted by the European editor until they appeared in a hard copy of the current issue, again delivered to them via post. And they also did not know how many papers originating in Europe were awaiting publication. The European editor likewise was in the dark as to the numbers and topics of articles that were under review or had been accepted from North American authors.

Editorial coherence was reestablished in 2005 when I became the journal's senior editor. Shortly before this, Springer had acquired Kluwer, and Springer's executives were anxious for *Public Choice* to shift to a new online manuscript-processing system. My predecessors still were dealing with the editorial status quo of hard copies of manuscripts and correspondence routed through Dordrecht, a scheme that I had had considerable experience with in my prior positions on the journal's masthead.[9] Peter Kurrild-Klitgaard, now a professor of political science at the University of Copenhagen, already had succeeded the incumbent European editor, and soon after my appointment, Duke University's

Michael Munger accepted my invitation to join the new editorial team at *Public Choice*. Although the journal began accepting and processing new submissions electronically on October 31, 2005, a transitional period of a year or more ensued during which we also dealt collectively with the stockpile of manuscripts already being processed in paper form. That backlog, to the editors' great and everlasting relief, has long since been cleared, and since late 2006, *Public Choice* has been fully live exclusively in cyberspace.

What is most important in my view is that the structure of the editorial process was reorganized coincident with my appointment so that I, for better or worse, make the final decisions on all manuscripts submitted to the journal. The remainder of this essay summarizes my experiences and the chief lessons that I have learned as the editor in chief of *Public Choice*, which remains among the top thirty-five economics journals and ranks even higher among the journals of political science. In so doing, I hope to supply authors of articles written with *Public Choice* in mind with some helpful advice and to comment on some of the trends, good and bad, that I see in today's extensive—and distinctive—literature that intersects the fields of economics and political science.

The Expanding Editorial Workload

Public Choice now has three associate editors—the aforementioned Peter Kurrild-Klitgaard, Peter Leeson of George Mason University, who agreed to replace Michael Munger after the latter decided to step down after five years of exceptional service, and Georg Vanberg, then of the University of North Carolina and now at Duke, who was added early in 2011.

When Gordon Tullock contracted with Martinus Nijhoff to publish and distribute *Public Choice* to libraries and individual subscribers around the globe, he also assigned the journal's copyright to that company. Those rights later transferred to Kluwer Academic Publishers and then on to Springer in the relevant clauses of their respective merger agreements. The editorship of *Public Choice* thus is somewhat unusual in the world of academic journals in two senses. First, the editors are appointed by the publisher and serve in their posts under written contracts with the same, typically for five-year terms renewable by mutual agreement, and Springer pays them honoraria on a yearly basis.[10] Second, no formal relationship exists between the journal and the Public

Choice Society. The association is loose, as we often say, although the senior editor of *Public Choice* is an ex officio member of the society's executive board and submits a report on the journal's activities during the previous calendar year at the board's (and society's) annual meeting in March.[11]

Manuscripts are submitted through the online Editorial Manager software system that Springer adopted. They first go to an editorial assistant, who now is based in Mumbai, who in turn transmits them to me. Usually within twenty-four hours, I either reject a paper without review (a so-called desk rejection) or assign it to one of the three associate editors. It goes to an associate editor if the topic seems potentially to be of interest to the journal's readers and if the presentation of the theory or empirical evidence is scientifically sound. Early on, I continued the traditional editorial practice of assigning papers to associate editors based on their geographic origins (at the time, usually Europe and North America), but that norm gradually was displaced as the number of manuscripts submitted from other regions and continents grew by leaps and bounds.

Nowadays, roughly six hundred new manuscripts are submitted to *Public Choice* every year, about the same as the average annual number of submissions received by the *Journal of Political Economy* from 1970 through 2000 (Ellison 2002, 974).[12] Although authors from western Europe and North America still account for more than half of the papers received by *Public Choice*, scholars based in Asia, South Asia, South America, eastern Europe, the Middle East,[13] and Africa increasingly think of the journal as a potential outlet for the results of their research. Ever more often than in the past, so, too, do political scientists.

Given the present diversity of the geographic origins and fields of study of the authors who send papers to *Public Choice*, I assign manuscripts to my editorial colleagues based not on the corresponding author's home country but on the associate editors' areas of academic expertise and current workloads. At that point, each of the associate editors undertakes another review, and occasionally they recommend that papers be rejected without review. If the associate editor thinks that the manuscript has merit and might eventually be worthy of publication, he is responsible for soliciting external reviews (in almost every case, we now seek two outside opinions, using a fairly standard double-blind method), reading the reports when they come in, and recommending that the paper be rejected after review or returned to the author to be revised and resubmitted.

In virtually all cases, I concur with the associate editor's recommendation (all three editors are very good!).[14] If not, I confer with the handling editor via email to reach a mutually agreeable editorial decision. The process is not perfect, as many authors would surely argue. We undoubtedly commit type 1 and type 2 errors. Although I do not agree with John Maynard Keynes on many things, he came close to stating what I see as a half truth when he remarked at a dinner commemorating his retirement as editor of the *Economic Journal* (*EJ*) that he "never rejected what deserved publishing" but had "published much that wasn't" (quoted in Shepherd 1995, 26). Bloomsbury group hubris (or perhaps postprandial port) may have caused Keynes to be overconfident in his ability recognize and accept for the *EJ* 100 percent of the papers that "deserved publishing."

Later scholars are not so sure that journal editors, including Keynes himself, are infallible. Joshua S. Gans and George B. Shepherd (1994, 167) list twenty-eight heavily cited contributions to the economics literature that were rejected initially one or more times by the editors of leading journals (also see Shepherd 1995). Among the "mighty fallen" are Nobel laureates Gary Becker, Fischer Black, Myron Scholes, James Buchanan, Paul Krugman, Robert Lucas, Franco Modigliani, William Sharpe, Paul Samuelson, and James Tobin. And the list could be longer. Although not a winner of the Nobel Prize in economic science, Gordon Tullock's influential article titled "The Welfare Costs of Tariffs, Monopolies, and Theft" (Tullock 1967), which launched an extensive literature on rent seeking,[15] made the rounds of the top journals, piling up rejection letter after rejection letter until it was published by the *Western Economic Journal* (now *Economic Inquiry*).

Type 1 errors (rejecting worthy papers) evidently are common, if not necessarily the order of the editorial day. Errors of type 2 (accepting unworthy papers) are, in my judgment, much less of a problem, except to the authors in question. As Keynes said elsewhere in the after-dinner remarks mentioned above, "I feel much clearer . . . about the demerit of the articles I reject than I do about the merit of those which are included [in the *EJ*]" (quoted in Shepherd 1995, 26).

For reasons outlined in the next section, decisions to reject manuscripts submitted to *Public Choice* typically are far easier to make than decisions to ask authors to revise and resubmit or decisions to accept articles for publication.[16] As I contend below, rejections usually are more the fault of the author than of the editors' failure to grasp the importance of the paper's potential contribution to the literature.

The Authorial Rubber Meets the Editorial Road

Journal editors do not really edit.
—Sam Peltzman (quoted in Shepherd 1995, 110)

At any one point in time, the three associate editors of *Public Choice* collectively have seventy-five to a hundred manuscripts in process. They include papers just submitted (for which referees must be identified), those awaiting receipt of external reviewers' reports, and those that are awaiting recommendations to the editor in chief (me). I used to think that editorial duties consumed about 40 percent of my time; now it is closer to 60 percent. Because of this heavy workload, authors who receive positive preliminary editorial responses that ultimately may lead to acceptance rather than to rejection have exercised due diligence prior to submission. Many do not do so.

As documented by Glenn Ellison (2002), the articles published by most academic journals are much longer nowadays than they were a generation ago: "At the *AER*, *JPE*, and *QJE*, articles are now twice as long as they were in 1970. At *Econometrica* and *REStud*, articles are about 75 percent longer," thereby reversing "a 70-year long trend toward shorter papers" (Ellison 2002, 966).[17] Ellison is concerned mainly with shedding light on what he calls the "slowdown of the economics publishing process," and to do so he tests and largely rejects several plausible explanations, including coauthorship,[18] the rising specialization and division of scholarly labor,[19] the growth in the size of economics profession, increases in the number of manuscript submissions, and increases in submissions that have been authored or coauthored by nonnative speakers of English, "who need more help to improve the readability of their papers" (Ellison 2002, 958).

Along the way, he makes an observation about the interactions between authors and journal editors that I find persuasive. Prior to 1970, "almost all initial submissions were either accepted or rejected; the noncommittal 'revise and resubmit' was reserved for exceptional cases" (Ellison 2002, 948). Today the "noncommittal" editorial decision is issued more frequently, and "authors, cognizant that they will have to revise later, send papers to journals prematurely" (989). They fail to have their manuscripts read and commented on by colleagues, who might uncover obvious errors in the underlying theory or in the empirical tests of it or supply suggestions for improvement in the paper's logical structure or exposition. It is not clear to me that some authors nowadays even read their own papers from start to finish prior to submission to a journal.

In what follows, I supply some advice to authors.

Write Well

Bad writing abounds in submissions to *Public Choice*. I doubt that the journal is unique in that regard. Many manuscripts received by me are flabby, take too long to get to the point, contain excessive numbers of tables, figures, and appendices, and provide far too many details that often will be of little or no interest to the article's readers, assuming that the paper ever appears in print. Long manuscripts, which I define as more than thirty pages of double-spaced text, including all front and end matter,[20] try the patiences of editors and referees, bog down the review process, and prolong the time between submission and initial decision.

Good, concise writing is especially important for a manuscript's abstract, which is the first thing that an editor will read during an initial review, is sent to prospective referees, and is the basis on which they decide whether to agree to supply reports and recommendations to the journal's handling editor. In about 150 words, that abstract must inform the reader about the topic addressed, perhaps contain a brief summary of the methods of analysis employed, and describe the paper's main findings. An abstract that is too wordy or unclear can easily result in a desk rejection or make it more difficult for editors to find willing referees.

Notwithstanding Sam Peltzman's apt remark at the head of this section, I do edit *Public Choice*. A manuscript passes through the editorial process at the associate editor level, is revised (almost always at least once), is returned to the referees, and is endorsed by both of them. Then the handling editor recommends "minor revisions" or "accept but incomplete." At that point, I take charge of the paper. I print a hard copy of the paper, read it carefully with red pen in hand, and email the corresponding author a detailed list (sometimes running to two or more single-spaced pages) of suggested line edits and, if needed, substantive comments on matters of content. Only after the authors have responded to my editorial corrections, am I prepared to accept the paper for publication.

Because authors know that revisions almost always will be requested, many submit manuscripts prematurely. They also learn over time that if their paper is at *Public Choice* and jumps the early editorial hurdles, then they will benefit from my hands-on attention to substance and exposition. Unfortunately, that knowledge strengthens the incentives for even worse writing up front. I devote considerable time to editorial duties to ensure that the articles published in the journal read well even when they are not path-breaking contributions to the literature. One reason that economists have reputations for being bad writers is that many journal editors no longer edit the papers that they publish.

As John H. Cochrane (2005, 12) writes, "Many economists falsely think of themselves as scientists who just 'write up' research. We are not; we are primarily writers. Economics and finance papers are essays. Most good economists spend at least 50% of the time they put into any project on writing. For me, it's more like 80%." Every paper submitted to a journal should tell a story (a nonfictional one, it is to be hoped) and have a beginning, a middle, and an end. Authors should tell readers what they are going to tell them, tell them, and then tell them what they have been told. If you know that you are not a good or careful writer, hire a professional copyeditor who might not help with the paper's technical details but can straighten out your syntax.[21]

Know Thy Audience
Public Choice is a specialized journal whose contents are devoted to the work of the members in good standing of the Virginia school, whose origins can be traced to the publication of *The Calculus of Consent: Logical Foundations of Constitutional Democracy* (Buchanan and Tullock 1962). Although the journal is the flagship of the field of what has often narrowly been defined as the application of the theories and methods of economics to the study of politics, the reach of *Public Choice* is far broader and encompasses nonmarket decision making more generally. The public-choice approach to the analysis of extramarket decisions begins by adopting methodological individualism, according to which only individuals are capable of making choices, given their own preferences and the constraints that bind those choices. Groups and other collective bodies (such as voters as a whole, political parties, committees, legislatures, nations, and international organizations) do not choose in any meaningful sense of that term.[22]

There are other approaches, grounded in economic theory, to the analysis of political institutions and the public policies that emerge from them. Prior to the public-choice revolution, for example, the "prevailing view of political scientists was that government is generally benevolent, often benign, and seldom dangerous" (Simmons 2011, 2). That mindset has been adopted by the contributors to the so-called new political economy, which originated in western Europe and the fragment of the eastern bloc that is still evident in Cambridge, Massachusetts, as exemplified in the recent work of, for example, Torsten Persson and Guido Tabellini (2002, 2005) and Daron Acemoglu and James Robinson (2005, 2012). Those scholars, able and famous as they may be, are in the process of reinventing the public-choice wheel without acknowledging the shoulders of the giants on which they stand.[23] One of the key defects in the new political economy is the idea that elected and appointed public officials have incentives, stronger or weaker, to cater to society's welfare, however that may be defined.

To motivate their theoretical models, these political economists frequently suppose the existence of a social planner who maximizes a social welfare function, despite the fact that such an objective function does not—and cannot—be specified without violating at least one of a handful of uncontroversial assumptions about how individual values might be aggregated into social choices (Arrow 1963).[24] Therefore, if your manuscript includes the terms *social planner* or *social welfare function*, it will be rejected without review. For similar reasons, I customarily desk-reject papers that do not engage the distinctive and extensive public-choice literature because manuscripts accepted for publication in *Public Choice* must acknowledge the relevant work contributed previously to that literature. One footnote mentioning Buchanan and Tullock (1962), as some authors seem to assume, does not suffice.

Remain Abreast of the Articles Published in *Public Choice*

Keeping up with the current literature of any field of economics used to be a daunting task. Given the fairly long delays between the date of a paper's acceptance and its appearance in print, readers of journal articles were limited to seeing the fruits of research projects that scholars had been working on one or two years earlier. Nowadays, though, manuscripts accepted for publication in academic journals are published online quickly. For *Public Choice*, that delay is at most two weeks following the corresponding author's return of corrected page proofs.

Gordon Tullock monitored and guided the development of the field of public choice by accepting manuscripts exploring new areas of research that he found to be novel or interesting, even if they fell below his current standards for acceptance and, presumably, by rejecting papers that traveled down well-trodden paths. The current editorial team of *Public Choice* pursues those same objectives, but editorial policies change, and acceptance decisions evolve over time in response to changes in the mix and volume of topics addressed by the manuscripts submitted to a journal.

The editors currently are not looking for the following topics (in no particular order):

• Political economy and orthodox public finance / public economics: As indicated at the end of the last section, manuscripts that do not engage the distinctive public-choice literature but instead rely on models and methods that assume the existence of a social-welfare-maximizing planner (benevolent dictator) or of a social-welfare function are not appropriate for *Public Choice*. Neither are papers that situate themselves in the mainstream of the traditional fields of public finance or public economics. The authors of such manuscripts receive desk rejections, along with suggestions for submission to one of the many other general-interest and field journals that provide more appropriate outlets for their research.

• Manuscripts that merely gild Tullock's lily: We have lowered the priority assigned to the umpteenth minor theoretical variation on Tullock's (1980) specification of a contest-success function that underpins his original rent-seeking insight (Tullock 1967), which has been extended and embellished ad infinitum over the past thirty years. Unless a new manuscript adds something novel or takes that literature in an entirely new direction, the editors, for the foreseeable future, will reject the paper without review.

• So-called happiness research: *Public Choice* has seen a spate of manuscripts recently that rely on survey-based measures of happiness either as a dependent or independent variable in cross-sectional regressions or panel data regressions, usually at the country level. The authors explore the economic and political determinants of happiness or ask whether happier nations are more politically stable. We have published some articles along those lines, but the editors now feel that the happiness construct is built on unacceptable interpersonal comparisons of (cardinal) utility and is fatally flawed.

• Econometric analyses of the effect of political and economic freedoms on income or growth: It is by now well established that freer nations (and freer U.S. states) are both richer and grow faster than their less free counterparts. Although the relative weights that can be attached to indexes of economic rights versus political rights, as well as the subcomponents thereof, are less certain, enough evidence supporting the overall growth-enhancing effects of good institutions has been reported to warrant downgrading priorities assigned to such research in the editorial review process. We nevertheless do not rule out considering research relying on such indexes, provided that it points the literature in one or more new directions.

The foregoing partial list is likely to change as time passes. The editors at *Public Choice* communicate with one another frequently. Decisions to downgrade or upgrade areas of research are made largely in response to the overall volume of submissions as well as to the mix of topics we see. Above all, we strive to accept and publish manuscripts that are interesting or novel or—consistent with Gordon Tullock's vision for the journal—might not get published anywhere else.

Why Edit?

I have asked myself that question many times, particularly on days when I have six to ten manuscripts to consider—and especially when I receive an email message from an author whose paper recently has been rejected. The online submission and manuscript processing system at *Public Choice* has many benefits in terms of shortening the delay between submission and initial editorial decision. But the factors that lengthen the turnaround time are the same as they were in the old days of academic journals. Some referees agree to review manuscripts but fail to turn in their reports within the requested thirty-day deadline, and some authors do not revise and resubmit their papers in a timely manner (we suggest thirty days if the revision if minor and forty-five days if it is major).

The first problem for journal editors, especially at the associate editor level, is dealing with referees who miss their deadlines. Because we strive to base decisions on two external reviews, if one referee fails to submit a report on time, then three options are available: wait another week or so to see if the report comes in, try to find an alternate reviewer, or decide based on one report. Although referees automatically receive reminders when their reports are overdue, the responsible associate editor always communicates independently via email with them to determine when the report will arrive. The associate editor's time would be better spent on reading other manuscripts. If a referee's report will arrive soon, then a recommendation can be submitted to me. But when a referee is unresponsive, the associate editor must decide whether to find a substitute, which resets the review clock by another thirty days, or make a decision based on one report. Dealing with referees is a major part of the associate editors' jobs and is the main reason for long delays in the review process.

Authors can be impatient and sometimes complain when an editorial decision has been prolonged. One consequence of the associate editors' desire to issue recommendations in a timely fashion is that, over time, they identify which potential reviewers can be relied on and which cannot. But associate editors cannot go back to the well too often and overtax reliable referees. If authors appreciated the editorial headaches that are created by overdue reviewer reports, they might themselves become better referees.

A second source of editorial frustration is that emails make it far too easy for authors to complain to editors about rejection decisions. They no longer need even to buy a first-class postage stamp. All editors commit type 1 errors, but asking them to revisit a decision to reject rarely results in an acceptance. I can recall only a handful of manuscripts submitted to *Public Choice* since 2005 for which a corresponding author's grievance (usually that a referee "had not read my paper") prompted me to change my mind. In those few cases, I invited the author to revise as he or she saw fit and resubmit and promised that at least one new referee would be asked to take a look at it. The odds are not very good for the aggrieved author, and the editor must spend extra time finding another referee, who generally confirms the initial decision to reject.

Scholarly journals traditionally fulfilled two complementary roles in the academic world—the verification (authentication) of research findings, using the system of peer reviews, and the dissemination of those findings (see, e.g., Tullock 2005, 107–134). The dissemination function largely has been usurped by the World Wide Web, which allows authors to post working papers online, by electronic journals that offer quick turnaround times but do not publish or distribute regular issues in a paper format, and by journals' increasingly common practice of granting online access to their subscribers to articles that have been accepted for publication and eventually will appear in print.

The verification of research findings thus is now the primary function of the traditional academic journal, and this cooperative enterprise involves authors, external referees, and editors. Editors exercise their own independent judgments, sometimes overruling the recommendations of peer reviewers and sometimes arguing among themselves about a particular manuscript's merits or demerits. It is an intellectually stimulating enterprise that keeps me continuously on my toes. Although Springer provides honoraria to the editors of *Public Choice*, if divided by the number of hours that we work on an annual basis, our publisher would be in violation of the minimum wage laws if we were its employees.

I edit not for the money but because of my commitment to the public-choice research program. I still cash the yearly check, though.

Helping to supply a collective good to my colleagues in that research program, which is transformed partly into a private good for the authors of the papers that the journal publishes, is why I edit.

I also edit because it is fun. As Postrel (1998, 183–185) writes, in referring to the work of psychologist Mihaly Csikszentmihalyi, "thinking is pleasurable. . . . It is 'better than anything else.'"[25] Every new manuscript submitted to *Public Choice* that reaches my court of last resort supplies a new challenge prompting me to ask myself rhetorically, "'how can I beat my record?'" (184). How, that is, can I do my job better? Eight years on, I am still am sliding down the proverbial learning curve, although perhaps its slope is less steep than it was at the beginning of my editorship.

Acknowledgments

This chapter benefitted considerably from the comments of Roberta Herzberg, Randall Holcombe, Peter Kurrild-Klitgaard, Peter Leeson, Michael Reksulak (who went into overtime), Randy Simmons, Diana Thomas, Robert Tollison, and Georg Vanberg on earlier versions of this essay. My friendly critics hereby are absolved of any blame for remaining errors, for which I accept full responsibility.

Notes

1. Gordon Tullock's backhanded compliment was voiced in the wake of the retirement as book review editor of my predecessor, the late William C. Mitchell, of whom Tullock (1991, 137) wrote that he was "markedly better in that role than anyone we ever had before and I'm sure better than anyone we could get to replace him." Touché.

2. The first two issues of *Papers on Non-Market Decision Making* did not carry publication dates. "Fall 1967" appears on the cover of volume 3 (Tullock 1991, 132).

3. Based on my own knowledge as an author of papers submitted to *Public Choice* and as Tullock's colleague at George Mason University during the mid-1980s, to which the Center for Study of Public Choice had by then relocated, Tullock commonly informed authors that he would accept their manuscript for publication in *Public Choice* if it had been rejected by at least two other journals.

4. "My experience here was unpleasant, although I gather completely normal" (Tullock 1991, 132).

5. During his editorial tenure, Tullock (1991, 132) handled "over 90 percent of the papers" submitted to *Public Choice* himself.

6. Friedrich Schneider of Johannes Kepler University of Linz was appointed in January 1990 as the journal's European editor to process the growing volume of submissions from scholars who were based in western Europe (Rowley 1991a, 202).

7. "From time to time, I . . . decided that some particular subject should be encouraged; hence, I . . . lowered my standards for that particular subject with the idea of making it obvious to bright young assistant professors that this is a particularly easy place to do research which will be published. And then, as I [received] more articles, I would raise my cutting level again but I have meanwhile changed the total structure of the discipline" (Tullock 1991, 138; also see Rowley 1991b).

8. The journal's two editorial positions actually were designated as one for Europe and, although occupied jointly, one for the "rest of the world." In the era before the globalization of scholarly research, "the rest of the world" as a point of origin for submissions to *Public Choice* comprised, for all practical purposes, Canada and the United States.

9. I had served as the journal's book review editor (1991–2004), acting European editor (2004), and joint coeditor (2004–2005).

10. The editorship of *Public Choice* thus changes hands in harmony with the traditional practice for selecting the president of the Public Choice Society. In accordance with the society's one-line constitution, the incumbent president, who serves a two-year term, designates his successor and then becomes a member of the executive board, comprised of all living past presidents. For a discussion of the single exception to that rule, see Stevens J. Brams, Michael W. Hansen, and Michael E. Orrison (2006). Tullock named his replacements at *Public Choice*, who in turn named theirs, subject to the publisher's implied veto power, which, to my knowledge, never has been exercised.

11. *Public Choice* also is one of the few academic journals that still publishes book reviews on a regular basis. Randall Holcombe of Florida State University succeeded me in that position, and Christopher Coyne of George Mason University followed him and now holds that post. The book review editor operates independently of the editorial process governing the acceptances of original research articles, commissioned editorial commentaries, and literature reviews.

12. *Public Choice* publishes sixteen regular issues annually in four numbered volumes. But we also from time to time commission and publish one or two guest-edited special issues every year. These are organized around themes of current interest (such as political blogs, transnational terrorism, and public choice at the local government level), celebrate important events (like the fiftieth anniversary of *The Calculus of Consent* in 2012) (Buchanan and Tullock 1962), or honor the scholarly work of major contributors to the public-choice literature.

13. Ever since the journal's founding, scholars who are based in Israel have submitted a small but steady stream of manuscripts to *Public Choice*.

14. Tullock (2005, 116) once wrote that "present-day editors of journals vary greatly. While the editor of a journal is seldom the leading figure in a field, he may come close to that level. At the opposite extreme, and more commonly, the editor may be simply a respected but ordinary worker in the field covered by his journal." Tullock and his successors have all been very active contributors to the public-choice literature.

15. Apparently not aware of her intellectual predecessor, Anne Krueger (1974) actually coined the term *rent seeking* in the title to an article that she published seven years after Tullock's paper appeared in print.

16. As Tullock (2005, 121) writes, "the prestige of a journal is affected by the articles it publishes; it is not affected by those it turns down."

17. For supporting evidence, see David N. Laband and John M. Wells (1998).

18. "In the 1970s only 30 percent of the articles in the top five journals were coauthored. In the 1990s 60 percent were" (Ellison 2002, 966).

19. According to Ellison (2002, 970–972), narrow specialization in subfields of economics may make it more difficult for authors to find colleagues who are willing to read and comment on their manuscripts prior to submission and for journal editors to evaluate submissions that address topics or use methods that are distant from their own fields of specialization. I don't buy either conjecture. First, email has reduced the cost of sending papers out for comment substantially, so authors do not have to rely solely on their departmental colleagues, none of whom may belong to the same subspecialty. Second, Ellison's other reason sounds like comments that are made in college or universitywide promotion and tenure review committees, when a candidate's champion asks how an economist can possibly evaluate the promotion or tenure application of someone from, say, physics. My reply is that I may not know much about physics but that I do know a well-crafted and tightly reasoned journal article when I see it. Much of that knowledge might be tacit and not capable of articulation. As Virginia Postrel (1998, 89) writes, "A swimmer cannot say how he stays afloat, nor an editor truly account for what makes an interesting, appropriate article."

20. Some authors try to game the system by submitting single-spaced manuscripts in small font sizes. Users of LaTeX are the worst offenders in that respect, and the eyesight of editors and referees suffers. Manuscripts can more easily be read and edited if they are double-spaced and are set in a font size no smaller than 11 point.

21. For some succinct and valuable tips on how to avoid these writing problems, see John H. Cochrane (2005). I also recommend highly Deirdre N. McCloskey (1999) as well as the classic writing reference, now in its fourth edition, William Strunk Jr. and E. B. White (2012). Among other lessons, Strunk and White advise every author to go on a "*which* hunt" to eliminate improper usages of that word when it is substituted incorrectly for *that*. As a matter of fact, the word *that* seems to be disappearing from the English language. I see many sentence constructions of the form "Assume the swan is black" instead of "Assume that the swan is black." Today's authors of scholarly articles also overuse many words, such as *high*, *higher*, *increased*, *increasingly*, and variants thereof when

they mean *larger, greater,* or just *more.* Few split infinitives are unsplit by authors nowadays.

22. For a recent introduction to the intellectual roots of public choice and summaries of some of the implications of the field's models and methods, see, for example, William F. Shughart II (2013).

23. For instance, a reference to James M. Buchanan and Gordon Tullock (1962) appears once—in a footnote—in Torsten Persson and Guido Tabellini (2005). There is no mention of either Buchanan or Tullock in the indexes to Daron Acemoglu and James Robinson's (2005, 2012) two latest books.

24. The differences between public choice and political economy probably are not as momentous (or as well known) as the clash between neoclassical theorists and Keynesians (Heilbroner and Milberg 1995). But unlike the new political economists, the Keynesians did not completely ignore their intellectual forebears or their contemporaries on the other side of the debate.

25. In the latter passage, Csikszentmihalyi quotes assembly-line worker Rico Medellin, who did the same task nearly six hundred times every working day. Summarizing some of Csikszentmihalyi's conclusions, Postrel (1998, 183–184) goes on to write that "people say they are happiest when they are completely absorbed by some activity that challenges their skills, provides feedback, has rules, and gives them a sense of control—when, in short, they are at play."

References

Acemoglu, Daron, and James Robinson. 2005. *Economic Origins of Dictatorship and Democracy.* Cambridge, MA: MIT Press.

Acemoglu, Daron, and James Robinson. 2012. *Why Nations Fail: The Origins of Power, Prosperity, and Poverty.* New York: Crown.

Arrow, Kenneth J. 1963. *Social Choice and Individual Values.* 2nd ed. New York: Wiley. First published 1951.

Brams, Steven J., Michael W. Hansen, and Michael E. Orrison. 2006. Dead Heat: The 2006 Public Choice Society Election. *Public Choice* 128 (3–4):361–366.

Buchanan, James M., and Gordon Tullock. 1962. *The Calculus of Consent: Logical Foundations of Constitutional Democracy.* Ann Arbor: University of Michigan Press.

Cochrane, John H. 2005. Writing Tips for Ph.D. Students. Available at http://faculty.chicagobooth.edu/john.cochrane/research/Papers/phd_paper_writing.pdf.

Durden, Gary C., Larry V. Ellis, and Steven W. Millsaps. 1991. Gordon Tullock: His Journal and His Scholarship. *Public Choice* 71 (3):171–196.

Ellison, Glenn. 2002. The Slowdown of the Economics Publishing Process. *Journal of Political Economy* 110 (5):947–993.

Gans, Joshua S., and George B. Shepherd. 1994. How Are the Mighty Fallen: Rejected Classic Articles by Leading Economists. *Journal of Economic Perspectives* 81 (1):165–179.

Heilbroner, Robert, and William Milberg. 1995. *The Crisis of Vision in Modern Economic Thought*. Cambridge: Cambridge University Press.

Krueger, Anne O. 1974. The Political Economy of the Rent-Seeking Society. *American Economic Review* 64 (3):291–303.

Laband, David N., and John M. Wells. 1998. The Scholarly Journal Literature of Economics: A Historical Profile of the *AER, JPE*, and *QJE. American Economist* 42 (2):47–58.

McCloskey, Deirdre N. 1999. *Economical Writing*. 2nd ed. Long Grove, IL: Waveland Press.

Persson, Torsten, and Guido Tabellini. 2002. *Political Economics: Explaining Economic Policy*. Cambridge, MA: MIT Press.

Persson, Torsten, and Guido Tabellini. 2005. *The Economic Effects of Constitutions*. Cambridge, MA: MIT Press.

Postrel, Virginia. 1998. *The Future and Its Enemies: The Growing Conflict over Creativity, Enterprise, and Progress*. New York: Simon & Schuster.

Rowley, Charles K. 1991a. A Changing of the Guard. *Public Choice* 71 (3):201–223.

Rowley, Charles K. 1991b. Gordon Tullock: Entrepreneur of Public Choice. *Public Choice* 71 (3):149–169.

Rowley, Charles K., and Daniel Houser. 2012. The Life and Times of Gordon Tullock. *Public Choice* 152 (1–2):3–27.

Shepherd, George B., ed. 1995. *Rejected: Leading Economists Ponder the Publication Process*. Sun Lakes, AZ: Horton.

Shughart, William F., II. 2013. James Buchanan and Gordon Tullock: A Half-Century On. In *Public Choice, Past and Present: The Legacy of James M. Buchanan and Gordon Tullock*, ed. Dwight R. Lee, 101–123. New York: Springer.

Simmons, Randy T. 2011. *Beyond Politics: The Roots of Government Failure*. Rev. and updated ed. Oakland, CA: Independent Institute.

Strunk, William, Jr., and E. B. White. 2012. *The Elements of Style*. 4th ed. White Plains, NY: Pearson Longman.

Tullock, Gordon. 1967. The Welfare Costs of Tariffs, Monopolies, and Theft. *Western Economic Journal* 5:224–232.

Tullock, Gordon. 1980. Efficient Rent Seeking. In *Toward a Theory of the Rent-Seeking Society*, ed. James Buchanan, Gordon Tullock, and Robert D. Tollison, 97–112. College Station: Texas A&M University Press.

Tullock, Gordon. 1991. Recollections of an Editor. *Public Choice* 71 (3): 129–139.

Tullock, Gordon. 2005. *The Organization of Inquiry: The Selected Works of Gordon Tullock*. Vol. 3. Ed. Charles K. Rowley. Indianapolis, IN: Liberty Fund. First published 1966.

Economics of Sports

16

The *Journal of Sports Economics*

Leo H. Kahane

Beginnings

This chapter, I suspect, is distinct from most others in this collection in that I am the editor of a journal and also one of its founders. The *Journal of Sports Economics* (*JSE*) was borne out of a 1997 conversation I had in the hallway at California State University at East Bay.[1] I had just put the finishing touches on my first sports economics paper (Idson and Kahane 2000), and I was discussing it with colleague Paul Staudohar, who had been writing in the field for many years. I noted to Paul that with the frequent appearance of sports economics papers in a variety of journals, perhaps the time had come for a journal devoted to the field. We began contacting folks who had written on sports economics topics in the past to see if they would be interested in serving on the editorial board of a journal devoted to the topic, and virtually everyone we contacted was excited at the prospect. Our list of board members was, in my view, impressive and included such notable economists as Jerry Hausman (Massachusetts Institute of Technology), Richard Gilbert (University of California at Berkeley), Roger Noll (Stanford University), Lawrence Kahn (Cornell University), Paul Weiler (Harvard University), Sherwin Rosen (University of Chicago), and Robert Tollison (then at the University of Mississippi).

Having never founded a journal before, I was at a bit of a loss about how to find a publisher. I contacted my former dissertation adviser at Columbia University, Doug Holtz-Eakin,[2] who at the time was serving as the editor of the *National Tax Journal*. I had a simple question for him: how does one start a new journal? He really did not have much advice as neither he nor anyone he knew had ever done so. Eventually, with the assistance of friend and coauthor Todd Idson (who was a faculty member at Columbia at the time), I wrote a proposal for the *Journal of*

Sports Economics and sent it out to a handful of publishing houses. Most showed interest in the project, but Sage Publications was the most enthusiastic and quickly offered a contract. By mid-1999, the *JSE* had come into existence, and the first issue appeared February 2000.

One of the challenges that researchers in sports economics face, and one that the *JSE* would face as well, is to have the discipline accepted as a legitimate field of economic research. We did not want the *JSE* to be perceived as an outlet for the sophisticated sports fan's analysis of sports statistics. Our goal was to publish serious, rigorous economic research that was related to sports. We envisioned publishing papers that would fall into one of two broad categories. One would emphasize the unique economics of sports markets, such as the structure of leagues, the issue of competitive balance, the role played by sports institutions (such as player unions and the National Collegiate Athletic Association), and unique legal arrangements (such as contracts restricting labor mobility and the antitrust exemption that Major League Baseball enjoys). The other category would be papers that use the abundant, amazingly detailed data generated by sports markets to focus on more general economic analyses. With the use of sports data, researchers can explore various economic theories, particularly in labor economics, that would go untested or poorly tested otherwise. Labor economist Lawrence Kahn (2000, 75) made this point in a *Journal of Economics Perspectives* piece:

> Professional sports offers a unique opportunity for labor market research. There is no research setting other than sports where we know the name, face, and life history of every production worker and supervisor in the industry. Total compensation packages and performance statistics for each individual are widely available, and we have a complete data set of worker-employer matches over the career of each production worker and supervisor in the industry. These statistics are much more detailed and accurate than typical microdata samples such as the Census or the Current Population Survey. Moreover, professional sports leagues have experienced major changes in labor market rules and structure—like the advent of new leagues or rules about free agency—creating interesting natural experiments that offer opportunities for analysis.

A sample of other economists using sports industries as a testing ground for general economic theories include Sherwin Rosen (1981), Ronald G. Ehrenberg and Michael L. Bognanno (1990), Arthur A. Fleisher III, Brian L. Goff, and Robert D. Tollison (1992), and Jerry A. Hausman and Gregory K. Leonard (1997).[3]

The inaugural issue of the *JSE* started with an introduction written by myself, Todd Idson, and Paul Staudohar. Our goal was twofold: we wanted to explain why we believed that the time had come for a journal devoted to sports economics, and we wanted to set out the scope for research that would appear in the journal. Our introduction was followed by an invited piece written by Simon Rottenberg, professor emeritus from the University of Massachusetts. Those familiar with the field know that Rottenberg wrote what is considered to be the first true sports economics paper in the 1950s (Rottenberg 1956).[4]

Growth

The *JSE* began as a quarterly publication with issues appearing in February, May, August, and November. The newness of the journal made the editing job a bit tense because there was not an established cache of manuscripts accepted for publication. The first year we received about fifty submissions, which was enough to get us through the year. Each year thereafter, the manuscript flow has increased, and now we receive approximately 120 submissions per year. The *JSE* also became affiliated with the International Association of Sports Economists (IASE), which was formed in Limoges, France, in 1999.[5] The years just after the founding of the *JSE* saw standard subscriptions numbering in the two hundred to three hundred range.

Interest in *JSE* has increased steadily over the years. Today the *JSE* has over four thousand subscribers of various types (both individuals and institutions). Furthermore, approximately seventy thousand separate articles were downloaded in 2011 (the latest complete year of data available).[6] As the manuscript flow increased, a backlog of accepted papers began to grow, which led to long time lags before accepted papers appeared in print. To address this problem, the *JSE* moved to six published issues per year beginning in 2007. The *JSE* has also created a formal affiliation with the North American Association of Sports Economists (NAASE).[7] The NAASE was founded in 2007 by a group of economists who had been regularly attending and presenting sports economics research at the Western Economic Association International (WEAI) conferences during the 1990s and 2000s. As part of the affiliation with the NAASE, each year (starting in February 2009) one issue of the *JSE* is devoted to publishing a selected number of papers presented at the WEAI in sessions sponsored by the NAASE. Over the past few years, special issues of the *JSE* have been devoted to specific topics, and their papers are invited and vetted by guest editors.[8]

One of the challenges that I face as editor of the *JSE* has to do with the journal's size. The *JSE* is what I would consider a small journal in comparison to most others. Larger journals typically have an editor, some coeditors, a book review editor, a managing editor, and editorial board members. At this time, the *JSE* is not large enough to warrant such a structure, and I carry out most of the editorial duties (except for reviewing manuscripts).[9]

The editorial process has several steps, beginning with the receipt of submissions. After a paper has been received and given a manuscript number, the next step involves looking over the paper to determine whether it is worthy of a full peer review. If a paper is not suitable for review, a rejection notice is sent out immediately. If it is worthy of review, the next step involves finding suitable reviewers. As I expect that most editors would agree, this is the second-most difficult and time-consuming task. The most difficult task is staying on top of reviewers and sending out periodic reminders to tardy referees. After their reports have been completed, the first-round decision needs to be made by carefully considering the viewpoints of the referees. Larger journals can accomplish most of these tasks by spreading their submissions out among the coeditors. In the case of the *JSE*, I do virtually all of these tasks.

Editing the *JSE* has recently become much easier with the move to an online submission process.[10] The Web site and associated software automates some of these tasks and sends me reminders, such as due dates. The downside, however, is that my communications with authors and referees have become much more impersonal.

Awkward Moments

Being new at the editing game, it did not take long for me to commit my first foul. I had decided that a legitimate, peer-reviewed economics journal should also publish book reviews, so for the second issue, I asked one of the editorial board members, a prominent sports economist, if he would review a book for the *JSE*.[11] The book I had in mind was written by another member of the editorial board (and also a top sports economist). The invitee happily agreed, and I looked forward to seeing his review. I shared this news with *JSE* cofounder Paul Staudohar, who was well acquainted with both the book author and book reviewer. His response was, "Geez, I hope he doesn't pan the book!" As it turns out, the book author and reviewer apparently had an ongoing feud of which

I was unaware, and sure enough, the review was harshly negative. As a courtesy to the author, I decided to warn him that a negative review was likely to be published in the next issue of the *JSE*. The author firmly requested that the review not be published because the reviewer had an axe to grind and would not produce an unbiased review of the book. Requests from me to the reviewer to tone down the language that he had used in the review were dismissed, and the reviewer stated that what he wrote was his honest opinion of the book. Being in the middle of all of this was quite stressful. After seeking consultation from various colleagues, I ultimately decided to publish the book review as-is. The basis for this decision centered on protocol: a highly qualified academic was asked to write a review of a book, and he did so. Furthermore, if we pulled the review because it was not favorable, then this would set the wrong precedent for future book reviews.[12]

Other awkward moments have occurred over the years that I imagine other editors have experienced. Several cases of plagiarism were detected by reviewers, and some cases involved otherwise well-respected academics. Responding to the authors in such cases is always a delicate matter. There have also been various struggles with the refereeing process. As noted earlier, the worst part of the editing job is hounding tardy reviewers (and as an author who has been on the other side of the process, I feel badly when the editorial decision drags on for six months or longer). Some referees accept my invitation to review a manuscript, promise to do the review after being reminded two months later, and then are ultimately apologetic when after five or six months, I notify them that their review is no longer needed. This is when I call in a favor from one of my more reliable reviewers or write a review of the paper myself (I ended up writing fourteen reviews in 2009).

Another problem that arises in the refereeing process is receiving diametrically opposed reviews from two highly qualified academics (such as "this paper is seminal and should be published immediately" and "this paper is awful and looks like it was written by an undergraduate"). In such cases, if I believe I am qualified, I serve as the tie breaker and write my own review; otherwise, I solicit a third opinion. All of this drags out the editorial process and wears on all parties involved. Lastly, I also struggle with reviews that are unnecessarily harsh and mean-spirited. (I once had a reviewer write that the author of a paper was so incompetent that he "should never have been born.") In such cases, I take the liberty of editing the language to make it more civil.

Future

My duties as editor of the *JSE* take up about a third of my working hours—a sizeable opportunity cost. But the experience being involved from the journal's beginning and seeing the *JSE* grow to become a recognized outlet for academic research has been very rewarding. I foresee several changes for the future. One is the editorial organization of the journal. As noted earlier, the *JSE*'s manuscript flow has grown considerably over the past decade. At some point, the workload will be too great for a single editor, and the next logical step will be to engage associate editors to shepherd subsets of the manuscripts through editorial process.

Another change that I expect to see in the future has to do with the source of manuscripts. The vast majority of manuscript submissions emanate from the United States and western Europe. We have had a handful of submissions from Japanese, Chinese, and South Korean authors, as well as a small number from South American writers. Because the *JSE* is now completely accessible online (from the submission process to online publication of papers), I hope and expect that we will see an increase in submissions from other parts of the world.

Lastly, contributors to the *JSE* (authors, editorial board members, and manuscript reviewers) have worked hard to make sure the journal is a respected outlet for serious economic research. Evidence of success in this regard has come in a variety of forms, including the prominence of the contributors and the quality of the published articles that have appeared in the *JSE*. In addition, the research appearing in the *JSE* has had a significant impact on the research published in other journals. For example, research published in the *JSE* has been cited by authors of papers appearing in top economics journals around the world, including *American Economic Review*, *Journal of Political Economy*, *Review of Economics and Statistics*, *Econometrica*, and the *Quarterly Journal of Economics*. Furthermore, after a lengthy examination period during which the *JSE* was assessed for its consistency in production, the journal received its first published impact factor. The *Journal Citation Reports* (Reuters Thomson 2012) computed the *JSE*'s impact factor for 2011 to be 0.718, ranking the *JSE* 170th out of 320 ranked economics journals.[13] This ranking puts the *JSE* in good company: *Contemporary Economic Policy* is ranked 194th and the *Southern Economic Journal* is ranked 185th. Our hope is that as time goes on, the *JSE* will continue gain the respect of economics academicians and to climb ever higher in the rankings.

Notes

1. Formerly known as California State University, Hayward.

2. By then, he had moved to Syracuse University.

3. These authors have written multiple papers in the field of sports economics and have been active reviewers for the *JSE*. The late Sherwin Rosen served on the journal's editorial board. Hausman and Tollison are both editorial board members.

4. In his 1956 paper, Rottenberg provides a rich economic description of the baseball labor market and in doing so develops a concept, referred to by sports economists as the "invariance proposition," which is seen as an early example of the Coase theorem, which came some four years later. For a careful examination of Rottenberg's seminal 1956 paper, see Rodney Fort (2005).

5. See The IASE's Web site at http://www.iasecon.net.

6. The *JSE* Web site can be found at http://jse.sagepub.com.

7. See the NAASE's Web site at http://www.kennesaw.edu/naase/index.html.

8. For example, the February 2006 issue, which was guest edited by Umberto Lago, Rob Simmons, and Stefan Szymanski, contained a collection of papers examining the financial crisis in European football. The February 2010 issue, guest edited by Rodney Fort, published a collections of papers devoted to the challenges of working with sports data.

9. As of 2007, Dennis Coates (University of Maryland, Baltimore County) took on the role as book review editor.

10. See the *JSE*'s online submission Web site at http://mc.manuscriptcentral.com/jsportsecon.

11. Names are withheld for this story, although enterprising readers could easily track them down.

12. To his credit, the book author accepted the decision and has remained a valued member of the *JSE* editorial board.

13. The impact factor for a given year is calculated as follows: (number of cites to *JSE* papers appearing in JCR-ranked journals for papers published in the previous two years) / (total number of citable papers published in the *JSE* over the previous two years).

References

Ehrenberg, Ronald G., and Michael L. Bognanno. 1990. Do Tournaments Have Incentive Effects? *Journal of Political Economy* 98 (6):1307–1324.

Fleisher, Arthur A., III, Brian L. Goff, and Robert D. Tollison. 1992. *The National Collegiate Athletic Association: A Study in Cartel Behavior*. Chicago: University of Chicago Press.

Fort, Rodney. 2005. The Golden Anniversary of the Baseball Players' Labor Market. *Journal of Sports Economics* 6 (4):347–358.

Hausman, Jerry A., and Gregory K. Leonard. 1997. Superstars in the National Basketball Association: Economic Value and Policy. *Journal of Labor Economics* 15 (4):586–624.

Idson, Todd L., and Leo H. Kahane . 2000. Team Effects on Compensation: An Application to Salary Determination in the National Hockey League. *Economic Inquiry* 39 (2):345–357.

Kahn, Lawrence M. 2000. The Sports Business as a Labor Market Laboratory. *Journal of Economic Perspectives* 14 (3):75–94.

Reuters Thomson. 2012. *2011 Journal Citation Reports*. Social Science Edition. Philadelphia: Reuters Thomson.

Rosen, Sherwin. 1981. The Economics of Superstars. *American Economic Review* 71 (5):845–858.

Rottenberg, Simon. 1956. The Baseball Players' Labor Market. *Journal of Political Economy* 64:242–258.

Economic Development

17

My Experiences as Editor of the *Journal of Developing Areas*

Abu N. M. Wahid

An introduction may not be irrelevant for this chapter. When I opened my email on June 13, 2012, I saw that a message had just arrived from Michael Szenberg and was waiting to be opened in my inbox. I was not expecting this email but recognized his name and opened the mail with much interest and enthusiasm. When I started reading the message, I was excited about what Michael had to say, and before I finished reading it, I had decided to accept his invitation to write an essay about my experiences as editor of the *Journal of Developing Areas (JDA)*.

Before I focus on my experiences as editor of the *JDA*, I must share the story of how I became an editor. In early 2000, I submitted a paper to the *JDA*. At that time, I knew that the journal was located in the College of Business at Western Illinois University, Macomb. Later, I was surprised to learn that the journal had gone out of business in 1999. For some reason, I had been fascinated by this journal since my days as a graduate student at the University of Manitoba.

Since the early 1980s, as a doctoral student and later as a young economics faculty member, I made several unsuccessful attempts to have at least one paper published in the *JDA*. When I heard that one of my preferred journals had stopped publication, I felt bad, not because my desire to be published in there would remain unfulfilled forever but because a good academic journal died too soon. I was aware of its quality and worldwide reputation. Almost immediately, I thought about the possibility of having the journal relocated to the College of Business at Tennessee State University (TSU). First, I discussed the matter with my friend and colleague Galen S. Hull, the then director of the Office of International Business Programs. He was overseeing several activities of the college with a Title III federal grant. In our first discussion about the possible move, he indicated that he would support including the journal as a separate line item on his next budget proposal for the Title III grant.

A few days later, I spoke with associate dean Millicent Lownes-Jackson and dean of the college Tilden Curry, who received the idea favorably and expressed their willingness to help relocate the *JDA* from Western Illinois to TSU. One day, Dean Curry took me to the office of the provost and the vice president for academic affairs, Augustus Bankhead, which led to the start of the actual initiative. The dean of the Business School at Western Illinois University reacted positively to my proposal and welcomed the idea of bringing the journal back to life. I asked the dean why the *JDA* went out of business at Western Illinois, and she said that when the university shifted its focus away from research and to undergraduate teaching, the administration decided to stop funding the journal.

After several rounds of negotiations, it appeared that Western Illinois was willing to hand over the periodical to us, so I wrote a detailed project proposal that highlighted the journal's importance in the field, the justification for its revival and relocation to TSU, and its academic and business prospects, including the initial budgetary and financial implications to TSU. The proposal recommended that the journal be supported by a Title III grant for five years, after which it would be on its own. I also proposed that if the relocation was completed before the end of 2001, then the first issue of the *JDA* in 2002 could be volume 36 (it was founded at Western Illinois in 1966). With a positive nod from the then president of the university James A. Hefner, the matter went to the legal advisers of both the universities, who considered the pros and cons of the move and drafted a simple formal agreement in writing. Western Illinois proposed that TSU pay it $36 as a token price for the journal (for the thirty-six years from 1966 to 2002). That was the only financial cost that TSU incurred for the transfer of the title, rights, and interests pertaining to the *JDA*. The transfer process went through smoothly and was completed in a relatively short period of time.

At that moment, I felt delighted and excited about becoming the editor of a respectable academic journal. I was naive, but I soon began to realize the serious responsibility and financial implications of the takeover and felt that my career could be negatively affected by the journal's fortunes. If I had known how challenging the editorship would be, I probably would not have dared to promote the move and handle the *JDA* single-handedly at TSU.

In those early days, I knew nothing about editing a journal or looking after the typesetting, promotion, marketing, sales, and accounts of the journal. But I told myself that looking backward was not an option and I must march forward. I took it seriously and focused on its success.

As editor of the *JDA*, my first job was to put together a strong international board of advisers, and I contacted people in academia on all continents at random. I picked Sir Partha Dasgupta's name from the Cambridge University faculty list and had an interesting conversation with him. I did not know that he was a big-name economist and the son-in-law of another great British economist, Nobel laureate James Meade. I also later came to know that Sir Dasgupta was of Bangladeshi origin, the same country in which I was born and raised. At that time, Sir Dasgupta was the dean of the School of Business at Cambridge. When I invited him to serve as a member of our international board of advisers, he asked me a question: "Being on your board, what will be my job?" I thought that if I asked him to promote the *JDA* in the United Kingdom or to write or review articles for our journal, he might turn down my offer. So I told him, "As a member of our board, you will not have to do anything for the *JDA*. You will just be on our committee. Everything else I will do." To my surprise, I heard a solid heavy voice: "If I have nothing to do, why do you want me to be on your board?" I understood what he meant and briefly concluded my conversation with him.

Along the way, I was fortunate to get positive response from people such as Kaushik Basu of Cornell University, Timothy Besley of the University of London, and the Nobel laureate Harvard professor Eric Maskin. When the international board of advisers was in place, I designed a *JDA* letterhead and began the long process of announcing to the world the revival and relocation of the *JDA*. I also developed a copyright form, check deposit slips, subscription invoices, payment receipts, and an Excel spread sheet for accounting purposes. I devised an easy and convenient accounting method that I continuously revise, based on my everyday experiences.

In 1999, when the *JDA* went out of business, it had over twelve hundred paid subscribers worldwide, and I expected that within two or three years, I would be able to recapture at least four or five hundred subscriptions. Later on, I realized that this estimate was overly optimistic and never had more than slightly over three hundred subscriptions for the print version. It was a period when libraries were increasingly switching from hard-copy subscriptions to online usage. A couple of years after the relocation, we joined Project MUSE of the Johns Hopkins University Press for its online dissemination. Since then, our print copy subscriptions have declined, our online subscriptions have increased, and we are experiencing a surge in our cash flow and revenue. In addition to Project MUSE, right now the *JDA* is available online with *JSTOR*, *ProQuest*, and *EBSCOhost*. The journal became self-sustainable slightly before my estimated target date.

Even in the early tough and rough days of the *JDA*'s journey, we paid attention to the academic quality of the journal and its design. We kept only the old name. We changed the shape, size, color, and design of the cover. Everything else was altered both in terms of looks and substantive contents. Before our takeover, the *JDA* was basically a multidisciplinary (a combination of economics, political science, and sociology) policy journal. To meet the needs of the time, we changed its focus to make it a more rigorous academic journal in the field of development economics. We decided that without some econometrics and empirical testing, no submission would even be considered as a full paper. Later, we started the Note section for which we consider noneconometric works, although every issue does not carry a note. The addition of the Note section to the *JDA* has its own interesting history, but it is not relevant for this piece.

When the first issue of the new *JDA* (volume 36) came out in the fall of 2002, readers, contributors, and libraries from around the world appreciated the resurrection, changes, and transformation that the journal had gone through. We decided that the *JDA* would try to stimulate in-depth and rigorous empirical and theoretical research on all issues pertaining to the process of economic development. We also committed ourselves to encouraging research on economic, social, urban/regional, and inner-city problems of the United States and other developed countries as well.

Reviewers have liked the evaluation criteria that I developed:

An abstract of 150 words must precisely and succinctly define the problem, briefly state the research methodology, describe empirical findings, and present simply the principal policy recommendations.

A section must list the JEL classification codes, the keywords, and the corresponding author's email address.

The introduction should give a solid background that provides a good beginning for understanding the whole paper.

The problem needs to be focused narrowly.

The research methodology must be current, sophisticated, and clearly explained.

The relevant literature must be reviewed comprehensively, and all relevant works must be critically connected.

The problem must be logically and meaningfully deduced from the review of literature, and the importance and significance of the problem must be fully elucidated.

The mathematical or econometric model must be theoretically sound and solid, and the data must be current, clean, and appropriate for the study.

The findings of the research must be discussed and interpreted in detail in correct perspectives.

The arguments employed throughout the paper must be logically consistent and empirically supported.

The tables, charts, and graphs must be simple and easy to understand.

The conclusion must be complete with a clear set of policy recommendations.

The list of references needs to be complete, up to date, and free from superfluous items.

The *JDA* has been published and distributed regularly and on time with few exceptions. Every year, I report to the dean about the academic progress and financial situation of the journal. Although everything has been running fairly smoothly, being an editor is not always fun. The job sometimes is pleasing and enjoyable, and at other times it is disappointing. First, I start with the downside of the job. In my opinion, the most difficult job for an editor is finding appropriate reviewers who keep their word by doing a thorough review job and turning in the evaluation report on time. Even when someone accepts a referee job and agrees to submit a review by a certain date, my experience has been that eight out of ten will be late, four out of ten will do a poor job, one or two out of ten will do a job that is not acceptable by any standard. In most cases, alternative referees will be warranted. Meanwhile, months will be lost, and authors will inquire about the status of their papers and grow increasingly frustrated, impatient, and irritated.

My experiences with authors and contributors are not terribly bad. Normally, they are friendly and cooperative. Most are patient as well. But a majority do not follow the journal's rules and policies and do not properly comply with editorial directions. A very few authors are too stubborn to understand that as editor, I have no control over what and when the referees write. I also have known a couple of authors who were angry with me because the referee recommended that his or her paper be rejected. I found them unreasonably nonacademic. Sometimes accepted manuscripts may give rise to problems. Some authors repeatedly write, "What volume and what issue is going to carry my article? When is it going to come out?" This is a problematic decision on the part of the editor. Once I make a commitment, I cannot breach it. At the same time, often it becomes impossible to accommodate all committed papers due to some factors totally beyond my control. I often face another dilemma with accepted manuscripts. Sometimes an author will insist that his or her piece must appear before such and such date to avoid jeopardizing a promotion or tenure decision. I always try to be sensitive to this issue and do my best to help my contributors, yet I cannot please them all.

In early 2002, I received a paper from a Greek corresponding author who had Greek and Russian coauthors. After the refereeing process, the paper was accepted. As I usually do with accepted manuscripts, I typeset the paper myself and forwarded it to the corresponding author for proofreading, correction, and final approval. The paper was returned to me as being proofread and corrected and came out in fall 2003 (volume 37, issue 1). About a month or so after the paper was published, I received an email from the Russian coauthor, who wrote something like this: "My name has appeared as Chapurko Yuri Alexandrovich of Kuban State University, Russia. This is not my correct name. My name is Yuri Chapurko. You have published my paper in my father's name. I am afraid that I may not get any credit for this work." I explained to him that the corresponding author had sent me proofread copy and therefore was responsible for the error. I never did learn how he dealt with his corresponding author and his own institution. The job of an editor requires sensitivity and delicacy as well as a sense of responsibility.

In this context, embarrassing errors have been made by great economists and editors such as Ragnar Frisch and John Maynard Keynes. Frisch served as the editor of the prestigious journal *Econometrica* for twenty-two years and occasionally published editorial comments on papers that were published in earlier issues of the journal. On one occasion, however, Frisch wrote and published a note on a paper by Michael Kalecki before the original article appeared in the journal, which caused Frisch some embarrassment. A similar incident happened with Keynes. In 1922, Nobel laureate economist Bertil Ohlin sent a paper to Francis Edgeworth for publication in the *Economic Journal*. At that time Edgeworth and Keynes were coeditors of the journal, and Edgeworth forwarded Ohlin's paper to Keynes for his opinion. After some time had passed, Ohlin received his manuscript back with a small handwritten note from Keynes saying, "This amounts to nothing and should be refused." Ohlin saved the note. When Ohlin conversed with Keynes on the subject matter of his rejected article, he felt that Keynes had turned down his paper without carefully reading it. In his autobiography, Ohlin notes that at that time Keynes was extremely busy with momentous multiple responsibilities.

But being an editor also has its good moments. After publication of a paper, an author might send me a thank-you note that says something like this: "Thank-you, Dr. Wahid, for accepting and publishing my paper in your esteemed journal. Due to this publication, you will be pleased to know that I have gotten tenure and promotion. Thank-you, again. If I can be of any help to you in any way in the future, please feel free to contact me." Notes like this make me feel good: my hard work is worth something, and I have at least helped someone in our shared profession.

I have two final feelings about the *JDA* that I would like to share. First, I could not publish in this journal as a graduate student or a faculty member. Now that I am the editor of the journal and as a result of my own policy, I still cannot publish an article in the *JDA* as an author or coauthor. So my early dream of publishing in the *JDA* has and will remain unfulfilled forever. My second feeling about the *JDA* is that I consider it to be one of my own babies. I brought it back to the world from near extinction, and I have been raising and nurturing it for more than a decade. Even now, when a new issue of the *JDA* comes fresh off the press, I sniff it, touch it, and open it to turn the pages. With every page, I feel as though my dreams are coming true. Seeing the print version of the *JDA* always lifts my spirits. If all other editors feel the same way about their periodicals, we need to think seriously about how to save the print versions of all journals from extinction despite the online onslaught that is ferociously approaching us.

Economics of Education

18

Potpourri: Reflections from Husband and Wife Academic Editors

William E. Becker and Suzanne R. Becker*

When we were invited to contribute to this series on experiences of journal editors in academe, Bill said to Suzanne, "I have stories to tell about poor scholarship and the possible demise of economic education as a scholarly activity, and you have stories to tell about dealing with professors, the maiming of the English language, and catching errors." We have been involved in economic education and the economics of education since 1973 and edited the *Journal of Economic Education* (*JEE*) for twenty years from summer 1989 to fall 2009. What follows is a snapshot of some of the more memorable experiences and observations that this married couple would like to share with younger scholars for their edification and enlightenment regarding scholarship.

Whose English?

I (Bill) have long been waiting for an opportunity to tell of the first time I heard of the distinction between economics education and economic education. In the early 1970s, Rendigs Fels (then secretary/treasurer of the American Economic Association and a founding editorial board member of the *Journal of Economic Education*) politely but firmly informed academic economists that the term *economic education* said "cheap education" and that we should be saying and writing *economics education*. In the 1980s, I was surprised by a visit from an elderly distinguished professor of English who took it upon himself to inform me that the *Journal of Economic Education* needed to be renamed the *Journal of Economics Education* because its title was an embarrassment to Indiana University.[1] In the 1990s, while I was visiting at the University of South Australia, a colleague sheepishly but repeatedly asked me if I knew the difference between the meaning of *economics education* and *economic education*.

In 2008, we (Bill and Sue) continued to edit authors who had been schooled in the Queen's English to the conventions of American English. When pushed, we learned to respond that if and when the American Economic Association and its *American Economic Review* and the Royal Economic Society and its *Economic Journal* change their names from the implied American Cheap Association's *American Cheap Review* and the Royal Cheap Society's *Cheap Journal* to the American Economics Association's *American Economics Review* and the Royal Economics Society's *Economics Journal,* then the *Journal of Economic Education* will consider changing its name but until that day it will follow the U.S. convention of *economic education.*

The debate about the hyphenation of two terms—*pre-test* or *pretest* and *post-test* or *posttest*—is also worth a word. Both *pre-war* and *prewar* mean "before the war," and both *post-war* and *postwar* mean "after the war." The *JEE* convention (and the convention of most documentation styles) is to eliminate the hyphen for compound words with prefixes. The journal uses *pretest* to represent the preintervention test and *posttest* for the test after the intervention. Even so, some authors resist the current trend toward combining words with their prefixes. In the *JEE*, we continued to encourage authors to use *pretest* and *posttest*, although it might be more accurate to refer to these tests as *pretreatment* and *posttreatment* test scores and avoid cavilers.

An Error: No Way!

Some of those who are most certain of their infallibility with the English language (and with mathematics as well) are assistant professors. When full professors make errors, they tend to appreciate editorial comments. For example, econometrician Asatoshi Maeshiro, one of Bill's former professors, was "very grateful for detailed editorial suggestions." He said that he admired our "editorial skills and dedication" when Sue caught an error in one of his equations.

In Sue's position as assistant editor, she edited manuscripts for publication. In this capacity, she read for thought, exposition, and grammar. She marked equations and figures for *Journal of Economic Education* conventions and style. She had the privilege of editing Paul Samuelson, who made no objection to her correction of a small mixed metaphor.

Occasionally, tables, figures, or appendixes survive a referee's and associate editor's recommendation to condense or delete, or authors continue to refer in their revised text to deleted material. Since 1989, the only *errata* page that the *JEE* has published was in winter 1997 to correct the duplication of a figure in the previous issue: two figures had different titles but the same line graph. The error was pointed out by a mentor (W. Lee Hansen) of the article's author (John Siegfried). Despite this error, Siegfried remains one of the journal's most frequent contributors, and Lee Hansen has continued to serve on the editorial board.

Rosalind Springsteen, who was the managing editor for the *JEE* at Heldref Publications from 1990 to 2008, liked to remind us of the limited number of scholars who dig into an author's mathematics. Her story was from her position at the *Monthly Labor Review*. During discussions on changes that were needed in articles with many equations, she would laugh and remember working with an author to make perfect a manuscript that had about fifty equations (in the days before computer equation editors). The article's author told her that only two people in the world would ever read all those equations, and "we already have."

Working with authors in the process of preparing their manuscripts for likely publication can be trying. Potential authors regularly are sent messages that call attention to their lack of clarity, need for double spacing, use of endnotes instead of footnotes, missing references, and missing camera-ready figures.

Cocky assistant professors who see little value in editing are a concern. Sue recalls a six-month exchange of communications with a young author who was either obtuse or recalcitrant over the production of a final acceptable copy. (In most cases, this revision process takes only two or three weeks.) After he argued over required changes, made excuses for his failure to deliver, and claimed that a version was sent but never arrived, the author did send a complete and acceptable copy, along with the following cheeky email: "Hi, I wanted to confirm I personally sent the corrected manuscript and CD via Priority Mail this afternoon, so you should have it Tuesday or Wednesday at the latest. If it doesn't show up by around then, please let me know promptly."

The advent of the LaTeX document preparation system has led some economists to believe that editorial expertise is irrelevant. We had one author who had a paper that made it through the referee process but later withdrew his manuscript when we informed him that editorial changes were required, including conformity with our reference style even if it did not conform to the style options that were available in LaTeX. He did not appreciate that our publisher would not typeset directly from his LaTeX source .tex and .bib files because copyediting was required. Although printing is now done electronically, we have learned that errors are reduced when the hard copy continues to govern in the editing, production, and printing process.

Sometimes the printed manuscript and the electronic files do not correspond to each other. One editorial query asked an author: "Why does panel B come before panel A in your table?" The author responded, "Nice catch!" His revision reversed the column heads but did not properly change the numbers in the corresponding columns. When brought to his attention, he wrote "That was sad. I corrected it in the other files but not the one you needed."

Sue recalls devoting hours each month in pre-Internet days in travel to or phone calls with the excellent and always helpful reference desk librarians at the Indiana University library verifying quotations, references, and missing citation details.[2] Authors continue to make errors in these things, but it is rare now that any reference check is not completed quickly with a few words typed into Google.

Poor Scholarship

Over the years, we have seen many examples of poor scholarship. Some are innocent little things, such as assistant professors who claim to advance the teaching of economics or econometrics without giving sufficient credit to someone who wrote on the topic before them. Some are possible oversights, such as authors whose article in another journal falsely claims that they had an article forthcoming in the *Journal of Economic Education*. As an example of mindless prose, consider the authors who wrote these sentences: "The most widely used equilibrium concept in noncooperative game theory is the Nash equilibrium. . . . The first application of the Nash equilibrium concept to firm behavior are the Cournot (1838) and Bertrand (1883) models of duopoly." Antoine Cournot and Joseph Bertrand were long dead when John Nash received his Nobel Prize in 1994. Needless to say, the authors were asked to rewrite.

Because of the overlap of issues among economic education, the economics of education, and education in general, it is not unusual to see authors rebottle wine with new labels. As editors of the *JEE*, we have not discouraged derivative articles (one piece being an extension of another) because journal audiences differ and the derivatives can be better than the original. On rare occasions, however, we have seen authors attempt to acquire another publication without indicating that one submission is an exact copy of the other. We are fortunate that referees catch this chicanery. We have never seen a case of plagiarism in which an author put his or her name on another's work. We have had cases where authors have asked to have their names removed from an article (none of those articles have been published in the *JEE*).

Some of those in schools of education with little or no formal quantitative discipline background are notorious for not recognizing, not understanding, or ignoring what economists have to say about education processes and institutions. When we asked one noted higher-education student-satisfaction guru to provide a copy of the data that he used for one of his published articles as well as a copy of the paper that was listed as the source for one of his regressions, he replied that it would take some time to find the information because he no longer had research assistance. He also noted that the cited paper never did get written.

That Damned Referee Process

Joshua S. Gans and George B. Shepherd (1994) provided a brief review of how and why leading economists have had their work rejected. Yet sometimes, journal editors are in the position of having to reject their own work, as I had to do as editor of the *JEE*. The *JEE* 2002 annual report[3] noted that when risk-adverse university officials are confronted with threats of government action and lawsuits regarding medical malpractice, they sometimes needlessly extend central oversight to student information that is gathered in classroom research and aimed at improving teaching and learning. I argued that centralized institutional review boards (IRBs) are an obstacle for faculty members who are interested in pursuing research on educational practices. To assess the extent to which economists and academics in general were familiar with the laws and regulations that are associated with students' rights, Jane Lopus, Paul Grimes, Rodney Pearson, and I conducted an online national survey. We wrote an article about economists' knowledge of students' rights and regulations and submitted it to the *JEE*, where it received a negative recommendation from an associate editor and his referees. As editor, I followed their recommendation, although like all rejected authors, I was unhappy and possibly even more so than my coauthors who received the letter. At one time or another, I have had to reject articles submitted from almost all the *JEE* associate editors, and none of them ever complained or formally questioned the decision, although we all have been unhappy with the outcome.[4]

Our study of economists and our more general study involving all social scientists were published respectively in the *American Economist* (Lopus et al. 2007b) and the *Journal of Empirical Research on Human Research Ethics* (*JERHRE*) (Lopus et al. 2007a). Both articles have stirred a significant amount of debate, which we believe is a desired outcome of any academic publication. For example, a coordinator at the U.S. Department of Education sent us a list of ten questions about the two articles (and blind-copied the editor of the *JERHRE*), but his commentary on each question suggested that his inquiry was a negative critique in support of his own department's agenda. When we suggested to him and the journal editor that he prepare his comments in the form of an article commenting on our work and submit it to the *JERHRE* so that the editor and referees could assess its merits and give us an opportunity to reply if his comments were published, we never heard from him again. The traditional peer-review process does guard against frivolous inquiries.

Associate Editors

At the *Journal of Economic Education*, almost all refereeing is overseen by the associate editors. Special recognition and thanks go to the associate editors of the *JEE* with whom we were fortunate to work, including Robin Bartlett, David Colander, William Goffe, Paul Grimes, Hirschel Kasper, Peter Kennedy, Kim Sosin, Myra Strober, William Walstad, and Michael Watts.

Finding highly visible and high-quality scholars to volunteer to serve as associate editors is no small task. These extremely busy academics already have high demands on their time, and we ask them to volunteer to do a job for which they will end up rejecting many more papers than can be accepted and in the process upsetting more authors than they could ever please. Getting an acceptance from two *JEE* associate editors is particularly memorable.

Some thirty years ago, when I was associate editor of the *JEE* research section, Peter Kennedy found something objectionable in the *JEE* and wrote to call it to my attention. My secretary located him so that we could talk. He was so shocked that we tracked him down at a family cottage that he agreed to write an article. When I became editor of the *JEE*, I used a similar tactic to persuade him to agree to become the associate editor of the *JEE* research section. I learned that like most good scholars, Peter responds favorably to the sincere efforts put forward by others.

For personal reasons, Hirschel Kasper requested to be relieved of duties as associate editor after twenty-two years of outstanding service. This necessitated finding a replacement on short notice. I immediately called David Colander but was turned down with a long list of reasons. David, however, made the mistake of volunteering to help me find the perfect replacement. After we spent a month or so discussing the plusses and minus of several scholars, I was able to demonstrate to David that he was the perfect scholar for the job and that no one else was as uniquely qualified. Once again, a good scholar responded favorably to persistent sincere efforts.

Economic Education and the Scholarship of Teaching and Learning

The *JEE*'s 1999 annual report[5] noted that the Carnegie Foundation was launching a multiyear project called the Carnegie Academy for the Scholarship of Teaching and Learning (CASTL), which was to promote the development of a scholarship of teaching and learning in academe to maximize the influence of work being done in varied educational settings (Hutchings and Shulman 1999). It seemed that CASTL, which is now associated with the scholarship of teaching and learning (SOTL), was to have discipline-based academics combine the latest ideas in their fields with current ideas about teaching and learning in a way that is made public, is open to critique and evaluation, and is presented in a form on which others could build. By the time of the *JEE*'s 2007 annual report,[6] SOTL had lost its way.

One problem confronting SOTL was that discipline-based inquiry into teaching and learning would not have credibility within the disciplines. As Lee S. Shulman (2004, 20), then president of the Carnegie Foundation for the Advancement of Teaching, wrote: "it is hard to deny that too often mainstream scholars in their disciplines marginalize these [discipline-specific educational research] journals, however well they perform their functions. I envision a time when we witness the incorporation of scholarly contributions on the teaching and learning of the disciplines in general periodicals in those fields, as well as in the specialized education journals."

Shulman did not provide documentation to support his allegation that scholars are marginalizing discipline-based journals devoted to the teaching of their respective subjects or the implication that scholarly contributions on the teaching and learning of the disciplines are not already appearing in the major field journals. But economists at major research universities who have done extensive work in economic education include Kenneth Elzinga (University of Virginia), Michael Salemi (University of North Carolina), John Siegfried (Vanderbilt University), and Michael Watts (Purdue University). The *Journal of Economic Literature* has featured articles on the teaching of economics that economists have used to advance their careers. Similar articles have been published primarily in the *Journal of Economic Education* and other major refereed journals in economics, such as the *American Economist*. For example, for Bill's *JEL* (September 1997) article on teaching economics at the college level, sixty-five of the eighty-two references were to academic journals (twenty-eight to the *JEE* and ten to the *American Economic Review*). In William Walstad's *JEL* (December 1992) article on the teaching of economics in high schools, seventy-eight of 141 were to academic journals (thirty-eight to the *JEE* and sixteen to the *American Economic Review*). Similarly, the classic *JEL* article "Research on Teaching College Economics: A Survey" by John J. Siegfried and Rendigs Fels (1979) documented path-breaking work in economic education going back to World War II. Mainstream economists clearly continue to be involved in the teaching of economics and to publish their work in the *JEE*.

Notes

* This is an abridged version of Becker and Becker (2011).

1. In the 1990s, when Jay Wilson was chair of Indiana University's department of economics, interest and time devoted to teaching implied lack of interest and less time devoted to research. This fallacious argument confuses the time constraint with production and desired outcomes (Becker 1979; Becker and Kennedy 2006). The *Journal of Economic Education*'s title gave the wrong impression. Fortunately, several colleagues (notably, Phillip Saunders and George von Furstenberg) and the dean of the College of Arts and Science, Morton Lowengrub, saw value in supporting the *JEE*.

2. The Indiana University library staff deserves special thanks for its service when an author's National Guard unit was deployed to Iraq. The IU librarians volunteered to find all missing references and returned them within a day.

3. http://www.indiana.edu/~econed.

4. The biggest sting in being rejected as an editor is that editors work hard helping others get their manuscripts published.

5. http://www.indiana.edu/~econed/anrtps/anrpt99/rep99/htm.

6. http://www.indiana.edu/~econed.

References

Becker, William E. 1979. Professorial Behavior Given a Stochastic Reward Structure. *American Economic Review* 69 (5):1010–1017.

Becker, William E., and Suzanne R. Becker. 2011. Potpourri: Reflections from Husband /Wife Associate Editors. *American Economist* 56 (2):74–84.

Becker, William E., and Peter Kennedy. 2006. The Influence of Teaching on Research in Economics. *Southern Economic Journal* 72 (3):747–759.

Bertrand, Joseph. 1883. Book review of *Theorie mathématique de la richesse sociale* and of *Recherches sur les principles mathématiques de la théorie des richesses*. *Journal de Savants* (September): 499–508.

Cournot, Antoine. 1838. *Recherches sur les principes mathématiques de la théorie des richesse* (*Researches into the Mathematical Principles of the Theory of Wealth*). Trans. Nathaniel Terry Bacon. New York: Macmillan, 1897.

Gans, Joshua S., and George B. Shepherd. 1994. How Are the Mighty Fallen: Rejected Classic Articles by Leading Economists. *Journal of Economic Perspectives* 8 (1):165–179.

Hutchings, Pat, and Lee Shulman. 1999. The Scholarship of Teaching. *Change* 31:11–15.

Lopus, Jane, Paul Grimes, William Becker, and Rodney Pearson. 2007a. Effects of Human Subjects Requirements on Classroom Research: Multidisciplinary Evidence. *Journal of Empirical Research on Human Research Ethics* 2:69–78.

Lopus, Jane, Paul Grimes, William Becker, and Rodney Pearson. 2007b. Human Subjects Requirements and Economic Education Researchers. *American Economist* 51:49–60.

Shulman, Lee S. 2004. Visions of the Possible: Models for Campus Support of the Scholarship of Teaching and Learning. In *The Scholarship of Teaching and Learning in Higher Education: Contributions of Research Universities*, ed. W. Becker and M. Andrews, 9–24. Bloomington: Indiana University Press.

Siegfried, John J., and Rendigs Fels. 1979. Research on Teaching College Economics: A Survey. *Journal of Economic Literature* 16:923–969.

Walstad, William B. 1992. Economics Instruction in High Schools. *Journal of Economic Literature* 30:2019–2051.

General Economics

19

Helping the Homeless: Reflections on Editing Journals outside the Mainstream

Geoffrey M. Hodgson

Some essays in this volume are distillations of the experiences of editors of prominent mainstream journals in economics. By contrast, this article concerns the experiences of an editor of less prestigious publications that might develop the subject in a different direction. Although concerns about rigor and quality are shared, the problems of carving out a space for new ideas in often adverse institutional circumstances are of special concern here. This essay combines reflections about the state of economics with an attempt to draw some lessons from personal experiences with the editing process.

Mainstream economics has come into a great deal of criticism. Many point to failures of analysis and prediction, illustrated allegedly by the role of economic models in the run-up to the 2007 credit crunch and the 2008 great crash. Another complaint is the lack of theoretical pluralism in the profession, but arguably, this has been at least partly alleviated since about 1990 by the mainstream incorporation of rival approaches, including behavioral and experimental economics (Davis 2006). A degree of pluralism in mainstream economics is evidenced by the fact that criticisms of the rationality assumption are now published in leading journals, whereas previously they were dismissed as outside the defining canons of the discipline. A third complaint—which itself comes in various forms—is that the priority given in the discipline to mathematical technique over real-world substance has stunted or distorted its scientific development (Ward 1972; Friedman 1991; Krueger 1991; Lawson 1997; Blaug 1998; Krugman 2009).

Mathematics is an indispensable tool. But leading figures in the profession—including Nobel laureates Wassily Leontief, Ronald Coase, Milton Friedman, Paul Krugman, and Douglas North—have claimed that the discipline is now driven excessively by technical and unempirical rather than real-world problems. Krugman (2009) put it particularly well, linking the problem of technique domination to theoretical and policy failures prior to the 2009 crash. Referring to "the profession's blindness to the very possibility of catastrophic failures in a market economy," he argued that "the economics profession went astray because economists, as a group, mistook beauty, clad in impressive-looking mathematics, for truth . . . economists fell back in love with the old, idealized vision of an economy in which rational individuals interact in perfect markets, this time gussied up with fancy equations. . . . Unfortunately, this romanticized and sanitized vision of the economy led most economists to ignore all the things that can go wrong."

But such critical statements are confined to a tiny minority. The discipline exhibits a deeply rooted culture that venerates mathematical technique over real-world substance. There is inadequate reflection on habitual assumptions or on the way that economists are trained as narrow technicians rather than broadly grounded social scientists. Some observers have reached pessimistic conclusions about the likelihood of economics becoming a more empirically grounded and practically oriented science (Earl 2010).

In the years before 1990, the disciplinary boundaries of economics were defined primarily in terms of core neoclassical assumptions such as utility maximization. Now the set of canonical core assumptions has become more flexible. But veneration of mathematical technique remains the obligatory credo.

Before 1950, this was not the case. Not only was economics defined more broadly as "the study of mankind in the ordinary business of life" (Marshall 1920, 1), but the economist was required to have some knowledge of key related disciplines. Alfred Marshall himself referred to his theoretical models as "toys" and argued that the mathematics should always be translated into words (Hodgson 2012). For John Maynard Keynes (1924, 322), an economist had to be broadly trained in a number of disciplines, including economics itself:

the master-economist must possess a rare combination of gifts. He must reach a high standard in several different directions and must combine talents not often found together. He must be mathematician, historian, statesman, philosopher—in some degree. He must understand symbols and speak in words. He must contemplate the particular in terms of the general, and touch abstract and concrete in the same flight of thought. He must study the present in the light of the past for the purposes of the future. No part of a man's nature or his institutions must lie entirely outside his regard.

Such sentiments were then widely acknowledged in our profession, and economists generally received a broader training. Today, one of the effects of the growing importance bestowed to mathematical technique rather than real-world substance has been to drive important integral or complementary disciplines to the fringes or even outside the curricula or research agendas of economics. I refer to the study of political history, economic history, social theory, philosophy, the history of economic thought, politics, law, and much else. Prestigious departments of economics hire mathematicians rather than polymaths.

How I Became Homeless

My parents and teachers trained me to question assumptions, and that has made life difficult for me as an economist. My undergraduate degree was in mathematics and philosophy. Mathematics made me a competent reader of mainstream economic theory. But philosophy made me question the assumptions behind the theoretical claims as well as the meaningfulness or value of the theoretical results. By the early 1980s, I had become an evolutionary and institutional economist.

I had come to the conclusion that institutions rather than production functions provided better explanations of differences in economic performance. Evolutionary economists from Thorstein Veblen (1898, 1909) to Richard R. Nelson and Sidney G. Winter (1982) had moved away from the mainstream world of equilibrium, tackled the technological and institutional factors behind economic transformation, and offered a more adequate conception of individual motivation.

Furthermore, the emergence of chaos and complexity theory stressed the limits of prediction in complex systems (Anderson, Arrow, and Pines 1988; Rosser 1999). Economics has to become more interested in causal explanation than the development of models with the primary purpose of prediction. Although it is now possible for mainstream economists to question the assumption of utility maximization, the mistaken notion that economics (or any science) is primarily about "correct predictions" (Friedman 1953) remains pervasive. Arguably, it has had arguably deleterious effects on economic theory (Frydman and Goldberg 2011; Hodgson 2011). The emergence of chaos theory and catastrophe theory in the 1980s demonstrated the limits to prediction, but these lessons have not permeated the profession sufficiently. We are all obliged for practical reasons to form expectations about the future. But real-world complexity limits the capacity to do anything more than offer experienced guesses. Studies of complex systems reinforce the view that economics needs to focus primarily on causal explanation and be less ambitious regarding prediction.

Publishing academic articles in institutional and evolutionary economics in the 1980s was more difficult than it is today. My many rejections were due to the scholarly limitations of my earlier work and also the unpopularity of such perspectives. Now the situation has changed dramatically, with an explosion of journals with a profusion of approaches. Institutions are frequently acknowledged, and the word *evolution* is widely employed.

But it is still very difficult to publish my kind of work in leading mainstream journals. For example, one particular modeling approach that I favor is agent-based simulation. Unlike most mainstream models, these simulations allow a wide heterogeneity of economic agents. They are intended as heuristic devices that focus on particular causal linkages and illustrate possible unexpected effects rather than make predictions about the future. They are typically unsuitable for predictive purposes because they are notoriously highly susceptible to parametric alteration. Agent-based models are rarely found in premier-league journals in economics, and I suspect that their predictive weakness is the main explanation for this.

As Marshall freely admitted, the appropriate use of mathematics enforces greater precision. My own experience with agent-based modeling shows that the specification of any behavioral algorithm prompts deep reflection on presumed relations and linkages. But my training as a philosopher taught me that conceptual precision is also vital. There is a remarkable lack of consensus in economics today on the meaning or definition of key terms, including *firms*, *markets*, and *institutions* (Hodgson 2002, 2006, 2008a, 2008b). Because of a dearth of philosophical training, the very meaning and purpose of a definition is misunderstood: it is often confused with description or abstraction. Economists are trained to venerate mathematical precision but not to sharpen the concepts that are necessary to link their mathematics to discourse about the real world.

This neglect of conceptual, methodological, and contextual issues is found in journals outside mainstream economics. Aping tendencies in economics itself and in pursuit of recognition and prestige, some nonmainstream journals in economics and business that are ostensibly interested in evolutionary, institutional, and other unorthodox themes seem to have developed a strong preference for technical or quantitative material, thereby making homeless the people who previously would have considered them as an outlet.

Any preference for broader approaches—for causal explanation over prediction, for substance rather than technique, for conceptual as well as mathematical precision, for agent-based rather than analytic models with questionable assumptions, and for a full and creative dialogue with other relevant academic disciplines—is unlikely to enhance one's career as an academic economist. Consequently, since 1992, I have made my home in business schools where broader approaches are at least tolerated.

Economics will not overcome its current limitations without seismic changes in the international organization and orientation of the social sciences. Sadly, the current economic crisis has not led to major changes (Hodgson 2009). The appropriate strategy is to play for the long term—to build up the foundations of an alternative theory that learns from disciplines outside economics and also offers a superior scientific understanding of real-world economies.

On Being an Editor and on Helping Others Who Are Homeless

I have refereed hundreds of research papers for dozens of academic journals. In addition, I have nominally served as an editor of some kind on about twenty journals with *economic* or *economics* in their titles. In most cases, my service, if any, has to been to add my name to the board and to help indicate the alignment of the journal, for good or ill. In a minority of cases, my role as an editor has been to accept a greater burden of refereeing.

For any journal, the role of the referee is vital. The quality of reports from referees is crucial in the decision process over the fate of a submitted article. Consequently, good decisions on the selection of possible referees are among the most important decisions to be made by an editor.

Although I have nominally been an editor for several journals, in only two cases have I had the power to make or regularly influence decisions over the choices of referees. I served as a member of the editorial collective of the *Cambridge Journal of Economics* (*CJE*) from 1993 to 2009. The *CJE* editors meet weekly in Cambridge on Friday lunchtimes and together make decisions over the appointment of referees and the fate of the submissions. Since 2004, I have been editor in chief of the *Journal of Institutional Economics* (*JOIE*), which first appeared in 2005. As

JOIE editor in chief, I make decisions jointly with four other editors, communicating regularly and primarily by email.

My experience with the *CJE* convinced me that the quality and viability of the journal depends a great deal on the choice of referees. If a paper on (say) economic history contains some econometrics, then referees should be appointed that cover both areas of expertise. But it is also advisable to seek opinions from both sympathizers and likely critics of the line of argument in the article. It is treacherous to confine the choice to in-group referees who are likely to endorse the approach in the paper. Finding two or three willing referees who together satisfy all these requirements is tricky, and typically editors themselves have also to be involved in the final assessment.

Clans are common in academia as well as in other spheres. Scientists are human and prefer the company of like-minded fellows to the scourges of critique. This tendency allows the mainstream to ignore forceful criticism. It also prevents those with dissident approaches from sharpening and developing their alternative views.

My experience has convinced me that every journal should develop and publish its policy concerning potential conflicts of interest. There should be rules disallowing a colleague in one university from refereeing the paper of someone in the same institution and disallowing a supervisor from refereeing the paper of a current or recent graduate student. Some journals (including *JOIE*) disallow submissions of full-scale articles from editors themselves. Sources of funding for any research should be disclosed and so on. Such rules cannot themselves solve the problems, but they help to benchmark moral standards and to protect authors and editors from accusations of impropriety.

But even with such efforts, the peer-review process is bound to be imperfect. Several notable casualties are recorded in the book *Rejected* (Shepherd 1995; see also Gans and Shepherd 1994). Peer review by anonymous referees is a widely criticized model. Alternatives such as open peer review have been developed. But as Winston Churchill said of democracy, peer review by anonymous referees is the worst system, except for all the others. I have yet to see a high-quality academic journal that does not use peer review by anonymous referees. But there are many anonymously refereed journals of low quality. Anonymous peer review may be necessary but is far from enough.

When *JOIE* was established, the following policy concerning mathematics was agreed on by the journal's founders: "Papers with some formal content will be considered if it is fully explained for a general readership, the mathematics is consigned as much as possible to appendices, the assumptions have sufficient grounding in reality, and the paper enhances our understanding of past, present, or feasible socioeconomic institutions. *JOIE* is not interested in the advancement of formal or econometric technique for their own sake."

Given that *JOIE* is not a specialist journal devoted to one approach or line of technical development and publishes essays on numerous topics from multiple disciplines and theoretical approaches (as long as they address economic institutions), the above policy on mathematics should have been uncontroversial. Surprisingly, it was criticized by some who claimed that it would lower the academic reputation of the journal. But the statement does not rule out the use of mathematics. It simply requires that mathematical exposition is accessible, is orientated toward reality, and does not constitute the main substance of the paper. The fact that some prominent scholars could object to such a policy on the grounds that it would undermine the journal's reputation is itself a symptom of some of the things that are wrong with our discipline.

The struggle to maintain high standards of scientific quality is vital, and there are additional reasons that it is important for dissident economists. The reigning establishment in any discipline is bound to attract criticism. This is even more likely to be the case in economics because it addresses the sources and distribution of wealth and serious concerns such as poverty and unemployment. Anyone who dislikes the perceived status quo in economics—in terms of prevailing policy or theory—is likely to become a dissent economist. The discontent may have scientific grounding, or it could stem from misunderstandings. People with both attributes are found in heterodox quarters. The battle for a better and more relevant economics has to deal with the double problem of mainstream disapproval and substandard social scientists among the critics.

One of the biggest and most stubbornly enduring mistakes is to confuse ideology with theory. All social science has ideological connotations and to a large extent is ideologically driven. This is unavoidable. But this does not mean that science is simply ideology, that promulgating ideology is doing science, or that science and ideology are the same thing. Economists on the left and right have fallen into this trap.

A version of this conflation arises when neoclassical economics is simply regarded as promarket economics. This depends on how *neoclassical* is defined. A prominent meaning, adopted by adherents as well as critics, is that neoclassical approaches involve utility-maximizing individuals, a focus on equilibrium, and an exclusion of radical information problems (such as uncertainty in the Knight-Keynes sense).

Although these assumptions place individuals and their incentives in pride of place, no economist has logically demonstrated that promarket conclusions flow from these assumptions. They do not imply that markets are efficient, for example. In fact, leading theorists—such as Léon Walras, Oskar Lange, Abba Lerner, John Roemer, and Jon Elster—have adopted these neoclassical assumptions and used them to promulgate some model of socialism. Obversely, Friedrich Hayek was not a neoclassical economist (he rejected both utility maximization and equilibrium and embraced radical uncertainty), yet he put forward a distinctive theoretical case for free markets. Neoclassical assumptions are neither necessary nor sufficient to establish promarket conclusions.

In my dealings as an editor, I have experienced colleagues arguing that this paper should be rejected because it reaches promarket conclusions or that this person should not be a referee or otherwise involved because he or she is a neoliberal. I know that mainstream economists also use ideological arguments, but I regard them as highly inappropriate in an academic context, from whatever quarter.

What matters is not the ideological profile of the paper or the person but the scientific quality of the arguments involved. Papers should be judged not by their policy conclusions but by the theoretical rigor and empirical relevance of the arguments that are used to establish them. Likewise, potential authors, referees, or editors should be judged by their intellectual and scientific capacities and not by their political inclinations. Sadly, some of my heterodox colleagues think differently.

With *JOIE*, decisions over the acceptance or rejection of a paper are made by a vote by the five editors. I would recommend this system because it pools specialist expertise and reduces the chances of an idiosyncratic decision by an editor.

A different question that has emerged frequently in my experience is the attitude to published citation metrics, in particular the Thomson-Reuters citation impact factor. It is widely accepted that these metrics are imperfect and to some degree may be manipulated. (The current *Wikipedia* entry on "impact factor" has a brief but useful discussion.) Emphasizing these flaws, some of my colleagues argue that that Thomson-Reuters listing and citation impact factors should be shunned or ignored.

There are several reasons why I think that this stance is deeply mistaken. First (and especially in non-Anglophone countries), Thomson-

Reuters listing is widely used as a minimal criterion of a reputable academic publication outlet. Failing to attain or maintain Thomson-Reuters listing is to make life more difficult for aspiring nonmainstream academics by denying them a potential publication outlet that is formally recognized by numerous academic institutions.

Second, it is a mistake to see Thomson-Reuters listing as intrinsically biased toward mainstream economics. Mainstream journals reap some citation advantage because the mainstream (by definition) constitutes the majority of the profession, not because of the Thomson-Reuters system of calculating impact factors. In fact, the impact factor is calculated by gathering citations from all social science publications and not simply from those in economics. Consequently, the impact-factor system encourages inter- and transdisciplinarity.

By contrast, highly technical and specialist articles in mainstream economic journals are less accessible across disciplines than a more discursive and clearly written piece. If it were not for the numerical superiority of technique-driven mainstream economists, they would receive lower citations.

Finally, several established heterodox journals in economics have citation impact factors of less than 1.0. Although heterodox journals are disadvantaged by problems of homelessness and the marked numerical inferiority of heterodox scholars, these low citation impact factors are ignored at their peril. It is not simply that a low-impact journal can be (and some have been) removed from Thomson-Reuters listing. A 2011 (two-year) impact factor of 1.0 means that on average an article published in that journal in the 2009 to 2010 period received only one citation in 2011 in any Thomson-Reuters listed journal. Thomson-Reuters now also publish a five-year impact factor that takes into account articles published the preceding five years. Generally, impact factors below 1.0 typically mean that many articles in that journal are insufficiently relevant to be cited by any author who publishes in any Thomson-Reuters-listed journal in closely succeeding years.

Thomson-Reuters citation impact factors should be monitored and not shunned. Efforts to develop alternative quality rankings that would favor heterodox journals ignore the problem that many published heterodox articles are simply ignored. Salvation does not lie in an alternative quality metric. In any case, it is unlikely to be employed, even by the heterodox minority. We are obliged to work within the citation system as it is and improve it where necessary and possible. Although maximizing the impact factor should not be the supreme aim, low impact factors should prompt deep strategic reflection by journal editors, advisers, and sponsors.

The primary concern is to publish relevant research of the highest possible scientific quality—papers that enhance our understanding of real-world phenomena and hence may directly or indirectly help to guide economic policy. To repeat: the citation metric is highly imperfect. I have come across many well-written papers of high scientific quality and importance that receive relatively low citation rates. Uncomfortable arguments that effectively challenge prevalent (mainstream or nonmainstream) assumptions are often ignored or forgotten. That does not mean that papers with challenging arguments should be rejected. Editors should take risks. If a paper fulfills the criteria of clarity, relevance, and scientific quality, then it should be published, even if low citations are anticipated.

The final topic that I wish to raise is the difficulty that is faced by potential authors whose first language is not English. Although I have some knowledge of other languages, I have never written an academic article in a language other than English, and I am aware of the additional hurdles in the way of writing in a nonnative language. But this does not mean that articles written in poor-quality English can be accepted by a journal. Clear communication is vital in any language.

The academic community in a non-Anglophone country has a choice—either to accept that English has become the global academic language and go with the grain or to resist and build up a cluster of academic journals in an alternative language. Either choice is understandable and honorable.

But what is unviable is some imagined halfway house where it is accepted that English is the global academic vernacular but few steps are taken to ensure that people are adequately trained and supported to write in that language. Many non-Anglophone academic communities understand this. Consequently, in many universities in continental northern Europe, social science courses are taught in English. In China—at least in urban areas—most people start learning English when they are about four years of age. By contrast, in many other (even developed) countries, the teaching of English in schools is of a poor standard, and relatively few Anglophone teachers are hired in universities or schools. It can be fully admitted that the teaching of foreign languages is often very poor in schools in both the United States and the United Kingdom, but both countries seem to hire a higher number of university teachers from abroad. I know of no systematic survey, but the reader may compare the relatively high number of non-Anglophone academics in any prominent

U.S. or UK economics department with the low number of academics of (say) non-Francophone origin in equivalent university departments in France. If an academic community in a country accepts that English has become the dominant global language, then it must develop and institutionalize academic competence in the English language.

Turning to the Future

With the growth of the Web and of alternative business models for journals—such as open access—the future for print journal publishing is uncertain. But I wish to make two forward-looking arguments based on my experience and judgment.

First, consider the future of the business model where a hard-copy journal is distributed to and is based on the membership of a scholarly association, with institutional subscriptions taken up by libraries. Multiple developments since the 1990s threaten this model. There has been a proliferation of scholarly associations, and many of them are now static or declining rather than growing. The large number of kindred associations puts constraints on their membership growth. In addition, more and more scholars are relying on the Web to do their research. Receipt of the hard copy of a journal has less of a premium. If one has access to a good electronic library, then this advantage of association membership is reduced.

This in turn creates problems for the promotion of a journal. The advantage of the association-based model is that the members will help to promote the journal and increase the number of institutional subscriptions. This very usefully supplements the marketing efforts of the journal publisher. Without a membership base, a journal has to rely on marketing and reputation alone.

The *Journal of Institutional Economics* is experimenting with a major modification of the association-based model. Originally, the journal was set up by the European Association for Evolutionary Political Economy (EAEPE). Its members receive the journal as part of their membership package. But the aim at the outset was also to involve other kindred associations. So a company was set up in 2004 with EAEPE initially as the sole shareholder. The holding company (Millennium Economics Ltd) has two more shareholders, one of which is the Society for the Advancement of Socioeconomics (SASE), and other associations have also been invited to be shareholders. It is hoped that the visibility, availability, and reputation of the journal will be enhanced by these affiliations.

My second argument is that the growing use of the Web and the exponentially increasing number of electronic journals will not circumvent the use of quality rankings in universities or overturn the hegemony of prestige journals in our discipline. Far from eroding the mechanisms of quality screening and authentication (including the use of citation impact factors), the enhanced availability of proliferating journals obliges readers to make even more use of them. We cannot read more than a tiny fraction of what is published in our area. We are thus increasingly impelled to rely on the imperfect judgments of others and on institutionalized mechanisms of quality accreditation. If we have any influence in this regard, then we should do our best to improve the quality of the accreditation processes and the information available.

I believe that *JOIE* has a future because institutions are the stuff of economic life. Social and economic life is made up of systems of rules, ingrained on habits. Individuals learn rulelike conditioned responses of thought or behavior. Institutions are basically shared and socially encompassing systems of rules. The importance of institutions in economic performance is now widely recognized, and major institutional studies have been published in leading journals of economics. Two Nobel laureates—Simon Kuznets and Gunnar Mydral—were influenced by the old or original institutionalism. Since then, Ronald Coase, Douglass North, Elinor Ostrom, and Oliver Williamson have all been awarded Nobel Prizes for their work in institutional economics. But the turn toward institutions requires a broadening of economics to embrace history, social theory, the methodology of economics, evolutionary theory, and much else. There is a place for journals such as *JOIE* that span multiple disciplines in pursuit of the common understanding of economically vital phenomena.

The transformation of economics into a more relevant and less technique-driven science is a long-term project that will not be completed in my lifetime. The shorter-term goals are to enhance the quality and constructiveness of criticism, to help the discipline develop in the right direction, and to build reputable homes for good, innovative research that serves these purposes.

Acknowledgments

The author thanks David Gindis, Patrick McCartan, and Barkley Rosser for helpful comments on a previous draft.

References

Anderson, Philip W., Kenneth J. Arrow, and David Pines, eds. 1988. *The Economy as an Evolving Complex System*. Reading, MA: Addison-Wesley.

Blaug, Mark 1998. Disturbing Currents in Modern Economics. *Challenge* 41 (3): 11–24.

Davis, John B. 2006. The Turn in Economics: Neoclassical Dominance to Mainstream Pluralism? *Journal of Institutional Economics* 2 (1):1–20.

Earl, Peter E. 2010. Economics Fit for the Queen: A Pessimistic Assessment of Its Prospects. *Prometheus* 28 (3):209–225.

Friedman, Milton. 1953. The Methodology of Positive Economics. In M. Friedman, *Essays in Positive Economics*, 3–43. Chicago: University of Chicago Press.

Friedman, Milton. 1991. Old Wine in New Bottles. *Economic Journal* 101 (1):33–40.

Frydman, Roman, and Michael D. Goldberg. 2011. *Beyond Mechanical Markets: Asset Price Swings, Risk, and the Role of the State*. Princeton, NJ: Princeton University Press.

Gans, Joshua S., and George B. Shepherd. 1994. How Are the Mighty Fallen: Rejected Classical Articles by Leading Economists. *Journal of Economic Perspectives* 8 (1):165–179.

Hodgson, Geoffrey M. 2002. The Legal Nature of the Firm and the Myth of the Firm-Market Hybrid. *International Journal of the Economics of Business* 9 (1):37–60.

Hodgson, Geoffrey M. 2006. What Are Institutions? *Journal of Economic Issues* 40 (1):1–25.

Hodgson, Geoffrey M. 2008a. Markets. In *New Palgrave Dictionary of Economics*. 2nd ed. Basingstoke: Macmillan. Online.

Hodgson, Geoffrey M. 2008b. Markets. In *The Elgar Companion to Social Economics*, ed. John B. Davis and Wilfred Dolfsma, 251–266. Cheltenham: Elgar.

Hodgson, Geoffrey M. 2009. The Great Crash of 2008 and the Reform of Economics. *Cambridge Journal of Economics* 33 (6):1205–1221.

Hodgson, Geoffrey M. 2011. The Eclipse of the Uncertainty Concept in Mainstream Economics. *Journal of Economic Issues* 45 (1):159–175.

Hodgson, Geoffrey M. 2012. Introduction. In *Mathematics and Modern Economics*, ed. Geoffrey M. Hodgson, xiii–xxxii. Cheltenham: Elgar.

Keynes, John Maynard. 1924. Alfred Marshall. *Economic Journal* 34 (3): 311–372.

Krueger, Anne O. 1991. Report on the Commission on Graduate Education in Economics. *Journal of Economic Literature* 29 (3):1035–1053.

Krugman, Paul R. 2009. How Did Economists Get It So Wrong? *New York Times,* September 2. http://www.nytimes.com/2009/09/06/magazine/06Economic-t.html. Retrieved October 2009.

Lawson, Tony. 1997. *Economics and Reality*. London: Routledge.

Marshall, Alfred. 1920. *Principles of Economics: An Introductory Volume*. 8th ed. London: Macmillan.

Nelson, Richard R., and Sidney G. Winter. 1982. *An Evolutionary Theory of Economic Change*. Cambridge, MA: Harvard University Press.

Rosser, J. Barkley, Jr. 1999. On the Complexities of Complex Economic Dynamics. *Journal of Economic Perspectives* 13 (4):169–192.

Shepherd, George B., ed. 1995. *Rejected: Leading Economists Ponder Over the Publication Process*. Foreword by Kenneth J. Arrow. Sun Lakes, AZ: Horton.

Veblen, Thorstein B. 1898. Why Is Economics Not an Evolutionary Science? *Quarterly Journal of Economics* 12 (3):373–397.

Veblen, Thorstein B. 1909. The Limitations of Marginal Utility. *Journal of Political Economy* 17 (9):620–636.

Ward, Benjamin. 1972. *What's Wrong with Economics?* London: Macmillan.

20

Econ Agonistes: Navigating and Surviving the Publishing Process

Steven Pressman

Let me begin this article with a brief summary of my qualifications. During my career, I have refereed nearly three hundred articles for professional journals and as a journal editor have made decisions on more than a thousand papers. I have edited several symposia and special issues for economics journals and for refereed journals in other disciplines. Since 1989, I have served as associate editor and book review editor of the *Eastern Economic Journal* and since 1995 have served as coeditor of the *Review of Political Economy*.

Part of the reason for my success is that when I was just beginning my professional career, I was extremely fortunate to have Ingrid Rima[1] as my mentor. I first met Ingrid at the annual meetings of the Eastern Economic Association in the early 1980s. At the time, I was a graduate student working on my doctoral dissertation, and Ingrid was editor of the *Eastern Economic Journal*. After we met, Ingrid sent me a few articles to referee, and when she saw I had a knack for doing them quickly and well, she sent me many more articles. By critically evaluating the work of others, I learned the sorts of things that referees look for and figured out the simple things that authors can do to minimize the probability of having their paper rejected. Finally, as I began publishing my own work and began accumulating referee reports rejecting my papers, I learned more about how to avoid rejections. Moreover, I learned not only what to say in a referee report to help authors improve the quality of their paper but also how to say things so that authors did not feel alienated, thus making them more likely to listen to my comments and suggestions.

As a reward for my hard work, Ingrid appointed me to the editorial board of the *Eastern Economic Journal*. Shortly thereafter, she made me book review editor and associate editor of the journal. These promotions enabled Ingrid to send me even more articles to referee without having to feel too guilty about all the work she was giving me.

In the 1980s, I also met John Pheby at an international conference. John wanted to start a new political economy journal and wanted a young, energetic U.S. economist with some editorial experience on his team. I seemed to fit the bill and helped John convince a publisher to take a chance on a new journal. Like Ingrid, John put me on the editorial board and relied on me for lots of refereeing. When John decided to relinquish the job as editor of the *Review of Political Economy*, I became one of his replacements.

Crapshoots and Triage

My extensive service over the years as both a referee and a journal editor has been first and foremost a learning experience. Perhaps the most important lesson I have learned, and the one I wish to stress here, is how the entire process is one part crapshoot and one part triage. These are reasonably good metaphors for what goes on when making decisions about submitted papers. *Crapshoot* emphasizes the somewhat arbitrary nature of getting a paper accepted for publication and the fact that getting a paper accepted depends on the luck of the draw regarding referees. *Triage* indicates the role that human judgment (mainly by editors) plays in determining which papers get saved and how many get saved.

Getting published is a crapshoot because even if you write a decent paper, the chances are good that a large fraction of scholars in the field will not see it that way. To make this point concretely, think about the large number of papers you have read (or started to read, making it through just a few paragraphs or pages), all the while wondering how this paper ever made it through the review process. The answer to this question is that some referees found something of value in these papers. Opinions will be split on many papers: some people will find something of value in them, and others will think that they are boring or riddled with errors.

Keeping things simple, a decent paper is defined here as one for which somewhere around 40 percent of the people who might be asked to referee it will see it in this light, something that is not far from the truth.[2] Under this assumption, getting a decent paper published becomes a crapshoot because it depends on who you get as a referee. To get your paper accepted, you need two referees who are favorably disposed to it, and the odds are against you. Looking only at probabilities, there is a greater than 80 percent chance that either or both referees will recommend rejecting your paper. On the other hand, there is around a 16 percent chance that you will get lucky and that both referees will recommend accepting your paper (after substantial revisions are made to it).

A good deal of evidence suggests that the refereeing process resembles a crapshoot. My favorite piece of evidence involves a clever and revealing experiment. Douglas Peters and Stephen Ceci (1985) selected twelve articles that had been published in prominent psychology journals. All were written by professors who worked at prestigious schools, and all were cited more than average in the eighteen to thirty-two months after each article appeared in print. Peters and Ceci then resubmitted these articles to the same journal that originally published them—with only a few minor changes. They changed the title of the paper, the author's name, and the institutional affiliation of the author. Most of the new institutional names were not actual universities or even made-up universities (such as the University of Southern North Dakota at Hoople) but were fictional organizations (such as the Southern North Dakota Human Potential Center).

The results were astounding (unless you are a jaded journal editor, in which case the results are probably not surprising). The twelve papers resubmitted to the same journal were handled by thirty-eight different editors and referees. Only three people recognized that the submitted paper had been previously published in that journal. This means that 92 percent of the referees and editors who looked at the paper failed to recognize that the journal they were working for had already published the paper they were examining. Because the chances are quite good that in at least one or two cases the paper was sent to the author of the original and resubmitted paper (because it likely had references to their own previous work), it is hard to come to any conclusion other than referees and editors do not read much and do not read much of what gets published in their journal.

Just as astounding (again, except for jaded journal editors) is the fate of the nine papers that made it through the review process without being detected as having been previously published. Of these nine papers, eight were rejected, generally for methodological flaws in the design of the study. Because these papers had appeared in print, were written by authors from top-tiered academic institutions, and had above-average citations, it is questionable that they contained serious methodological flaws that would preclude publication. Something else must have been going on.

One clue about what went wrong arises from the fact that the journals evaluating these twelve resubmitted articles did not employ double-blind refereeing. The referees knew who the author of each paper was, and they knew where they worked. The one paper that was accepted for publication listed the name of a made-up university as the home of its made-up author. It was the only resubmitted paper sent from a university address.

Numerous studies have documented that nonblind refereeing leads to biases in whether papers get accepted or rejected. Female authors, for example, have a lower probability of getting their papers accepted, controlling for all sorts of other factors (Ferber and Teiman 1980). In addition, reviewers are strongly biased against manuscripts whose results conflict with their own theoretical perspective (Mahoney, 1977). The Peters and Ceci study reveals a bias concerning the institution at which one works. Anecdotal evidence from years of talking informally to other editors confirms this latter bias. Many editors and many referees that I have spoken to over the years seem to believe that colleagues at an author's academic institution have vetted a paper before it is sent off for publication. They also believe that people who are employed at a good academic institution must be good economists and so are more favorably disposed to accept their papers.

Such assorted biases, while anomalies to rational economic man, have been shown again and again to exist in experimental economics and in the field of economics and psychology. Daniel Kahneman was awarded a Nobel Prize in 2002, in large part for demonstrating the rich array of human biases in real-world situations (for more on Kahneman and this work, see Pressman 2006). These biases make the refereeing process a crapshoot. Having a decent paper published becomes a matter of being assigned two referees with biases that lean toward your paper rather than against it and having them find something of value in it.

But the publication process is also akin to triage. Like the wounded in war, after papers have been shot full of holes by referees, it is time for editors to earn their keep. Although many people describe editors as gatekeepers (Berkenkotter 1995), a much better description would be that editors serve as mentors. Alas, not every paper can be mentored into print; some decisions must be made, and some papers must be rejected.

After receiving referee reports, editors typically put papers into one of three categories. Some they have no choice but to reject. These papers have received mainly negative reports. They are like the soldiers who do not make it to the operating room because their wounds are too extensive and they will not likely survive, even with immediate and intensive treatment. This is the largest category of papers. Based on personal experience as well as conversations with other editors, this group comprises 50 to 75 percent of all the papers submitted to most journals. Other papers are accepted (after some revision) because they receive a set of positive reports. These papers do not make it to the operating room immediately because they have only minor injuries and will more than likely survive the process. But their authors do receive encouraging letters from editors, imploring them to follow the suggestions of the referees and resubmit their paper. By far, this is the smallest category of papers that editors must deal with, making up 10 percent or so of the total.

The remaining 30 percent or so of the papers under review fall into the middle category. These papers can be saved with a lot of hard work. The editor decides which papers go into the operating room and which papers are passed on to the editor of some other journal. Virtually no editor can publish all of the papers in this category because in any given year a journal has a limited number of pages and can publish only so many articles. To work with all authors would be extremely time consuming and would soon lead to such a long publication queue that submissions would suffer. On the other hand, publishing only the papers that referees praise highly will result in too few articles and conspicuously slim journal issues. Consequently, all the in-between papers cannot be rejected and cannot be revised and published. This is the hard work of the editor—deciding which papers to try to save and which authors to work with on their papers.

Navigating and Surviving the Process

Understanding the refereeing process makes it easier to navigate and survive it. Toward this end, here are three tips for authors who are looking to maximize their chances of being published in a system that is partly a crapshoot and partly triage.

First, history is important, and it is important in several ways. Before you submit any article, it is essential that you do your homework and know the history of the journal where you are sending your paper. There is no point wasting your time, the time of referees, and the time of editors by sending your paper somewhere inappropriate. In addition, as David Smyth (1994) has pointed out, an important part of your homework involves proofreading your paper carefully to make sure that there are no misspellings, grammatical errors, math mistakes, or other obvious errors. These are clear indicators that you are not serious, not careful, and do not want your paper published. They greatly reduce the chances that you make it to the operating table of the triage process.

You also need to make sure that you have up-to-date references in your paper and that you refer to articles previously published in the journal where you are submitting your paper. When your latest reference is several years old, you signal that your paper has been rejected many times already and has not been updated or revised. Also make sure to reference authors who have published on your topic in any journal where you plan to send your paper. As Daniel Hamermesh (1994, 156) notes, editors tend to send papers to people who have submitted and published in the journal. These people are the likely referees of your paper, and like most academics, they want their work to be read and acknowledged. Failure to do your homework here greatly increases your chances of getting rejected.

History is also important for another reason. Many topics will likely to be of interest at some point in time but of less interest at other times. Fiftieth and hundredth anniversaries are always good opportunities to summarize and evaluate some literature or the work of some economist. They are a time for reflecting on the past. They open the door for papers that might otherwise get rejected because the paper mainly summarizes and evaluates previous work but does not add very much that is new. Anniversaries, however, call out for such assessments.

One good example of this is a recent conversation that I had with my colleague, Robert Scott. Robert is interested in the economic ideas of Kenneth Boulding. He has written on Boulding and environmental economics and has talked about doing a book on Boulding. Because 2010 was the hundredth anniversary of Boulding's birth, I suggested to Robert that he should contact journal editors about a possible symposium on Boulding to be published in 2010 and also to consider writing an article that is part biographical and part an assessment of Boulding's contributions to economics.

Taking this route does not mean just paying attention to birthdays. You should also be aware of the dates when key articles and books were published. Kenneth Arrow's (1963) paper on the economics of health care, the one that began health economics as a field in its own right, will be fifty years old in December 2013. And for those inclined toward even more esoteric subjects, 2013 also marks the 175th anniversary of Antoine Cournot's *Researches into the Mathematical Principles of the Theory of Wealth* (1838), the first work to bring the differential calculus into economic analysis and the first attempt to use calculus to analyze the pricing behavior of firms (Cournot 1960). What better time than 2013 for an examination of the role of mathematics in economic analysis?

My second tip is to be a good referee. As John Ziman (1968, 111) notes, "the referee is the lynchpin about which the whole business of Science is pivoted." By far the hardest part of the entire process is finding expert referees who will review articles in a timely fashion, advise the editor about what to do with the paper, and provide good suggestions so that authors can improve their paper (no matter how good or bad it is).

Alas, good referees are harder to find than good men. Refereeing is a thankless job, despite what the acknowledgments say at the end of journals each year. There are few rewards for those who do a lot of refereeing and try to be conscientious. There are no financial benefits and no gains in reputation. To the contrary, the time spent refereeing takes away from time that could be spent writing things that might bring fame and fortune. To be even more cynical, one main reward for doing a good refereeing job is that your comments will get ignored and you will get even more papers to look at. This is probably why economists are reluctant to serve as referees. Surveying a number of journal editors, Hamermesh (1994, 158f.) reports that 5 percent of people who are sent papers never submit a report, while nearly 20 percent turn down the papers they are asked to review. These figures are pretty close to what I have experienced over the years, with things getting worse over time.

Consequently, journal editors are always looking for referees, and their help is always greatly appreciated. For those who want to help, a good strategy is to contact editors, send them a brief statement of your willingness to referee, and list your main areas of interest. You should also attach a copy of your curriculum vitae so that the editor can see the things you are working on and have done.

Despite its drawbacks, serving as a referee has its benefits. Journal editors are human, and reciprocity is a fundamental, deep-seated human trait. Editors are more likely to help those they know and those who have helped them. So good referees are more likely to make it to the operating table and more likely to be published.

What makes a good referee? The two things most important to an editor are being prompt and providing helpful comments. As an editor, I always have many papers to deal with and many more referees looking at all these papers. I do not want have to remind people that they owe me a referee report. I also do not want to decide whether I can trust you to produce something for me in another few weeks or whether I should cut my losses and ask someone else. Late reports from referees also result in difficult interactions with authors who are awaiting a response on their papers and who sometimes have tenure or promotion decisions hanging in the balance.

Most important, editors want a report that helps the author. The goal of the review process should be to help authors write a better paper, whether or not it gets published. In short, be a mentor. Alas, the review process often fails abysmally here. Referees frequently deliver *ad hominem* attacks, using the paper as a piñata, rather than constructive suggestions for improving the piece. Self-interested referees advance their own work and the work of their friends and allies and try to prevent others from getting published.

When I referee a paper, I start by saying a few positive things about the paper. When I am done with the report, I put it down for a week or two and come back to it with a fresh eye. At this time, I do my final revisions, attempting to improve the tone of the report as well as clarify my main points, which I try to limit to three main things that would improve the paper (regardless of my views about whether it should be published). This is a good model, and editors and authors would be very grateful if most referees followed it.

My third tip for navigating the refereeing process comes via Sidney Weintraub. Sid was a founding editor and coeditor of the *Journal of Post Keynesian Economics*. He taught at the University of Pennsylvania from 1950 until his death in 1983, except for a brief interlude at the University of Waterloo in Canada.[3]

I first met Sid when I was applying for Ph.D. programs in economics. After being accepted at Penn, I took the train to Philadelphia to sit in on classes and meet some faculty. Although I did not consider myself a neoclassical economist, I felt the need to learn the standard economic approach well—whether or not I agreed with it. My hope was to get a good grounding in neoclassical theory at Penn but to also learn about the post-Keynesian alternative from Sid. Sid's advice to me was to follow my heart—focus on what really interested me, rather than on what I felt I needed to learn, and use that to inspire my work and my writing.

I next ran into Sid several years later at a cocktail party at an annual American Economic Association conference. He remembered our meeting at Penn and his advice to me. I told him that I was currently working on my dissertation and was ready to start sending out articles for publication. Sid then provided me with the three keys to his success—

persevere, persevere, persevere. This advice I now pass on, along with some perspective on what this means.

First, to persevere in a crapshoot with the odds stacked against you means developing a tough skin. Remember, at good journals, acceptance rates are 20 percent or less, and this figure is just an average. They include both senior, established scholars and recent Ph.D.s. With a 20 percent acceptance rate on average, the rate will be closer to 30 percent for senior people who have more experience getting published but close to 10 percent for those who are just starting their career and have less experience and fewer professional contacts. In practice, it means you are likely to get five to ten rejections before you get an acceptance—even if you have a decent paper.

Rejection should not trigger a major psychological depression. You need to pick yourself up off the ground, dust yourself off, and move on. To help keep yourself going in the face of numerous rejections, you can look at some of the voluminous literature on how to have articles published in refereed journals. The study by Peters and Ceci (1985), described earlier, is one good antidote. Also useful to combat the rejection blues is the research that shows reviewers to be biased against results that are contrary to their theoretical perspective (Mahoney 1977). There is also the literature on famous articles in economics that were rejected numerous times (Shepherd 1995; Gans and Shepherd 1994). Finally, you might want to consult some of the scholarly literature on journal refereeing, which finds that inexperienced referees tend to think that their job is to find flaws in the articles they are given to assess (Ashford 1996, 124), that referees tend to stress the limited aspects of the manuscript through detailed and harsh comments (van Lange, 1999), and that referees tend to think they are impressing an editor with their toughness in the hopes of gaining a position on the journal editorial board (Bedeian 2004).

After you conquer the initial outrage and hurt feelings over being rejected, it is time to move on. Moving on involves one of two things. You can send your paper immediately to another journal, or you can revise it before you send it elsewhere. This brings us to the second meaning of *persevere*—learning from the referee reports and editor comments that you receive. It means dealing intelligently with referee comments—knowing when and how to make changes to your paper and when to try another journal.

Always try to learn something from the referee reports that you receive. Usually there is something of value in them, no matter how badly put or how hostile the tone. Make use of this. Just because you think that the referees are idiots does not mean that you should be one also. But make your changes quickly, and send out the paper again.

If you are given an opportunity to revise your paper, correspond with the editor if you have any questions, and feel free to disagree with the referees by making a case to the editor. If you revise your paper, it is best to respond with a list. Point by point, tell the editor how you have dealt with each of the changes that the referees have requested. If you did not make changes, state your case, and provide your evidence. Be polite. On several occasions during my career, I have had a paper accepted when I was able to make a strong case to the editor (with documentation) that a referee was mistaken on a particular point. I then had the editor siding with me rather than the referee and probably got the benefit of the doubt on a couple of other points of contention. On yet other occasions, I have had the editor side with a referee who (I thought) was wrong and should have been overruled, but that is the right of the editor and a sign for you to try another journal.

Unfortunately, many authors receive revision requests that they do not agree with. Comments by the referees and the editor can be nearly as long as the paper itself (Spector 1998), and sometimes they try to force the authors to write a paper that the referees want (Leblebici 1996). Especially disturbing is the fact that, over time, journals are requiring authors to make more and more revisions and larger revisions (Ellison 2002, 948). Even worse, it seems that almost a fourth of revise-and-resubmit invitations lead to authors to revise their paper in a manner that they felt included errors or made things incorrect (Bedeian 2003). Bruno Frey (2003) has quipped that many authors must prostitute themselves when following the suggestions of referees and editors in order to get their articles accepted and published.

If you feel that this is what is happening in your case, then it is time to move on to another journal. Unless and until authors start to reject revise-and-resubmit invitations from journals, this situation will not improve. At times, however, difficult tradeoffs are involved in making such a decision. Starting with a new journal always means a year lag (more with a rejection or two) before you get another opportunity to revise. Here more than anywhere, you probably need some good advice from a more senior and established scholar. But the important thing is that you have a strategy for your paper, maintain some confidence in yourself and the paper, and move forward with it (one way or another).

Finally, *persevere* means working hard—writing continuously and having ideas that you are interested in and want to explore. It means revising your papers again and again so that they read well and flow well because you take pride in your work and what you are doing. (It is not unusual for me to do twenty or more revisions after I have a good first draft, and each one improves the argument and the readability of my paper.)

Here Sid's advice on publishing dovetails with his advice to me concerning graduate school. If you find something that is in your heart and that you want to do, then you will work hard at it, and you will likely do it well. On the other hand, if nothing excites you and you cannot find anything that you want to write about, then perhaps you are in the wrong profession.

Let me end with one bit of good news and encouragement for you: if you are reading this chapter, it is not likely that you fall into the latter category.

Notes

The author thanks Guldem Gokcek and Robert Scott for comments on an earlier version of this paper.

1. For more on Ingrid Rima, see Stanley Bober and Steven Pressman (1992) and Pressman (2007).

2. The real world is more complex. Referees can waffle, and revise-and-resubmit recommendations can come with various degrees of support. However, I think that the simple bifurcation of support publication or not support publication is useful and accurate, especially when it comes to cover letters sent to editors.

3. For more on Weintraub, see Johann Deprez and Will Milberg (2000) and Paul Davidson (1983).

References

Arrow, Kenneth. 1963. Uncertainty and the Welfare Economics of Medical Care. *American Economic Review* 53 (5):941–964.

Ashford, Susan. 1996. The Publishing Process: The Struggle for Meaning. In *Rhythms of Academic Life: Personal Accounts of Careers in Academia*, ed. P. J. Frost and M. S. Taylor, 119–127. Thousand Oaks, CA: Sage.

Bedeian, Arthur G. 2003. The Manuscript Review Process: The Proper Roles of Authors, Referees, and Editors. *Journal of Management Inquiry* 12:331–338.

Bedeian, Arthur G. 2004. Peer Review and the Social Construction of Knowledge in the Management Discipline. *Academy of Management Learning & Education* 3:198–216.

Berkenkotter, Carol. 1995. The Power and Perils of Peer Review. *Rhetoric Review* 13:245–248.

Bober, Stanley, and Steven Pressman. 1992. Ingrid Hahne Rima: An Appreciation. *Eastern Economic Journal* 18:125–128.

Cournot, Antoine Augustin. 1960. *Researches into the Mathematical Principles of the Theory of Wealth*, trans. Nathaniel Bacon. New York: Kelly. First published 1838.

Davidson, Paul. 1983. An Appraisal of Weintraub's Work. *Eastern Economic Journal* 9:291–294.

Deprez, Johan, and Will Milberg. 2000. Sidney Weintraub (1914–1983). In *A Biographical Dictionary of Dissenting Economists*, ed. P. Arestis and M. Sawyer, 702–709. Cheltenham, UK: Elgar.

Ellison, Glenn. 2002. The Slowdown of the Economics Publishing Process. *Journal of Political Economy* 110:947–993.

Ferber, Marianne, and Michelle Teiman. 1980. Are Women Economists at a Disadvantage in Publishing Journal Articles? *Eastern Economic Journal* 6: 189–193.

Frey, Bruno. 2003. Publishing as Prostitution? Choosing between One's Own Ideas and Academic Success. *Public Choice* 116:205–223.

Gans, Joshua, and George Shepherd. 1994. How Are the Mighty Fallen: Rejected Classic Articles by Leading Economists. *Journal of Economic Perspectives* 8:165–179.

Hamermesh, Daniel. 1994. Facts and Myths about Refereeing. *Journal of Economic Perspectives* 8:153–163.

Leblebici, Huseyin. 1996. The Act of Reviewing and Being a Reviewer. In *Rhythms of Academic Life: Personal Accounts of Careers in Academia*, ed. P. J. Frost and M. S. Taylor, 269–274. Thousand Oaks, CA: Sage.

Mahoney, Michael. 1977. Publication Prejudices: An Experimental Study of Confirmatory Bias in the Peer Review System. *Cognitive Therapy and Research* 1:161–175.

Peters, Douglas, and Stephen Ceci. 1985. Peer-Review Practices of Psychology Journals: The Fate of Published Articles, Submitted Again. *Behavioral and Brain Sciences* 5:187–255.

Pressman, Steven. 2006. *Fifty Major Economists*. 2nd ed. London: Routlege.

Pressman, Steven. 2007. Ingrid Rima and Post Keynesian Macroeconomic. In *Post Keynesian Macroeconomics: Essays in Honour of Ingrid Rima*, ed. M. Forstater, G. Mongiovi, and S. Pressman, 1–11. London: Routledge.

Shepherd, George, ed. 1995. *Rejected: Leading Economists Ponder the Publication Process*. Sun Lakes, AZ: Horton.

Smyth, David J. 1994. How Not to Get Your Article Published. *Eastern Economic Journal* 20:471–473.

Spector, Paul E. 1998. When Reviewers Become Authors: A Comment on the Journal Review Process. *Research Methods Forum* 3:1–4.

van Lange, Paul. 1999. Why Authors Believe That Reviewers Stress Limiting Aspects of Manuscripts: The SLAM Effect in Peer Review. *Journal of Applied Social Psychology* 29:2550–2566.

Ziman, John. 1968. *Public Knowledge: The Social Dimensions of Science.* Cambridge: Cambridge University Press.

21

Tales from the Editor's Crypt: Dealing with True, Uncertain, and False Accusations of Plagiarism

J. Barkley Rosser Jr.

I am writing this in December 2010, my final month as editor of the *Journal of Economic Behavior and Organization* (*JEBO*), having first assumed this position effectively in August 2001.[1] It has been a mostly rewarding experience but has become increasingly time-consuming as submissions have approximately doubled over this period. To handle a substantially increased workload, I have become better at doing things more quickly, and this has been helped by the move from snail mail to the electronic handling of matters. It has been fascinating to see what people submit to the journal and to influence, even if in a small way, the direction of the profession of economics. I have also gotten to know many interesting people—members of my editorial board, authors, submitters, and referees—that I would not have known if I had not been editor. Although it will be a relief not to have all this constant responsibility and work, I confess that I shall miss it.

As other editors can attest, aside from the workload, many other things that are not so pleasant accompany the job of journal editor. It is well known that some authors complain when their papers are rejected for publication. This is par for the course and goes with the territory. Another hassle involves getting referee reports back and being able to make decisions without making authors wait too long. This also goes with the territory, although many editors have tried many methods to have reports sent back to them sooner.

These problems are common to most editors, but others are more unusual. One of the most challenging problems I have dealt with is one that other editors have also handled, although in my case it got a lot worse than in most. This is the problem of accusations of plagiarism.

The Problem of Plagiarism in Academic Publishing

The Enders and Hoover Study

In 2004, Walter Enders and Gary Hoover published a useful, interesting, and much-discussed study in the *Journal of Economic Literature* on the responses by journal editors to accusations of plagiarism. Their study was triggered by the experience that one of them had as a referee. After an editor sent this author a paper to referee, he found many sentences in it that were similar or identical to sentences in one of his own published papers. He returned the paper to the editor with a copy of his own paper. The editor noted the possibility of plagiarism, discussed the matter with counsel, rejected the paper without bringing any charges of plagiarism to the author, invited the author to submit papers in the future, and did not even acknowledge any kind of problem. Appalled at this editor's tepid response to evidence of plagiarism, the would-be referee was inspired to investigate further the views of editors on the matter, which resulted in the *JEL* paper.

Enders and Hoover sent questionnaires to 470 editors and received 130 replies. They asked editors about what constitutes plagiarism and what they felt the appropriate responses to established acts of plagiarism should be. They offered five possible examples of plagiarism with four possible replies for each ("Not at all," "Not likely," "Likely," and "Definitely"). For each the five possible acts of plagiarism, I list which of these four responses received the most votes:

"Unattributed sentences (several)" was viewed as "Likely" by 47 percent.

"Unattributed proof (derivation) from working paper" was viewed as "Definite" by 63 percent.

"Unattributed proof (derivation) from published paper" was viewed as "Definite" by 72 percent.

"Unattributed idea" was viewed as "Not Likely" by 45 percent (although the "Likely" plus "Definite" together constituted 51 percent, a bare majority).

"Use of privately collected data without permission" was viewed as "Definite" by 51 percent.

Thus, a majority found all of these to be "Likely" or more, although only just barely for the category of "Unattributed idea."

With the same possible four replies, the study authors then asked about the "appropriateness" of four possible responses to discovering plagiarism in a submitted paper:

"Notify the original author (if possible)" received 78 percent for "Definitely."

"Notify plagiarist's department chair, dean, provost, etc." received 42 percent for "Not Likely." Adding "Not at all" reached a total of 53 percent, another bare majority.

"Ban future submissions to journal from plagiarist" received 45 percent for "Definitely."

"Public notice of plagiarism" received 50 percent for "Not Likely" and another 19 percent for "Not at all," making it the least popular possible response.

Both Enders and Hoover along with other commentators especially focused critically on the apparent unwillingness of the 53 percent to notify the plagiarist's department chair, dean, or provost.

Regarding the frequency of observing plagiarism, they reported that on average an editor could expect to observe a case of it slightly less frequently than once every other year. A majority of their respondents would like to have a code of ethics for economists. They also discussed a variety of related issues regarding different forms of plagiarism, some of which I discuss below, as well as the relevance of copyright laws, which are sometimes applicable. Finally, they found that a solid majority of journals, 81 percent, do not have formal policies regarding how to deal with plagiarism.

Many observers and commentators in the econoblogosphere and elsewhere have expressed dismay and shock at this. The general view is that editors are cowards or wimps for not more vigorously moving to punish plagiarists. However, fear of litigation brought by one who is accused of plagiarism is complex. It is not always easy to prove plagiarism, and editors often disagree about what constitutes plagiarism. These cases can be complicated. It also matters who is accused and who is accusing. Many respondents were more likely to let off very junior people on grounds that they do not know the norms yet and should be given another chance after a slap on the wrist rather than a career-destroying public humiliation and excoriation.

Egregious Examples of Plagiarism

Although many cases of suspected plagiarism are ambiguous and difficult to determine, some are clearer than anything discussed by Enders and Hoover. I am aware of a case in another discipline where a prominent professor frequently served on U.S. National Science Foundation (NSF) panels judging grant proposals. On more than twenty occasions, this individual maneuvered to have grant proposals rejected, stole ideas from the proposals, and published them. Eventually, one grant writer realized that this had happened and complained to both the professor's dean and NSF. The latter instituted a formal investigation that led to the uncovering of the widespread nature of this professor's activities, which were duly reported to the dean in question. This professor was stripped of tenure and fired.

Another surprisingly widespread example of blatant plagiarism is to take someone else's published paper; replace the abstract, introduction, conclusions, or other minor sections with different wording; and submit it to a different journal. Generally, the way this is done is to pick a paper that can be published in different disciplines or in very different subfields of a given discipline. This was done by someone who was hired from outside at my university to be department chair of another department. After about a year of employment, this individual was discovered to have done this and was fired.

Another variation on this is to find articles previously published in foreign languages, translate them into English, and submit them as one's own to journals in the field. During the Soviet period, this practice was quite common going the other way: papers were translated from English into Russian and were published in Russian-language journals without any attribution to the original author. Quite recently, an East Asian physicist was found to have made a cottage industry of finding physics papers originally published in Russian-language journals, translating them into English, and submitting them to English-language journals, perhaps an ironic revenge on the former Soviets. This physicist was not from China, but it has been alleged that some academic institutions in China encourage this sort of thing to enhance the international reputations of their institutions through English-language publications, although this strategy is backfiring, and it is my understanding that it is being discouraged by higher authorities in China at this time.

These sorts of cases are unequivocal and in most countries will result in severe professional consequences for the plagiarist when discovered. However, now I move to the murkier sorts of examples, where I draw on my own personal experiences. I refer to all individuals involved in these matters by letters only, which should not be construed as having anything to do with their actual names.

Words and Phrases

The first case I discuss did not involve a submission to *JEBO* but was presented to me privately for my advice by a member of the *JEBO* editorial board, Professor E, who was a good friend of mine. While we were at a conference, he asked me to go to lunch with him and one of his coauthors whom I knew through other connections. They showed me two papers—a recently published paper by Professor F, a moderately prominent individual whose work I was acquainted with, and a paper that they had written and that had been published earlier. They pointed out numerous distinctive words and phrases that appeared in both papers, although the paper by Professor F made no citation of the work by E and his coauthor (and E and F had briefly served in the same department together). I was convinced that the evidence indicated that plagiarism had occurred.

However, when they asked for my advice on what they should do about it, I acted like the tepid and timid editors who were discussed by Enders and Hoover. I warned them of the threat of litigation by the likely plagiarist. Although there were indeed quite a few of these similar uses of key words and phrases, it could easily be argued that all of this was simply an accident, a parallel, like Newton and Leibniz simultaneously discovering the calculus. They would have to show that Professor F had actually read their paper, and this might be hard to do. How could they prove he had stolen these words and phrases from them, especially if it were to go to a court of law?

They were disheartened by my advice and in the end did nothing. Although I have not discussed this now somewhat ancient matter with Professor E, I noticed in a recent paper of his that he was citing something by Professor F, who is indeed somewhat prominent. So I guess he has decided to live with the matter, however much it may still annoy him.

As for me, however, I did put Professor F on my private "no publish" list. He has submitted only one paper to *JEBO* since that time, but I desk-rejected it, barely looking at it, while not informing him that there was anything special or out of the ordinary regarding his desk rejection.[2] To this day, he has no idea that he was accused of plagiarism by Professor E, that I accepted the accusation, and that he is banned.

I conclude this section by relating a curious event. I had not met Professor F prior to hearing the accusation against him, but some years later, I was pressured into discussing a paper by him at a conference. When I finally met him, I found him to be an exceptionally arrogant and unpleasant individual, which bolstered my conviction that he was indeed a plagiarist or had been on at least one occasion. I confess that I was rather harsh in my commentary on his paper, and although none of my comments were unjustified, I delivered the more negative ones with somewhat greater vigor and force than I would have if I was not convinced that he was an otherwise unpunished plagiarist.

Fun and Games with Galley Proofs

As anyone who has published much knows, there are multiple stages in the process of publishing a paper in a journal. The paper is submitted. It must get past the editor's possible desk rejection. It then must pass through the gauntlet of refereeing and recommendations by board members and various referees, usually with one or more rounds of revisions. Then it is proofread and corrected. Then it is sent off for production and further copyediting. Then galley proofs are sent to the authors. Only after those are returned is the paper published, initially in an electronic form before it appears in a specific print issue with volume and page numbers and all that. Generally, this final form mostly will be accessed electronically, even for journals that have a print version as well, such as is the case with *JEBO*. In the midst of all these stages, fun and games can happen.

The fairly prominent Professor M submitted a paper as lead author with two junior and less prominent coauthors. After the usual rounds of refereeing and revising, the paper was accepted for publication. It made it past the stage of galley proofs being sent and returned and had gone up publicly in electronic form, although not yet in the version with a definite date and volume number and not yet in the printed hard-copy version. During the galley-review stage, Professor T submitted a comment on this paper. Then after the galley proofs were sent back and the version appeared publicly but not fully officially, Professor T sent a complaint alleging plagiarism by M and his coauthors and demanding that I punish them by going to their professional superiors to report their plagiarism.

The alleged plagiarism had taken the following form. When Professor T submitted his initial comment to me, he also sent a copy of it to Professor M. The comment made several points, but the most important and devastating showed that a proof in the paper was flawed. In his complaint to me, Professor T noted (which I had not been aware of) that Professor M had changed the galley proofs to correct the flaw but did not cite the input by Professor T.

At this point, I raised this matter with Professor M, who happens to be another rather arrogant individual and who initially denied any wrongdoing. I involved the associate editor who had handled the paper, and he also initially supported Professor M by denying that there was anything wrong with the initial proof although Professor M had indeed corrected it. I determined that Professor T's complaint was valid and that indeed the original proof had been flawed. In the end, I required M and his coauthors to revise their paper to add a citation and thanks to Professor T for having assisted in the formulation of this proof, which involved a central argument of the paper.[3] I also published the comment by Professor T, although without his correction of the proof. This turned into quite a wrangle, and all the parties involved complained every step of the way. The whole process took more rounds to resolve than I care to report on in any detail. In any case, I never raised this matter with the professional superiors of Professor M or any of his coauthors, even if I think that I managed to arrange a satisfactory outcome in the end in which a possible instance of plagiarism was avoided before it could actually fully occur.

Plagiarism or Bumbling Miscommunication by Junior Economists?

Another difficult case bore similarities to the previous case, and after initial demands for punishment, I managed to arrive at an outcome in which outright plagiarism again was avoided. The case involved two junior people, one a fresh assistant professor (Professor P) and the other a graduate student (Grad Student Q). Their major professors and some of their committee members became involved in the discussions and negotiations over what should be done in this situation.

Professor P submitted a paper that was accepted after a round of revisions. After its acceptance but before it had gotten to the galley proof stage, I received a complaint from Grad Student Q about the paper, which he had apparently seen listed on Professor P's Web site as "forthcoming in *JEBO*." The two were about a year apart as starting cohorts of graduate students at different schools, but they pursued similar topics, had come into communication with each other a few years prior to these events, and sent papers back and forth to each other. The introduction to Professor P's paper cited one of Q's papers as providing useful work on the topic without clearly specifying how this was done. But Grad Student Q claimed that a crucial theorem in P's paper appeared in one of Q's earlier unpublished papers and that he had sent a copy of this paper to P when they were both grad students. The two papers did not present precisely identical proofs, but the theorem in P's paper was very close to the one in Q's paper. Q demanded that P be reported to his new department chair, dean, and so on.

Yet again, the situation proved to be more complicated than it appeared on the surface. Grad Student Q had not published his original paper or even tried to submit it anywhere. He had put it aside and essentially abandoned it. His committee had decided he should focus on a slightly different aspect of his topic, and his subsequent work on his nearly completed dissertation no longer included this theorem or its proof, although it drew on its results in a more general way. The theorem in question was sitting in a working paper that Grad Student Q was making no effort to do anything with. Nevertheless, when Q saw that Professor P was publishing a paper with a theorem and a proof that were similar to a theorem and proof that appeared in a paper that Q had sent to P and that P was not citing his work, he understandably became upset.

I began to communicate with both P and Q, and both of their advisers became involved. P and Q communicated diplomatically with each other (with all involved cc'ed), but separately they complained to me about the conduct of the other. They did not react in a furious or nasty way as those involved in the previous section did, where things became unpleasantly contentious. This became more a matter of working things out so that all could be appeased without any plagiarism actually occurring. The major professors also were working to this end by encouraging communication between P and Q. They were embarrassed by what had come about and wished for a diplomatic outcome. All of us seniors who were involved advocated for these two to collaborate on their research efforts, although I fear that this has not come to pass and that bad blood remains between P and Q.

In the end, I was able to persuade Professor P to revise his paper to include a citation to this almost abandoned unpublished paper by Grad Student Q, noting the similarity between the two theorems and their proofs. Q later submitted a different paper, which I published. I think that the major professors were pleased, even if the two juniors were not fully satisfied. To this day, I remain uncertain whether Professor P was consciously plagiarizing or whether some sort of mistake or miscommunication occurred. In any case, this was one of those cases that some editors referred to in Enders and Hoover, where on the grounds that a junior person had not been properly informed of professional norms, he was given another chance without suffering severe consequences for his questionable conduct.

The Difficult Matter of Self-Plagiarism

Legally and ethically, what has come to be called "self-plagiarism" is not true plagiarism, which involves intellectual property theft of some sort. Writers cannot steal from themselves. However, most editors believe that each paper they publish in their journals should contain at least something that is new to that paper, although in the case of review essays, this may amount to a new presentation of how previously published ideas relate to one another.

We try to avoid publishing papers that are essentially identical to others that an author is publishing, although many economists engage in the unfortunate practice of submitting nearly identical papers to several journals. There is also a norm against submitting the same paper to more than one journal at the same time. Many journals indeed demand that writers declare that the paper that they are submitting to one journal is not currently under consideration at another journal. It may be that this norm is ultimately unreasonable or even ridiculous,[4] but it is widely accepted within the economics profession. This acceptance certainly plays a role in the phenomenon of self-plagiarism, given the widespread pressures to publish as frequently as possible.

Although some economists publish papers in various subfields of economics or even in multiple disciplines, many economists and probably a majority of untenured faculty work on narrowly defined research programs that usually are derived from their Ph.D. theses. Many such research programs effectively involve the study of a single basic idea. Thus, given the constraints and rules that exist, the researcher must map out carefully what is to appear in each paper in the developing research program. There may be a common theoretical core to all the papers, but each must provide a new twist or angle, new data set, new empirical technique, or variation on the theory itself combined with variations in these other areas. So it is not necessarily wrong to have portions of papers that are very similar, possibly even identical word for word, across different papers by an author (or group of coauthors) for portions that present the core idea or ideas that underpin the entire research program. But something else needs to be distinctive in each paper. Sometimes it is a fine line regarding just how important or distinctive a point might be, which makes it difficult to judge when "self-plagiarism" is occurring.

Several times during my editorship, I have rejected papers when an associate editor or a referee has reported that there is a "substantially identical" paper by the same author that is either forthcoming in another journal or has already appeared in print elsewhere. Although not strictly plagiarism, there is clearly a problem when a submitted paper lacks anything sufficiently new to warrant publication. For me, a red flag in this matter is a failure to cite the other paper or papers. Authors need to explain exactly where a particular paper fits into their research program, and even though some frown on self-citation, some self-citation is needed to help clarify this point. Although papers U, V, and W may show a certain point, paper X adds to what those papers have shown with the following new material and points. This sort of thing is missing in the cases of clear self-plagiarism, even if the papers are not identical and the authors cite some of their other papers. But the crucial papers that are very similar somehow are lost in the shuffle of this citing. Their authors try to pretend that they do not exist.

I confess to having considerable sympathy with those who engage in these practices, particularly those who are seeking tenure and promotion under pressure to meet certain arbitrary numerical goals of publications within a tight time constraint. It can be difficult to know how finely to slice and dice the ideas in a given research program and still maintain some originality of publishable importance in each further morsel that is produced. Slipping over the line into unpublishable self-plagiarism is all too easy. Although it certainly is not in the same league as true plagiarism, it is a vice to be avoided.

I substantially blame the combination of constraints and broader trends in the profession for the emergence of this problem. It was not always thus, and in Europe the older view and approach persisted longer than in the United States, where I am afraid this pressure to publish, publish, and publish more initially developed.[5] In this regard, I close this section with an extended quotation from a Swedish economist friend who is now an emeritus professor and decidedly of the old school, Tönu Puu (2006, 31–32):

European university culture, until the 1960s, heavily depended on seminars, where various members of the staff, working with entirely different topics, communicated their results. For that reason the staff members had to keep a broad perspective on their disciplines. Relatively little was regarded as being worth publishing, and national and local "schools" were established, which made visits to other environments really interesting.

We tend to look down on the previous generation as they published relatively little. This fact, however, does not imply that they worked little or were less creative. It might just signify that they were more choosy about what they regarded as being significant enough to merit publication.

After large scale production ideals from the US overtook the European style, everything is produced for immediate publication, even the relatively insignificant ideas. If it is publishable, it is not insignificant, and the number of journals will expand to allow for ever-increasing publications. The number of journals, which has exploded accordingly, conveniently provides for the space. We still have seminars, but we read already published or accepted papers, which we do not want to criticize, and we hardly expect anybody else at the department to understand our whole message. Travel and change of department only results in new personal relations, not new ideas; it may be that we would urgently need new more interdisciplinary scientific fora in the future just in order to provide for encounters with the unexpected ideas we need to secure creativity.

Dealing with an Aggressively Public but False Accusation of Plagiarism

Plagiarists can be crafty about how they steal others' ideas, but some people also make false accusations of plagiarism. They can create fronts to cover their role in the making of such accusations to avoid possible litigation, even as they may arrange to have their charges become public in an effort to garner publicity and sympathy for themselves for professional gain. Editors and others can be cautious about aggressively charging authors with plagiarism, which may reflect a fear of possible litigation. Those who succeed in constructing defenses against such possible litigation may get away with conduct that is not nearly as widely condemned as plagiarism itself but that can become at least as damaging. In this section, I recount my experience with an aggressive false charge of plagiarism, although I must accept that the person behind these accusations to this day probably considers himself to be fully in the right and unjustifiably scorned in his efforts to gain recognition and acceptance for his charges. He almost certainly was ultimately responsible (while denying it) for having nasty messages about me sent to my editorial board and all of my colleagues in my college, including my dean, charging me with unethical conduct for allowing one of those he considers to be a plagiarist to coedit a special issue of *JEBO*, which included a paper by him as well. I call this individual Professor X.

I call the three accused individuals Professors A, B, and C in order of their seniority and prominence, and there also is a Dean D. I proceed by laying out a timeline of the events that involved me directly.

Although I am convinced that Professor X is behind the false charges against A, B, C, D, and me, he has steadfastly maintained that he is not and continues to do so today. Indeed, he has declared that he disapproves of what transpired, even though an enormous amount of evidence indicates that he was responsible. These denials, along with the fact that the accusations were made by a supposed organization, have protected him from litigation by A, B, or C or their respective universities. Also, it is impossible to prove a negative, but after substantially more investigation than I am going to report on in this section, I am thoroughly convinced that Professors A, B, and C are not guilty of plagiarism in this case.

Not long after I became editor of *JEBO*, I received an email message that was sent to multiple recipients, many of them editors. It was supposedly from a group calling itself the Global Network for Research Integrity (GNRI). The message was many pages long and claimed that Professors A, B, and C had plagiarized the work of Professor X, in particular a concept that X was argued to have introduced to the world in its scientific formulation initially in the early 1990s in a paper that was published in *Journal 1*. The message described the careers of A, B, and C and charged them with committing plagiarism and conspiring to cover up their plagiarism by manipulating databases and pressuring others into joining them in this effort, including various guilty editors. The message named the editors of *Journal 2*, which in the early 2000s had published the supposedly most egregious paper by A, B, and C. The recipients of this message were urged not to publish anything by these alleged plagiarists.

I began to receive these messages on a semiregular basis every several months or so. Each new one added more material, including supposed personal items about A, B, and C's relationships and adding more villains, such as Dean D at Professor A's prominent university, who supposedly was forced to resign and move to an obscure institution in Idaho because of his supposedly fiendish efforts to aid A, B, and C in covering up their evil conspiracies and gaining grant monies and public attention that Professor X supposedly deserved.

This was before I had any dealings of my own with Professors A, B, or C, but being a stickler on such matters, I decided to check on these charges on my own. Many of the accusations seemed impossible to check or were nonsensical, but crucial to the matter of whether A, B, and C were guilty as charged was the matter of whether they had actually read any of the papers by Professor X on this topic. They discussed the topic starting in the late 1990s and used some of the methodology that X proposed in an early 1990s paper in *Journal 3*, which laid out his argument more fully and applied it empirically to make regional measures of this concept.

A major piece of Professor X's argument that A, B, and C were aware of his work was the claim that "they used a large number of the same references as the work they plagiarized." I decided that this was something that I could check on without too much effort and did so. When dealing with papers that deal with very similar topics or arguably the same topic, some overlap in references is expected, particularly regarding what could be considered the fundamental literature. And indeed, I found such overlap. However, for the two crucial papers, there was only a 40 percent overlap for the period prior to 1990. I found this insufficient to prove that the accused authors had read the earlier paper. The next time I received a message from GNRI, I replied that I had investigated its claims and found them unconvincing and that I did not wish to receive any more messages.

Some time later, a colleague of Professor A suggested that I publish a special issue based on a certain conference, and he proposed that Professor B should coedit the special issue. I agreed, despite knowing about the charges that had been made against B and also knowing that Professor C was slated to contribute a paper to the special issue. I published the special issue, including a paper coauthored by B that would become one of the most cited papers in *JEBO* following its publication. Although I was convinced of the innocence of B and C, I made sure that the concept that X claimed to have invented would not appear in the issue at all in order to avoid any controversy.

I received a message that was also sent to my entire editorial board and all my college colleagues, including my dean. The message was eleven pages long and began with the following:

BARKLEY ROSSER: YOUR LACK OF ETHICS IS DESPICABLE. YOU HAVE SUPPORTED PLAGIARISTS [B] AND [C], AND PUBLISHED THEIR WORK IN JEB&O [SIC] (DATE). WE WILL EXPOSE YOU AND YOUR LACK OF ETHICS. SHAME ON YOU.

What followed was an expanded version of messages that I had previously received. It included new guilty parties as participants in the vast web of alleged conspiracies. Thirty other persons besides A, B, and C now were part of this supposed conspiracy against X, including numerous deans, university presidents, and prominent economists.[6] The message concluded with a description of the GNRI as consisting of a supposedly enormous global network of students and researchers who all needed anonymity and who all were dedicated to defending the honor of Professor X, even though GNRI's messages claimed that X "refused to talk to our network."

Let me begin with this last point—the nature and identity of GNRI. To the best of my knowledge, GNRI has no identity beyond the promulgation of this particular case. It does not appear on any Google searches by either its full name or its initials. If a Google search is done on the concept in question, two sites appear where much shorter versions of "the case" are made. Neither of these sites actually identifies itself as being the GNRI. Although Professor X has continued to claim complete separation from the GNRI, I was informed by someone at Professor A's university that the school's investigation had found that at least some of these messages were sent from Internet cafés in cities around the world at times when Professor X was visiting those cities.

Furthermore, Professor X to this day maintains a Web site under his name that explains his reasons for claiming that he invented the scientific version of the concept in question.[7] After much discussion of the concept and justifications of why he is the inventor of it as a scientific concept, even though it had appeared in print previously, the body of the introduction to his Web site concludes with remarks about "Some authors who have profited" from using the concept after they introduced it as new in the late 1990s, without naming those parties. The section concludes with a "Notice" declaring that he "strongly rejects the sending of anonymous e-mails" by any group and that he is not a member of any such group that does this.

After this message was sent to many people around the world (several times), I engaged in a lengthy investigation of my own, communicated with many of the involved parties, and became convinced that Professor X was behind the GNRI. My email to him described the message that I had received, argued that it was ultimately baseless in its charges, and urged him to use his influence with the GNRI to make it stop sending scurrilous and potentially libelous messages. I sent copies of this message to his department chair, dean, provost, and university president, along with some of the parties named in the message, including Professors B and C (I have never dealt with A directly). I also sent a message to my board of editors presenting my side of the case and spoke privately with many colleagues at my college, including my department head, my dean, and a professor of business ethics, who urged me to act vigorously in reply.

Unsurprisingly, Professor X responded angrily, made threats, and proclaimed his lack of connection with the GNRI and disapproval of its messages. However, I simply persisted in my line, making it clear that if Professor X did not urge the GNRI to cease its attacks, I would continue to send messages complaining about them to him and his professional superiors, just as had been done to me. This went back and forth several times, but eventually the volley petered out. GNRI sent a few more messages that mostly attacked the editors of *Journal 2* (whom I had kept informed of my actions), but it has now been at least two years since I have heard of any such message from the mysterious GNRI. It may well be that Professor X convinced the GNRI that its efforts on his behalf were backfiring and were doing his case more harm than good.

One member of my editorial board had told a prominent blogger about the matter, and the blogger wanted to write a story on it that would be picked up by the *New York Times*. I urged him not to do so, and he did not. Professors B and C and I felt that Professor X wanted the press to provide him with an opportunity to make his case in a "he said, she said" manner.[8] Professor X is not even a professional economist. He is in a department of social ecology at a midlevel state university, and his original papers on the subject were published in journals rarely read by professional economists,[9] which is another reason I have been willing to believe that Professors A, B, and C were unaware of his work when they initially failed to cite any of it after they began their work on the matter in 1999. Professor X was not entirely without a case. His two papers in the early 1990s, particularly the second (and these were followed up by others less notable), were indeed the first to use the concept in question in a particular way. He deserves to be cited for these papers, and starting in the early 2000s, Professors A, B, and C began to cite X's early 1990s papers in their papers on the subject, crediting him with having done valuable work on it in the United States. The GNRI's Web version of the case declares that Professors A, B, and C have refused to recognize the work of Professor X. The GNRI sent me a message that implicitly recognized that A, B, and C's version was somewhat different than X's version (they "reworked the concept").

Professor X recognized that others had used the term that he claimed ownership of in publications prior to 1990, but his Web site and later GNRI messages argued that these usages were not "scientific" but simply "figures of speech." I have been unable to find anyone using the precise term in question earlier in this context, but there would have been plagiarism by A, B, and C only if they had known of Professor X's work. There was a late 1990s review of the literature on this topic that provided a lengthy list of references but did not include X's early 1990s papers, which is further evidence that it was reasonable to expect that in the late 1990s A, B, and C could have also been unaware of X's work and also were probably unaware of the literature review, which first appeared prior to their first paper on the topic. After they became aware of these works, they began citing them in a reasonable fashion.

Conclusions

Plagiarism is a difficult problem, and accusations of plagiarism are regularly made to journal editors, who oppose plagiarism and seek to avoid facilitating it. However, given disagreements over what plagiarism is and the threat of litigation from those who might argue that they have been falsely accused, editors tend to tread cautiously when presented with such accusations. Most editors support a code of ethics for the economics profession, and such a code of ethics would undoubtedly include strongly injunctions against plagiarism.

Plagiarism is a serious ethical issue, but so is the rarer phenomenon of false accusations of plagiarism, which can seriously damage the careers of innocent persons.[10] Based on my own experiences in receiving accusations of unethical conduct because I published work by people who were falsely accused of plagiarism, my recommendation is that such false accusations should be treated as being as unethical as plagiarism itself and that those who make such accusations should be confronted as forcefully as possible with the falsity and unjustified nature of their conduct and condemned accordingly.

Acknowledgments

I wish to thank my colleagues on my editorial board and at my university; Jeroen Loos at Elsevier, the journal publisher at the time, who supported me when I was publicly accused of unethical conduct for allowing an accused plagiarist to coedit and publish a paper in the journal I edited; and some commentators who will remain anonymous.

Notes

1. For Elsevier, the publisher of the *Journal of Economic Behavior and Organization*, I served the final portion of my predecessor's term, Richard H. Day, in late 2001. Day was a cofounder of the journal in 1980. I officially became editor on January 2, 2002. I have served two four-year terms, plus an extra year added onto the final term.

2. In recent years, we have desk-rejected about 50 percent of submitted papers.

3. I learned much more about the topic of the paper and became aware that there are sharply divided views about the arguments in the paper. My associate editor strongly favored Professor M's position, and Professor T was on the other side. A history of conflict between these parties came out in the various exchanges and complaints by all those involved. To this day, I have not made up my mind about the ultimate right or wrong of the competing sides in this controversy over the economic ideas involved.

4. It is acceptable to submit the same book proposal to multiple book publishers, and there is no obvious reason that it is not acceptable to submit papers to multiple journals. Also, some disciplines (such as law) allow the practice, but most do not. The job of an editor is simplified by not having multiple submissions, but it is not clear that multiple submissions involve anything unethical, unless the writer lies on the form asking if the paper is being simultaneously submitted to another journal. In this case, the lie is the problem, not the act of multiple submissions.

5. For a broader discussion of trends in the relationship between American and European economics, see J. Barkley Rosser Jr., Richard P. F. Holt, and David Colander (2010).

6. This list contained so many distinguished individuals that I began to feel proud to be on it, much as if I had awakened in 1974 to learn that I was on Richard Nixon's enemies list.

7. Professor X's Web site makes a big deal about how he has copyrighted this concept, so I minimize quoting from it directly.

8. Professor A is tenured and a chaired full professor. Professors B and C were both junior and untenured at the time that the group initially made its accusations. Both B and C suffered substantially from delays in being considered for tenure, from time wasted in responding to the accusations, from pain experienced by their families and friends, and from the substantial costs borne by their universities in investigating the charges, which all were found to be false.

9. Although I have cited work in both of these journals, few economists do. *Journal 1* was largely a psychology journal, although it published the occasional economics or management paper, perhaps because a leading economist was on its board at the time. Its readership was so low that it later merged with another journal, in which I published a paper in the mid-1990s. *Journal 3* is one of the leading mathematically oriented journals in its field, and Professor X's paper in it was much better than the earlier one, although this journal also is rarely read by economists, and mostly by regional economists, with none of Professors A, B, or C fitting into that category.

10. These accusations brought much pain and distraction for Professors A, B, and C, who needed to defend themselves to their professional superiors at great length and cost. They were exonerated, but no one can give them back the time spent on this painful and ridiculous matter. Their arguments were ultimately accepted, and the actions of the anonymous group were discredited. To the best of my knowledge, Professor X has avoided any overt censure or other punishment, other than what he has brought on himself by maintaining his Web site.

References

Enders, Walter, and Gary A. Hoover. 2004. Whose Line Is It? Plagiarism in Economics. *Journal of Economic Literature* 42:487–493.

Puu, Tönu. 2006. *Arts, Sciences and Economics: A Historical Safari*. Heidelberg: Springer-Verlag.

Rosser, J. Barkley, Jr., Richard P. F. Holt, and David Colander. 2010. *European Economics at a Crossroads*. Cheltenham: Elgar.

22

An Instructive Case in Referencing, Priority Conflict, and Ethics: The Role of an Editor in a Scholarly Journal

Michael Szenberg

If you torture the data sufficiently, it will confess to anything.
—Ronald H. Coase

Projection: A defense mechanism in which one attributes to another person one's own wishes and qualities and thereby does not experience them as one's own.
—Sigmund Freud

Cognitive dissonance: A state of conflict and discomfort occurring when existing beliefs are contradicted by new evidence. One way the individual(s) seek to relieve the discomfort is by denying the existence of the evidence.
—L. Festinger

A story is told of a master who was asked by his young disciple how to proceed in his unquenchable thirst for truth. The teacher did not reply but continued to walk in the field with his assistant in silence until they came to a stream. Suddenly, the teacher seized the student and thrust his head beneath the water, where he held it for several moments. Sputtering and surprised, the student asked the meaning of this. The master replied: "When you want the truth as much as you panted for air, you will find it."

It is an editor's role to probe and dissect and to do so in a way that does not encourage distortions or embellishments. To fulfill this role suitably, the editor must adhere to a high standard of ethics. The assessment and especially the scrutiny of the publication process are of vital concern to scientists because scholarly journals are the mainstays of scientific communication, and publication in them by academicians is the primary route to professional advancement.

This chapter reviews a controversy concerning citation and priority of publication that arose between the authors of two different articles on the same subject published in two different journals, and it also discusses the role played by the editor of a journal. Both authors and editors are essential for the publishing transaction to take place. Yet even under the best of circumstances, the editor has disproportionate power in this relationship because he or she views the job as routine, whereas the writer views it as an emergency.

In 1992, I served as one of four editor panelists at a session called "Publishing in Economic Journals: Selection Criteria, Refereeing, Processes, and procedures" at the Convention of the American Economics Association. During the session, I raised the issue of multiple submissions, and after the session, the eminent economist Gordon Tullock remarked that the time had come for an editor to support the multiple submission procedure. This remark sparked my interest in writing a piece on the subject, and I decided to juxtapose editors' arguments on the pros and cons of multiple submissions. Both articles appeared in the *American Journal of Economics and Sociology* (AJES) (Szenberg 1994).

In response to my article, two authors complained to the editor of *AJES*. that I had failed to cite one of their articles in favor of multiple submissions. They complained to the editor if *AJES* about what they seemed to feel was plagiarism on my part. As I pointed out to the editor, multiple submissions had been discussed in the journals and in the profession for many years, far antedating anything that these authors published on it. In the early 1970s, I was involved in discussions on multiple submissions at meetings of editors of economic journals, and I also practiced it. For many years, journals and books directed at writers have regularly included discussions of the subject. Furthermore, in the editorial note that accompanied the articles on multiple submissions, the editor of *AJES* wrote that the subject had been frequently discussed by journal editors, authors, and potential authors at academic conferences. Neither the *AJES* editor nor I ever claimed that the idea was original with us.

Although discussions of this topic can be traced to the 1970s (as I have done), the complaining authors do not cite anyone for the point made in their 1982 paper and insist that anyone raising similar points after that date must cite their article. They also claimed that I should have cited their main article because it was published by a journal that I edit. In fact, I do not think that editors are obliged to promote any article that incorrectly claims to be the first contribution in writing on a subject.

Calvin Peters (1976) was the first to have argued in writing for multiple submissions, and following the practice of citing original sources, I cited his 1976 article (noting that Peters "was the first to raise the issue of multiple submissions"). The Peters article generated a discussion among academics ("Replies to Calvin Peters" 1976) for and against multiple submissions on the pages of the *American Sociologist*. Among the key words included in Peters's article were "ethics, efficiency, promptness, mobility, security, and restraint of trade" (Peters 1976). The two authors included similar key words in their article but do not cite the Peters article, the "Replies to Calvin Peters," or any contributions on multiple submissions that were published prior to their piece. In my article, I thank another eminent student of the journal industry, David Laband, for providing me with his unpublished manuscript dealing with the review process, including the subject of multiple submissions. Laband's key words parallel those of Peters and the two authors in question. Laband also cites Peters and also does not cite the two authors' article.

In 1971 (eleven years before publication of the complaining authors' article), I submitted my first lengthy manuscript on the diamond industry (Szenberg 1973) to several publishers at the same time. I continued this practice of multiple submissions with all my other books, one of which (Szenberg, Lombardi, and Lee 1977) was published five years before the piece. So their claim to originality on this point was disproved. (Incidentally, although I advocate eliminating the exclusivity of journal submissions, I have always offered my articles to journals on an exclusive basis.)

Despite my response, the editor of *AJES* published the two authors' comment, which again ignored the existence of the 1976 Peters article and other earlier contributions and suggested that these authors are convinced that the idea of multiple submissions started with them.

The executive board of the society that appointed me to the editorship of the *American Economist* evaluated all of the materials relevant to this controversy and gave me their unanimous support.

Fortunately, the scientific enterprise has a great capacity for self-correction and is very effective at uncovering mistakes over time. Most editors possess discriminating moral intelligence, dispassionate reflection, and intellectual independence. Editors of scholarly journals, even if encumbered by self-absorption and a sensational bent, must preserve their reputation for truth, candor, common sense, and decency and avoid being hotly partisan for one side instead of a disinterested, detached gatekeeper.

To develop sustainable relationships between author and editor, the critical element of listening must be incorporated into the matrix. Hearing alone is not sufficient. Learning through talk (and this includes self-inquiry, a form of inner dialogue about what is the right thing to do) can take place only when both parties listen with sensitivity and empathy. Only then can a workable, salutary, and balanced relationship between author and editor exist. In times of conflict, the editor should serve as a bridge between warring factions and strive for magnanimity on both sides. To avoid or diminish erratic reasoning, self-contradictions, and misjudgments, editors must be disposed to listen to others and have the capacity to censure their own actions, however difficult this may be. Otherwise, we diminish ourselves. Editorial character must combine judgment and experience with an attachment to integrity, prudence, and respect for others and an ability to internalize a high degree of moral sensibility so that narrow interest and expediency are recognized, discounted, and shelved. In the case of the article in question above, both the journal editor and the managing editor were replaced within three months, after being forced to publish my very brief rejoinder.

Concluding Remarks

When it comes to conflicts over priorities, editors sometimes encounter scholars who exhibit "deviant behaviors" and harbor "wish fulfilling beliefs and false memories that we describe as illusions" (Merton 1963a, 81). Eugene Garfield, founder and chair emeritus of the Institute for Scientific Information and editor of *The Scientist*, once referred me to what an eminent social observer writes about cryptomnesia or unconscious plagiary (Merton 1963b, 273):

Cryptomnesia . . . subjects the scientist to the ever-present possibility that his most cherished original idea may actually be the forgotten residue of what he had once read or heard elsewhere. This fear may give rise to either of two conflicting patterns of behavior: in some cases, it may lie behind the emphatic insistence of any imaginative mind that he is beholden to no one else for his newfound ideas. This pattern of a possibly cryptomnesic scientist who protests-his-originality-too-much, not knowing whether he is right or not, differs of course from the pattern of the-lady-who-doth-protests-too-much, knowing as she does that her act will belie her words. In other cases, the scientist who knows that cryptomnesia can occur may assume that he has unwittingly assimilated an idea which he once believed to have been original with him. This may hold for big ideas or small ones.

In his address given at the 1960 annual meeting of the American Association for the Advancement of Science (AAAS), Sir Charles P. Snow (1960, 257) had this to say about the desire in science to pursue truth:

Without that desire there is no science. It is the driving force of the whole activity. It compels the scientist to have an overriding respect for truth, every stretch of the way. That is, if you are going to find what is there, you mustn't deceive yourself or anyone else. You mustn't lie to yourself. At the crudest level you mustn't fake your experiments.

Unfortunately, the centers that create and disseminate knowledge often become microcosms of scholarly irrationality whose inhabitants are not immune to the corrupting influences of power, close friends, and status. As one physicist observes, "The image of noble and virtuous dedication to truth that scientists have traditionally presented to the public is no longer credible" (Dyson 1995, 33. Politicians, editors, administrators, and other professionals sometimes think that they are unaccountable to others and rely on emotional opinions from the top down rather than on common sense or on facts from the ground up. As they become entangled in a web of their invention, they deny the possibility that their firmest convictions might be mistaken and attempt to arrive at conclusions too quickly.

I like to think that both writers and journal editors can benefit from this comment that John Steinbeck (1962) made in his Nobel Banquet acceptance speech: "The ancient commission of the writer hasn't changed. He is charged with exposing our many grievous faults and failures, with dredging up to the light our dark and dangerous dreams for the purposes of improvement."

References

Coase, R. H. 1995. *Essays on Economics and Economists*. Chicago: University of Chicago Press.

Dyson, F. 1995. The Scientist as Rebel. *New York Review of Books*, May 25, 33.

Simultaneous Submission of Manuscripts. 1975. *Sociological Quarterly* 15 (2):163.

Festinger, L. 1985. *A Theory of Cognitive Dissonance*. Stanford, CA: Stanford University Press [originally published in 1957].

Freud, Sigmund. 1938. *The Basic Writings of Sigmund Freud*. Trans. and ed. A. A. Brill. New York: Modern Library.

Merton, R. K. 1963a. The Ambivalence of Scientists. *Bulletin of the Johns Hopkins Hospital* 112:77–97.

Merton, R. K. 1963b. Resistance to the Systematic Study of Multiple Discoveries in Science. *European Journal of Sociology* 4 (2):237–282.

Peters, C. 1976. Multiple Submissions: Why Not? *American Sociologist* 11 (3):165–168.

Replies to Calvin Peters. 1976. *American Sociologist* 11 (3):168–179.

Snow, Charles P. 1960. The Moral Un-Neutrality of Science. Address to the American Association for the Advancement of Science, New York, December 27.

Steinbeck, John. 1962. Nobel Prize Banquet Acceptance Speech, Stockholm, December 10.

Szenberg, M. 1973. *Economics of the Israeli Diamond Industry*. Introduction by Milton Friedman. New York: Basic Books.

Szenberg, M. 1994. Disseminating Scholarly Output: The Case for Eliminating the Exclusivity of Journal Submissions. *American Journal of Economics and Sociology* 53 (3):303–315.

Szenberg, Michael, J. W. Lombardi, and E. Y. Lee. 1977. *The Welfare Effects of Trade Restrictions*. Foreword by Robert E. Baldwin. New York: Academic Press.

23

An Editor's Life at the *Journal of Economic Perspectives*

Timothy Taylor

In spring 1984, I was a disgruntled graduate student of the standard make and model on my way to bailing out of Stanford University's Ph.D. program in economics with what I regarded as a consolation master's degree. I was clueless about my future career path, except that it seemed clear that my road would not travel through academia. In 1986, I started working as managing editor of the *Journal of Economic Perspectives* (*JEP*). In fall 1988, I moved back to Stanford and into an office in the department of economics with my own full-time assistant in the neighboring office. When moving back to Stanford, I had the mind-bending experience of rejoining friends with whom I had entered graduate school, who were just then finishing their doctoral degrees and heading out to first jobs. A year later, in fall 1989, I found myself lecturing to five hundred students in Stanford's Economics 1 class with ten graduate students as teaching assistants.

This chain of events seemed wildly improbable to me even as it was happening, and the passage of time has not dimmed its serendipity. In this chapter, I tell the story of how I went from an academic car crash in graduate school to spending the last twenty-five years as the managing editor of a prominent academic economics journal. Part of my personal history is also the history of the origins and mission of the *Journal of Economic Perspectives*, an academic journal with the distinctive mission of presenting essays on cutting-edge topics, often by prominent authors, and doing so in an expository style that minimizes specialized technique and jargon and thus is accessible to a broad readership of economists. Along the way, I offer some thoughts about graduate school in economics, the mindset needed for aggressive editing, and the role of editors in academia.

Graduate School Crash and Burn

After graduating in 1982 from Haverford College, a twelve-hundred-student liberal arts college on the Main Line of Philadelphia (as the guidebooks say), I enrolled in Stanford University's graduate program in economics. I refer to my two years in economics graduate school as "the two worst years of my life." These years were not tragic: I learned an enormous amount and made some lifelong friends. But it was hard to wake up every day feeling like a mutated combination of fish out of water and gerbil on a treadmill.

Although I did not realize it at the time, some of my difficulties were systemic. A few years after it was too late to do me any good, Hirschel Kasper (1991) reported the results of a study of nine liberal arts colleges—Amherst, my own Haverford, Middlebury, Oberlin, Smith, Swarthmore, Wellesley, Wesleyan, and Williams—and their experiences in sending students to economics Ph.D. programs. Historically, these colleges had each produced undergraduates who completed two or three economics Ph.D.s per year, but by the late 1980s, these colleges were sending about one person a year to an economics Ph.D. program, and that person often did not complete the program.

Why did this dramatic change occur? Kasper (1991, 1098) emphasizes a substantial shift in graduate education in economics: "Two decades ago a significant segment of first year graduate theory was a review for liberal arts graduates of advanced undergraduate theory, as evidenced by the fact that the graduate courses made use of textbooks written by undergraduate faculty." But this situation changed dramatically (Kaspar 1991, 1102): "The gap mentioned earlier between undergraduate and first year graduate theory arises from the increased emphasis on technical methods at the graduate level, with an apparently corresponding decrease in emphasis of economic analysis. The emphasis during the first year on techniques, with too little announced justification for them, strikes liberal arts graduates, whose interest in economics is partly fueled by social concerns of the consequences of economic problems, as an approach which is, at best, misplaced."

My Haverford education was excellent along a number of dimensions. I read widely across the classic literatures of economics and political science. In particular, I developed my ability to read sympathetically— that is, to assume that knowledgeable and profound thinkers almost never say idiotic things, although they may often make difficult or subtle points that at first reading seem unclear or inconsistent or contradictory.

A sympathetic reading leaves open the possibility that the author is less than clear but persuades the reader not to dismiss or negate the text for that reason and instead to draw out whatever lessons and analytical frameworks are available.

The small class sizes and individual attention at Haverford along with the particular classes I selected also encouraged sheaves of writing. In those precomputer years, I typed hundreds of pages on Eaton's "Corrasable Bond" paper, correcting errors with a pencil eraser. I wrote columns for the school newspaper. I wrote early and final drafts of many ten-, twenty-, and forty-page papers. I designed an individual study class with the head of the freshman writing program (thank you, Joanne Hutchinson) in which I wrote a fifteen-page paper each week, she commented extensively on the writing, and then the following week I rewrote the first paper and produced a new first draft. I wrote multiple drafts of a two-hundred-page senior thesis on how to think about fairness in the federal income tax.

But when it came to mathematical background, I was woefully underprepared for graduate school in economics. I had had a semester of econometrics, a year of calculus, and a semester of linear algebra. This mathematics background was more than most Haverford economics majors had at that time. As Kasper (1991, 1099) wrote: "Changes in the mathematics requirement at Haverford are illustrative of the changes which occurred at all nine colleges. In 1974 no Haverford economics course required any calculus; in 1984 one semester of calculus was required for the intermediate microeconomics course; and by 1989, calculus was required in both intermediate micro and macro, plus an advanced field course." I scored highly on the math portion of the GRE, but when it came to the mathematical demands of Stanford's Ph.D. program, I was carrying a cheese grater to knife fight.

When a student and a graduate program are a bad fit, no one comes out looking good. To many of the faculty in Stanford's graduate program, I am sure that I looked like just another drowning graduate student. Maybe I was drowning from lack of effort, lack of background, lack of brainpower, or lack of interest. Frankly, it did not seem to matter too much to anyone to find out. From my point of view, I felt as if I had drifted into a parallel universe where instead of actually studying the economy, I was studying a set of mathematical and statistical tools that one might use if at some point in the future one desired to study the economy. The years from 1982 to 1984 were eventful economic times. The United States was emerging from a decade of oil shocks, repeated recessions, and unemployment and inflation rates that had topped out in double digits. Huge budget deficits and trade deficits were developing. "Supply-side economics" was in the news. Deregulation of airlines, trucking, banking, and many industries was underway. Paul Volcker was changing the rules for how to conduct monetary policy. The country was only about a decade into its experience with floating exchange rates. Japan's economy seemed inexorably on the rise, with South Korea's not far behind. The Latin American debt crisis was underway. But those topics—any real-world topics—were essentially absent from our first-year curriculum.

Kasper (1991, 1105) summarizes the issues facing graduates of liberal arts colleges in economics programs in this way:

> We conclude that the graduate programs no longer attract the same numbers of top liberal arts graduates as they once did in large part because graduate study is no longer merely the advanced specialization of the undergraduate field, but instead has nearly become a discipline distinct from undergraduate study, especially from the perspective of first year graduate students. The emphasis on technique, at the expense of less attention to the analytical issues of economics, tends to depreciate the importance of the intuitive and creative talents of the liberal arts graduates.

As I was fighting through graduate school, working hard and hating my days, many students offered reassurance of this general form: "Everyone hates the first year of graduate school. It's actually pretty pointless, and you won't ever use most of what you learn. It's just a set of hoops you need to jump through so that you can do interesting work later on." I recognized a substantial element of truth in this message, and perhaps in some galaxy far, far away, this message could be viewed as inspirational. But for me, this well-meant reassurance felt like an acknowledgment that I was living through an intellectual hazing ritual, which made the whole experience feel even grimmer.

My personality and temperament were ill-suited for graduate school in other ways as well. In graduate school, I discovered that by the standards of academic researchers, I am intellectually impatient. Some years later, I ran across a paper by Xavier Sala-i-Martin (1997) called "I Just Ran Two Million Regressions." As I read the paper, I thought to myself: "That's one reason I wasn't suited for graduate school. Let *him* run the two million regressions. I want to be the person who comes along after the work is done and learns about what he's done—maybe over lunch." I have a grasshopper mind. I like to hop from one subject to another. In the second year of Stanford's graduate program, various topics were pretty interesting to me for about six weeks. Then I began to feel that I pretty much knew what I wanted to know on that subject, diminishing returns had set in, and I was ready to move along to some other field of economics.

A friend of mine who attended graduate school in library science once told me that a librarian needed to be like the Missouri River—a mile wide and a foot deep. In other words, librarians did not need to know a whole lot except how to find everything they might want to look up. Conversely, most research economists are closer to a crevasse in an ice field—say, a mile deep but only a foot wide. (As the old joke goes, experts know more and more about less and less until they know everything about nothing.) I am most comfortable with a mix of breadth and depth—call it a quarter mile deep and a quarter mile wide. In many areas of economics, I know more than the nonspecialists in that area but decidedly less than the specialists.

I did learn an enormous amount of economics in my two years at Stanford. On my best days, I remained fuzzy on how semicontinuity differed from hemicontinuity and demicontinuity along with why I should care. My efforts to sketch a quick macromodel or to derive a new maximum likelihood estimator were weak. But I spent considerable time working my way through the lengthy first-year reading list, which was heavily weighted toward classic articles of the previous few decades. In terms of doing well on the end-of-year comprehensive exams, this careful reading was largely time wasted. The comprehensive exams were all about fluidity in applying and interpreting mathematical techniques, not about developing a broad understanding of the modern evolution of the economics literature. In this way as in others, my intellectual approach was dysfunctional for graduate school but has turned out to be highly useful as a journal editor.

An Interlude in the Newspaper Business

Thanks to a newspaper executive who was willing to take a chance on a economics grad student (thank you, Rob Elder), I left graduate school for a job as an editorial writer for the *San Jose Mercury News*, which was the main daily newspaper in Silicon Valley. I loved that job. I have opinions to burn. After the straitjacket of graduate school, I especially liked the intellectual freedom and the focus on current events. Silicon Valley was taking off in the mid-1980s, which meant that I could find local angles on any number of issues related to high technology, R&D,

finance, competition policy, international trade, and the environment. I look back at my time as an editorial writer at the *Mercury News* with great affection. It had great people and a great work environment, and it was a great time to be in that particular job. It also taught me two professional lessons in particular that have been essential for my later work as managing editor of *JEP*.

First, the newspaper business taught me about writing as a professional drill. You wake up in the morning, walk to your front door, pick up the morning paper, see a headline, and know that in about six or seven hours you will have written a short essay on the subject—an essay that will be on the breakfast tables of 300,000 households the next morning. You do not have any excuses for not finishing the essay. The newspaper cannot be printed with a white space because you did not feel quite up to finishing your piece. You need to adjust the length of what you write. You may start off thinking that you are going to fill ten column inches of space, but an hour before deadline, you may find that you only have six inches or perhaps twelve inches. You write three to five of these unsigned editorials each week, along with occasional signed op-ed columns.

I once read a sentiment (which I remember as being attributed to Ernest Hemingway, although I have never been able to track down a source for the quotation) to the effect that "the first 500,000 words that anyone writes is garbage." Well, writing something like two thousand words per week works out to about a hundred thousand words per year. After my Haverford writing experience, I must have finished out my time at the newspaper near the brink of that 500,000 word minimum.

My second major lesson from my time at the *Mercury News* is that I learned some useful reading habits. My job at the newspaper required a broad awareness of what economists were thinking about the events of the day so that I would be ready to churn out those daily editorials as events dictated. I began regularly reading reports from the Congressional Budget Office, publications from the regional Federal Reserve banks, the annual *World Development Report* from the World Bank, the *Economic Report of the President* from the Council of Economic Advisers, and newsletters and articles from think tanks like the Brookings Institution and the Cato Institute. When the president's budget proposals were unveiled each year, I spent a day or two going through the *Historical Tables* and the *Analytical Perspectives* volumes. When the *U.S. Statistical Abstract* arrived each year, I spent a day doodling around the pages, looking at levels and trends. When these sources or the issues of the day led to the research literature, I spent a day in the Stanford library stacks tracking down working papers and journal articles. Sometimes this reading turned into an immediate unsigned editorial or op-ed, but often it just deepened my own background in economics.[1]

The *Journal of Economic Perspectives* Is Born

In the summer of 1985, while I was working at the *Mercury News*, I heard an intriguing rumor from Tim Bresnahan, a Stanford economist (and Haverford alumnus) for whom I had worked as a research assistant during my second year in graduate school. Tim had been talking with Joseph Stiglitz, who used to come out to Stanford for a summer institute each year, and Tim had heard that Joe was expecting to become the editor of a new and different economics journal. His intention was to present sophisticated economics in a relatively nontechnical way to the broad audience of academic economists. Joe had been asking if anyone knew of someone who was knowledgeable about technical economics but who was primarily a writer. I am sure that other people were at the intersection of those Venn diagram circles, but most of them were securely perched in jobs that they did not want to leave. I was ready to take a chance. Tim passed along my name to Joe, we talked, and by early 1986, I was planning to move to Princeton University to take the job as managing editor of a new and as yet unnamed journal of the American Economic Association.

I will always owe Joe Stiglitz an enormous debt of gratitude. First and foremost, he was willing to hire me as managing editor of the *Journal of Economic Perspectives*. I am not sure that I would have hired myself. I probably would have looked for someone other than a twenty-six-year-old who had never run anything before.

I learned an enormous amount from Joe. He has the extraordinary gift of great economists, which is that when Joe explains the intellectual structure of how he looks at a problem or a situation, it seems like the only sensible way that anyone could ever look at it. Joe also has remarkable breadth across many fields of economics. Just rubbing shoulders with him on a regular basis was an education.

Working with Joe opened other doors for me. For example, I worked with Joe on the first edition of his *Principles of Economics* textbook, which was published in 1991. This experience led to opportunities to teach the introductory economics class at Stanford and later at the University of Minnesota. Winning student-voted teaching awards led to offers to record lectures for the Teaching Company, a for-profit firm that sells lectures to the adult education market. It also led, through a winding road that is a story in itself, to a chance to write an introductory textbook of my own that was published in 2007.[2]

Finally, Joe treated me as a partner in the founding of the journal. I was a junior partner, to be sure, but the difference between a junior partner and a subordinate or an underling is very real. Maybe I am hypersensitive about being treated as if I matter. That was an issue for me in graduate school. But with Joe, I always felt that my opinion was heard and heeded, whether or not the eventual decisions went the way I preferred.

When I was hired as managing editor of a new economics journal, the journal was just an idea. It lacked a title, and the mission of the journal was ill-defined. Joe, coeditor Carl Shapiro, an editorial assistant named Carolyn Moseley, and I sat down together and looked at different fonts, kerning and leading, page sizes, and weights of paper and cover stock. We looked at many other journals to see where they placed the table of contents, what running heads they used at the top of pages, where they put page numbers, where they listed qualifications of authors and acknowledgments, and other details. We carried around samples of different colors and designs for the cover. We thought about the desired length of articles and issues. In short, we invented the *Journal of Economic Perspectives* from the ground up.

I am not sure how many economics journals existed in 1986, but the American Economic Association currently indexes over a thousand academic journals of economics. From the start, the *Journal of Economic Perspectives* was intended to be a different kind of economics journal. Most academic journals serve two functions: they certify that the author has written a paper of quality, which is useful for promotion decisions and grant applications, and they serve as metaphorical file cabinets for storing worthy papers so that they are relatively easy to refer to and to locate when needed. Both functions are important, but neither function implies that readers will actually sit down to browse through the articles in a given issue, not even for a prominent journal. Even scanning the abstracts at the start of the article is more than many economists actually do. If people are active in research in a certain field, they should almost always be aware of research in their field from seminars and working papers and discussions with colleagues—well before the finished draft of the paper struggles through final revisions, typesetting, and the long wait for actual publication.

In contrast, the *Journal of Economic Perspectives* was intended to publish articles that could be read—not articles that could be figured out given a sufficient investment of time and energy. All economists (with the possible exception of Joe Stiglitz and a few others) are nonspecialists in most fields. Rather than behaving as yet one more standard double-blind refereed journal, the *JEP* would invite its authors. The comments from the editors and coeditors would all be signed rather than anonymous. And rather than just making comments such as "This section needs tightening up," "This argument isn't quite clear," or "The discussion here seems repetitive," a hands-on editor (me) would work through every line of every paper. Thanks to the miracle of floppy disks in 1987 and now to the even greater miracle of email attachments, editors could do more than just scrawl red-ink comments in the margins of pages. We could make revisions directly to the text by clarifying, trimming, cutting, and expanding. The revised text could then be returned to the author for further changes. After someone has accepted an invitation from the *JEP* to write, we are committed to working through an editing process with them. As long as *JEP* authors are willing to be responsive to comments and feedback, we eventually will be willing to publish their articles.

When the journal started, one main concern was whether the often high-powered academics who were being invited to write for *JEP* would accept this kind of interactive editing or whether we would confront a volcanic outburst of temper at least once every full moon. But the hope of the *JEP* editorial process, which has proved true over time, is that this kind of direct hands-on interaction is actually effective in getting to a readable final draft in a way that does not make everyone crazy. Instead of receiving general comments about making a manuscript shorter or clearer, authors receive specific suggestions. Many authors will throw out or overrule 10, 20, or even 50 percent of the advice they get. But by accepting most of the advice, their article is typically finished after one or two revisions and does not drag on through multiple revisions, which can easily lead to bad feelings. As many authors have noted, it is always hard to revise your own work, so having someone else do the first edit allows authors to return to the manuscript feeling less stale and more productive. Also, because authors know that their article will appear in the journal—and typically with much shorter delays than they experience with other journals—they generally have been willing to work with our editorial process to mold the article into shape.

But although the *JEP* editorial process has worked well, by and large, it does require striking a balance. Detailed hand-on editing requires caring a great deal, being confrontational with authors about things that matter, not caring too much about things that are less important, and having sufficient perspective to see the difference. Arthur Plotnik (1986, 1) describes this balancing act in his *Elements of Editing: A Modern Guide for Editors and Journalists*: "What kind of person makes a good editor? When hiring new staff, I look for such useful attributes as genius, charisma, adaptability, and disdain for high wages. I also look for signs of a neurotic trait called compulsiveness, which in one form is indispensable to editors, and in another, disabling." Humorist Ambrose Bierce (1911) also conveyed the necessary editorial combination of aggressive interventionism while soothing the savage author when he defined *editor* in his *Devil's Dictionary,* in part, in this way:

editor: . . . a severely virtuous censor, but so charitable withal that he tolerates the virtues of others and the vices of himself; who flings about him the splintering lightning and sturdy thunders of admonition till he resembles a bunch of firecrackers petulantly uttering his mind at the tail of a dog; then straightway murmurs a mild, melodious lay, soft as the cooing of a donkey intoning its prayer to the evening star. . . .

Here I discuss three aspects of the mindset of a tough but tender editor—the nuts-and-bolts aspect, the confrontational aspect, and the peacemaking side.

The Nuts-and-Bolts Aspect of Editing

One central and perhaps undervalued aspect of hands-on editing is working on the nuts and bolts of the writing. Nuts-and-bolts editing does not challenge the substance of an article but instead seeks to smooth the presentation. In many cases, authors barely notice that nuts-and-bolts editing has been done, except for a warm and fuzzy feeling that by some alchemy their words now read more clearly than before.

As an extreme example of nuts-and-bolts editing, consider the problems posed in editing the papers of Jeremy Bentham, the utilitarian philosopher and occasional economist. Bentham wrote perhaps fifteen pages in longhand almost every day of his adult life. His admirers gathered some of his work for publication, but much was simply stored in boxes, primarily at the library of University College, London. In 1941, an economist named Werner Stark was commissioned by the Royal Economic Society to prepare a comprehensive edition of Bentham's economic writings, which in turn are just a portion of his overall writings.

In the three-volume work that was published eleven years later, Stark (1952) wrote in the introduction:

The work itself involved immense difficulties. Bentham's handwriting is so bad that it is quite impossible to make anything of his scripts without first copying them out. I saw myself confronted with the necessity of copying no less than nine big boxes of papers comprising nearly 3,000 pages and a number of words that cannot be far from the seven-figure mark. But that was only the first step. The papers are in no kind of order: in fact it is hard to imagine how they ever became so utterly disordered. They resemble a pack of cards after it has been thoroughly shuffled. . . . . The pages of some manuscripts, it is true, were numbered, but then they often carried a double and treble numeration so that confusion was worse confounded, and sometimes I wished there had been no pagination at all. In other manuscript collections the fact that sentences run uninterruptedly from one sheet onto another, is of material help in creating order out of chaos. I was denied even this assistance. It was one of Bentham's idiosyncrasies never to begin a new page without beginning at the same time a new paragraph. But I cannot hope to give the reader an adequate idea of the problems that had to be overcome.

Stark's lamentations would chill the heart of any editor: "Bentham was most unprincipled with regard to the use of capitals"; "After careful consideration, it was found impossible to transfer the punctuation of Bentham's manuscripts on to the printed page. When he has warmed to a subject and is writing quickly, he simply forgets to punctuate "; and so on.

The technology of word processing has blessedly deleted most the problems that confronted Stark. Articles for the *JEP* arrive in an electronic form that is suitable for editing. Modern economists may be guilty of irrelevance, ponderous prose, unnecessary technical detours, and an occasional run-on sentence, but few dispense with punctuation and capitalization altogether, and page numbering is automatic these days. But some of the difficulties that I encounter in my editorial work are worse than Stark's. Stark was trying to produce a literal draft of what Bentham had written. My task is to suggest revisions as aggressively as necessary to make the draft readable by our broad target audience of generalist economists. Jeremy Bentham was long dead and in no position to object to any decisions that Stark made. My authors are very much alive and kicking. This difference calls to mind the description of an editor's "Platonic ideal of the perfect contributor—the writer who hands in his article and is then run over by a bus before he can complain about the editing" (Ferguson 2007). When an author sends me a paper that promises in the first sentence "to disambiguate" any questions I might have on a certain subject (the example is not hypothetical), I need to confront the author directly.

Nuts-and-bolts editing can take on a mechanical feeling. No, we will not have five pages of introduction that previews what will be said in the following five pages of text. Just say it. No, we will not publish an article that is eighty-eight pages in length when we requested one of twenty-five. No, we will not suddenly change the philosophy of the journal and decide to publish a blizzard of mathematical equations and statistical results. No, we would prefer not to repeat the same thought in every other paragraph. No, you may not *italicize* for emphasis *every* fifth sentence or *every* tenth word. No, we will not ask our typesetter to create new fonts for your particular article. No, we do not need twenty figures and tables in your article. No, you may not start every other sentence with a version of "there is," "this is," "that is," or "it is." No, not everyone thinks in the passive voice.

Many academics have had the experience of editing something at some time but mostly as a side dish rather than a steady diet. It is difficult to convey how time-consuming intensive editing can be. On a tough article—where *tough* can refer either to how little I know about the topic or how much work the exposition needs—I may edit a page an hour. On an easier one, I might cover three pages an hour. The *JEP* publishes about a thousand total pages per year, with about five hundred words per page, so that is a total of about 500,000 published words a year. Original drafts tend to be longer than we ask for, so I cut at least 100,000 words each year (and some of my economic value-added happens through subtraction). I started running the journal at age twenty-six, so I could potentially end up doing it for a total of forty years (or more). If the journal stays about the same size, my life's work could end up being the purification of perhaps 20 million words—and the outright elimination of millions more.

Part of the editor's credo or compulsion is that even if no individual nuts-and-bolts change matters, the accumulation of these changes does matter. No article was ever sunk by a few inelegant sentences. But I long ago was struck by a comment in E. B. White's introduction to *The Elements of Style* (Strunk and White 1979, xvi), where he described a central belief of his mentor, William Strunk: "Will felt the reader was in serious trouble most of the time, a man floundering in a swamp, and that it was the duty of anyone attempting to write English to drain this swamp quickly and get his man up on dry ground, or at least throw him a rope." In my case, I try to bear in mind the broad and nonspecialist target audience of the *JEP*—the faculty members who are dipping into a subject that is not their specialty either out of curiosity or because they need to prepare a lecture or explain something to undergraduate students; economists who are not based at research institutions but would like some access to what research economists are thinking; older economists who are interested in current developments in the field; graduate students who are sampling possible topics to pursue further; advanced undergraduate students; economists outside academia who are perhaps in government, in private business, or at a think tank and are checking the research literature; and specialists who are interested in how another specialist would lay out the key arguments and intuition of a topic. Economics can be hard, and readers of economics often struggle. As an editor, I fix in place the ropes that can help the climb to understanding.

The Confrontational Side of Editing

At some point, nuts-and-bolts editing inevitably slides into content editing, and here a new set of pitfalls arises. Authors for *JEP* may have difficulties with clarity of expression, but they are acknowledged experts in their fields. Even when what they have written is convoluted or nonsensical to me—and presumably would read that way to many other nonspecialist economists as well—I must operate on the assumption that behind what looks to me like garble is a cohesive and substantially correct insight. My problem is that I am not grasping that insight, even if it might be perfectly clear to another specialist in the subject. My first step in this situation is to struggle for a sympathetic understanding of the author's meaning in my own terms. Sometimes this requires spending time Web surfing through working papers or taking a trip to the library to look up past articles on the subject. At this level, editing academic prose becomes a sort of wrestling match. My primary opponent is not the author but rather my own ignorance of the subject and my ego— which would prefer to blame the author for any lack of clarity rather than to feel inadequate myself. People with offices near mine over the years have become used to the sight of me pacing in the hallways, head down, sometimes gently kicking the wall.

In some cases, I face considerable temptation to give up on the process. I sometimes wish for the near-dictatorial editorial powers of John Maynard Keynes, who, among his other accomplishments, served as editor of the *Economic Journal* from 1911 to 1943. (I occasionally contemplate the year 2019, when my term as managing editor of *JEP* would total thirty-three years and would equal Keynes's tenure as editor.) In the earlier, simpler times of Keynes's editorship, he often turned down papers as he saw fit, sometimes with barbed commentary. In one rejection letter, Keynes wrote (as quoted in Moggridge 1990): "it seems to me clear that your article, in its present shape, is half-baked and not fit for publication. I have not been able to spare time to read it carefully enough to know whether there is anything in it at the bottom. But I find it a bit of a rigmarole, of which I fear the reader would make little or nothing. It is neither clear what you are driving at nor where you arrive. And behind all that lies my doubt as to whether the method you are employing is capable of helping much with this particular problem." To another rejected author, Keynes wrote (Moggridge 1990): "I am inclined to return to the opinion that the article is pretentious, misleading, inconclusive and perhaps wrong. I would rather have cheese to a weight equal to the paper it would occupy in 5,000 copies of the *Journal*." I like to think that I could write such letters. But Keynes was not only capable of dazzling turns of phrase but also had earned the professional right to arrogance, which I have not.

But my job is also different from that of Keynes or of any editor at a standard peer-reviewed journal. I am not trying to make judgments on the overall value of the article. That decision was made when we decided to invite the author to write for *JEP*. Instead, I view myself a stand-in for readers everywhere. I sometimes call myself, only half-joking, the "designated dummy" of the *JEP*. If an argument does not read clearly and make sense to me, then it cannot be published in the pages of the journal.

Proper editing needs an element of personal confrontation. A good editor must be willing to confront the author's ego, even when it sometimes means trespassing on the social niceties of a personal relationship with the author. The editorial function is a shaky three-legged relationship in which the editor mediates between the author and an unseen readership. Someone in this ménage à trois of author, editor, and reader needs to point out possibly helpful nips and tucks in the exposition and to insist on major surgery when necessary. The readers are invisible and powerless; they do not see the article until after publication. Authors are presumably doing the best that they can, given their abilities as writers, the other constraints on their time, and their inner fears about belonging to the ranks of academia, being correct, and being perceived within academia both to belong and to be correct. If an editor does not speak up on behalf of the future readers, no one else is in a position to do so.

Management guru Peter Drucker described the necessarily intrusive aspect of editing in a discussion of newspaper editors (as quoted in Jenkins 2007): "Every first-rate editor I have ever heard of reads, edits and rewrites every word that goes into his publication. . . . Good editors are not 'permissive'; they do not let their colleagues do 'their thing'; they make sure that everybody does the 'paper's thing.' A good, let alone a great editor is an obsessive autocrat with a whim of iron, who rewrites and rewrites, cuts and slashes, until every piece is exactly the way he thinks it should have been done."

This level of aggressiveness in editing does not seem appropriate to me for an academic journal, although some *JEP* authors might feel that they have been treated in this way (you know who you are, and I apologize). Newspaper editing is ultimately a commercial product whose goal is to attract readers, In academic journals, the articles are ultimately the responsibility of the author. But even with this difference, my editor's mission is that the papers should be reworked as necessary to conform with the mission of the journal and with the needs of readers. As one of my former coeditors, Brad De Long. said of the *JEP* editorial process: "We can't always make a silk purse out of a sow's ear, but we can usually make a rayon handbag."

The Peacemaking Aspect of Editing

In the minds of nonacademics, academia is all about the free-flowing give-and-take of ideas—a blend of open arguments, fair-minded criticisms, and honest responses, all conducted in a spirit of good faith. Most academics, however, have passed through their formative years from elementary school to college as the smartest person in the room. They are in the habit of being correct. As budding academics progress through graduate school and into research and classrooms, being right becomes not only a habit but an important element of professional success. For many academics (I sidestep here the question of whether it is a majority or only a substantial minority), criticism can feel like a declaration of war. An editor who has the temerity to suggest that an argument is unclear, that the length of a paper can be reduced, or that a table or figure is unnecessary may be stepping into a minefield.

My own strategy is a mixture of politeness, good humor, and occasional groveling. I bear in mind the story of a note that Alexander Gerschenkron wrote to Abram Bergson, asking for comments on a paper that was written by a third party (in Dawidoff 2002, 142): "Let me have your criticism, general and particular, and let me have it promptly"; a postscript added, "Criticisms are to be submitted in the form 'I suggest the following change' never in the form: 'This does not make sense' or similar." In that spirit, my own comments on *JEP* papers rely heavily on "I don't understand" rather than "This is wrong." I occasionally preface my comments with: "A question based on raw ignorance here. . . ." When a paper has some especially strong elements or when part or all of a draft is especially well written, I try to say so, hoping that in the overall karma of my editorial lifetime, some honestly positive words where possible will offset the reality that most comments have an inevitably negative tone.

But it is possible to apply the soft soap too liberally. Academic legend tells of a rejection letter once received from a Chinese economics journal (Bernard 1990, 44, as quoted in Gans and Shepherd 1994, 178):

We have read your manuscript with boundless delight. If we were to publish your paper, it would be impossible for us to publish any work of lower standard. And as it is unthinkable that in the next thousand years we shall see its equal, we are, to our regret, compelled to return your divine composition, and to beg you a thousand times to overlook our short sight and timidity.

I confess that I have my own, milder versions of this flattering response, which have the advantage of being true. For example, I can often honestly say to authors that while the terminology or explanation in their current draft would be fine for an audience of specialists, it will not work well for our readership of generalist economists. That message contains an implicit deference to their authority as a member of the insider community of specialists. In other cases, we are offered ideas for papers that may turn out to be standard economic arguments at some point but are not yet established in the research literature. In that case, I can honestly say to the authors that while their work is potentially excellent, it is not yet "ripe" for a generalist journal like *JEP*.

At its best, content-related editing becomes a kind of partnership in which authors become comfortable with a fundamental incongruity: they did not write the paper in the way that it finally appears in *JEP*. Left to their own devices, they would not have written the paper in that way. But nonetheless, all elements of the final product remain truly and distinctively their own.

The Role of the Editor in Academic Life

No child dreams at night of growing up to be an editor. No graduate student works for a doctorate in the hope of becoming an editor. No class in economics graduate school teaches editing. In the academic triumvirate of research, teaching, and service, the job of editing is presumably bundled as a subset of service, together with student advising, membership on the hiring committees, and a willingness to give talks when requested at the local Chamber of Commerce or Kiwanis club. But many economists end up with aspects of editing at some point in their careers, either as journal editors, referees, or book editors. A scan of recent issues of the *Journal of Economic Literature* suggests that about a third of all books that are published in economics are edited volumes. Because academic disciplines record their results in journal articles, editors shape what is in those articles and how they are expressed. In the publish- or-perish academic world, editors and referees hold one of the keys to professional success and even survival.

Compared to what I do in editing articles for *JEP*, much of the academic editing that occurs in economics journals or in conference volumes seems shallow and serves a binary gate-keeping function—separating acceptable from unacceptable but often little more. I occasionally see drafts of articles with a few words of comment scattered here and there. The general tone is something like this: "Liked your paper a lot. The third section could be tightened up a little, and I'm not sure about the point at the bottom of p. 19. Hope to see you at the conference next month." This kind of editing is more a polite social interchange than any meaningful attempt to improve the paper. But to be fair, many of these papers are aimed at a specialist readership. The papers are also receiving feedback from colleagues, seminar participants, and journal referees. The overall effect of this process can help to produce a research paper that is suitable for publication in a journal or conference volume, even if it would not lead to a paper suitable for a more generalist readership like *JEP*.

Even after twenty-two years, I deeply enjoy my work as managing editor of the *Journal of Economic Perspectives*. For a generalist economist with a grasshopper mind, like me, it is hard to imagine a job with a better-fitting combination of interest, autonomy, flexibility, and security. I remember the early days of *JEP* when we were not sure that anyone would want to write for the journal, that anyone would accept being edited, or that we would be able to produce a stream of issues. Now I meet professors who grew up with the journal as a presence in their lives, beginning with reading lists in their own undergraduate days and continuing up to their assignments for their own students today. My professional insecurities are not about whether I enjoy my work or I am good about it but about whether the work has sufficient social value.

One afternoon, after finishing my work on one manuscript and lacking the strength to start immediately on another, I attempted to provide for myself an economic rationale to justify my salary. There are various ways to think about my social product. For example, because I cut the length of articles, there could be a savings of paper and mailing costs. My editing might simplify the task of professors as they put together reading lists or update and amend lecture notes. My editing might help readers develop greater understanding for the amount of time that they invest in an article. As a simple metric, let us say that as a result of my editing, typical readers save an hour of time, either because they can read the published articles in *JEP* more quickly than they could have read the original drafts or because the journal saves them time in gathering entries for a reading list or information for a lecture. Say that the number of readers of *JEP* for a given issue is five thousand (roughly a quarter of the circulation) and that the value of the time of the typical reader is $40 per hour. (In keeping with my own graduate school experience, we will ignore any benefits to students and count their time as worth zero.) With four issues per year, my editing saves $800,000 worth of time per year, which comfortably exceeds my annual salary and is almost equal to the entire annual budget for the journal.

But one of my conceits as an editor is that my work does not just contribute to saving the time and energy of readers in the dissemination of knowledge but also contributes to the development of knowledge itself. Many of us carry around an implicit image of academic knowledge as a ladder, where new discoveries add an extra rung, or perhaps as a mountaintop, where new discoveries make the peak just a little taller. The implication is that the privileged task of creating knowledge is a matter of extending farther up the ladder or mountain and that all else is a secondary matter of filling in the gaps. But a full and mature under-standing of any field is not one-dimensional in this way. Knowledge is not a ladder to be climbed. There is not one way up, and there is not one clear sense of how to advance. Knowledge is a terrain or an ecosys-tem to be explored, and that exploration can be done from multiple angles and perspectives by using different tools and approaches.

In some broad sense, most of economics can be found in Adam Smith's *The Wealth of Nations* (1776). But the process of bringing lucidity, clari-fication, terminology, definiteness, and a recognition of the limits, param-eters, and interconnections of arguments is all part of knowledge, as well. I once read a paper in which the author referred to an earlier article on the same subject by saying, "This point was first made in a virtually impenetrable paper by _____." The sentiment seemed appropriate to me: give credit to the originator, but also take note that the original exposition was hardly the last word on explicating or understanding the issues.

The economist/philosopher Jeremy Bentham, he of the terrible penmanship, once commented on the process of intellectual discovery in a passage that John Maynard Keynes (1964, 353) later called Bentham's "finest passage": "The career of art, the great road which receives the footsteps of the projectors, may be considered as a vast, and perhaps unbounded plain, bestrewed with gulphs. . . . Each [gulf] requires a human victim to fall into it ere it can close, but when it once closes, it closes to open no more, and so much of the path is safe to those who follow."

For those of us who live in Minnesota, the unavoidable image evoked by this passage is an ice-covered lake, where drifting snow obscures potential cracks, holes, and open water. Knowledge seekers (the "projectors," as Bentham calls them) are exploring this terrain. Some move so quickly that they shoot right over holes in the ice. Others barely miss holes without realizing it. Some venture into areas where the ice begins cracking under them and then leave so quickly that they are not quite sure what was wrong. Still others fall through, but by doing so they help the rest of us understand what path to follow. The projectors deserve credit for reaching out into new areas. But just because an author has taken the first steps into a new terrain does not mean that the ground has been fully explored or fully understood. As someone who spends his work life confronting academic articles that test and extend the limits of my knowledge, I know all too well that sense of falling into a gulf, struggling for a while, and then laboriously climbing out—only to repeat the process a few pages later. If you are an editor, you hope to mark such gulfs clearly, build over them, find ways around them, smooth out rough spots, and create a broader, safer path for the readers who will follow.

Notes

1. After I left the *Mercury News*, I kept a connection with colleagues there. For a number of years afterward, especially after I moved back to California in 1988, I wrote twenty to twenty-five signed op-ed columns each year for the paper, along with an occasional unsigned editorial. Many signed columns are available at my Web site at http://www.timothytaylor.net.

2. My courses for the Teaching Company include "Economics: An Introduction," "America and the New Global Economy," "A History of the U.S. Economy in

the Twentieth Century," and "Legacies of Great Economists." My textbook, *Principles of Economics: Economics and the Economy*, was published in 2007 and is, to my knowledge, the first mainstream principles of economics text that is freely available over the Web. Perhaps over the next few years the publisher, Freeload Press, can make a profit with a combination of selling advertising at the Web site, charging for advertising-free downloads of the book, and charging for inexpensive ad-free paper copies. For more details on these projects, see my Web site at http://www.timothytaylor.net.

References

Bernard, Andre, ed. 1990. *Rotten Rejections*. London: Penguin Books.

Bierce, Ambrose. 1911. *The Devil's Dictionary*. http://www.thedevilsdictionary .com.

Dawidoff, Nicholas. 2002. *The Fly Swatter: How My Grandfather Made His Way in the World*. New York: Pantheon.

Ferguson, Andrew. 2007. Man of Letters. *Wall Street Journal*, December 20. http://online.wsj.com/public/page/news-lifestyle-arts-entertainment.html.

Gans, Joshua B., and George B. Shepherd. 1994. How Are the Mighty Fallen: Rejected Classic Articles by Leading Economists. *Journal of Economic Perspectives* 8 (1):165–179.

Jenkins, Holman W., Jr. 2007. From My Sweet Press Lord: We'll Take the *Washington Post*, Please. *Wall Street Journal*, June 6. http://online.wsj.com/public/page/ news-opinion-commentary.html?id=110010174.

Kasper, Hirschel. 1991. The Education of Economists: From Undergraduate to Graduate Study. *Journal of Economic Literature* 29 (3):1088–1109.

Keynes, John Maynard. 1964. *The General Theory of Employment, Interest, and Money*. New York: Harcourt, Brace, Jovanovich [originally published 1936].

Moggridge, Donald E. 1990. Keynes as Editor. In *A Century of Economics: One Hundred Years of the Royal Economic Society and the Economic Journal,* ed. John D. Hey and Donald Winch, 143–157. London: Basil Blackwell.

Plotnik, Arthur. 1986. *The Elements of Editing: A Modern Guide for Editors and Journalists*. New York: Macmillan.

Sala-i-Martin, Xavier. 1997. I Just Ran Two Million Regressions. *American Economic Review* 87 (2):178–183.

Stark, Werner, and Jeremy Bentham. 1952. *Economic Writings: Critical Edition Based on His Printed Works and Unprinted Manuscripts*. London: Allen & Unwin.

White, E. B. 1979. Introduction. In William Strunk Jr. and E. B. White, *The Elements of Style*. New York: Macmillan [originally published 1957].

The Journal Editorial Cycle and Practices

24

The Journal Editorial Cycle and Practices

Lall B. Ramrattan and Michael Szenberg

Editors and authors both recognize that way that journals function needs to improve. Scholarly journals are the mainstays of scientific communication, and publication in them by academicians is the primary route to promotion, tenure, salary increases, recognition, and mobility. The scrutiny and assessment of the publication process is therefore of vital concern to the scientific community. The purpose of this volume is to relay editorial insights that will enlighten the academic stakeholders as well as the general public.

The literature on journal editorial practices is limited. Fritz Machlup (1962, 7) was one of the first to point out the importance of analyzing the "production of knowledge," which included periodicals. He referred to "disclosure, dissemination, transmission, and communication." In George B. Shepherd's 1994 book, *Rejected: Leading Economists Ponder the Publication Process*, authors shared their experiences of how they dealt with their rejected manuscripts. The works of Joshua S. Gans and Shepherd (1994) and Gans (2001) are also in that vein, sharing significantly overlapping information on the subject. This book goes beyond the scope of those works and delves into the various phases of journal editing cycle from the editors' perspectives.

A journal editorial cycle involves phases of rejection, revision, acceptance, publication, and risk management to reduce the chance of publishing unworthy papers. The journal editors allocate their efforts within various process groups in order to initiate, plan, execute, and control or monitor those phases of publication. This volume reviews the shared and unique experiences of editors in the various activities of those process groups.

The contributing editors were asked to reflect on their editorial environment, share the fruits of their experiences for both seasoned and aspiring writers, and disseminate that knowledge to the public. They explain how they steer the course of their discipline by rejecting and accepting articles. Some editors explain how they cope with the complexities in their organization and operations. For instance, editors now receive many more manuscripts than in pre-Internet years, which, given the scarcity of resources available, creates an informational overload and the possibility that poor manuscripts might be accepted and worthy manuscripts might be rejected. The contributors reveal their experiences as well as their vision of how this organizational matrix is structured and implemented.

The first part of this volume deals with common and specific issues about journal editing. The second part examines the initiation, planning, execution, and controlling stages of journal editing.

Variety of Experiences

This work presents the experiences of the editors of prestigious journals such as the *American Economic Review*, *Journal of Economic Literature*, *Journal of Finance*, and *Review of Economic Studies* and other journals to provide a balanced and insightful perspective on the issue. Coleridge's definition of *beauty*—"Beauty is Multeity in Unity"— is appropriate.

As expected, the nature of editors' experiences varies by the nature of their journals. Journals differ by their underlying qualitative criteria, the compensation characteristics of their editors and editorial staff, and their technical or readable nature. We validated some of the major hypotheses in the literature and found that administrative efforts by journal editors are significantly correlated with the quality of a journal (Ramrattan and Szenberg 2003).

Some editors maintain a journal's quality through skepticism. In this function, they abide by George J. Stigler's (1988, 65) dictum that a deeply skeptical attitude may lead to the right formulation of ideas. Such an orientation supports an editor's role as a gatekeeper to the kingdom of knowledge. In that role, editors wield their power "either to help or to prevent a specific study from being published, since they decide who the referees will be" (Colander and Brenner 1992, 40–41). Several editors perform desk rejections, which preempt the refereeing process. Steven Pressman, coeditor of *Review of Political Economy*, has a contrarian view to this practice and believes that editors should act more like mentors than as gatekeepers.

Finally, it is the nature of some journals to be dedicated to a single paradigm, and these journals might be reluctant to publish unorthodox papers. Until recently, the paradigm for the *Journal of Industrial Economics* organized articles according to structure, conduct, and performance analysis. Now industrial economics is analyzed through the lenses of game theory or case studies. Journals are also partial to scientific approaches, which are often divided into falsifiable hypotheses or validation of ideas. An author who is not conscious of the journal's archetype will be unlikely to find a home for his or her article.

Conforming Experiences with the Expectations of the Literature

An editor's decision process can be seen as being either probabilistic or deterministic. The chief editor usually sends out an article to two or three referees, each with a different probability of returning a successful review. Alternatively, the article may be sent to a particular referee who is known for certain review traits—fair, biased, tough, critical, or easy. There still remains the possibility that the editor may hold onto the article and not send it out to the referees for immediate review or reject it for not being cogently written, for having faulty logic, or for not sharing some elements of the journal's paradigm.

The traditional literature divides experiences into the categories of positive (science), normative (belief), and art (practical) criteria. Editors may emphasize one aspect over another to the extent of degenerating the other two over time: "Art advises, prescribes and directs; science observes, describes and explains," but both art and science must take into account "the freedom and cognitive nature of the human will" (Walras 1969, 58, 62). The Walrasian viewpoint about the human will can be articulated as a gatekeeping role where the editors exercise their will to believe and their will to determine which article to accept or reject. For instance, John M. Keynes rejected Milton Friedman's first paper on elasticity (which was critical of Arthur Pigou's stance) by sending it for review to Pigou. Pigou, for obvious reasons, had no will to believe Friedman's point of view (Gans 2001, 37).

Editors may look for articles that are empirical, complex, simple, and aesthetic. Gerard Debreu (1983, 203), a Nobel laureate in mathematical economics, wrote that he was "grateful to Roy Radner for his objection to an inesthetic feature of the first version" of his "Excess Demand Function" article. I have noted that "Words that express aesthetic values, such as 'beautiful,' 'ingenious,' 'simple,' 'graceful,' and 'elegant,' appear increasingly in the writings of scholars [including editors]. Although aesthetic criteria are hardly clear, for some, these qualities are expressed by the dictum 'less is more'" (Szenberg 1998, 4)

The contributors to this volume also recognize that authors are driven by the need to "publish or perish." When this principle makes a "game of citations and peer approval that are supposed to certify to the scientist's standing in the scholarly world, the game takes on an aesthetic dimension for scholars" (Szenberg 1998, 6). This drive to publish contributes to the increasing volume of articles, underscoring the remark that the "function of the editor is perhaps more important than ever before" (Medema, Cardoso, and Lodewijks 2002, 194). The need to publish or perish also elevates the risk that the production of more research may have "less effect on scholarship over time" (Weintraub 2002, 11). Journal editors must therefore exercise their authority in that capacity: "editors have much power either to help or to prevent a specific study from being published, since they decide who the referees will be," and this idea is reinforced by the finding that "when the same proposals were resubmitted to a different set of reviewers . . . more than 25 percent of the decisions were reversed" (Colander and Brenner 1992, 40–41).

The technical complexity of journal articles continues to be elevated by journal editors. The Commission on Graduate Education in Economics (COGEE) (1991) found that the subject matter of economics has become increasingly technical and that journals have not abandoned essential formalism in their content. Starting with John R. Hicks (1946, 61) and Paul Samuelson (1947, 257), new complexities in static and dynamic changes in equilibrium estimates and in underlying parameters have increased the complexity of journal articles as well as editors' efforts to discern them. The American Economic Association founded the *Journal of Economic Perspectives* to provide the specialist with a nontechnical source to keep abreast with the literature at a time when many journals were not giving up on their formalism.

Several editors in this book express a preference for empirical analysis, most likely aligning themselves with David Hume, who stated that if something cannot be measured, then it is better to cast it to the flames. Using information from seven journals, Daniel S. Hamermesh (1994, 58–61) examined a myth that unknown authors are treated somewhat unfairly and that editors send unknown authors' work to referees whose opinions they do not trust.

Controversy: Scheduling and Other Issues

A schedule itemizes when the review process will begin and end. A pitfall in this schema is that some tasks that are sequenced could be done in parallel fashion. This point has been was commented on by several authors (Szenberg 1994; Pressman 1994; Azar 2006). I argued that the processing time could be shortened by allowing authors to make concurrent submissions to multiple journals. When an author submits an article and it is not accepted, the process has to be restarted with another journal. Although the practice of multiple submissions is an exception rather than the rule, information technology has brought the two sides closer, diffusing conflicts that may arise from this. Leaving out the lower and upper outliers that are shown in the journals that are listed in table 24.1, the average review time in 2012 is 3 to 6.5 months, with a standard deviation of about a month. Given the absence of a standard to measure this against, it can be inferred that review time has declined significantly. Several contributors to this book, such as John Pencavel (chapter 5), point out that a year is an excessive period for acceptance of a paper. For some editors, such as William A. Barnett (chapter 10), associate editors keep their own turnaround times. If the turnaround time for associate editors slows significantly, then at the end of their term, the position is offered to someone else. As a result, no overall information

Table 24.1

Review time at economics journals, 2012 (months)

Names	Optimistic	Mean	Pessimistic	Beta mean	Beta STD
Journal of Economic Issues	3	6	12	6.50	1.50
*Journal of Economic Education**	2	12	36	14.33	5.67
Land Economics	3	4	6	4.17	0.50
Economic Inquiry	2	3.5	9	4.17	1.17
Eastern Economic Journal	2.5	4.5	6.5	4.50	0.67
Journal of Behavior and Organization	3	6	12	6.50	1.50
Journal of Economic Perspectives	0.75	1.1	1.6	1.13	0.14
American Economist	2.5	4	7	4.25	0.75
Review of Industrial Organization	2	3	6	3.33	0.67

Note: * Mode for optimistic estimate used for nonreporting.
Source: Direct email survey to authors from the author.

on the distribution of turnaround times for the journal as a whole was aggregated.

Editors vary in their rejection rates, as well. Some carry out desk rejections, while others follow the recommendations of their referees. They are also aware that some weak articles make it through the editorial process. How does an editor guard against this? For Pencavel (chapter 5), one way of dealing with this is "to play it safe. . . . to turn away potentially controversial papers, those that receive mixed reviews, and those that are out of the mainstream."

Four years ago, the *American Economist* received a submission that was accompanied by a letter from a Nobel Prize–winner who supported the article. The author argued that his approval should serve as an alternative to the refereeing process. I had to reject his idea and noted Marcel Proust's method of dealing with unsolicited manuscripts: "whenever Proust was asked to evaluate a manuscript, he always enclosed the following letter: 'Divine work. It is a work of genius. I would not change a word. I take my hat off for you. All the best, Marcel Proust.' The novelist wrote the same laudatory note to all potential writers who contacted him. When confronted about what he was doing, Proust said that he did not have time to read the submitted material because it interfered with his writing. By telling young authors that their work was that of a genius, he made sure that they would not return their revised papers to him with changes" (Szenberg, Ramrattan, and Gottesman 2006, 10). Such Proustian letters should be taken with a grain of salt. As for the paper, it was accepted eventually for publication after two major revisions.

Not all editors look for original contributions. For William E. Becker and Suzanne R. Becker (chapter 18), "it is not unusual to see authors rebottle wine with new labels." According to Pencavel (chapter 5), "The *JEL*'s role is not so much that of publishing articles containing original frontier research but that of communicating an important class of scholarship to a wider intellectual community and of providing dispassionate assessment of that scholarship."

Initiation Phase

One piece of invaluable information that comes out of this effort is the answer to the question "How does one become a journal editor?" Lawrence J. White (chapter 9) was asked to join the *Journal of Industrial Economics* and the *Review of Industrial Organization* based on his varied work experiences and publications in industrial organization, which formed his editorial viewpoint.

Timothy Taylor (chapter 23) became an editor of the *Journal of Economic Perspectives* at the age of twenty-six. He found graduate education at Stanford to be boring, and after working as a reporter for the *San Jose Mercury News*, he was recommended to Joe Stiglitz to be the managing editor of the *Journal of Economic Perspectives*, a journal that specializes in taking sophisticated economics and turning it into enjoyable and popular reading.

For Pencavel (chapter 5), breaking into a journal editorship required some preparatory training. He wrote "In effect, my years as an associate editor were something of an apprenticeship to an eminent and honorable scholar, and I benefitted greatly from the training and education I received from Moe [Abramovitz]." Pencavel considers his editorial effort to be "largely a labor of love. No doubt, I worked hard at the position. I took a deep personal interest in the well-being of the journal and invested much effort in it." At the same time, being motivated by a desire to enhance his knowledge, he also solicited articles that he wanted to learn from.

Barnett (chapter 10) writes that his editorship grew out of a conflict situation that arose between two journals. Steven Pressman (chapter 20), on the other hand, took the journeyman's path: he started as an associate editor and eventually was offered the editor's position. And so was I (Szenberg, chapter 22), after receiving the Irving Fisher award. I was first offered a coeditorship with an economist who served as the managing editor, but the managing editor refused to share his duties, so the board voted for me to serve as the sole editor.

Planning

Editors bring specific goals to their editorships. White's (chapter 9) objective was to provide a "top-tier journal" through the publication of "good, informative, thought-provoking papers." Pencavel (chapter 5) provided potential authors with specific instructions on how to write a research article. He asked that the paper should not read as though "X (1980) claimed this, Y (1984) argued that, and Z (1989) responded in this way." He insisted and planned for well-reasoned arguments in articles, observing that "after scholars put down these arguments and claims in writing, they often become attached to their papers almost as parents are to their babies."

A journal's plan has milestones for meeting publication deadlines. Papers are selected to make each issue of the journal a unique piece. A cursory look at some of the journals indicates that ranking authors and pieces on economic issues of the day vie for the lead article positions. Editorial pieces are usually placed upfront.

In other instances, readability is important. The objectives of the *Journal of Economic Perspectives* and the *Journal of Education* are "thought, exposition, and grammar."

Execution

Although most editors did not describe their journals' organizational structure, it does vary. According to R. Preston McAfee (chapter 3), the *American Economic Review* utilizes "excessive organization" in the editorial process. Its staff in Pittsburgh accepts online submissions and forwards them to editors. The editors then assign papers to coeditors who are experts in their fields. Papers are also assigned to avoid conflict of interest. Thus, editors of the *American Economic Review* practice a matrix type of organization that has a mixture of functionality and project characteristics.

Many journals adopt the double-blind review process even though it is not difficult to identify the authors of the papers via the Internet. Some editors practice desk rejections depending on their standards, topics, paradigm, audience, and other factors. For White (chapter 9), "authors want a reasonably rapid initial editorial decision from a journal; if the initial decision is negative, a clear explanation why and helpful comments for improvement from referees; if the initial decision is positive (an invitation to revise and resubmit), clear instructions from the editor as to what is expected and how to interpret the referee reports; and a high probability that the revise-and-resubmit process will involve only a few rounds and will have a favorable ultimate outcome."

Some journals, such as *Macroeconomic Dynamics* and the *American Economist*, make their journals user-friendly by interviewing eminent economists and publishing their life and work philosophies. Barnett (chapter 10) explains that the drive for his journal was "the explosive growth in high-quality, scientific research in macroeconomics throughout the world." As such, he focuses on interviewing technical persons, such as Wassily Leontief, James Tobin, and Franco Modigliani. Reflecting on the scope of these interviews, one finds rays of spontaneous thought from minds that "breathe and dream of economics."

The *Journal of Economic Perspectives* is unique in its execution. As Timothy Taylor (chapter 23) explains, "rather than just making comments such as 'this section needs tightening up,' 'this argument isn't quite clear,' or 'the discussion here seems repetitive,' a hands-on editor (me) would work through every line of every paper." This also means that he changes the paper electronically. As he quotes from William Strunk: if a man is drowning in a swamp, "it was the duty of anyone attempting to write English to drain this swamp quickly and get his man up on dry ground, or at least throw him a rope." Pressman (chapter 20), in line with Taylor (chapter 23), thinks of the editorial process as "one part crapshoot and one part triage." He is referring to the arbitrariness of the referee selection process and the desire to save a paper in the process. Becker and Becker (chapter 18) are meticulous about checking facts: "Sue recalls devoting hours each month in pre-Internet days in travel to or phone calls with the excellent and always helpful reference desk at the Indiana University library verifying quotations, references, and missing citation details."

Control

White (chapter 9) controls his flow of articles by "leaning more toward empirically oriented articles." He is meticulous about "extreme data points" and respect for the data. Papers that do not measure up empirically meet with a "desk rejection." He injects himself into the review process: "My letter includes my own instructions in addition to the referees' reports." Pencavel (chapter 5) mentions the aphorism that the "the referee is always right." He finds that "it is not a bad rule of thumb for an editor to act as if the referee's claims are correct and to ask the author of the paper to explain the argument more carefully so that a diligent referee should not draw the wrong inference."

Taylor (chapter 23) explains that the *Journal of Economic Perspectives* requires authors to accept the editor's revisions: "Many authors will throw out or overrule 10, 20, or even 50 percent of the advice they get. But by accepting most of the advice, their article is typically finished after one or two revisions and does not drag on through many multiple revisions, which can easily lead to bad feelings." He also holds that a good editor must be able to confront the egos of authors. Becker and Becker (chapter 18) are strict regarding their journal's style requirements: "We had one author who had a paper that made it through the referee process but later withdrew his manuscript when we informed him that editorial changes were required, including conformity with our reference style even if it did not conform to the style options that were available in LaTeX."

I try to be tactful in communicating rejections. Here is a representative rejection letter for the *American Economist*:

Dear _____,

Attached please find the referee's report on your submission. He or she finds that the paper is well written but does not offer anything novel to warrant publication. I hope that this does not discourage you from future submissions. We all face rejections, and a famous study found that successful people face more rejections than unsuccessful people. I have a motto that I am guided by and share with friends and students: "Rejections energize me."

Best wishes and kindest regards,

Michael

Conclusions

Journal editors in economics are guided by art, correspondence, coherence, or ontology principles, including paradigms and positive research program methodologies. The most that the author can do is make sure that the manuscript is sent to the right journal because editors usually defend some paradigm. After that hurdle is cleared, the authors can think of editors as gatekeepers or mentors.

The characteristics of journal editors can be grouped into a few general types. As grouped by Axel Leijonhufvud (1973), a leading macrotheorist, editors can be viewed as belonging to a tribe with caste (fields) and status (transitivity) considerations that are arrayed by "Grads, Adults, and Elders" and operate under a "Totems and Social Structure." This complex subject matter generates scientific research that is kept in check by nonscientific considerations, thereby underscoring the varying role of the editors.

Both the gate-keeping role and the mentorship role of editors are significant. Both aspects were important in the publishing of David Ricardo's *Principles of Political Economy and Taxation* (1817). The editor, James Mills, asked Ricardo to revise his submitted chapters several times despite the author's reluctance. Mills also insistently encouraged Ricardo to complete the work. It is as if Mills saw Ricardo's hidden talents. Their creative interaction forged a masterpiece in economics. Such an exemplar of economic editing should remain paramount for all times.

References

Azar, Ofer H. 2006. The Academic Review Process: How Can We Make It More Efficient? *American Economist* 50 (1):37–50.

Colander, David, and Reuven Brenner. 1992. *Educating Economists*. Ann Arbor: University of Michigan Press.

Commission on Graduate Education in Economics (COGEE). 1991. *Journal of Economic Literature* 22 (3): 1035–1053.

Debreu, Gerard. 1983. *Mathematical Economics: Twenty Papers*. Cambridge: Cambridge University Press.

Gans, Joshua S. 2001. *Publishing Economics: Analyses of the Academic Journal Market in Economics*. Northampton, MA: Elgar.

Gans, Joshua S., and George B. Shepherd. 1994. How Are the Mighty Fallen: Rejected Classic Articles by Leading Economists. *Journal of Economic Perspectives* 8 (1):165–179.

Hamermesh, Daniel S. 1994. Facts and Myths about Refereeing. *Journal of Economic Perspectives* 8 (1):153–164.

Hicks, John R. 1946. *Value and Capital*. 2nd ed. Oxford: Clarendon Press.

Leijonhufvud, Axel. 1973. Life among the Econ. *Western Economic Journal* 11 (3):327–337.

Machlup, Fritz. 1962. *The Production and Distribution of Knowledge in the United States*. Princeton, NJ: Princeton University Press.

Medema, Steven G., Jose Luis Cardoso, and John Lodewijks. 2002. Heaven Can Wait: Gatekeeping in Age of Uncertainty, Innovation, and Commercialization. In *The Future of the History of Economics*, ed. E. Roy Weintraub, 190–207. Durham, NC: Duke University Press.

Pressman, Steven. 1994. Simultaneous Multiple Journal Submissions: The Case Against. *American Journal of Economics and Sociology* 53 (3):317–333.

Ramrattan, Lall B., and Michael Szenberg. 2003. Ranking of Economics Journals: A Statistical Survey and Analysis. *American Economist* 47 (1):82–90.

Samuelson, Paul. 1947. *Foundations of Economic Analysis*. Cambridge, MA: Harvard University Press.

Shepherd, George B. 1994. *Rejected: Leading Economists Ponder the Publication Process*. Sun Lakes, AZ: Horton.

Stigler, George J. 1988. *Memoirs of an Unregulated Economist*. New York: Basic Books.

Szenberg, Michael. 1994. Disseminating Scholarly Output: The Case for Eliminating the Exclusivity of Journal Submissions. *American Journal of Economics and Sociology* 53 (3):303–315.

Szenberg, Michael, ed. 1998. *Passion and Craft: Economists at Work*. Foreword by Paul A. Samuelson. Ann Arbor: University of Michigan Press.

Szenberg, Michael, Lall Ramrattan, and Aron Gottesman. 2007. Ten Ways to Know Paul A. Samuelson. *American Economist* 51 (2):3–7.

Walras, Leon. 1969. *Elements of Pure Economics*. Trans. William Jaffe. New York: Kelley.

Weintraub, E. Roy. 2002. *The Future of the History of Economics*. Durham, NC: Duke University Press.

Contributors

Richard V. Adkisson Professor and department head for the Economics, Applied Statistics, and International Business Department, New Mexico State University, Las Cruces

Journal of Economic Issues

Richard G. Anderson Vice president, Federal Reserve Bank of St. Louis, Missouri

Journal of Money, Credit, and Banking

William A. Barnett Oswald Distinguished Professor of Macroeconomics, University of Kansas, Lawrence, and director, Center for Financial Stability, New York City

Macroeconomic Dynamics

Suzanne R. Becker Former assistant editor, *Journal of Economic Education*

Journal of Economic Education

William R. Becker Professor emeritus of economics, Indiana University, Bloomington

Journal of Economic Education

Daniel W. Bromley Anderson-Bascom Professor Emeritus of Applied Economics, University of Wisconsin, Madison

Land Economics

William G. Dewald Professor of economics emeritus, Ohio State University, Columbus, and retired director of research, Federal Reserve Bank of St. Louis, Missouri

Journal of Money, Credit, and Banking

Antony W. Dnes Senior associated scholar, Mercatus Center, George Mason University, Fairfax, Virginia, and past chair and professor of economics, University of Hull, UK

Managerial and Decision Economics

Zvi Eckstein Dean, School of Economics, Herzliya, and professor of economics, Tel Aviv University, Israel

European Economic Review

Richard Friberg Jacob Wallenberg Professor of Economics, Stockholm School of Economics, Sweden

Scandinavian Journal of Economics

Esther Gal-Or Professor of business administration and economics and Glenn Stinson Chair in Competitiveness, University of Pittsburgh, Pennsylvania

European Economic Review

Craufurd Goodwin James B. Duke Professor of Economics emeritus, Duke University, Durham, North Carolina

History of Political Economy

Thorvaldur Gylfason Professor of economics, University of Iceland, Reykjavik

European Economic Review

Campbell R. Harvey Professor of finance, Fuqua School of Business, Duke University, Durham, North Carolina, and a research associate of the National Bureau of Economic Research, Cambridge, Massachusetts

Journal of Finance

Geoffrey M. Hodgson Research professor in business studies, University of Hertfordshire, UK, and director, Group for Research into Organizational Evolution (GROE), University of Hertfordshire, UK

Journal of Institutional Economics

Cambridge Journal of Economics

Leo H. Kahane Professor of economics, Providence College, Providence, Rhode Island

Journal of Sports Economics

R. Preston McAfee   Economist at Google, former J. Stanley Johnson Professor of Business, Economics, and Management, California Institute of Technology, Pasadena

American Economic Review

John Pencavel   Pauline K. Levin-Robert L. Levin and Pauline C. Levin-Abraham Levin Professor in the School of Humanities and Sciences, Department of Economics, Stanford University, Stanford, California

Journal of Economic Literature

Gerard Pfann   Professor of economics, Maastricht University, the Netherlands

European Economic Review

Steven Pressman   Professor of economics and finance, Monmouth University, West Long Branch, New Jersey

Eastern Economic Journal
Review of Political Economy

Lall B. Ramrattan   Instructor of economics, University of California, Berkeley Extension

The American Economist

J. Barkley Rosser Jr.   Professor of economics and Kirby L. Cramer, Jr. Professor of Business Administration, James Madison University, Harrisonburg, Virginia

Journal of Economic Behavior and Organization

Paul H. Rubin   Samuel Candler Dobbs Professor of Economics, Emory University, Atlanta, Georgia, and research fellow, The Independent Institute, Oakland, California

Managerial and Decision Economics

William F. Shughart II   J. Fish Smith Professor in Public Choice, Jon M. Huntsman School of Business, Utah State University, Logan

Public Choice

Robert M. Solow   1987 Nobel Prize winner in economic sciences and former professor of economics, Massachusetts Institute of Technology, Cambridge, Massachusetts

Daniel F. Spulber   Elinor Hobbs Distinguished Professor of International Business, Kellogg School of Management, Northwestern University, Evanston, Illinois, and research director, Searle Center on Law, Regulation and Economic Growth, Northwestern University, Chicago, Illinois

Journal of Economics & Management Strategy

Michael Szenberg   Distinguished Professor of Economics, Lubin School of Business, Pace University, New York, New York

The American Economist

Timothy Taylor   Managing editor, *Journal of Economic Perspectives*, Macalester College, St. Paul, Minnesota

Journal of Economic Perspectives

Abu N. M. Wahid   Professor of economics, Tennessee State University, Nashville

Journal of Developing Areas

Michael Watts   Professor of economics and director, Purdue Center for Economic Education, Krannert School of Management, Purdue University, West Lafayette, Indiana

Lawrence J. White   Robert Kavesh Professorship in Economics, Leonard N. Stern School of Business, New York University, New York

Journal of Industrial Economics
Review of Industrial Organization

Jürgen von Hagen   Professor of economics, University of Bonn, Germany

European Economic Review

Fabrizio Zilibotti   Professor of macroeconomics and political economy and academic director of the UBS International Center of Economics in Society, Department of Economics, University of Zurich, Switzerland

Review of Economic Studies
Journal of European Economic Association

Index